BLACKSTONE'S GUIDE TO

The Human Rights Act 1998

Third Edition

BLACKSTONE'S GUIDE TO

The Human Rights Act 1998

John Wadham, Helen Mountfield and
Anna Edmundson

OXFORD
UNIVERSITY PRESS

OXFORD

UNIVERSITY PRESS

Great Clarendon Street, Oxford OX2 6DP

Oxford University Press is a department of the University of Oxford.
It furthers the University's objective of excellence in research, scholarship,
and education by publishing worldwide in

Oxford New York

Auckland Bangkok Buenos Aires Cape Town Chennai
Dar es Salaam Delhi Hong Kong Istanbul Karachi Kolkata
Kuala Lumpur Madrid Melbourne Mexico City Mumbai Nairobi
São Paulo Shanghai Singapore Taipei Tokyo Toronto
with an associated company in Berlin

Oxford is a registered trade mark of Oxford University Press
in the UK and in certain other countries

Published in the United States
by Oxford University Press Inc., New York

© John Wadham, Helen Mountfield, and Anna Edmundson 2003

The moral rights of the authors have been asserted

Crown copyright material is reproduced under Class Licence Number CO1P0000148
with the permission of HMSO and the Queen's Printer for Scotland

Database right Oxford University Press (maker)

First published by Blackstone Press 2003

British Library Cataloguing in Publication Data

Data available

Library of Congress Cataloging in Publication Data

Data available

ISBN 0–19–925453–2

1 3 5 7 9 10 8 6 4 2

Typeset in Times
by Cambrian Typesetters, Frimley, Surrey
Printed in Great Britain
on acid-free paper by
Antony Rowe Ltd, Chippenham

Contents Summary

Contents

Preface to the Third Edition

In the preface to the first edition of this book we wrote:

> The Human Rights Act 1998 will have a momentous impact on our legal system . . . It will affect every area of law in England and Wales . . . No law student or legal practitioner will be able to ignore its effect.

And even before the Act came fully into force in England and Wales this proved to be the case, with Lord Hope declaring in the House of Lords case of *R v DPP ex parte Kebilene* [2000] 2 AC 326 that:

> although the 1998 Act is not yet in force, the vigorous public debate which accompanied its passage through Parliament has already had a profound effect on thinking about issues of human rights. It is now plain that the incorporation of the European Convention on Human Rights into our domestic law will subject the entire legal system to a fundamental process of review and, where necessary, reform by the judiciary.

During the two-year period between the Human Rights Act ('the 1998 Act') receiving Royal Assent and its coming into force, every judge was trained, at least to a basic level, in the 1998 Act and its implications; civil servants and public authorities started to examine their practices and procedures to see whether they complied with the 1998 Act; and commentators started to prophesy chaos in the legal system with a 'field day for crackpots, a pain in the neck for judges and legislators, and a goldmine for lawyers' (Lord McCluskey's now infamous speech in the House of Lords debate on the Bill).

The 'unfounded predictions that the 1998 Act would cause chaos in our legal system' (Lord Steyn in *R v Lambert* [2001] 3 WLR 206) have not resulted in the courts being swamped with unmeritorious applications. The excellent research carried out by Francesca Klug and her colleagues at the Human Rights Act Research Unit (see further Chapter 10, 'Researching Human Rights Jurisprudence', and Klug and O'Brien, 'The first two years of the Human Rights Act' [2002] PL 649) illustrates that European Convention ('the Convention') rights have been raised in domestic courts and tribunals of all kinds and at all levels. The Human Rights Act Research Unit examined 316 cases in the period from July 1975 to July 1996 in which the Convention was cited and found that in only 11 cases did the international instrument influence statutory interpretation. Using a similar methodology, the Unit has examined the flow of cases in the first 18 months of the Act's life and estimates that, in the higher courts, the Convention affected the outcome, reasoning, or procedure in 318 cases out of the 431 cases in which it was cited. A claim based on the 1998 Act was upheld in 94 of these cases and remedies were granted in 91 of them.

The impression that emerges of the initial impact of the 1998 Act is that human rights arguments are mostly used to add to, bolster, or put a fresh slant on pre-existing lines of challenge rather than being used to bring completely free-standing claims. This is borne out by the research of Varda Bondy for the Public Law Project, *The Impact of the Human Rights Act on Judicial Review* (Public Law Project, 2003). However, the 'tentacles' of the 1998 Act (see David Steel J in *Mousaka Inc v Golden Seagull Maritime* [2002] 1 WLR 395) have reached throughout English law and influenced public, criminal, family, and even commercial law. The standard of review for judicial review cases involving human rights is now 'proportionality' rather than the much criticized '*Wednesbury* unreasonableness'; the criminal law tests in relation to evidence have been re-written in cases such as *Lambert* and *R v A*; and, in family law, new rules and practice directions have been introduced as a direct result of breaches of Convention rights. It is also clear that the 1998 Act has had a significant impact on legislative interpretation, the development of the common law, and the judicial review of public bodies. The rule of statutory construction under the 1998 Act has meant that Convention rights have had an effect on cases between private parties—most famously in the 'privacy' cases between newspapers and publishers and celebrities (for example, *Douglas and Zeta-Jones v Hello!*, *Campbell v Mirror Group Newspapers*).

Although it could be argued that the Human Rights Act is just another statute (it is not entrenched, neither does it have any explicit higher-order status), there has been judicial recognition of its constitutional significance. Laws LJ (*obiter*), in *Thoburn v Sunderland City Council* [2003] QB 151 (the 'Metric Martyrs' case), placed it in a category of 'constitutional statutes' which included Magna Carta and the European Communities Act 1972. Unlike ordinary statutes, which may be impliedly repealed, Laws LJ argued that constitutional statutes may not. There are other reasons why the Human Rights Act has profound constitutional significance. This is partly because the strong obligation (in s. 3 of the 1998 Act) to read all UK legislation compatibly with European Convention rights brings domestic legislation under intense judicial scrutiny. Most importantly, the 1998 Act imports the notion that in a democratic society, government action is limited, as 'the recognition of the need to adhere to the rule of law by protecting human rights is essential to the proper functioning of democracy' (Lord Woolf's speech to the British Academy, 15 October 2002). This model of limited government insists that fundamental rights must be protected, even if the majority of the electorate (as represented by Parliament) decides otherwise. The Human Rights Act does not go as far as allowing the courts to strike down legislation that violates fundamental Convention rights—the compromise which preserves parliamentary sovereignty is that courts can issue a declaration of incompatibility with Convention rights. The rationale is that ministers then come under considerable political and moral pressure to amend legislation which offends against fundamental rights. The end result is that these provisions in the 1998 Act have brought about a significant cultural change in our legal system. Previously, British citizens merely had 'negative' rights to freedom which consisted of the rights that were left over after all the law's prohibitions had been obeyed. Since the 1998 Act came into force on 2 October 2000, they now have 'positive' rights to protection from violations of their fundamental rights by the acts or omissions of public bodies.

The substantive legal developments over the last two and a half years receive detailed examination in the main part of this guide, but two underlying debates have had a profound impact on developments since the Act came into force. The most pronounced of these debates was triggered by the horrific events of 9/11. As we have grappled with the heightened threat of international terrorism and the potential it may have to wreak havoc in the United Kingdom, the 1998 Act (and the partially incorporated Convention) have become the target of unwarranted attacks. In the immediate aftermath of events, Parliament enacted the Anti-Terrorism, Crime and Security Act 2001. This allowed for the unlimited detention of foreign nationals who were suspected of being involved in international terrorism and required the United Kingdom to enter a derogation from the European Convention so as not to breach Article 5 (the right to liberty and security of person). To date, the United Kingdom is the only Council of Europe state to have deemed it necessary to enact emergency legislation and derogate from the Convention on the grounds that there exists a 'war or other public emergency threatening the life of the nation' (Article 15).

Criticizing these measures, Professor Conor Gearty has pointed out ('Cry Freedom', *The Guardian*, 3 December 2002) that the protection of civil liberties:

> does not make Britain vulnerable, or more vulnerable, to terrorist attack because arrested persons are given access to their lawyers, because the prosecution is required to prove the commission of some objective crime, or because detention without trial is generally frowned upon.

Similarly, Lord Woolf (in his lecture to the British Academy) has warned of the dangers of scoring an 'own goal' in the fight against terrorism, and reminded us that the 1998 Act is not a suicide pact which prevents terrorists from being brought to justice—instead it helps to reduce the risk of undermining the values which make democracy worth defending. We agree with these observations and advocate the use of alternative measures such as surveillance and vigilant law enforcement (using existing frameworks such as the Regulation of Investigatory Powers Act 2000) instead of prolonged detention without trial.

Despite the drastic measures contained in the Anti-Terrorism, Crime and Security Act, it appears that even these may not be considered strong enough by politicians to 'contain' the terrorist threat. In early 2003, following a series of unfavourable decisions of the courts, both the Home Secretary and the Prime Minister raised the possibility that the UK might withdraw from the Convention because of difficulties with the obligation under Article 3 (the right not to be subject to torture, inhuman, or degrading treatment) which prevents the return of asylum seekers to countries where they would face a real risk of torture. Article 3 (unlike Article 5) cannot be derogated from, nor a fresh reservation entered without withdrawing from the Convention altogether. Leading members of the Conservative

Party have labelled the Human Rights Act and Convention a 'problem' and pledged themselves to either renegotiation or withdrawal from the Convention. This potential 'denunciation' of the Convention has been dissected by David Pannick QC and Shaheed Fatima (in an opinion for Liberty), who concluded that withdrawing from and then re-ratifying the Convention for the purposes of entering a reservation against Article 3 would not be permitted under the Convention. It is also doubtful whether Britain could withdraw from the Convention while remaining a member of the EU—all members being signatories to the Convention—and it appears that the Government has subsequently dropped plans to carry these threats through. Regardless, these attacks on the Convention and the Human Rights Act are worrying, both for their inaccuracy and because they threaten seriously to undermine the development of a human rights culture in the United Kingdom.

Far from being opposed to the protection of society and the democratic ideal, human rights principles can help to protect society from panic in times of emergency. Lord Scarman memorably said, in the context of the troubles in Northern Ireland, that it is precisely when fear is stalking the land that bills of rights are needed most. What legislation other than the Human Rights Act can provide the coherent framework for parliamentary and judicial scrutiny of new laws proposed in times of emergency? The Act measures the proposed provisions against the key standards of necessity and proportionality, and forces ministers to justify their proposals and decisions at times when emotion and fear threaten to overwhelm rational thinking. When the Human Rights Bill was introduced into the House of Lords by the then Lord Chancellor, Lord Irvine, he expressed his conviction that it would 'deliver a modern reconciliation of the inevitable tension between the democratic right of the majority to exercise political power and the democratic need of individuals and minorities to have their human rights secured'. It is to be hoped that the Government continues to view the constitutional settlement that is the Human Rights Act in this light and protect its provisions from being unnecessarily limited.

During these particularly testing times the judiciary has had a difficult, and often controversial, balancing exercise to undertake. The second underlying development which has limited the potential impact of the 1998 Act concerns the widely-held fear that it would further politicize the judiciary, lead judges into 'legislating', and undermine the notion of a balance between the three branches of power. Undoubtedly, highly sensitive issues have had to be determined by the courts under the 1998 Act. Some of these issues would not have come under such close judicial scrutiny prior to the Act. But Convention arguments and judicial scrutiny of highly sensitive political and human rights issues are not, in themselves, new (for example, *R v Secretary of State for the Home Department ex parte Brind* [1991] 1 AC 696, which excluded Sinn Fein politicians from media appearances but allowed actors to stand in). The Human Rights Act, and the attitude of the Government and media to it, have, however, heightened the political debate about the appropriate roles of various constitutional actors. Since October 2000, judges have come under fierce attack from politicians and parts of the media as, for example, 'dictators in wigs' (*Daily*

Mail) after upholding human rights complaints. However, as Lord Lester has said:

> It is the function of Parliament to make the law, of the executive to carry it out under law, and of the judiciary to interpret and apply the law. By enacting the Human Rights Act 1998, Parliament required the courts, where possible, to interpret and apply both statute law and common law compatibly with the fundamental rights and freedoms protected by the European Convention. ('Don't Blame the Judges', *The Guardian*, 25 February 2003)

The phenomenon of 'judicial deference' indicates that, perhaps overly aware of this potential criticism, judges have been erring on the side of caution. 'Judicial deference' occurs when judges, not wishing to offend against the constitutional principle of the separation of powers, defer to the executive's judgment in certain situations—most commonly those cases involving politically sensitive issues revolving around national security, asylum, and resource allocation questions. This deference is justified in a limited sense—in that there are occasions when primary decision-makers may be better qualified than the courts to make a decision on an issue which they are asked to adjudicate upon. However, these should be confined to cases with facts which concern high political, economic, social, or national security situations; and even within these spheres, 'context is everything' (Lord Steyn in *R v Secretary of State ex parte Daly* [2001] 2 WLR 1622). Legitimate 'judicial deference' is part of the process of setting an appropriate level for constitutional review in which a number of factors are taken into account when deciding questions of fundamental rights. The creep of the language of 'margin of appreciation' into this debate, and any discussion of the development of a 'domestic margin of appreciation', is not justified. In the Convention, the doctrine of 'margin of appreciation' is employed to delimit a supra-national court's powers given that it cannot, as a domestic court could, enter into a fresh examination of the facts and socio-political context which has given rise to the issue in question. The 1998 Act ushered in a new era that requires judges to scrutinize, where appropriate, decisions of the executive so as to carry out the duty imposed on them by Parliament to read all legislation, so far as it is possible to do so, compatibly with Convention rights. If judges defer excessively to the executive in inappropriate circumstances it is unlikely that they will be fulfilling the role that Parliament envisaged for them, and the Act's stated intention to 'give further effect to rights and freedoms guaranteed under the European Convention on Human Rights' will be seriously undermined.

Four years after the first edition of this book, in which we asserted that the effect of the Human Rights Act would be 'momentous', were we right? There is little doubt as to the significance of the Human Rights Act as seen by the reach of the statute into all areas of domestic law. Strasbourg principles and interpretative approaches to executive scrutiny, in particular the concept of proportionality, have been steadily imported into domestic law. What Sedley LJ (*Freedom, Law and Justice* (London: Sweet & Maxwell, 1999)) has described as a 'human rights dye' has begun to rinse all UK law and effect considerable change. This book charts the growth of these developments in the Human Rights Act's infancy and hints at future developments in the protection of human rights in the United Kingdom. As the 1998 Act becomes an integral part of our legal landscape we hope to see enhanced protection of fundamental rights through the development of a human rights culture, in which the Convention rights act as a floor beneath which rights protection cannot sink and not as a ceiling to our aspirations.

ACKNOWLEDGEMENTS

Since the first edition of this guide, the list of acknowledgements we ought to make has grown. The long list of names is recorded in full in the previous editions, and we remain enormously grateful to everyone with whom we have discussed the Act and incorporation of the Convention into domestic law over the past decade.

Those who contributed important intellectual stimulus and who require a special mention include Francesca Klug (LSE), Lord Lester of Herne Hill QC, Anne Owers (formerly of JUSTICE and now HM Chief Inspector of Prisons), Jonathan Cooper (formerly of JUSTICE and now at Doughty Street Chambers), Keir Starmer (of Doughty Street Chambers), and especially those many friends and colleagues at Matrix with whom we have debated our ideas. They know who they are. Tony Jennings QC suggested important additions to our coverage of the impact of the Act on the criminal law for which we are very grateful. Since the first edition in 1998 many of our colleagues have produced their own books on the Human Rights Act which are more ambitious, wide-ranging, and comprehensive in their analysis of the scope of human rights law than this introductory text is intended to be. We draw attention to their work in Chapter 10 of this book and hope that this introduction to the Human Rights Act whets the reader's appetite for further exploration of this fascinating area of law.

We are particularly grateful to JUSTICE for allowing us to use their work in dissecting Hansard in Appendix 4—Jonathan Cooper and Adrian Marshall William's *Legislating for Human Rights: the Parliamentary Debates on the Human Rights Act* (London: Hart Publishing, 2001) contains a much more detailed analysis of this material.

We would especially like to thank Gillian Ferguson, who juggled volunteering at Liberty with work on the Matrix Research Panel to write the substantially enhanced Chapter 8, 'Convention Rights and the Human Rights Act'. This, and her wider contributions to the writing process, helped enormously to improve the structure of the book as a whole. We owe her a significant debt.

Lastly, we particularly thank Alistair MacQueen (formerly of Blackstone Press) for commissioning the first edition of the guide, David Stott (formerly of Blackstone Press and OUP), and Annabel Macris, Meg Zawadzki, Becky Allen, and Catherine Minahan (the OUP team), who bore with us through rescheduled deadlines and somehow managed to maintain their calm, charming manners throughout.

The law is up to date to 1 March 2003, and we have been able to include some additional, later cases, such as the discussion of the *ProLife Alliance* case and *Wilson v First County Trust* in the House of Lords, in the final stages.

Any mistakes in the text—of course—are ours.

John Wadham, Helen Mountfield, and Anna Edmundson
July 2003

Table of Cases

Tables of Legislation

1

INTRODUCTION

Rights have been a central theme throughout the history of legal and political thought. Legal philosophers and writers have grappled with the complex implications of the concept over many centuries. What is a 'right'? There are many facets to the debate scrutinizing the forms of rights, their status as legal or moral claims, and their philosophical basis which are beyond the scope of this book (detailed discussions can be found in: Tuck, *Natural Rights Theories: Their Origins and Development* (Cambridge: Cambridge University Press, 1979); Hart, *The Concept of Law* (Oxford: Clarendon Press, 1961); and Dworkin, *Taking Rights Seriously* (London: Duckworth, 1978)). Despite different perspectives on the debate, however, common threads are discernible in the theorists' writings. For example, it is generally accepted that a number of different elements are contained within the concept of a 'right'. When discussing Dworkin's theories on rights, Clayton and Tomlinson point out that contained within a right is both a 'positive' and a 'negative' element:

> The status of a right entails that a person is both entitled to stand on his own right *and* to require others to be duty bound to respect it. It means, for example, that when a person asserts his right to privacy, he has a claim right which others are duty bound to respect; and also that he has a liberty right to privacy which entitles him to insist on an entitlement to be let alone. (*The Law of Human Rights* (Oxford: Oxford University Press, 2000), 20)

Equally, it is accepted by theorists that rights and responsibilities are inextricably linked. In *The Rights of Man* (1791) Tom Paine asserted that 'a Declaration of Rights is, by reciprocity, a Declaration of Duties also . . . whatever is my right as a man, is also the right of another; and it becomes my duty to guarantee, as well as to possess'. For Paine, rights are not purely the preserve of the 'selfish' individual but are vital to a healthy civil society.

English lawyers have traditionally been sceptical of the idea of human rights as a 'positive' concept, preferring instead to focus on the 'negative' conception of liberties. The former Prime Minister John Major proclaimed 'we have no need of a Bill of Rights because we have freedom'. However, that 'freedom' traditionally consisted of residual leftovers after all the law's prohibitions had been obeyed, and offered no protection against the acts or omissions of public bodies that harmed fundamental rights.

The rapid development of international human rights law since the 1950s has offered English lawyers a different perspective. The events of the Second World War and the horrors of the Holocaust led thinkers and politicians (including H.G. Wells and the Roosevelts) to frame new covenants drawing on concepts of rights to try to ensure that such atrocities would never occur again. The first major convention that dealt with human rights, the Universal Declaration on Human Rights (1948), recognized civil and political rights as well as economic, social, and cultural rights. In 1966, the UN-sponsored International Covenant on Civil and Political Rights (ICCPR) was opened for signature. In the same year, the International Covenant on Economic, Social and Cultural Rights (ICESCR) was drawn up, but, unlike the ICCPR, the rights contained within it are subject to the availability of resources and the obligations are to be 'progressively realized'. Doubts about the universality and practicability of economic and social rights have been expressed and the nature of the ICESCR accommodates these concerns (see Steiner and Alston, *International Human Rights in Context* (Oxford: Oxford University Press, 2000)). A range of other legal instruments aimed at securing key human rights for specified groups of people (including women, ethnic groups, children, and refugees) and at protecting particular thematic rights (for example, the UN Convention against Torture) have since become an integral part of international law. These treaties and conventions articulate a range of different rights that combine the twin concepts of 'positive' and 'negative' rights, and strive to achieve a balance between individuals' rights and their linked responsibilities.

The development that has had the biggest impact on the United Kingdom today, and on international human rights jurisprudence more broadly, has been the European Convention for the Protection of Human Rights and Fundamental Freedoms (the Convention). Although the United Kingdom was among the first signatories to the Convention in 1951, moves to make it part of domestic law are of more recent origin. Part of the reason for this is the British political and constitutional tradition. 'Freedom', as it has emerged in this tradition, rests largely on the (negative) freedom from Government interference rather than on positive human rights guarantees enshrined in a written constitution or human rights instrument.

1.1 HUMAN RIGHTS IN THE UNITED KINGDOM BEFORE THE 1998 ACT

1.1.1 Rights in English Common Law before the 1998 Act

In 1215 the Magna Carta was drafted, which introduced the concepts of due process and trial by jury. In 1688, the Bill of Rights emerged from the 'Glorious Revolution' and limited the monarch's powers, in most respects, to those permitted by Parliament. In the eighteenth and early nineteenth centuries, many ideas that we regard as central to the rule of law—such as a philosophy of liberty and the notion of the freedom of the press—were developed by English thinkers such as Tom Paine, John Locke, and J.S. Mill. But despite their political writings and contemporary events such as the French Revolution and the American Declaration of Independence, Britain did not adopt a comparable 'Declaration of the Rights of Man'. Until 1998, Britain was almost unique among developed democracies in having no written constitution and no positive guarantees of rights.

The foundation of our liberties has been a negative one, outlined in the nineteenth-century theory of residual rights articulated by Dicey. The doctrine holds that individuals may say or do whatever they please provided they do not transgress the substantive law or infringe the legal rights of others. In other words, 'we are free to do everything except that which we are forbidden to do by law'. Further, the Crown and other public authorities may not do anything unless they are so authorized by a rule of common law (including the royal prerogative) or statute, and thus may not interfere with individuals' liberties.

As well as these residual freedoms, classical writers such as Blackstone, in *Commentaries on the Laws of England*, and Dicey identified a separate body of fundamental rights in English common law (including the right to personal security, the right to personal liberty, and the rights to private property, to freedom of discussion, and to assembly). These 'guarantees' of fundamental rights were protected by the common law presumption of legality, which holds that rights cannot be removed by Parliament except by express words (see Chapter 2). These fundamental rights were recognized by the courts as part of the common law, the 'birthright of the people' and part of the compact between monarch and Parliament (see *Halsbury's Laws of England*, 4th edn, 8(2), 'Constitutional Law and Human Rights'). Dicey argued that this system of residual rights worked well, as Parliament, elected by the people, was the only body which could legislate rights out of existence. But this belief has not been borne out by experience.

The enormous growth of the power of public and quasi-public bodies over the lives of individuals during the twentieth century has diluted the power of Parliament to scrutinize legislation—if , indeed, it ever had such omnipotence. Since Dicey was writing, the way in which power is distributed in modern society has altered fundamentally. It is no longer accurate to talk of constitutional power being shared between the legislative, executive, and judiciary alone. The imposition of strict parliamentary party-political discipline has also meant that the executive's power within the legislature is often unchallenged, and the growth of quasi-public bodies performing privatized functions of Government has led to a re-allocation of public power amongst a variety of different constitutional actors.

In any case, as J.S. Mill observed in *On Liberty*, democracy is not in itself a guarantee against the tyranny of the majority over unpopular minorities. In the notorious *East Asian Africans Case* (1981) 3 EHRR 76, the European Commission of Human Rights found that the Commonwealth Immigrants Act 1968, passed to stop British passport holders in East Africa who were fleeing persecution in their home countries coming to the United Kingdom, was motivated by racism. Parliament was also prone to legislating to remove fundamental rights as, for example, in the Criminal Justice and Public Order Act 1994, when the newly created offence of 'trespassory assembly' limited individuals' common law right to assemble (one of the fundamental rights identified by Dicey). Relying on the common law alone to protect rights has inherent problems as courts are unable to extend the law (or 'legislate') in completely new fields since only incremental development is permitted.

For further reading, see Allan, *Constitutional Rights and the Common Law: Law, Liberty and Justice* (Oxford: Clarendon Press, 1993) and Singh, *The Future of Human Rights in the United Kingdom* (London: Hart Publishing, 1998).

1.1.2 European Convention Rights in the United Kingdom before the 1998 Act

The Convention was drafted with a significant input from English lawyers. The United Kingdom ratified the Convention in 1951 and recognized the individual right of petition in 1966. But the positive guarantees of 'fundamental rights' contained in the international Convention in which the United Kingdom was so instrumental, have been found by the European Court of Human Rights (ECtHR) to have been violated by successive Governments in a surprising number of cases (see the partial list in Hunt, *Using Human Rights Law in English Courts* (London: Hart Publishing, 1997, Appendix 1). Part of the difficulty was the inability of the judiciary to consider and develop English law consistently with the Convention. Under the dualist principles of English law, international treaties ratified by the UK Government, such as the Convention, did not have legal effect domestically because they had not been incorporated into domestic law by an Act of Parliament.

However, even before the Human Rights Act 1998 came into force—indeed, even before the Bill was drafted—it was possible for Convention principles to have an impact on domestic law either indirectly (through judgments against the United Kingdom in Strasbourg), or directly (through the use of legal arguments based on the Convention in English courts).

Over the last five decades the Convention has, indirectly, had an increasing impact on the development of the English law. Findings of violations against the

United Kingdom have led to several changes being made to primary legislation. The Strasbourg Court's judgment in *Sunday Times v United Kingdom (No. 1)* (1980) 2 EHRR 245 was an important factor leading to the reform of the law of contempt by the Contempt of Court Act 1981. The violation of the right to respect for private life in Article 8, found by the ECtHR in the telephone-tapping case of *Malone v United Kingdom* (1984) 7 EHRR 14, led to the enactment of the Interception of Communications Act 1985.

The judiciary was also able directly to consider the provisions of the Convention in cases before the domestic courts. The most important pre-Act uses of the Convention were as follows:

(a) As an aid to the construction of legislation in cases of ambiguity. For example, in *R v Secretary of State for the Home Department ex parte Brind* [1991] 1 AC 696. There is a presumption that Parliament does not intend to act in breach of international law (and the specific treaty obligations the UK Government has committed to on behalf of the Crown), so where there is ambiguity in a statute the courts will construe the law consistently with these international treaty obligations.

(b) To establish the scope of the common law where it is developing and uncertain, or where it is certain but incomplete. For example, in *Derbyshire County Council v Times Newspapers Ltd* [1992] QB 770, where because the common law had conflicting judgments, Article 10 informed the House of Lords' decision that a local authority could not bring an action for libel as it would offend against the freedom of expression protections in the Convention.

(c) To inform the exercise of judicial (as opposed to administrative) discretion. For example, in *R v Khan* [1996] 3 WLR 162, the House of Lords held that a trial judge may have regard to the Convention as a material consideration in exercising the discretion conferred by s. 78 of the Police and Criminal Evidence Act 1984 as to whether to exclude evidence.

(d) To inform decisions on Community law taken by domestic courts. For example, in *Johnston v Chief Constable of the Royal Ulster Constabulary* [1987] QB 129, where the European Court of Justice (ECJ) took Articles 6 and 13 into account in determining that the applicant did not have an effective remedy in her sex discrimination case. The ECJ has declared that the general principles of EC law include the protection of fundamental rights. This means that not only should English judges have regard to the Convention when dealing with questions of fundamental rights in EC law, but also that ECJ judgments involving fundamental rights are to be regarded as authoritative when domestic courts grapple with questions of EC law. These issues are discussed in detail in Chapter 7.

These techniques continue to be important, and should also still be used in relation to other international treaties that have not been incorporated into English law. For a more detailed analysis of how this is done, see Hunt, *Using Human Rights Law in English Courts* (London: Hart Publishing, 1997); Beloff and Mountfield,

'Unconventional Behaviour? Judicial uses of the European Convention on Human Rights in England and Wales' [1996] EHRLR 467.

1.2 THE INCORPORATION OF THE CONVENTION

The initial justifications advanced by Parliament for not giving full effect to the provisions of the Convention included concerns that the constitutional doctrines of parliamentary sovereignty and the separation of powers would be irreparably harmed. In particular, commentators were worried that judges would wield too much power and that the difficult societal questions about balancing conflicts of interests would be resolved by unelected, unaccountable judges rather than through political debate by elected MPs. Opponents also argued that it was an unnecessary step given that rights were already adequately protected by the common law, and indeed the incorporation of the 'vague', general principles of the Convention would be a retrograde step for the protection of rights in the United Kingdom as the 'flexibility' of the unwritten constitution would be constrained.

Over the past 50 years, those views on the incorporation of the Convention into domestic law slowly changed, culminating in the Human Rights Act 1998. Supporters of a Bill of Rights had long argued that the common law safeguards for rights were inadequate and open to abuse because of their vulnerability to constant change from party politics. The glaring facts that the United Kingdom was one of a handful of western democracies which did not have a written Bill of Rights, and that British citizens were forced to undertake a lengthy and expensive route to enforcing their Convention rights in Strasbourg, were also unavoidable. Supporters pointed out that the strict party discipline imposed on the parliamentary political parties did not allow for a fully independent legislature, and so a Bill of Rights was needed to deal with what Lord Hailsham called an 'elective dictatorship'. The debate on a Bill of Rights during this period was not the preserve of one political party or political philosophy. In the late 1940s the main British protagonists of what become the Convention were Conservatives such as Winston Churchill and Harold Macmillan. Equally, it was the Labour Attlee Government that ratified the Convention in 1951, the Churchill Government that ratified the First Protocol in 1953, and the Labour Government of Wilson that accepted the right of individual petition to the ECtHR in 1966.

In 1968, the publication of the pamphlet *Democracy and Individual Rights* by Anthony Lester (now the Liberal Democrat peer Lord Lester QC), effectively opened the debate in a contemporary context. Lester suggested that incorporating the Convention was only a first step for enshrining human rights guarantees but would be no more than an interim measure. In subsequent years, the issue of incorporating the Convention was debated a number of times from a variety of political perspectives. An important step forwards was made in 1974, when Sir Leslie Scarman (the cross-bencher Lord Scarman) wrote of the need for an instrument to challenge the sovereignty of Parliament and to protect basic human rights which could not be adequately protected by the legislature alone. Scarman was in favour of entrenchment. He believed that only by making a Bill of Rights superior to the machinations of Parliament could such fundamental rights be protected (see the Hamlyn Lectures series, in particular *English Law—The New Dimension*).

In 1975, the Labour Party National Executive Committee unveiled a *Charter of Human Rights*. This document advocated an unentrenched Human Rights Act. This 'unentrenched' proposal was regarded as insufficient by many who considered that such an Act would offer inadequate protection to individual interests against the growing power of the state. In particular, many Conservatives (including Sir Geoffrey Howe (now Lord Howe), Sir Leon Brittan, and Roy Jenkins (the late Lord Jenkins)) preferred the concept of a Bill of Rights with entrenched clauses that would prevent even Parliament from granting the executive excessive power over the lives of individuals.

In 1976, the Liberal Democrat Lord Wade moved a Bill in the House of Lords which proposed to entrench the Convention as a part of all existing legislation and to make it an entrenched part of all subsequent enactments unless Parliament specifically legislated otherwise. Lord Wade and Lord Harris continued to be the chief advocates for a Bill of Rights in the Lords. In 1978, a House of Lords Select Committee examined the arguments for and against legislation to incorporate the Convention and create a Bill of Rights. However, traditional constitutional views prevailed, and particularly a concern about the idea of judges deciding 'human rights' cases. The fear was that this would remove the judiciary from its traditionally impartial role, supposedly beyond politics, and embroil it in (party) political questions.

In 1993 there was a clear shift in Labour Party policy, and the leadership (now under John Smith) started to voice more enthusiasm for a Bill of Rights (see, for instance, Francesca Klug, *A People's Charter: Liberty's Bill of Rights* (London: National Council for Civil Liberties, 1991); Michael Zander, *A Bill of Rights?* (London: Sweet & Maxwell, 1996)). The Labour Party conference in October 1993 had adopted a policy supporting a two-stage process to implement mechanisms to enforce rights. The first included the incorporation of the European Convention of Human Rights, entrenching this set of rights by the use of a 'notwithstanding clause' procedure. This was similar to the Canadian Charter of Rights and Freedoms, and would have led to the Convention overriding domestic law unless Parliament expressly provided for it to apply notwithstanding that it would violate the human rights instrument. The conference also advocated the establishment of a human rights commission to monitor and promote human rights. Tony Blair MP set out his views in *The Guardian*, 16 July 1994, and reaffirmed the need for strengthened incorporation and the idea of a 'notwithstanding clause'.

Lord Lester of Herne Hill continued his human rights work in the Lords by introducing a Bill in November 1994. The Bill did not receive support from the

Conservative Government. Particular aspects of the proposed Bill were criticized by the Law Lords, but they supported incorporation in so far as it allowed United Kingdom judges to interpret human rights away from Strasbourg. The fact that a Human Rights Bill had received any support from the Law Lords was a significant development.

By December 1996, Jack Straw MP and Paul Boateng MP had published a Consultation Paper, *Bringing Rights Home*, setting out the Labour Party's plans to incorporate the Convention if they won the election due in 1997. Whereas the 1993 policy had advocated incorporation to be followed by a second stage in the form of a home-grown Bill of Rights, the Consultation Paper deferred the second stage, and the five key issues posed by the paper concerned only the incorporation of the Convention. In May 1997, Labour won a landslide victory, on a manifesto which included a commitment to incorporate the Convention into domestic law. The debate then turned to *how* the Convention should be incorporated, and in particular to whether it should be permitted to override statutes, subject to a 'notwithstanding' clause. The unique solution adopted in the Human Rights Act 1998 is the subject of Chapters 3 to 6 of this book.

1.3 THE HUMAN RIGHTS ACT AS A CONSTITUTIONAL INSTRUMENT

The Human Rights Act has been described by Lord Bingham as 'an important constitutional instrument' (*Brown v Stott* [2001] 2 WLR 817, at 835). It is generally agreed that the 1998 Act is a constitutional statute as it conditions the legal relationship between citizen and state in a general, overarching manner and enlarges or diminishes the scope of what we would now regard as fundamental constitutional rights (see Laws LJ in *Thoburn v Sunderland City Council* [2002] 2 WLR 247). The English tradition of regarding the sovereignty of the democratic Parliament as being the cornerstone of its (unwritten) constitution, and the fact that the Convention was to be enforceable in the courts, created some concerns in the debates before the 1998 Act came into being.

1.3.1 Parliamentary Sovereignty and Entrenchment

The doctrine that Parliament is the supreme legal power has been influential on English law through the writings of Coke, Blackstone, and, more recently, Dicey (see Wade, *Administrative Law* (Oxford: Oxford University Press, 2001). The doctrine has several elements. According to the theory, the sovereign legislature (the Queen, the Lords, and the Commons) can make and repeal any legislation whatsoever, so that no Parliament can bind its successors. As a result, it is impossible to 'entrench' particular legislation (for example, a Bill of Rights) by specifying that it would be repealable only under some specially safeguarded process. A corollary is that no act of the sovereign legislature could be invalid in the eyes of a court, because Parliament alone has the legal and political power to make laws. The potency of the doctrine has been diluted by the changes to the domestic legal system effected by the European Communities Act 1972, but it still carries some force. The problem with the doctrine is that courts do not have ultimate power fully to protect rights, and have no power to ensure that Parliament will not, in future, legislate such rights out of existence. To protect fundamental rights, some form of 'entrenchment' is necessary.

The solution adopted in the Human Rights Act is a complex one, reflecting a delicate political compromise between 'incorporating' Convention rights and retaining parliamentary sovereignty. The rule of construction in s. 3 of the Act places courts under a strong interpretative obligation to read and give effect to all legislation, whether primary or secondary, old or recent, in a way which is compatible with Convention rights 'so far as it is possible to do so'. Section 4 makes it clear that if a conflict between the provisions of a piece of legislation and Convention rights cannot be overcome, higher courts will have to make a declaration of incompatibility. The court cannot 'strike down' the offending Act and it still remains operative. The scheme of the HRA means that the only legal effect of a declaration of incompatibility is to permit (but not oblige) a minister to amend the impugned legislation by a 'remedial order' under s. 10. If the declaration of incompatibility is not accepted by the Government, and there is no overwhelming parliamentary pressure to change the law, there is no domestic legal obligation to change the law (see Chapter 6, 'Human Rights Act Remedies for Breaches of Convention Rights'). Further, s. 6(3) excludes Parliament from the definition of 'public authority' so that it is not bound by the provisions of the Act. This form of legislation for human rights is not as strong as the 'Canadian model', which gives courts the power to strike down primary legislation but allows the legislature to enact measures for a limited period 'notwithstanding' its contravention of provisions in the Charter of Fundamental Rights and Freedoms. It is, however, much stronger than the 'New Zealand model' which imposes only a weak obligation upon courts to 'prefer' an interpretation of legislation which is consistent with the Bill of Rights Act over an inconsistent one if possible.

Ultimately, the 1998 Act protects the principle of parliamentary sovereignty, because it does not permit the Convention to be used so as to override primary legislation: if a statute is clear in its terms, and clearly incompatible with the Convention, courts must give effect to it. Equally, if the terms of the primary legislation require subordinate legislation made under it (which will usually be in a statutory instrument) to be interpreted in a way which means that the subordinate legislation is incompatible with the Convention, it must still be given effect even though this may result in a breach of a Convention right. For more details see Bamforth, 'Parliamentary Sovereignty and the Human Rights Act 1998' [1998] PL 572.

1.3.2 Politicizing the Judiciary?

Montesquieu's influential notion of the 'separation of powers' describes his view of the proper distribution of power within a constitution between the legislature, executive, and judiciary. It suggests that the three branches of Government must balance functions between them to prevent an abuse of power. The theory has been adopted by important English jurists: 'Parliament makes the laws, the judiciary interpret them' (Lord Diplock in *Duport Steels Ltd v Sirs* [1980] 1 WLR 142). Many thinkers have warned against the perils of giving an excess of political power to an unelected and unaccountable judiciary. The best-known exponent of this cautious approach to written Bills of Rights is Griffith, *The Politics of the Judiciary*, 5th edn (London: Fontana Press, 1997).

During the passage of the Human Rights Bill some commentators, such as Ewing in 'The Human Rights Act and Parliamentary Democracy' [1999] MLR 79, particularly feared the politicization of the judiciary and an encroachment on the notion of parliamentary sovereignty because of the strong approach to statutory construction required by s. 3 of the 1998 Act. However, the law has been no stranger to politically controversial cases over the centuries. Recent examples are cases such as *R v Secretary of State for the Home Department ex parte Brind* [1991] 1 AC 696, which excluded Sinn Fein politicians from media appearances but allowed actors to stand in, and *Airedale NHS Trust v Bland* [1993] AC 789, which determined that the life-support machine of one of the Hillsborough stadium collapse victims should be turned off. English judges have always had to decide cases in areas of political controversy, and the Human Rights Act has ushered in only a different degree of scrutiny, not a different kind. Indeed, one of the important effects of the Act has been to focus public attention and debate on the proper nature and scope of the judicial function.

In response to recent criticisms of judicial 'activism', Lord Woolf has reminded us that:

> judges are only doing what they have to swear to do on appointment and that is to give a judgement according to law. The law now includes the HRA. By upholding the HRA the courts are not interfering with the will of Parliament. On the contrary, when they interfere, the judges are protecting the public by ensuring that the Government complies with the laws made by Parliament. The courts are therefore acting in support of Parliament and not otherwise. ('The Impact of Human Rights', Speech at Oxford Lyceum, 6 March 2003)

Lastly, s. 19 is an important provision in balancing the role of the executive, Parliament, and the courts. It presumes that new legislation is to be (and can be) read compatibly with the Convention. When legislation is introduced into Parliament for a second reading, the introducing minister must make a statement that, in his or her view, the legislation is compatible with the Convention, or make a statement that although the legislation is not compatible with the Convention the Government still wishes to proceed. It is unlikely that Governments will often wish to state publicly that they are acting incompatibly with an internationally binding human rights instrument, though they have been prepared to do so on occasion. Where a 'section 19' statement is made, Parliament has the opportunity to thoroughly examine the minister's assertion before the Bill is passed (with the help of reports of the Joint Parliamentary Committee on Human Rights—see 1.5.2 below). In order that s. 19 statements become powerful democratic tools for scrutinizing Bills, we hope that Parliamentarians will press for detailed assurances of compatibility from the Government, rather than accepting generalized, uninformative statements that Bills are Convention compliant (for a critique of the initial operation of s. 19 see Wadham, 'The Human Rights Act: One Year On' [2001] EHRLR 620). A s. 19 statement of compatibility also gives a strong indication to the judiciary that the Government intended its new legislation to be human rights compliant and that the judges are able to proceed with their judicial scrutiny with that intention in mind.

In the first three years since the 1998 Act came into force, judges seem to have been acutely aware of criticism of the kind discussed above, and have erred on the side of caution rather than judicial activism. The development of a notion of 'judicial deference', which considers when it is appropriate (and when it is not) for courts to defer to decisions made by other constitutional bodies such as the legislative, executive, or administrative branches, has been a contentious one since the 1998 Act came into force and is considered in detail in Chapter 4 below.

Ultimately, the 1998 Act entrusts the judiciary with the task of ensuring that legislation and executive action do not infringe individuals' Convention rights and freedoms any more than absolutely necessary. This has led some commentators to identify the nascent development of a 'dialogue' between the various branches of Government (see Edwards, 'Judicial Deference under the Human Rights Act' (2002) 65 MLR 859), as has already developed under the Canadian Charter of Rights and Freedoms. This 'dialogue' takes place when a court, in reviewing legislative and executive action, requires justification within the terms of the Convention for the law or action in question, and considers the explicit reasons advanced by the executive and legislature for any limitations on these fundamental rights. The final word, however, still rests with Parliament or the executive. In the Canadian case of *Vriend v Alberta* [1998] 1 SCR 495, Iacobucci J concluded:

> . . . a great value of judicial review and this dialogue among the branches is that each of the branches is made somewhat accountable to the other. The work of the legislature is reviewed by the courts and the work of the court in its decisions can be reacted to by the legislature in the passing of new legislation . . . This dialogue between and accountability of each of the branches has the effect of enhancing the democratic process, not denying it.

This concept of 'dialogue' is the most appropriate method for evaluating the interaction between Parliament, the executive, and the judiciary under the new constitutional arrangement ushered in by the Human Rights Act.

1.4 HUMAN RIGHTS IN THE UNITED KINGDOM AFTER THE 1998 ACT

1.4.1 The Convention in the United Kingdom after the 1998 Act

The Human Rights Act 1998 makes the Convention far more central to the practice of law in Britain. Until it came into force, there was no overriding presumption that Parliament intended in the past and in the future to legislate so as to conform with the rights protected by the Convention. The use of the Convention was limited to cases where the law was ambiguous. Public authorities had no duty to exercise administrative discretion in a manner which complied with the Convention, nor even to have regard to the rights contained in the Convention as 'relevant considerations' when reaching a decision (*R v Secretary of State for the Home Department ex parte Brind* [1991] 1 AC 696), except where they had expressly stated that they would do so (for example, *Briton v Secretary of State for the Environment* [1997] JPL 617). The Act changed that. Its purpose is to extend the ways in which the Convention can be used before domestic courts while retaining the existing ones. It is described in its long title as 'An Act to give *further* effect' to the rights and freedoms guaranteed under the Convention (emphasis added).

1.4.2 The Effects of the 1998 Act

The Act creates a statutory general requirement that all legislation (past or future) be read and given effect in a way that is compatible with the Convention. The effect of the Human Rights Act 1998 on English law is the subject of Chapters 3 to 5, where the features of the Act are set out in more detail. In summary, in *all* cases in which Convention rights are in question, the Act gives 'further effect' to the Convention, whether the litigants are private persons or public authorities. It does this in three ways:

(a) by obliging courts to decide all cases before them (whether brought under statute or the common law) compatibly with Convention rights unless prevented from doing so either by primary legislation, or by provisions made under primary legislation which cannot be read compatibly with the Convention (s. 6(1) to (3));

(b) by introducing an obligation for courts to interpret existing and future legislation in conformity with the Convention wherever possible (s. 3);

(c) by requiring courts to take Strasbourg case law into account in all cases, in so far as they consider it relevant to proceedings before them (s. 2(1)).

The overall scheme of the Act is discussed in detail in Chapter 3 'The Framework of the Human Rights Act'. In summary the 1998 Act is underpinned by the specific provisions in the following sections:

(a) *Section 6* which requires public authorities—including courts—to act compatibility with the Convention unless they are prevented from doing so by statute. This means that the courts have their own primary statutory duty to give effect to the Convention unless a statute positively prevents this.

(b) *Section 3* contains the overriding objective of the Act. This is to weave the Convention into the existing legal system, so that all courts will consider Convention arguments and interpret any legal issue consistently with them if possible.

(c) *Section 2* requires any court or tribunal determining a question that has arisen in connection with a Convention right to take into account the jurisprudence of the Strasbourg organs (the European Court and Commission of Human Rights and the Committee of Ministers). This jurisprudence must be considered 'so far as, in the opinion of the court or tribunal, it is relevant to the proceedings in which that question has arisen', whenever the judgment, decision, or opinion to be taken into account was handed down.

(d) *Section 7* of the Act creates new, directly enforceable rights against public bodies, and against quasi-public bodies which have some public functions when they are acting in the sphere of those public functions. It introduces a new ground of illegality into proceedings brought by way of judicial review, namely, a failure to comply with the Convention rights protected by the Act, subject to a 'statutory obligation' defence. It creates a new cause of action against public bodies that fail to act compatibly with the Convention. Finally, Convention rights are available as a ground of defence or appeal in cases brought by public bodies against private persons (in both criminal and civil cases). Only persons classified as 'victims' by s. 7 of the Act are able to enforce the duty to act compatibly with the Convention in proceedings against the authority, and only victims will have standing to bring proceedings by way of judicial review.

(e) *Section 8(1)* gives a court a wide power to grant such relief, remedies, or orders as it considers just and appropriate, provided they are within its existing powers.

(f) *Section 11* prevents the Act being used to diminish any greater rights protection that previously existed. It enables litigants who, because they are not victims of the decision, cannot challenge a public body's decision directly using the Act's provisions. Nonetheless, they are able to rely on the court's s. 3 interpretative obligations and use Convention arguments in the circumstances in which this was possible before the Act was brought into force (see 1.2 above).

1.5 THE INSTITUTIONAL FRAMEWORK—CREATING A CULTURE OF RIGHTS

Many commentators, including the authors, hoped that the Human Rights Act would have a broad impact on our political and social (as well as legal) culture. So, for example, Francesca Klug's excellent book *Values for a Godless Age* (Harmondsworth: Penguin, 2000) not only explains 'the story of the United Kingdom's New Bill of Rights' but also highlights the importance of creating a new culture to respect and protect human rights and make the Act work for every citizen, not just those who have the resources to pursue litigation.

There are two 'dimensions' to this new culture—ethical and institutional. The ethical dimension involves individual members of society developing an understanding that they enjoy certain rights by virtue of being human (not merely as a contingent gift of the state); *and* that with these rights comes the responsibility to respect the human rights of other individual citizens. Developing an institutional human rights culture involves mainstreaming fundamental principles into the design and delivery of policy, legislation, and public services so that decisions taken by public authorities such as schools and hospitals are proportionate, rational, and respectful of fundamental rights. The obligation on public authorities imposed by the Human Rights Act goes beyond non-interference with rights and requires such bodies to take active steps to protect people's rights against interference by others (see 2.3.2 below).

1.5.1 Government Implementation of the 1998 Act

An estimated £4.5 million was invested in judicial training for the introduction of the Human Rights Act, and on preparing public authorities for implementation. This task was led by the Human Rights Unit at the Home Office. It was assisted by a Human Rights Task Force, the purpose of which was to maintain dialogue between the Government and non-governmental organizations (NGOs) on the readiness of public authorities for implementation. The Task Force continued to meet until April 2001, and had a particular role in supporting the training and development of public and judicial authorities, and in the production and dissemination of guidance on good practice and publicity. It also aimed to raise general awareness, especially amongst young people, of the rights and responsibilities flowing from incorporation, and thus to help to build a human rights culture in the UK.

Following the general election in 2001, responsibility for human rights, along with freedom of information and data protection, was transferred from the Home Office to the Lord Chancellor's Department (LCD). In June 2003, as part of the Government's plans to modernize the constitution and public services, the Prime Minister announced the creation of a new Department for Constitutional Affairs (DCA). This will incorporate most of the responsibilities of the former LCD, including human rights.

The extent to which the Human Rights Act has altered the institutional culture of Whitehall, and of public authorities generally, is the subject of heated political, as well as legal, debate. The Constitution Unit at the University of London undertook a detailed examination of the steps taken by the Government to implement the Human Rights Act. A comprehensive overview of the progress up to the transfer of responsibilities to the LCD can be found in Jeremy Croft's article, 'Whitehall and the Human Rights Act' [2001] EHRLR 392.

1.5.2 A Human Rights Committee in Parliament

The Labour Party Consultation Paper, *Bringing Rights Home*, and the White Paper, *Rights Brought Home* (see Appendix 3), both said that 'Parliament itself should play a leading role in protecting the rights which are at the heart of parliamentary democracy'. A Human Rights Committee has proved to be a fundamental part of this. The idea of a Human Rights Committee in Parliament originated in Francesca Klug's *A People's Charter: Liberty's Bill of Rights* (London: National Council for Civil Liberties, 1991). Klug's suggestion was that the new committee might conduct inquiries on a range of human rights issues relating to the Convention, and produce reports to assist the Government and Parliament in deciding what action to take. It might also range more widely, examining issues relating to the other international obligations of the United Kingdom, such as proposals to accept new rights under other human rights treaties. Another main task proposed for the committee was to conduct an inquiry into whether a Human Rights Commission is needed and, if so, how it should operate.

The Joint Parliamentary Committee of Human Rights (a Select Committee consisting of members of both Houses of Parliament) (JCHR) was not appointed until January 2001. Its terms of reference are to consider:

(a) matters relating to human rights in the United Kingdom (excluding consideration of individual cases); and

(b) proposals for remedial orders made under the fast-track legislative procedure (s. 10) of the Human Rights Act, including whether the special attention of Parliament should be drawn to them.

The JCHR has generally been recognized to carry out important work, including prolific scrutiny of important bills. It has had an important influence on Parliament and, in particular, on controversial and human-rights sensitive pieces of legislation such as the Anti-Terrorism, Crime and Security Act 2001. In the 2001–2002 session, it also decided to establish an inquiry into the case for a Human Rights Commission in the United Kingdom. For a detailed account of the work of the body to date, see Lord Lester's (a member of the JCHR) article, 'Parliamentary Scrutiny of Legislation under the Human Rights Act 1998' [2002] EHRLR 432.

1.5.3 A Human Rights Commission?

One of the aspects of the Human Rights Act 1998 which was most criticized during its passage through Parliament was the decision not to set up a Human Rights Commission at the same time. The White Paper, *Rights Brought Home*, states that more consideration would have to be given to the relationship of a new Commission to the existing bodies set up to promote anti-discrimination legislation—the Equal Opportunities Commission, the Commission for Racial Equality, and the Disability Rights Commission. Clearly, financial constraints were also a factor.

The option of setting up a Human Rights Commission in future has not been ruled out. The recommendation in the JCHR's Sixth Report of Session 2002–2003 was that the case for setting up such a Commission was compelling. Without it, the development of a 'culture of understanding of rights and responsibilities' envisaged by the original proposals had been significantly stalled (see also Wadham, 'The Human Rights Act: One Year On' [2001] EHRLR 620, for a detailed critique of the initial steps taken by the public sector to institute this culture of human rights and the need for a body to spur on future developments).

1.6 THE FUTURE OF HUMAN RIGHTS PROTECTION IN THE UNITED KINGDOM

The partial incorporation of the Convention into domestic law is not the end of a debate on a Bill of Rights. Both the Convention and the 1998 Act have gaps in their protection of human rights which will need addressing in the future in order fully to realize the Government's pledge in 1997 to 'bring rights home'.

1.6.1 Weaknesses of the Convention

The Convention was drafted in the aftermath of the Second World War and, although it is a 'living instrument' (see Chapter 2), it is not a contemporary document as the values it embodies are only those already current 50 years ago. It has a number of deficiencies that might have been expected to be remedied in a statute designed to protect human rights at the beginning of the twenty-first century. For example, it does not contain a right to freedom of information; the anti-discrimination provision is 'parasitic' in that it applies only where another Convention right has been violated; there is little specific recognition of children's rights; and it does not contain an absolute prohibition against self-incrimination for criminal defendants. (For further discussion see Wadham, 'Why Incorporation of the European Convention on Human Rights is Not Enough', in Gordon and Wilmot-Smith (eds), *Human Rights in the United Kingdom* (Oxford: Oxford University Press, 1996); and Wadham and Taylor, 'Bringing More Rights Home' [2002] EHRLR 713.)

In addition, the type of Convention rights which are enforceable in the UK courts are limited in range compared with the nature of rights more broadly, and offer little protection to social and economic rights. See, for example, the South African Constitution, which contains a right to adequate housing and a right of access to health care, social security, and emergency medical treatment, and a right to an environment which is not harmful to health or well-being. The Convention (and thus the Human Rights Act) has no such explicit protection for these types of rights.

1.6.2 Weaknesses of the 1998 Act

The omission of Article 13 of the Convention from the Human Rights Act is a significant weakness. Article 13 is the 'remedies' provision. It provides:

> Everyone whose rights and freedoms as set forth in this Convention are violated shall have an effective remedy before a national authority notwithstanding that the violation has been committed by persons acting in an official capacity.

Non-governmental organizations and legal bodies pressed for the inclusion of Article 13, in order to ensure that effective protection would be given to rights. The Government argued in Parliament that the inclusion of Article 13 was unnecessary as the Bill itself provided sufficient procedures and remedies to ensure that the other rights in the Convention could be enforced. It was also clear that the Government was of the opinion that the inclusion of Article 13 might be something of a 'wild card' in the hands of the judiciary. Despite this non-inclusion, where Article 13 plays a part in the Strasbourg jurisprudence, courts will be obliged by s. 2 to have regard to it when a question arises under the Act 'in connection with' a Convention right. It is therefore clear that the courts will be able to have regard to Article 13 and the jurisprudence founded on it (see the former Lord Chancellor, Lord Irvine's, response to Lord Lester of Herne Hill, Hansard HL, 18 November 1997, col. 477). Whether this will allow the courts to consider this as part of the intention behind the Act under *Pepper v Hart* [1993] AC 593, was debated in the House of Commons (Hansard HC, 20 May 1998, col. 980).

This is not purely a technical argument and may be important in certain cases. For example, in *Chahal v United Kingdom* (1996) 23 EHRR 413, the right to an effective remedy was crucial to the judgment of the Court. This was a case involving the detention and threatened deportation of a Sikh activist who the Government said was a terrorist. The key question in the case was whether, given that the Government claimed that the details of the case against him could not be disclosed to protect national security, the courts could provide an effective remedy. It was decided that there was no effective remedy, and as a result of that case the Government enacted the Special Immigration Appeals Commission Act 1998, which creates a new special right of appeal in such cases.

1.6.3 Future Developments?

There are, therefore, still steps that need to be taken towards ensuring that human rights are fully protected in the UK. Despite its previous manifesto commitment to a comprehensive Bill of Rights, it is unlikely that the Labour Government will take any concrete proposals forward in the near future to extend the scope of the protection currently offered. The EU Charter of Fundamental Rights (see Chapter 7) does contain a number of social and economic rights (including rights of access to medical care and environmental rights), but it is unlikely that, at least for the present time, the Charter will be legally enforceable in domestic courts. Nor is it likely that other human rights instruments which bind the UK in international law will be incorporated into domestic law in the foreseeable future.

Nonetheless, the greatest domestic developments in human rights may come from increasing awareness of, and recourse to, the other international human rights treaties that the United Kingdom has ratified and the diverse range of protection that they offer. There is no doubt that incorporation of the Convention has opened the eyes of English lawyers and judges to the creative ways in which international legal obligations interact with domestic laws. Although treaties such as the ICCPR and the Convention on the Rights of the Child are not directly enforceable in the English courts, they are increasingly likely to offer interpretative guidance to courts and to inspire new developments in similar ways to those in which the Convention was used by the judiciary prior to incorporation.

Despite the criticisms expressed above, the Human Rights Act is a tremendously positive development for the protection of human rights in the United Kingdom. We agree wholeheartedly with Lord Irvine, who has called for this constitutional statute to be celebrated:

> The Act represents one small manageable step for our Courts; but it is a major leap for our constitution and our culture. It has transformed our system of law into one of positive rights, responsibilities and freedoms, where before we had only the freedom to do what was not prohibited . . . It has breathed new life into the relationship between Parliament, Government and the Judiciary, so that all three are working together to ensure that a culture of respect for human rights becomes embedded across the whole of our society. ('The Human Rights Act Two Years On', Durham University lecture)

2

THE FRAMEWORK OF THE EUROPEAN CONVENTION ON HUMAN RIGHTS

2.1 INTRODUCTION

The European Convention for the Protection of Human Rights and Fundamental Freedoms is a treaty agreed by states that are members of the Council of Europe. The Council of Europe was established in 1949 as part of the Allies' programme to 'reconstruct durable civilization on the mainland of Europe'. Today it has over 40 members with a wide variety of political traditions, including many former Communist states from Eastern Europe. The United Kingdom ratified the Convention in 1951 but, unlike many of the other signatories, did not set about incorporating the Convention rights into domestic law. Incorporation was thought to be unnecessary, as it was believed that the rights safeguarded by the Convention already flowed from British common law. The Convention came into force on 3 September 1953.

The rights guaranteed by the Convention are based on those outlined in the UN Universal Declaration of Human Rights (1946), but their content and the permitted limitations to the rights are more specific in reflection of the states' intention that they are to be directly legally enforceable. A key feature of the Convention, as an international human rights instrument, is that it provides a mechanism for individuals to enforce it against states that allow the right of 'individual petition', as well as allowing states to bring proceedings against one another. In 1966 the United Kingdom granted the right of individual petition. This has meant that, even before its incorporation into domestic law, the Convention offered individual litigants in Britain the possibility of redress in international law where their civil liberties had been infringed by the state, and where no adequate remedy could be provided by the domestic courts. (It is important to appreciate that as a matter of international law, the Convention creates rights against states, not as against private individuals.)

The Convention originally established three bodies to monitor human rights within the countries that had ratified it. These bodies were the European Commission of Human Rights (ECmHR), the European Court of Human Rights (ECtHR), and the Committee of Ministers. All were based in Strasbourg. Until November 1998, the first two bodies heard complaints from individuals about violations of their rights. The ECmHR exercised a 'screening' function, and could refer cases to the ECtHR for a final determination. However, Protocol 11 to the Convention brought major changes to the Strasbourg system. From November 1998, the ECmHR ceased to exist. Instead, a one-tier system was introduced in which all cases are dealt with by different divisions of the ECtHR. Decisions of the ECtHR are binding on the country concerned. See Chapter 10, 'Researching Human Rights Jurisprudence', for more details of these changes and their effect on the Strasbourg adjudication system.

The Convention's provisions guarantee most, but not all, civil liberties, including the right to life, freedom from torture, freedom from arbitrary arrest, the right to a fair trial, the right to respect for private life, freedom of religion, freedom of expression, and freedom of assembly and association. These protected rights are mostly civil and political in complexion (with the notable exceptions of the right to property and the right to education in Protocol 1). The dividing line between economic rights and civil and political rights is not sharply demarcated and, to 'safeguard the individual in a real and practical way' (*Airey v Ireland* (1979) 2 EHRR 305), the interpretation of Convention rights may extend into the sphere of social and economic rights. The detailed content of these rights are considered in Chapter 8.

The traditional English law method of legal analysis has been to adopt a 'black-letter' approach, closely defining the scope and content of a power or requirement in the text of a legislative provision. But the Convention is quite unlike a United Kingdom statute, and the Strasbourg organs do not interpret Convention rights in the same way as English judges traditionally construe domestic statutes. The broad nature of the terms of the Convention has led to the development of a sophisticated jurisprudence built upon underlying principles and interpretative techniques which the Strasbourg organs have used to 'flesh out' the scope of the rights. Domestic lawyers will have to become accustomed to these principles and a different way of working, and it is true to say that, since the Human Rights Act 1998 has come into force, English judges are beginning to adopt some of the European analytical techniques.

2.2 INTERPRETING THE CONVENTION

The interpretative principles set out below should not be treated in isolation with one given more importance than another—they are part of single, complex jurisprudential exercise to ensure that the 'object and purpose' of the Convention are fulfilled.

2.2.1 'Object and Purpose'

The Convention is an international treaty and so should be interpreted in accordance with Articles 31 to 33 of the Vienna Convention on the Law of Treaties 1969. Article 31(1) states:

> A treaty shall be interpreted in good faith in accordance with the ordinary meaning to be given to the terms of the treaty in their context and in light of its object and purpose.

The Convention is intended to be interpreted purposively, that is, to give effect to the Convention's central purposes. The text, preamble, annexes, and related agreements and instruments of the contracting states are relevant to determining what these are, and the ECtHR has held that the 'objects and purpose' of the Convention include:

(a) the 'maintenance and further realization of human rights' (from the preamble) and the 'protection of individual human rights' (*Soering v United Kingdom* (1989) 11 EHRR 439);

(b) the promotion of the ideals and values of a democratic society (*Kjeldsen, Busk Madsen, Pedersen v Denmark* (1979) 1 EHRR 711), which supposes 'pluralism, tolerance and broadmindedness' (*Handyside v United Kingdom* (1976) 1 EHRR 737) so as to achieve a balance between individual and group interests which 'ensures the fair and proper treatment of minorities and avoids any abuse of a dominant position' (*Young, James and Webster v United Kingdom* (1982) 4 EHRR 38);

(c) the rule of law (*Golder v United Kingdom* (1979) 1 EHRR 524).

As the essence of the Convention is to protect the fundamental rights of persons from violation by contracting parties, limitations or qualifications of the rights set out in the Convention are to be narrowly construed and the ECtHR will try to:

> seek the interpretation that is most appropriate in order to realise the aim and achieve the object of the treaty; not that which would restrict to the greatest possible degree the obligations undertaken by the parties. (*Wemhoff v Germany* (1968) 1 EHRR 55, para. 8)

2.2.2 Effectiveness Principle

The Convention is intended to guarantee rights that are not merely 'theoretical and illusory' but 'practical and effective' (*Marckx v Belgium* (1979) 2 EHRR 330, at para. 31). The ECtHR is concerned with the reality of the individual's position and will 'look behind appearances and examine the realities of the procedure in question' (*Deweer v Belgium* (1980) 2 EHRR 439).

In order for some rights to provide 'effective' protection in accordance with the 'object and purpose' of the Convention, it may be necessary to read an element into a right that is not expressly provided for. An example of reading in these 'implied rights' can be found in the ECtHR's interpretation of Article 6 in *Golder v United Kingdom* (1979) 1 EHRR 524. In that case a prisoner complained that he could not get to court at all—a right not expressly contained in the text of Article 6. The ECtHR considered that to interpret Article 6 as merely providing procedural guarantees in the course of existing proceedings would enable contracting parties to remove the jurisdiction of the courts in relation to certain claims and thus undermine the protection of the right. To correct this the ECtHR held that the right of access to the courts constituted 'an element which is inherent in the right stated by Article 6(1)' (para. 35). Examples of other rights implied into Article 6 to ensure the 'effective' protection of individuals' rights include: the right to have a judgment enforced (*Hornsby v Greece* (1997) 3 EHRR 250); the right to be represented by a competent lawyer (*Artico v Italy* (1980) 3 EHRR 1); and the right to legal aid in civil cases in specific circumstances (*Airey v Ireland* (1979) 2 EHRR 305). More detail on the specific protections afforded by Article 6 can be found in Chapter 8.

The ECtHR has also recognized that in order to secure truly effective protection, certain rights must be read as imposing obligations on the state to take action to ensure that they are protected. This doctrine of positive obligations is considered more fully at 2.3.2 below.

Additionally, the principle of effectiveness not only means that rights must be given their full weight (including where necessary implying rights and obligations into the text), but equally that, in the case of qualified or limited rights, any exceptions are very narrowly construed.

2.2.3 Autonomous Concepts

Some specific Convention terms are 'autonomous', in the sense of having a particular meaning defined by the ECtHR, and the concepts they contain may go beyond their ordinary or domestic meaning. This is necessary both so that there is uniformity of meaning and understanding across the different national legal systems of the parties to the Convention, and to protect human rights from the possibility of being undermined by manipulation of terms by contracting states.

Examples of these autonomous concepts include the free-standing definitions of 'criminal charge' and 'civil rights and obligations' under Article 6. The ECtHR has laid down classification criteria to identify when these are engaged, which do not depend solely on the domestic law classification. Other concepts, such as 'private life' and 'family life', have developed incrementally since 1950 to ensure that the protection offered by the Convention is 'effective'. Further consideration of these terms is found in Chapter 8.

2.2.4 Dynamic Interpretation

The Convention need not—indeed, should not—be interpreted as it would have been by those who drafted it 50 years ago. It is a 'living instrument which . . . must be interpreted in the light of present-day conditions' (*Tyrer v United Kingdom* (1978) 2 EHRR 1, at para. 31). As such its meaning will develop over time and new case law will develop in an organic way without old case law being specifically overruled. Thus, when an English court is considering the meaning and effect of a decision of the European Commission of Human Rights or the European Court of Human Rights, it must nevertheless interpret the Convention by the standards of society today, and not those when the Convention was drafted. The doctrine of precedent must not be used slavishly in this field and older cases should be treated with caution.

An example of the 'growth' of the Convention to accommodate changing social attitudes is reflected in the case law surrounding the Article 8 rights of transsexuals. In *Rees v United Kingdom* (1986) 9 EHRR 56, the ECtHR considered that the rule that a transsexual could not alter her birth certificate to reflect her gender re-assignment did not, by the standards of the mid-1980s, contravene Article 8. But it was conscious of the seriousness of the problems and distress faced by people in that situation and stated:

> The Convention has always to be interpreted and applied in the light of the current circumstances. The need for appropriate legal measures should therefore be kept under review having regard particularly to the scientific and societal developments.

In the subsequent cases of *Cossey v United Kingdom* (1990) 13 EHRR 622, and *Sheffield and Horsham v United Kingdom* (1998) 27 EHRR 163, the ECtHR adhered to its earlier decision (albeit by a diminishing majority in each case). However, in the recent case of *Goodwin v United Kingdom* (2002) 35 EHRR 18, the lack of legal recognition of the applicant's new gender did result in a violation of Article 8, and the ECtHR stated that:

> It is of crucial importance that the Convention is interpreted and applied in a manner which renders its rights practical and effective, not theoretical and illusory. A failure by the Court to maintain a dynamic and evolutive approach would indeed risk rendering it a bar to reform or improvement. (para. 74)

2.2.5 Recourse to Other Human Rights Instruments

Increasingly, the ECtHR has taken into account any relevant rules of international law applicable between the parties when interpreting the Convention. For example, in *T and V v United Kingdom* (2000) 30 EHRR 121, the ECtHR relied in part on the UN Convention on the Rights of the Child and the Standard Minimum Rules for the Administration of Juvenile Justice ('Beijing Rules') to find that the United Kingdom's procedures for trying children charged with serious crimes did not enable the defendants to participate fully and effectively in the trial process and so violated their Article 6 rights to a fair trial.

This approach assists in the interpretation of the provisions of the Convention itself (which shares many similarities with other landmark human rights treaties) and provides useful evidence of present standards when considering how to interpret the Convention as a 'living instrument'. Chapter 10 gives details of the types of resources that may be of use and how to find them.

Broadly, Council of Europe instruments such as Conventions and Resolutions of the Parliamentary Assembly, the European Social Charter, and separate European Union materials may be relevant (for a detailed examination of the interrelationship between EC/EU law and the Convention see Chapter 7). In addition, UN human rights instruments such as the International Covenant on Civil and Political Rights, the Convention on the Elimination of all Forms of Racial Discrimination, and other standards and 'general comments' from the human rights bodies of the UN have been used to help determine the scope of fundamental human rights.

2.3 THE SCOPE OF CONVENTION RIGHTS

2.3.1 Absolute, Limited and Qualified Rights

Rights protected by the Convention may be loosely categorized as 'absolute' rights capable of no derogation, or those which may be limited or qualified. These terms do not connote precise categories but a way of seeking to understand the nature and structure of the Convention rights. The rights protected under the Convention are framed in very wide terms.

Some rights—such as the protection from torture in Article 3—are absolute. There are no circumstances in which torture can be performed in the interests of the state. No derogations from the Article are permitted. There is no balancing of the right against public interest. In *Chahal v United Kingdom* (1996) 23 EHRR 413, the ECtHR was asked to consider the United Kingdom's attempt to expel a suspected Sikh terrorist despite the real risk of his being subjected to torture in the receiving country. The ECtHR held:

> Article 3 enshrines one of the fundamental values of a democratic society. The Court is well aware of the immense difficulties faced by States in modern times in protecting the community from terrorist violence. However, even in these circumstances, the Convention prohibits in absolute terms torture or inhuman or degrading treatment or punishment irrespective of the victim's conduct.

However, many of the core rights are subject to limitations and qualifications. 'Limited rights', such as those protected by Article 5, can be restricted under explicit and finite circumstances. These rights set out the content of the right at the beginning of the Article itself, and also specify the exact limitations on its scope. Other rights subject to limitation in this way include Article 4(2) and (3) (prohibition on forced labour), Article 5 (right to liberty and security of the person), Article 7 (no punishment without law), Article 12 (right to marry), and Protocol 1, Article 2 (right to an education). However, any limitations are to be construed narrowly, as a wide interpretation 'would entail consequences incompatible with the notion of the rule of law from which the whole Convention draws its inspiration' (*Engel v Netherlands* (1976) 1 EHRR 647, para. 69).

The 'qualified rights' tend to be those which most obviously raise the conflicts with the overall interests of society or the rights of others—for example, the right to respect for private life (Article 8) and the right to freedom of expression (Article 10) may sometimes overtly compete. They are both therefore qualified rights, because their scope is necessarily qualified by the effect that their protection has on the rights of others (see too, *Kroon v Netherlands* (1994) 19 EHRR 263; *Soering v UK* (1989) 11 EHRR 439). Other qualified rights are Article 9 (in so far as it relates to *manifestation* of religious beliefs), Article 11 (freedom of assembly and association) and Protocol 1, Article 1 (right to peaceful enjoyment of possessions).

'Qualified rights' are usually set out in two parts in the text of the Convention. The first sub-paragraph sets out the substantive right, and it is then qualified in the second sub-paragraph of the Article. For example, Article 8(1) states: 'Everyone has the right to respect for his private and family life, his home and his correspondence.' This is the presumed right, but a number of limitations and exceptions to it are set out in Article 8(2):

> There shall be no interference by a public authority with the exercise of this right except such as is in accordance with the law and is necessary in a democratic society in the interests of national security, public safety or the economic well-being of the country, for the prevention of disorder or crime, for the protection of health or morals, or for the protection of the rights and freedoms of others.

The precise terms of the limitations attached to the different qualified Articles vary (contrast, for example, Article 10(2) with Article 8(2)), but the judicial method for considering them is the same.

The restrictions and limitations that can be applied to the Convention rights are considered in detail at 2.4 below.

2.3.2 Positive Obligations

The principal purpose of the Convention is to protect individual rights from infringement by states, and this is achieved by the imposition of so-called 'negative' obligations on the states, which require them to refrain from interference with the rights in question. However, the ECtHR has recognized that positive steps may need to be taken by the state to provide the legal or institutional structures or resources needed to protect human rights. For example, to provide laws which prevent private parties from infringing individual rights, or to provide free legal assistance in criminal cases under Article 6(3)(c), or (to an extent) institutions to provide education under Protocol 1, Article 2.

This is because it is not just the state which is capable of infringing the rights of others. Even rights which initially look as if they are merely negative freedoms may in fact require the state to take certain positive, protective steps in order to guarantee the essence of the right from violation by both state and non-state actors. Unfortunately, the ECtHR has expressly declined to develop any 'general theory' of positive obligations, and thus attempts to extract key principles from the jurisprudence of the ECtHR to locate them in a coherent framework have been subject to some controversy. However, it is now accepted that the Convention does impose positive obligations on states, and the only remaining questions are when and to what extent they should be imposed.

The legal basis for reading the Convention in a way which imposes positive obligations is a combination of: the overarching duty on states in Article 1 'to secure to everyone within their jurisdiction' the rights and freedoms set out in the Convention; express wording in some Articles (for example, the right to life 'shall' be protected by law); the principle set out in Convention case law that protection of rights is intended to be 'practical and effective' not merely theoretical; and the right to an adequate remedy for arguable breaches of Convention rights under Article 13. The cumulative effect is that the state cannot merely adopt a 'hands off' approach, by which it refrains from interfering with Convention rights, but rather is under an obligation to create an institutional and juridical structure in which human rights are positively protected from interference, whether by state or non-state actors.

For example, in *Platform Ärtze für das Leben v Austria* (1991) 13 EHRR 204, the applicants (a group of anti-abortion protestors) complained to the ECtHR that their rights to freedom of association were infringed because their marches were attacked and effectively halted by counter-demonstrators. The Austrian Government argued that it, as a state, had not interfered with the applicants' rights and therefore was not responsible for any breach of Article 11. The ECtHR disagreed and held that the freedom of peaceful assembly required the state to take positive steps to prevent counter-demonstrators from disrupting a demonstration, since otherwise, it would itself inhibit the reality of the right to demonstrate: 'Article 11 sometimes requires positive measures to be taken, even in the sphere of relations between states if need be.' Effective policing was required to enable the applicants to exercise their Article 11 rights free from the attacks of counter-demonstrators.

Starmer ('Positive Obligations under the Convention', in Jowell and Cooper (eds), *Understanding Human Rights Principles* (London: Hart Publishing/JUSTICE, 2001) has argued that there are five main positive duties under the Convention:

(a) a duty to have in place a legal framework which provides effective protection for Convention rights;

(b) a duty to prevent breaches of Convention rights;

(c) a duty to provide information and advice relevant to a breach of Convention rights;

(d) a duty to respond to breaches of Convention rights;

(e) a duty to provide resources to individuals to prevent breaches of their Convention rights.

Thus the types of legal and administrative measures that the ECtHR has held are necessary for effective respect of Convention rights are varied. Article 2 provides that the right to life 'shall be protected by law', and this has been interpreted as an obligation on the state to:

> secure the right to life by putting in place effective criminal law provisions to deter the commission of offences against the person, backed up by law enforcement machinery for the prevention, suppression and sanctioning of breaches of such provisions. (*Osman v United Kingdom* (2000) 29 EHRR 245)

Although the ECtHR has drawn back slightly from this position in recent cases, it is still accurate to assert that not only is the state required to adopt an adequate system of law to deter and punish individuals guilty of violating the Convention rights of others, but it is also recognized that the police (see *Osman*) and other relevant public bodies (for example, local authorities in *Z v United Kingdom* (2002) 34 EHRR 3) can be under a positive obligation to take reasonable operational measures to prevent a violation of individuals' rights under Articles 2 and 3. Further, in *Aydin v Turkey* (1998) 25 EHRR 251, the procedural element inherent in Article 2 was read with Article 13 (the right to an effective remedy) to impose an additional obligation on the state to investigate fully the conduct of individuals who had been suspected of an involvement in torture and killings.

In recent cases the ECtHR has begun to recognize that access to relevant information can help individuals to protect their Convention rights. In *Guerra v Italy* (1998) 26 EHRR 357, the ECtHR established that, on the specific facts of the case, the respondent state was under a positive obligation to provide information to the applicants who lived near a 'high risk' chemical factory and who were very likely to be adversely affected by environmental pollution. In *McGinley and Egan v United Kingdom* (1999) 27 EHRR 1 (para. 101), the ECtHR held that when a government engages in hazardous activities, such as nuclear testing, which might have hidden adverse effects on the health of those involved, 'Article 8 requires that an effective and accessible procedure be established which enables persons to seek all relevant and appropriate information'.

When determining whether or not a positive obligation exists, the ECtHR will have regard to 'the fair balance that has to be struck between the general interest of the community and the interests of the individual, the search for which balance is inherent in the whole of the Convention' (*Goodwin v United Kingdom* (2002) 35 EHRR 18). A number of factors may have a bearing on the extent of any positive obligation, including whether the right in question is broadly or narrowly defined; whether essential aspects of a right are at issue; the extent of any burden that may be imposed on the state; and the uniformity of views or practices in other contracting states. However, one of the most important factors taken into consideration by the ECtHR is the severity of the effect of the omission on the applicants' rights (particularly their fundamental rights such as those protected by Articles 2 and 3, or their intimate rights such as those of 'private and family life' protected under Article 8). The more serious the effect, the more likely it is that the state is to be under an obligation to take steps to prevent or punish those effects.

For a more detailed examination of the scope of the doctrine see Starmer (above, and *European Human Rights Law* (London: LAG, 1999), Chapter 5).

Positive Obligations and the Domestic Context
The first domestic cases on the scope of positive obligations have fallen into two categories—those under Article 2 and those under the ambit of Article 8.

Positive obligations arguments arising from the right to life have been most successful in domestic courts. For example, these positive duties under the Human Rights Act resulted in a court ordering an independent investigation into the death of a prisoner in *R (Wright) v Secretary of State for the Home Department* [2001] EWHC Admin 520. The procedural obligation to conduct an independent and effective investigation into an alleged death in breach of Article 2, was also addressed by the Court of Appeal in *R (Amin) and R (Middleton) v HM Coroner for Western Somersetshire* [2001] EWHC Admin 1043. The Court of Appeal did not find that the doctrine of positive obligations went as far as requiring an independent public inquiry into the circumstances of a death in custody (despite the requirements laid out in *Jordan v United Kingdom* (2001) 11 BHRC 1). However, the Court did find that the procedural obligations under Article 2 could encompass deaths resulting from negligence, and effective protection required a departure from the pre-Human Rights Act position. This new approach based on positive obligations required the Coroners Rules to be re-interpreted to include a 'rider' allowing a coroner to direct the jury to consider a verdict of neglect. With both cases on appeal to the House of Lords the exact scope of positive obligations under Article 2 and the Human Rights Act is yet to be decisively determined.

The nature of positive obligations was considered by the House of Lords in *R (Pretty) v DPP* [2002] 1 AC 800, a case questioning whether the applicant, a sufferer of terminal Motor Neurone Disease, could claim a right to die under Articles 2 and 8 of the Convention. Lord Bingham stated that the question of whether a positive obligation exists depends on striking a fair balance between the general interests of the community and the interests of the individual, and Lord Hope reiterated that striking this fair balance involved an assessment of proportionality. Lord Hope stated that a public authority will have acted proportionately if it proves: (i) that the objective which is sought to be achieved is sufficiently important to justify limiting the fundamental right; (ii) that the means chosen to meet the objective are rational, fair, and not arbitrary; and (iii) that the means used to impair the right are no more than is necessary to accomplish that objective and are as minimal as reasonably possible. Diane Pretty's application was not upheld by either the House of Lords or Strasbourg ((2002) 12 BHRC 149). The ECtHR adopted a cautious approach to her request by refusing to imply a right to die by assisted suicide into Article 2.

It initially appeared as if the doctrine of positive obligations would receive its most significant application and development under the ambit of Article 8, see *W and B (Children)* [2001] EWCA Civ 757. In the context of care order proceedings, the Court of Appeal recognized that a child's rights under Article 8 could be jeopardized by the omission, as well as action, of public authorities. The Court inferred from the concept of positive obligations (which was 'inherent in Article 8') a new obligation in respect of a child 'deprived of a life with his family of birth'; relevant public authorities were required to take 'adequate steps' to secure his family life with a new 'family for life'. Using the interpretative obligation in s. 3 of the Human Rights Act, it was held that in these circumstances the court was actively required to monitor and supervise progress of a local authority's implementation of a care plan where there was reason to suspect Convention rights were at risk. However, this approach received short shrift on appeal to the House of Lords ([2002] UKHL 10), with Lord Nicholls stating that:

> In my view this line of argument is misconceived. Failure by the state to provide an effective remedy for a violation of Article 8 is not itself a violation of Article 8. This is self-evident. So, even if the Children Act does fail to provide an adequate remedy, the Act is not for that reason incompatible with Article 8.

The faltering start for 'positive obligations' in the domestic courts, particularly the extent to which Article 8 may impose a positive and enforceable duty, is likely to be re-visited in the near future.

2.4 LIMITATIONS AND RESTRICTIONS ON CONVENTION RIGHTS

The Convention seeks to balance the rights of the individual against other public interests. But the object of human rights jurisprudence in democratic systems is not simple majoritarian rule. The rule of law is also required to ensure that democracy does not mean that the tyranny of majority causes disproportionate interference with the rights of minorities. Once a complaint has been shown to engage a primary right, the Strasbourg institutions consider the limitations and qualifications upon it in order to determine whether there has been a violation.

The Convention seeks to ensure that the limitations that the majority may place upon an individual's protected rights, in the name of the common or competing interests, are imposed only if they are:

(a) prescribed by law; and

(b) intended to achieve a legitimate objective; and

(c) necessary in a democratic society (that is, proportionate to the end to be achieved).

The underlying principles of legality, proportionality, and necessity have been developed in Strasbourg case law and underpin the approach to determining whether any interference with Convention rights is legitimate.

There are different types of restrictions on the scope of Convention rights and, after considering the general principles which govern all restrictions, this chapter goes on to examine these different categories: restrictions expressly permitted under

Articles 8(2), 9(2), 10(2), and 11(2); restrictions expressly permitted by Articles 5 and 12, and by Protocol 1, Article 1; restrictions impliedly permitted under Article 6 and Protocol 1, Article 3; those restrictions specifically provided for by a valid reservation or derogation; and the restrictions under Articles 16 and 17.

2.4.1 Underlying Principles

Legality
The concept of the rule of law is a core concept in the Convention. It is described in the preamble to the Convention as part of the 'common heritage' that the signatories share, and is one of the 'fundamental principles of a democratic society' (*Iatrides v Greece*, 25 March 1999, para. 62). Rights and freedoms can compete, and states may limit citizens' rights or curtail their freedoms for certain specified and legitimate purposes. But no matter how desirable the end to be achieved, no interference with a right protected under the Convention is permissible unless the citizen knows the basis for the interference because it is:

(a) set out in an ascertainable law which is
(b) accessible and
(c) certain.

In the absence of such detailed authorization by the law, any interference, however justified, will violate the Convention. In Strasbourg jurisprudence, a derogation must also have an ascertainable legal basis, that is, be 'prescribed by law' or 'in accordance with the law'.

The phrases 'prescribed by law' or 'in accordance with the law' mean that there must be an ascertainable legal regime governing the interference in question. It is not acceptable for an interference with a Convention right to occur without any legal regulation (for example, *Halford v United Kingdom* (1997) 24 EHRR 523 regarding office phone-tapping). This obviously includes statute law, but the ECtHR has ruled that secondary legislation (*Barthold v Germany* (1985) 7 EHRR 383); applicable rules of EU law (see *Groppera Radio AG v Switzerland* (1990) 12 EHRR 321); the common law (*Sunday Times v United Kingdom* (1979–80) 2 EHRR 245); and even rules of a professional body (*Barthold v Germany*, above) may be sufficient if validly made and available to those bound by them.

But the phrases mean more than a simple search for a national legal rule that permits the derogation. To be 'prescribed by law' for Convention purposes, the starting point is that there must be a basis for what is done in national law. But this is no more than a starting point. The idea of a lawful action is also 'imbued with a Convention idea of the essential qualities of law' (Harris, O'Boyle, Warbrick, *The Law of the European Convention on Human Rights* (London: Butterworths, 1995)). A national rule will not constitute a law for Convention purposes unless it has appropriate 'qualities' to make it compatible with the rule of law (see *Kopp v Sweden* (1999) 27 EHRR 91, paras 55 and 64).

The Strasbourg Court explained the concept in *Sunday Times v United Kingdom* (1979–80) 2 EHRR 245, at para. 49:

> Firstly, the law must be adequately accessible: the citizens must be able to have an indication that is adequate in the circumstances of the legal rules applicable to a given case. Secondly, a norm cannot be regarded as a 'law' unless it is formulated with sufficient precision to enable the citizen to regulate his conduct.

The accessibility rule is intended to counter arbitrary power by providing that a restriction cannot be justified, even if it is authorized in domestic law, unless the applicable law is published in a form accessible to those likely to be affected by it. Internal guidelines from Government departments or agencies probably do not fulfil the accessibility requirement unless they are published or their content made known (*Govell v United Kingdom* [1999] EHRLR 121).

The certainty rule is intended to enable individuals likely to be affected by a restriction on their rights to understand the circumstances in which any such restriction may be imposed, and to enable such individuals to foresee with a reasonable degree of accuracy the consequences of their actions.

For instance, in *Malone v United Kingdom* (1984) 7 EHRR 14, the applicant's telephone was tapped by the police. At the time when this took place, the only regulation of the practice was an internal code of guidance produced by the police which was not public. The European Court of Human Rights took the view that Mr Malone was not therefore able to assess whether or not his telephone conversations would be listened to, or what the basis in law for the surveillance might be. The common law was inadequate in this case, as was clear from the failure of Mr Malone's proceedings in the High Court (*Malone v Metropolitan Police Commissioner* [1979] Ch 344). Accordingly, the interference violated the Convention because it was not prescribed by law. (The Interception of Communications Act 1985 was introduced as a result of this case.)

What is sufficiently certain will depend on the circumstances and absolute certainty is not required. In the *Sunday Times* case the ECtHR said that:

> . . . whilst certainty is highly desirable, it may bring in its train excessive rigidity and the law must be able to keep pace with changing circumstances. Accordingly, many laws are inevitably couched in terms which, to a greater or lesser extent, are vague and whose interpretation and application are questions of practice.

Applying this principle, the ECtHR accepted that the common law relating to contempt of court was formulated with sufficient precision to satisfy the requirements of the Convention. In *Wingrove v United Kingdom* (1997) 24 EHRR 1 and *Müller v Switzerland* (1991) 13 EHRR 212, which were cases involving freedom of expression, the ECtHR accepted that the concepts of blasphemy and obscenity were not capable of precise definition. In *Kokkinakis v Greece* (1993) 17 EHRR 397, the ECtHR recognized that many statutes were imprecise in their wording, and accepted there was a need to avoid excessive rigidity in interpretation and to allow definitions to keep pace with changing circumstances.

The Concept of Legality and the Domestic Context

The Convention concept of legality is capable of having a substantial effect on the development of English law. It can be used as a powerful democratic tool for accountability: to ensure that the executive legislates accessibly, creating a positive and foreseeable legal basis for its actions, and to strengthen the powers of the courts to restrain interference with fundamental rights.

The most rigorous domestic analysis of the English common-law concept of 'legality' is contained in the pre-Human Rights Act, House of Lords cases of *R v Secretary of State for the Home Department ex parte Pierson* [1998] AC 539 and *R v Secretary of State for the Home Department ex parte Simms* [2000] 2 AC 115. *Simms* concerned prison rules (made under statute) that restricted face-to-face interviews between prisoners and journalists. The House of Lords held that, literally construed, the rules did permit restrictions on such interviews, but that a blanket ban curtailed fundamental rights and was therefore *ultra vires*, because a power to curtail fundamental freedoms cannot be implied without the use of express words or necessary implication. Parliament must, in Lord Hoffmann's words (at p. 341):

> squarely confront what it is doing and accept the political cost. Fundamental rights cannot be overridden by general or ambiguous words. This is because there is too great a risk that the full implications of their unqualified meaning may have passed unnoticed in the democratic process. In the absence of express language or necessary implication to the contrary, the courts therefore presume that even the most general words were intended to be subject to the basic rights of the individual. In this way the courts of the United Kingdom, though acknowledging the sovereignty of Parliament, apply principles of constitutionality little different from those which exist in countries where the power of the legislature is expressly limited by a constitutional document.

Although this English concept of a 'legal basis' for executive interference with rights is broadly in line with the approach identified in the Strasbourg case law, there remain differences which need to be resolved. For example, human rights law may require the domestic courts to develop a *positive* concept of legality. In *Ammann v Switzerland* (2000) 30 EHRR 843, a businessman had a call from a woman in the former Soviet embassy in Berne. The call was intercepted by the Federal Public Prosecutor's office, which made an entry in its security index, noting that Mr Ammann was a businessman, a contact with the Russian embassy, and that espionage was established. The Strasbourg Court held that this interference with Mr Ammann's Article 8 rights was not 'in accordance with the law' because the Swiss legal provisions relied upon did not contain specific and detailed provisions on the gathering, recording, storing, or destruction of the data to comply with the requirement of foreseeable application, or to permit proper safeguards against abuse. Notwithstanding the existence of a domestic legal basis for it, the interference was held not to be 'in accordance with the law'.

There is a stark contrast, however, between the approach in *Ammann* and that adopted by the English Court of Appeal in a case decided a few days later (but before the Human Rights Act came into force)—*R v Secretary of State for Health ex parte C* [2000] 1 FLR 656. That case concerned a challenge to the legality of an index which the Department of Health made available to employers, of people about whom there might be doubts as to their suitability to work with children. There was no statutory basis for this index, the existence of which was regulated only by Departmental Circular. The Court of Appeal held that the Crown, as a corporation with legal personality, had 'the same capacities and liberties' as a natural person, but could not infringe private rights of others without lawful authority. Since no one had a right to a job (justiciable under Article 6 of the Convention), the index was not unlawful. The concept of legality used in this decision is the Diceyan idea that the Crown can do anything which is not made illegal by some countervailing private right. Using the Convention concept of legality, however, the 'negative freedom' for the Crown to do what it likes is unlikely to provide a sufficient positive legal basis to allow interference with rights (for example under Article 8 of the Convention).

The first House of Lords case which laid out the proper approach to determining whether a measure is 'prescribed by law' in accordance with the Convention was *R v Shayler* [2002] UKHL 11. Lord Hope confirmed that there were three distinct questions: whether there is a legal basis in domestic law for the restriction; whether the law or rule in question is sufficiently accessible to the individual who is affected by the restriction, and sufficiently precise to enable him to understand its scope and foresee the consequences of his actions so that he can regulate his conduct without breaking the law; and, lastly, whether the measure was applied arbitrarily or was not proportionate.

It appears that one long-term effect of the incorporation of the Convention into English law, therefore, may be to shift our constitutional thinking, so that those exercising executive power, and those scrutinizing it, analyse the issue not in terms of the Crown's liberty to act (in a negative sense), but seek instead a positive legal basis for state interference with citizens' freedoms. For a more detailed account of the areas of potential change in English law see Mountfield, 'The Concept of a Lawful Interference with Fundamental Rights', in Jowell and Cooper (eds), *Understanding Human Rights Principles* (London: Hart Publishing/JUSTICE, 2001).

Legitimate Aim

In order to provide a defence to a claim under the Convention, any interference by a public authority with a Convention right capable of qualification must be directed towards an identified legitimate aim. Without a legitimate aim there is no justification for the interference. Gordon (in 'Legitimate Aim: A Dimly Lit Road' [2002] EHRLR 421) argues that in applying the test for the qualification of rights under the Convention, the question of whether there is a 'legitimate aim' for an interference with rights has wrongly been dealt with cursorily. He argues that this complex test requires separate and dedicated attention before the 'proportionality' of any measure can be properly examined.

In Articles 8, 9, 10, and 11 the legitimate aims are set out in the second part of each Article. The sorts of aims which are 'legitimate' are the interests of public safety, national security, the protection of health and morals and the economic well-being of the country, or the protection of the rights and freedoms of others. These restrictions should be read with Article 18 of the Convention, which provides that: 'The restrictions permitted under this Convention to the said rights and freedoms shall not be applied for any purpose other than those for which they have been prescribed.'

The Convention provides a large number of acceptable reasons for restricting rights, and they have a wide scope. It is not difficult for a country facing an allegation of a breach of human rights to find a reason relevant to any case. The Strasbourg authorities have had difficulty in assessing allegations made by applicants that the legitimate aim identified by the respondent was not the 'real' aim of the restriction. For example, in *Campbell v United Kingdom* (1992) 15 EHRR 137, a prisoner complained about the authorities opening his correspondence with his lawyer. He argued that the real reason was to assess the contents. The Government claimed that the interference was for the purposes of the prevention of disorder or crime. While finding that there had been a breach of Article 8, the ECtHR saw no reason to doubt that there had been a legitimate aim for the interference. More than one aim can be identified by a respondent state, although only one is necessary to defeat the claim.

Other Convention provisions, such as Article 6, may sometimes permit implied restrictions so long as they are 'necessary in a democratic society'. In these cases, the Strasbourg Court adopts a more rigorous approach to the identification of a legitimate aim and has held that 'only indisputable imperatives can justify interference with enjoyment of a Convention right' (*Chassagnou v France* (1999) 29 EHRR 615).

Legitimate Aim and the Domestic Context

Like the ECtHR, it seems that the domestic courts will not require a precise reading of the 'legitimate aims' contained in Articles 8–11. In *The ProLife Alliance v BBC* [2002] EWCA Civ 297, the anti-abortion group sought to persuade the Court of Appeal that a prohibition on freedom of expression ostensibly underpinned by considerations of 'taste, decency and offence' could have no legitimate aim as the 'rights of others' were not engaged by these considerations. The Court of Appeal rejected this approach and, observing that the ECtHR took a broad approach to the question, asserted that 'the factors of taste, decency and offence cannot be treated as categorically irrelevant to the judgment of a prohibition upon free expression'. The House of Lords ([2003] UKHL 23), however, reversed this decision and so the application of a broad approach to identifying a legitimate aim remains in question.

In *Wilson v First County Trust* [2003] UKHL 40, the House of Lords held that recourse to Hansard was permissible as part of the 'sociological assessment' of the aim which it was said constituted the justification for a particular measure, and its proportionality, albeit that this exercise should be approached cautiously.

Proportionality

The final important concept Strasbourg institutions draw on when assessing whether a Convention right has been improperly violated is that of proportionality. As the ECtHR put it in the case of *Soering v United Kingdom* (1989) 11 EHRR 439:

> . . . inherent in the whole of the Convention is a search for the fair balance between the demands of the general interest of the community and the requirements of the protection of the individual's human rights. (para. 89)

The principle of proportionality is concerned with defining that 'fair balance'. Proportionality arises in a number of different contexts and has subtly different meanings depending on these contexts. It is most commonly associated with the balancing exercise that the ECtHR adopts when determining claims under Articles 8–11. It is also the yardstick by which the scope of limitations on implied rights are measured (see 2.2.2 above for examples); it is used when determining whether a positive obligation should be imposed on a contracting state (see 2.3.2 above); and is relevant to the prohibition of discrimination under Article 14 (see 8.14).

However, the most common Convention approach to deciding whether a particular qualification of a right is justified is set out in the three-fold test in *Sunday Times v United Kingdom* (1979–80) 2 EHRR 245:

(a) whether the interference complained of corresponded to a 'pressing social need'; and

(b) whether it was 'proportionate to the legitimate aim pursued'; and

(c) whether the reasons given by the national authority to justify it were 'relevant and sufficient'.

This means that even if a policy which interferes with a Convention right might be aimed at securing a legitimate aim of social policy, for example, the prevention of crime, this will not in itself justify the violation if the means adopted to secure the aim are excessive in the circumstances. The importance of the aim in question and the actual situation which is subject to dispute are important: 'action for the prevention of crime may be directed against homicide or parking offences: the weight of each compared with the right sought to be limited is not the same' (Harris, O'Boyle, and Warbrick, *The Law of the European Convention on Human Rights* (London: Butterworths, 1995), 297).

Where the Convention allows restrictions on rights it not only requires them to be justified by a legitimate aim (see p. 33 above) *and* to be proportionate to the need at hand, it also requires the interference to be 'necessary in a democratic society'. In *Sunday Times v United Kingdom* (see above), the ECtHR examined the phrase 'necessary in a democratic society' and held that:

> whilst the adjective 'necessary' is not synonymous with 'indispensable', neither does it have the flexibility of such expressions as 'admissible', 'ordinary', 'useful', 'reasonable' or 'desirable'; rather it implies a 'pressing social need'.

This 'pressing social need' is a stringent standard: the state's desire to protect a legitimate aim does not allow it to restrict the right of the individual disproportionately—the state cannot use 'a sledgehammer to crack a nut'. In addition, that 'pressing social need' must accord with the requirements of a democratic society, which supposes 'pluralism, tolerance and broadmindedness' (*Handyside v United Kingdom* (1976) 1 EHRR 737). The state must show that there is a legitimate purpose for restricting a Convention right and that the actual restriction employed does not go beyond what is strictly necessary to achieve that purpose.

An example of the necessity doctrine is contained in the case of *Dudgeon v United Kingdom* (1981) 4 EHRR 149. The applicant in that case challenged the law that was then in force in Northern Ireland which made sex between consenting gay men a criminal offence. The ECtHR accepted that the law in question interfered with the exercise of the applicant's right to respect for private life as set out in Article 8(1) and was prescribed by law. The ECtHR went on to consider the other issues that arose from Article 8(2), that is, the objectives said to be served by that law, and whether it was a proportionate response to them. It stated that 'the Court recognizes that one of the purposes of the legislation is to afford safeguards for vulnerable members of society, such as the young, against the consequences of homosexual practices' and accepted that this was then a legitimate aim. However, it went on to say, at para. 60, that:

> It cannot be maintained in these circumstances that there is a 'pressing social need' to make such acts criminal offences, there being no sufficient justification provided by the risk of harm to vulnerable sections of society requiring protection or by the effects on the public. On the issue of proportionality, the Court considers that such justifications as there are for retaining the law in force unamended are outweighed by the detrimental effects which the very existence of the legislative provisions in question can have on the life of a person of homosexual orientation like the applicant. Although members of the public who regard homosexuality as immoral may be shocked, offended or disturbed by the commission by others of private homosexual acts, this cannot on its own warrant the application of penal sanctions when it is consenting adults alone who are involved.

Several other factors have also been relevant to the ECtHR's proportionality balancing exercise. Non-exhaustive examples of such factors include:

(a) The extent to which the interference impairs the 'very essence' of a right. The greater the right is interfered with the more likely it is that there will be a breach of the Convention (see, for example, *Dudgeon v Ireland* (above) and *Rees v United Kingdom* (1987) 9 EHRR 56). The nature of some rights means that the state will need to demonstrate 'particularly serious reasons' to justify an interference with, for example, an intimate aspect of private life.

(b) Whether a less restrictive alternative, yet equally effective, measure was available to the state to achieve the legitimate aim pursued. For example, in *Campbell v United Kingdom* (1992) 15 EHRR 137 (see p. 34 above for the facts of the case), the ECtHR held that the blanket opening of all prisoners' mail was disproportionate because the less intrusive measure of opening only those letters reasonably considered to contain prohibited material would have achieved the same aim.

(c) Whether there were any effective safeguards or legal controls over the measures in question. This includes the adequacy of compensation or legal remedies for those affected by the measures.

In addition, the test of proportionality also contains within it its own concept of procedural fairness. An infringement of a qualified right is much less likely to be a proportionate response to a legitimate aim if the person affected by the action was not consulted, or not given the right to a hearing, than if he or she was given such opportunities. The ECtHR has stated that:

> whilst Article 8 contains no explicit procedural requirements, the decision-making process leading to measures of interference must be fair and such as to afford due respect to the interests safeguarded by Article 8. (*McMichael v United Kingdom* (1995) 20 EHRR 205)

In many cases the greater rights set out in Article 6 will apply, but even where they do not the Convention will impose similar duties where possible. Thus, for instance, a decision to make a place of safety order and to remove a child from its parents may be justified on its merits, but if the parents (and in some circumstances the child) can be consulted and/or attend or be represented at the hearing of the court that takes this decision, then their Article 8 right to family life is less likely to be violated. In such a case Article 6 may not apply because this interim decision is not the 'determination' of the issue. Nevertheless, their right to family life has been interfered with, even if only for a temporary period. If it is possible to allow the family to participate in the decision-making process, this in itself is more likely to comply with the proportionality test in Article 8 irrespective of the outcome (for example, see *W v United Kingdom* (1988) 10 EHRR 29; and *Buckley v United Kingdom* (1997) 23 EHRR 101).

The final element of the proportionality test involves the ECtHR's assessment of whether the state's reasons for interfering with the right are 'relevant and sufficient' (*Jersild v Denmark* (1995) 19 EHRR 1). The ECtHR will look at the state's evidence or factual basis for believing that there was a real danger to the interest which the state claims there was a pressing social need to protect. Where no evidence is adduced in support of the reasons given for a restriction, a breach of the Convention is almost inevitable (*Autronic AG v Switzerland* (1990) 12 EHRR 485).

For detailed examinations of this key concept, see Eissen, 'The Principle of Proportionality in the Case Law of the Court', in Macdonald, Matscher, and Petzold (eds), *The European System for the Protection of Human Rights* (The Hague: Kluwer Law International, 1993), and McBride, 'Proportionality and the European Convention on Human Rights', in Ellis (ed.), *The Principle of Proportionality in the Laws of Europe* (London: Hart Publishing, 1999).

The Doctrine of Proportionality and the Domestic Context
The Convention test of whether the measure adopted by the member state is proportionate is more stringent than that traditionally used in English law. This is because the Convention starts with a presumption that a right contained in the first part of a Convention Article should be respected, it does not require a decision-maker to have 'taken leave of his senses' before the Court can intervene.

Before the commencement of the Human Rights Act 1998, the test for challenging the actions of public authorities by way of judicial review was that they must be unlawful or 'irrational': in Lord Diplock's often quoted explanation of *Wednesbury* unreasonableness 'a decision which is so outrageous in its defiance of logic or accepted moral standards that no sensible person who had applied his mind to the question to be decided could have arrived at it' (*Council of Civil Service Unions v Minister for the Civil Service* [1985] AC 375, at p. 410). It was very hard to challenge a decision on this basis, although in later cases, where fundamental rights were at stake, the test was redefined so that the greater the interference with fundamental rights, the greater the level of scrutiny required: see the formulation in *R v Ministry of Defence ex parte Smith* [1996] QB 517. But even this reformulated level of scrutiny was insufficient to meet the requirements of Article 13 of the Convention: see *Smith and Grady v UK* (1997) 29 EHRR 493 and the decision of the Grand Chamber in *Hatton v United Kingdom* (App. No. 36022/97) 8 July 2003.

The concept of proportionality has been filtering into English law for many years. In English courts, judges have generally come across it in the context of European Union law. For example, in *R v Secretary of State for Employment ex parte Equal Opportunities Commission* [1995] 1 AC 1, the House of Lords, having identified that a particular social measure (different service periods for full-time and part-time workers in order to qualify for the right to claim employment protection) had an effect on a higher proportion of women than men, then analysed the evidence which the Government had put forward to support the assertion that this was an 'appropriate and necessary' way of advancing the policy objective it had identified (promoting part-time work opportunities). The House of Lords found insufficient evidence of this. The language used in Convention case law is slightly different, but the concept of proportionality—and the Continental legal traditions from which it has derived—are very similar in both EU and Convention law.

Likewise, in the Privy Council case of *de Freitas v Permanent Secretary of Ministry of Agriculture, Fisheries, Land and Housing* [1999] 1 AC 69, Lord Clyde examined the phrase 'reasonably justifiable in a democratic society' and, after drawing on jurisprudence from the Canadian Charter of Rights, held that the three necessary conditions a state must prove to justify restricting a fundamental right are:

(a) the legislative objective is sufficiently important to justify limiting the right;

(b) the measures designed to meet the legislative objective are rationally connected to that objective; and

(c) the means used to impair the right must be no more than is necessary to accomplish the objective.

In the first House of Lords case on Convention proportionality, *R (Daly) v Secretary of State for the Home Department* [2001] 2 WLR 1622, it was confirmed that proportionality required the court to examine the questions set out by the Privy Council in *de Freitas* (see above). Lord Steyn then went on to underline the 'material difference' between the Convention principle of proportionality and *Wednesbury* unreasonableness:

(a) First, proportionality may require the reviewing court to assess the actual balance which the decision-maker has reached, not merely whether it is within the range of rational or reasonable decisions.

(b) Secondly, the proportionality doctrine may go further than the traditional grounds of review as it may require attention to be directed to the relative weight accorded to the interests and considerations.

(c) Thirdly, even the domestic 'heightened scrutiny' test developed in *R v Ministry of Defence ex parte Smith* [1996] QB 517 to deal with human rights cases cannot necessarily be approximated with the proportionality test employed by Strasbourg (see *Smith and Grady v United Kingdom* (2000) 29 EHRR 493).

However, Lord Steyn emphasized that proportionality does not mean a shift to a merits review, and that the intensity of the review will depend on the subject matter in hand, even in cases involving Convention rights. Since *Daly* there have been a number of cases which have sought to identify the intensity of review that is required, and this constantly evolving area of domestic human rights case law is examined in detail at 4.5.3.

Fordham and de la Mare, 'Identifying the Principles of Proportionality', in Jowell and Cooper (eds), *Understanding Human Rights Principles* (London: Hart Publishing/JUSTICE, 2001) offer a detailed examination of the types of issues that English courts may encounter when grappling with the principle. Clayton, 'Regaining a Sense of Proportion: The Human Rights Act and the Proportionality Principle' [2001] EHRLR 504, and Blake, 'Importing Proportionality: Clarification or Confusion' [2002] EHRLR 19, both contain critiques of some of the emerging domestic case law on proportionality.

2.4.2 Express Limitations under Qualified Rights—Articles 8–11

The 'qualified rights' tend to be those which most obviously raise conflicts with the interests of society or the rights of others—for example, the right to respect for private life (Article 8) and the right to freedom of expression (Article 10) may sometimes overtly compete. They are both therefore qualified rights, because their scope is necessarily qualified by the effect that their protection has on the rights of others (see, *Kroon v Netherlands* (1994) 19 EHRR 263; *Soering v United Kingdom* (1989) 11 EHRR 439).

The 'qualified rights' contained in Articles 8–11 of the Convention are set out in a broadly similar form. The first paragraph of each Article sets out the broad scope of the right and the second paragraph then sets out the specific circumstances in which the state can restrict that right.

A restriction will be compatible with the Convention only if: it is 'in accordance with the law' (the concept of legality is discussed at 2.4.1 above); the interference is directed towards an identified legitimate aim (in Articles 8, 9, 10, and 11 the legitimate aims are the interests of public safety, national security, the protection of health and morals and the economic well-being of the country, or the protection of the rights and freedoms of others); and the aim is 'necessary in a democratic society' (which encompasses the 'pressing social need' and proportionality tests discussed at 2.4.1 above).

2.4.3 Express Limitations on Limited Rights

'Limited rights', such as those protected by Article 5, can be restricted in explicit and finite circumstances. These rights set out the content of the right at the beginning of the Article itself and also specify the exact limitations on its scope. In addition, the ECtHR has added a requirement of proportionality.

For example, in *Winterwerp v Netherlands* (1979) 2 EHRR 387, the ECtHR examined the detention of the applicant under the ambit of Article 5(1)(e) (which permits detention of 'persons of unsound mind'). The ECtHR held that in addition to the clear requirements under the second limb of Article 5, the state also had to show that the applicant was affected by a mental disorder which was 'of a kind or degree warranting compulsory confinement' and that the lawfulness of continued confinement depends on 'the persistence of such disorder'.

Other rights subject to limitation in this way include Article 12 (right to marry), and Protocol 1, Article 1 (protection of property). However, any limitations are to be construed narrowly, as a wide interpretation 'would entail consequences incompatible with the notion of the rule of law from which the whole Convention draws its inspiration' (*Engel v Netherlands* (1976) 1 EHRR 647, para. 69).

2.4.4 Impliedly Permitted Restrictions

In general the ECtHR is unwilling to imply restrictions into the Convention, and where express restrictions are provided for (as discussed above) there is no scope for implied restrictions. In order to ensure the practical effectiveness of rights, the ECtHR has sometimes found it necessary to imply additional specific elements, and in these cases it has recognized that, occasionally, certain rights carry with them implied limitations. However, the ECtHR has stressed that its guiding principle is that these restrictions must not undermine the effective protection of the right in question. These restrictions do not originate from the express language of the Convention and their application to individual cases has been curtailed by the Strasbourg Court.

An example of these implied rights and restrictions can be found in the ECtHR's interpretation of Article 6. In *Golder v United Kingdom* (1979) 1 EHRR 524, a prisoner complained that he could not get to court at all—a right not expressly contained in the text of Article 6. The ECtHR considered that to interpret Article 6 as merely providing procedural guarantees in the course of existing proceedings would enable contracting parties to remove the jurisdiction of the courts in relation to certain claims and thus undermine the protection of the right. To correct this the ECtHR held that the right of access to the courts constituted 'an element which is inherent in the right stated by Article 6(1)' (para. 35). However, the Court went on to add that as this is a 'right which the Convention sets forth . . . without . . . defining it, there is room, apart from delimiting the very content of any right, for limitations permitted by implication' (para. 38). In *Ashingdane v United Kingdom* (1985) 7 EHRR 528, the ECtHR held that this right may be subject to restrictions, but that limitation on the right of access to court:

> will not be compatible with Article 6(1) if it does not pursue a legitimate aim and if there is not a reasonable relationship of proportionality between the means employed and the aim sought to be achieved.

Implied limitations must not impair the essence of the right, or render it ineffective and any restrictions need to be measured against the Convention's underpinning principles of 'legitimate aim' and 'proportionality'. The ECtHR has read implied restrictions into the right to education under Article 2 of Protocol 1, and into election rights under Article 3 of that Protocol. In *Osman v United Kingdom* (2000) 29 EHRR 245, the ECtHR considered the rules governing police immunity from negligence claims and their compatibility with Article 6 of the Convention. The ECtHR found that while they pursued a legitimate aim (the avoidance of defensive policing and diversion of resources), they were disproportionate as they amounted to a blanket immunity without regard to the merits of individual cases.

Both Van Dijk and van Hoof (*Theory and Practice of Human Rights*, 3rd edn (The Hague: Kluwer Law International, 1998), 576–7) and Clayton and Tomlinson (*The Law of Human Rights* (Oxford: Oxford University Press, 2000), at paras 6.114 to 6.122) discuss this controversial doctrine of 'inherent limitations' in more detail. Whilst they both accept that there may be implied limitations to what would otherwise be unqualified rights, they rightly argue that their use should be restricted so as not to breach the underlying principles of the Convention as set out in Articles 1 and 18. Article 18, which is incorporated into domestic law under s. 1(1) of the Human Rights Act 1998, states that the restrictions permitted under the Convention shall not be applied for any purpose other than those for which they have been prescribed.

2.4.5 Restrictions Specifically Provided for by Reservations and Derogations

Reservations
Article 57 entitles states to make reservations in respect of rights contained in the

Convention. A reservation to an international treaty is a device used by a signatory state to reserve particular policies or law in order to exempt them from challenge under the instrument. They are often used as a temporary measure, which gives states time to bring their laws into line with the requirements of the Convention. Reservations can be made only at the time of signing or ratification and must comply with Article 31(1) of the Vienna Convention on the Law of Treaties, which states:

> A treaty shall be interpreted in good faith in accordance with the ordinary meaning to be given to the terms of the treaty in their context and in the light of its objects and purpose.

A reservation is likely to be invalid if it seeks to circumvent key terms or underlying principles contained within the treaty in question.

There is currently one reservation by the United Kingdom to the Convention, which pertains to the second sentence of Protocol 1, Article 2 (which requires education to be provided in conformity with parents' religious and philosophical convictions). The United Kingdom has accepted this provision only so far as it is compatible with the provision of efficient instruction and training and the avoidance of unreasonable public expenditure (the full text of the reservation is set out in Part II of sch. 3 to the Human Rights Act—see Appendix 1). However, the United Kingdom's reservation must meet the requirements of Article 57(2) of the Convention and not be couched in terms that are too vague or broad for it to be possible to determine their exact scope and meaning (*Belilos v Switzerland* (1988) 10 EHRR 466). Some commentators (for example, Emmerson and Simor, *Human Rights Practice* (London: Sweet & Maxwell, 2000), para. 1.024) are sceptical as to whether the validity of the reservation would withstand challenge, given the language used by the United Kingdom.

Derogations

Article 15(1) of the Convention states:

> In time of war or other public emergency threatening the life of the nation any High Contracting Party may take measures derogating from its obligations under this Convention to the extent strictly required by the exigencies of the situation, provided that such measures are not inconsistent with its obligations under international law.

This enables states to restrict the exercise of some of the rights and freedoms without violating the Convention. Any derogation must be proportional to the threat and must be necessary to deal with the emergency. As a matter of international law, a state, by lodging a derogation in Strasbourg, can, to the extent that the derogation is lawful under Article 15, avoid a particular obligation in particular circumstances. Article 15 does not allow derogations from Article 2 (the right to life), Article 3 (freedom from torture), Article 4(1) (slavery and servitude), and Article 7 (retrospective criminal penalties).

The United Kingdom has, in the past, used Article 15 in relation to Northern Ireland, and until February 2001 there was a derogation in force which allowed the police to detain people under the Prevention of Terrorism (Temporary Provisions) Act 1989 for up to seven days. In *Brogan v United Kingdom* (1988) 11 EHRR 117, the ECtHR decided that periods of longer than four days' detention for interrogation without access to a judge violated the requirement to bring the suspect before a judge 'promptly' as set out in Article 5(3). The lawfulness of this derogation was then subject to an unsuccessful challenge (*Brannigan v United Kingdom* (1993) 17 EHRR 539). However, with the introduction of judicial authorization for extended detentions in the Terrorism Act 2000, this particular derogation was withdrawn.

Following the events of 11 September 2001, and domestic legislation introduced in Parliament, the United Kingdom lodged a new derogation from the Convention with Strasbourg. The text of this derogation is set out in the amended sch. 3 to the Human Rights Act (see Appendix 1) and sets out the Government's view that:

> there exists a terrorist threat to the United Kingdom from persons suspected of involvement in international terrorism. In particular, there are foreign nationals present in the United Kingdom who are suspected of being concerned in the commission, preparation or instigation of acts of international terrorism, of being members of organisations or groups which are so concerned or of having links with members of such organisations or groups, and who are a threat to the national security of the United Kingdom.
>
> As a result, a public emergency, within the meaning of Article 15(1) of the Convention, exists in the United Kingdom.

This allows the United Kingdom to derogate from Article 5(1) of the Convention. The Anti-Terrorism, Crime and Security Act 2001 gives the Government an extended power to arrest and detain a foreign national where it is intended to remove or deport the person from the United Kingdom but where this is not possible as it would contravene the Convention (Article 3 prohibits a state from returning a person to a place where he or she may face ill-treatment, irrespective of whether the person is a danger to the removing state: *Chahal v United Kingdom* (1996) 23 EHRR 413). As a result, extended detention, which would ordinarily be unlawful under the Convention and the Human Rights Act, can be used by the state. The legality of the derogation is currently being challenged in the domestic courts. Commentators have queried the necessity of the measures given that, despite the international nature of threats from terrorism, the United Kingdom is alone among Council of Europe countries in derogating from the terms of the Convention (see Tomkins, 'Legislating Against Terror: The Anti-Terrorism, Crime and Security Act 2001' [2002] PL 205).

The mechanism in the Human Rights Act by which these derogations take effect domestically is considered in more detail at 8.15.2 below.

2.4.6 Restrictions under Articles 16, 17, and 18

The rights contained in the Convention are subject to express restrictions in three specific areas:

(a) Article 16 (restrictions on the political activities of aliens);

(b) Article 17 (restrictions on activities aimed at the destruction of Convention rights); and

(c) Article 18 (prohibition on using Convention restrictions for an improper purpose).

The exact scope of these Articles is considered in detail in Chapter 8.

2.5 MARGIN OF APPRECIATION

2.5.1 Overview of the Doctrine

In essence, this means that a state is allowed a certain freedom to evaluate its public policy decisions, though subject to review by the Strasbourg institutions. The phrase has been much used in Strasbourg jurisprudence, and it is important to understand the role it plays in the decision-making of the ECtHR. However, the concept should not be used by the domestic courts. This is because it is important to understand that Strasbourg case law lays down a minimal 'floor' of human rights protection, not an optimal 'ceiling'. The jurisprudence from Strasbourg will need careful consideration before it is applied by domestic courts, because there may be questions in those cases which the Strasbourg organs abstained from deciding but which the domestic courts must decide.

The approach of the Strasbourg Court is comparable to the way in which the European Court of Justice sometimes approaches the question of whether derogations from European Union law rights are 'requisite and necessary': it states that this question of proportionality is one for the judgment of the courts of the member states, but is prepared to set out the sort of factors which they should take into account (for example, in *Nolte* [1975] ECR I-4625; *Keck* [1993] ECR I-6097). It is worth noting that, in European Union law, it is the national courts, not the national executives, which have the power to decide whether derogation from a EU law right is 'necessary'.

The Convention is an international human rights instrument, policed by an international court. The Strasbourg institutions have to be sensitive to the need for 'subsidiarity', that is, to ensuring that the member states' own political and cultural traditions are respected. For example, what may offend religious sensitivities in one country may be an aspect of free speech in another.

When determining whether a social policy aim is legitimate, therefore, or whether the means adopted to achieve it are 'necessary in a democratic society', the Commission and Court have recognized limits to their own competence to judge the issue. They have done this by giving the state a so-called 'margin of appreciation' in assessing the extent to which a signatory has violated the Convention.

The extent of the discretion the Strasbourg institutions will allow the state depends on the policy area involved. States have been allowed a broader margin of appreciation in cases involving national security or public morality, or where there is no general Europe-wide practice, but a narrower one in other types of cases.

The margin of appreciation doctrine was developed by the ECtHR in *Handyside v United Kingdom* (1976) 1 EHRR 737 (following the initial notion developed by the ECmHR in *Lawless v Ireland* (1970) 1 EHRR 15). The *Handyside* case concerned the publication in England in 1971 of the *Little Red School Book*, which was intended for children and included a section on sex. The police seized the books and a forfeiture order was obtained on the grounds that the books contravened the Obscene Publications Act 1959. The applicant claimed a violation of Article 10 (freedom of expression) and the Government argued that the restriction was necessary for the purpose of the 'protection of morals'. The Court accepted that the limitation was 'prescribed by law' and thus had to decide whether the limitation in question was proportionate and 'necessary in a democratic society'. The Court stated (at paras 48 and 49):

> By reason of their direct and continuous contact with the vital forces of their countries, state authorities are in principle in a better position than the international judge to give an opinion on the extent of these requirements as well as on the 'necessity' of a 'restriction' or 'penalty' intended to meet them. . . .

> Nevertheless, Article 10(2) does not give the contracting states an unlimited power of appreciation. The Court, which, with the Commission, is responsible for ensuring the observance of those states' engagements (Article 19), is empowered to give the final ruling on whether a 'restriction' or 'penalty' is reconcilable with freedom of expression as protected by Article 10. The domestic margin of appreciation thus goes hand in hand with a European supervision.

The use of this doctrine has sometimes led the Court to draw back from finding violations in cases by holding that the question of the proportionality of a response is within the 'margin of appreciation' of the national institutions. This is particularly so when considering cases under Articles 8–11: see the decision of the Grand Chamber in *Hatton v United Kingdom* (App. No. 36022/97, 8 July 2003). The doctrine has also been used when the Court has tried to assess the positive obligations in the Convention, for example, in the assessment of evidence by the courts in Article 6 or the right to peaceful enjoyment of property in Article 1 of Protocol 1. For a detailed examination of how the margin of appreciation doctrine has affected different Convention rights, see [1998] 19 *Human Rights Law Journal* 1 (Special Issue on Margin of Appreciation).

It has been argued that the doctrine is a necessary aspect of sensitivity to the different democratic traditions in member countries. However, many commentators consider that the idea has been used as a sloppy way of refusing to face the question of proportionality (see, for example, Lord Lester of Herne Hill QC, 'Universality Versus Subsidiarity: A Reply' [1998] EHRLR 73). A former judge of the Court has also trenchantly criticized the doctrine as allowing the Court to evade its responsibility to articulate the reasons why its intervention in particular cases may or may not be appropriate (see R. St J. Macdonald, 'The Margin of Appreciation', in Macdonald, Matscher, and Petzold (eds), *The European System for the Protection of Human Rights*, 3rd edn (The Hague: Kluwer Law International, 1993)). Partly as a result of such criticisms, the Court's Deputy Registrar has called for the identification of practical factors and criteria to help determine the boundaries of the doctrine in different cases. This criteria-based approach would, he argues, help to counter the dangers of conceding a wide margin of appreciation to national decision-makers, and he points out that: 'judicial self restraint should itself be exercised with restraint if the universal standards are not to be diluted or sacrificed in favour of national diversity' (Mahoney, 'Marvellous Richness of Diversity or Invidious Cultural Relativism?' [1998] 19 *Human Rights Law Journal* 1).

The adoption of such an approach would allow the Court to be sensitive to the context of individual cases without giving too great a weight to particular factors, or by declining to adjudicate on certain matters on the basis of subject matter alone.

2.5.2 Margin of Appreciation and the Role of the National Court

The margin of appreciation should be regarded as an international doctrine. It has no place in domestic arrangements for protecting human rights and should not be used when the Convention is applied by national courts. It was created to allow national judicial bodies a degree of flexibility; to enable an international judicial review system to give due weight to local political and cultural traditions; and to take into account the geographical, cultural, philosophical, historical, and intellectual distance between the judges in Strasbourg and local institutions. The domestic courts do not need the doctrine because this gap does not exist. They can give sufficient deference to the sphere in which there may be policy choices for the executive by use of the concept of proportionality. If domestic courts translate the international law concept of the 'margin of appreciation' into domestic law, the judges are likely to fail in their statutory duty, which is to decide for themselves whether a public body's decision constitutes a disproportionate infringement of human rights.

The English courts must themselves apply the doctrine of proportionality. While recognizing a discretionary area of judgment, as discussed above, this is not so lax a test as *Wednesbury* unreasonableness (see Hunt, Singh, and Demetriou, 'Is There a Role for the Margin of Appreciation after Incorporation of the ECHR?' [1999] EHRLR 15; and Pannick, 'Principles of Interpretation of Convention Rights under the Human Rights Act 1998 and the Discretionary Area of Judgment' [1998] PL 545). A detailed discussion of the interaction between proportionality and deference under the Human Rights Act can be found in 'Judicial Deference to Decisions of Public Authorities' in 4.5.3.

In the first case on the Human Rights Act to reach the House of Lords (*R v DPP ex parte Kebilene* [1999] 3 WLR 972) this position was confirmed. Lord Hope stated that the doctrine of margin of appreciation:

. . . is an integral part of the supervisory jurisdiction which is exercised over state conduct by the international court. By conceding a margin of appreciation to each national system, the court has recognised that the Convention, as a living system, does not need to be applied uniformly by all states but may vary in its application according to local needs and conditions. This technique is not available to the national courts when they are considering Convention issues arising within their own countries. But in the hands of the national courts also the Convention should be seen as an expression of fundamental principles rather than as a set of mere rules. The questions which the courts will have to decide in the application of these principles will involve questions of balance between competing interests and issues of proportionality . . .

As the margin of appreciation has no part in the domestic application of the Convention, the courts in this country will have to look again at some of the cases decided in Strasbourg. Many cases, for instance, raising issues under Article 10, have not led to a finding of a violation precisely because a margin of appreciation was allowed by the Court. In the absence of such a margin, domestic courts must not use these cases as authority for the proposition that there is no violation. They will have to decide for themselves whether there is a breach of the Convention by undertaking a proper analysis of what, in a domestic context, is 'necessary in a democratic society'.

3

THE FRAMEWORK OF THE HUMAN RIGHTS ACT

3.1 INTRODUCTION

The Human Rights Act 1998 is a special statute imbued with constitutional significance. It is described in its long title as an Act to 'give further effect' to the rights and freedoms guaranteed under the Convention.

Since the 1998 Act came into force it has altered the interpretation and use of the common law and all other legislation in cases involving human rights issues. The overriding objective is to weave the Convention into the existing legal system, so that all courts will consider Convention arguments, and rights which could have been obtained in Strasbourg can be secured in national courts, while minimizing disruption to the existing legal system. The method adopted, however, is a complex one reflecting a delicate political compromise between 'incorporating' Convention rights and retaining parliamentary sovereignty.

The Act creates a general statutory requirement that all legislation, primary or secondary, whenever enacted, must be read and given effect in a way which is compatible with Convention rights *whenever possible*. This principle of construction, contained in s. 3 of the 1998 Act, requires generous and progressive interpretation to give effect to the purpose of this constitutional statute. If it is not possible to interpret legislation in a compliant way then the higher courts may declare the legislation to be incompatible with the Convention.

This new principle of construction applies to all litigation, whether or not a public body is involved. It can, therefore, affect the rights of private persons between themselves. But the Act does not directly create a new cause of action for 'breach of the Convention' against private bodies.

However, by virtue of s. 6, the Act requires public authorities—including courts—to act compatibly with the Convention unless they are prevented from doing so by statute. This means that the courts have their own primary statutory duty to give effect to the Convention unless positively prevented from doing so. Section 7 gives the 'victim' of any act of a public authority which is incompatible with the Convention power to challenge the authority in court using the Convention to found a cause of action or a defence.

This chapter summarizes the key sections of the Human Rights Act, and outlines its effects. The Human Rights Act mechanism, and its operation in cases concerning private litigants and public authorities, are analysed in more depth in Chapter 4. Procedural issues concerning the bringing of a claim against a public authority are the subject of Chapter 5.

3.2 OVERVIEW OF THE PROVISIONS OF THE 1998 ACT

The Human Rights Act is a short, and elegantly drafted, piece of legislation. It is nonetheless helpful to approach it schematically rather than simply reading the sections in the order in which they appear. The overall scheme is as follows.

3.2.1 Section 1 and Sch. 1—Definition of Convention Rights

Section 1 and sch. 1 define the 'Convention rights' which have been incorporated, subject to any designated derogations or reservations (see Chapter 2). Article 1 (the obligation on contracting states to the Convention to 'secure' Convention rights to 'everyone within their jurisdiction') and Article 13 (the right to an effective remedy in a national court) are not specifically designated as 'Convention rights' within this definition.

3.2.2 Section 2—Interpretation of Convention Rights

Section 2 requires any court or tribunal determining a question that has arisen in connection with a Convention right, to 'take into account' the jurisprudence of the Strasbourg organs (the European Court and Commission of Human Rights and the Committee of Ministers). This jurisprudence must be considered 'so far as, in the opinion of the court or tribunal, it is relevant to the proceedings in which that question has arisen', whenever the judgment, decision, or opinion to be taken into account was handed down.

3.2.3 Section 3—Interpretation of Legislation

Section 3 requires primary and subordinate legislation to be read and given effect in a way which is compatible with Convention rights, 'so far as it is possible to do so', whether the legislation in question was enacted before or after the Human Rights Act

1998. Section 3 is a general requirement, addressed to any person reading the legislation, not just to courts. This strong interpretative obligation is one of the most important provisions in the 1998 Act and is examined in detail below.

3.2.4 Section 19—Statements of Compatibility

In the interpretation of primary legislation which post-dates the Human Rights Act 1998, s. 19 assists with the presumption that legislation is to be (and can be) read compatibly with the Convention. Section 19 of the Act requires a minister of the Crown with conduct of any Bill, before its second reading, either to make and publish a 'statement of compatibility', or openly to make a statement that he or she is unable to state that the legislation is compatible with the Convention rights. The rationale behind the provision is that the Government will not often wish to state publicly that it is acting incompatibly with an internationally binding human rights instrument. Where a minister has stated that the legislation is compatible with the Convention, this may assist the courts in finding a compatible meaning.

3.2.5 Sections 4, 5, 10, and Sch. 2—Incompatibility of Legislation

If it is *not* possible to read legislation so as to give effect to the Convention, s. 3(2)(b) and (c) provide that this does not affect the validity, continuing operation, or enforcement of the legislation. In such circumstances, however, s. 4 empowers the higher courts to make a 'declaration of incompatibility'. The Crown has a right under s. 5 to intervene in proceedings where such a declaration may be made. Section 10 and sch. 2 provide a 'fast-track' procedure by which the executive can act to amend legislation to remove incompatibility with the Convention, where a declaration of incompatibility has been made. These provisions are described in more detail in Chapter 5.

3.2.6 Section 6—Acts of Public Authorities

Section 6 makes it unlawful for a public authority to act in a way which is incompatible with a Convention right unless it is required to do so by primary legislation, or by secondary legislation made under it, which cannot be interpreted compatibly with the Convention. However, in order to preserve the sovereignty of the legislature, a 'public authority' does not include either House of Parliament, and 'act' does not include a failure to legislate. Section 6(3)(a) makes courts and tribunals public authorities, and so subject to their own primary duty to act compatibly with the Convention. By virtue of s. 6(3)(b) and 6(5), a body whose functions are partly public and partly private is a 'public authority' in relation to its functions 'of a public nature' but not in relation to acts which are private in nature. Such bodies are called 'hybrid' bodies in this book, and the implications of these terms are examined in detail in Chapter 4.

3.2.7 Section 7—Proceedings Against Public Authorities

Section 7(1)(a) permits a victim of an act by a public authority which infringes a Convention right to bring proceedings 'in the appropriate court or tribunal'. Section 7(1)(b) permits a person to rely on the Convention right or rights concerned in any legal proceedings against the public authority. Section 7(5) imposes a limitation period for bringing proceedings under s. 7(1)(a). Section 22(4) provides that s. 7(1)(b) can be used as a *defence* whenever the act in question took place, but proceedings may be instigated under s. 7(1)(a) only in relation to acts committed after the Act came into force on 2 October 2000.

The 'appropriate court or tribunal' for bringing proceedings against public authorities, and incidental jurisdictional matters such as the remedies which such courts or tribunals may provide, have been laid down in rules made by the Secretary of State concerned or the Lord Chancellor (s. 7(2) and (9)–(12)). These rules and relevant practice directions are contained in Appendix 2 of this book.

Section 7(1) may only be used by a person who is or would be a 'victim' of the unlawful act, as defined in s. 7(7). Section 7(3) provides that in proceedings brought by way of judicial review, the claimant is to be taken to have a sufficient interest in relation to the unlawful act only if he is, or would be, a victim of it.

3.2.8 Section 8—Judicial Remedies

Section 8(1) gives a court a wide power to grant such relief, remedies, or orders as it considers just and appropriate, provided they are within its existing powers. By virtue of s. 7(11), the powers of existing courts or tribunals may be enlarged by order. Damages may be awarded in civil proceedings, but s. 8(2) provides that such damages may only be awarded by a court which has power to order the payment of damages or compensation in civil proceedings. By virtue of s. 8(3), damages may be awarded only if necessary to afford 'just satisfaction', and s. 8(4) provides that in determining whether to award damages and the amount to award, the court must take account of the principles applied by the European Court of Human Rights in relation to awards of compensation under Article 41 of the Convention.

3.2.9 Section 9—Judicial Acts

Section 9 focuses on how the 'public body' provisions operate against courts which have allegedly acted contrary to the Convention. Proceedings in respect of judicial acts under s. 7(1)(a) may be brought only by exercising a right of appeal, or as prescribed by rules. However, awards of damages may be made against the Crown if they are necessary to compensate a person as required by Article 5(5) of the Convention.

3.2.10 Section 11—Safeguard for Existing Human Rights

Section 11 provides, for the avoidance of doubt, that reliance on Convention rights (as specified in the Act) does not restrict reliance on other legal rights, or procedural methods of enforcing them.

3.2.11 Section 12 and 13—Respect for Freedoms

Sections 12 and 13 provide specific assurances as to the respect that will be afforded to freedom of expression and freedom of thought, conscience, and religion: these are 'comfort clauses' for sections of the press and certain religious organizations. See the discussion at 4.3 below.

3.2.12 Designated Derogations and Reservations

The 1998 Act provides for limited 'designated derogations and reservations' from the effect of the Convention under ss. 1(2), 14 to 17, and schs 2 and 3. The provisions in the Convention which allow the protection of human rights to be limited are considered at 2.4.5 above. The mechanism in the 1998 Act by which these derogations take effect domestically is considered in more detail at 8.15.2 below.

3.3 SUMMARY OF THE EFFECTS OF THE 1998 ACT

In summary, the wide-reaching effects of the Human Rights Act 1998 are that:

(a) In *all* cases in which Convention rights are in question, the 1998 Act gives 'further effect' to the Convention, whether the litigants are private persons or public authorities. It does this in three ways:

i.   by obliging courts to decide all cases before them (whether brought under statute or the common law) compatibly with Convention rights unless prevented from doing so either by primary legislation or by provisions made under primary legislation which cannot be read compatibly with the Convention (s. 6(1) to (3));

ii. by placing an obligation upon courts to interpret existing and future legislation in conformity with the Convention wherever possible (s. 3);

iii. by requiring courts to take Strasbourg case law into account in all cases, in so far as they consider it is relevant to proceedings before them (s. 2(1)).

(b) The 1998 Act does not make Convention rights *directly* enforceable against a private litigant, nor against a 'hybrid' public body (that is, a body which is not obviously public in form but which has some functions of a public nature) if it is acting in a private capacity. But in cases against a private litigant, or hybrid body acting in exercise of its private-law functions, the 1998 Act still has an effect on the outcome, because the court:

i.   is obliged to interpret legislation in conformity with the Convention wherever possible;

ii. must exercise any judicial discretions compatibly with the Convention; and

iii. must ensure that its application of common law or equitable rules is compatible with the Convention.

(c) Section 7 of the Act creates new, directly enforceable rights against public bodies, and against hybrid public bodies (which have some public functions) when they are acting in the sphere of those public functions. First, it has introduced a new ground of illegality into proceedings brought by way of judicial review, namely, a failure to comply with the Convention rights protected by the Act, subject to a defence that there is a clear statutory obligation to act incompatibly with the Convention. Secondly, it has created a new cause of action against public bodies which fail to act compatibly with the Convention. Thirdly, Convention rights are now available as a ground of defence or appeal in cases brought by public bodies against private persons (in both criminal and civil cases). Chapter 4 of this guide considers these provisions more fully. Section 7 can be used only by 'victims' of violations of the Convention, the term 'victim' being defined in s. 7(7).

(d) However, even a litigant who is not defined as a 'victim', and so cannot challenge a public body's decision directly using the provisions of the 1998 Act, is able to rely on the court's obligation under s. 3 of the Act, to interpret legislation compatibly with the Convention where possible, and to use Convention arguments in the circumstances in which this was possible before the Act was brought into force (s. 11).

(e) The 1998 Act does not permit the Convention to be used so as to override primary legislation: if a statute is clear in its terms, and clearly incompatible with the Convention, courts must give effect to it. Equally, if the terms of the primary legislation require subordinate legislation made under it (which will usually be in a statutory instrument) to be interpreted in a way which means that the subordinate legislation is incompatible with the Convention, it must still be given effect even though this may result in a breach of a Convention right. To that extent, parliamentary sovereignty is preserved (s. 3(2)(b) and (c)). But if legislation cannot be read so as to comply with the Convention, the higher courts have the power to issue 'declarations of incompatibility', and a fast-track procedure exists whereby the Government can legislate to remedy such incompatibility (ss. 4 and 10 and sch. 2).

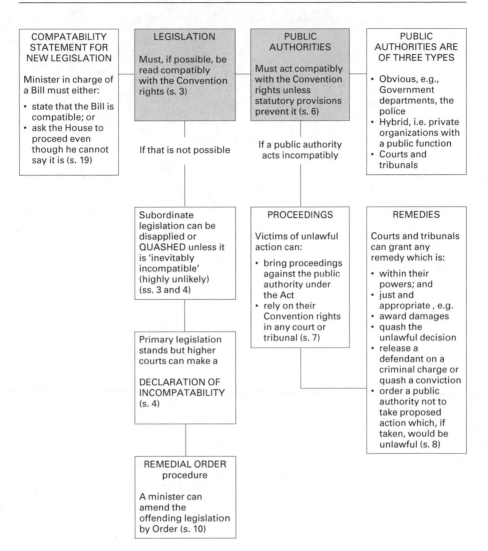

FIGURE 3.1.   Human Rights Act 1998—Key Provisions

Source: Human Rights Act 1998 Study Guide (2nd edn, 2002) (Crown copyright). Available at www.lcd.gov.uk/hract/studyguide/downloads/hract-study.pdf.

4

THE OPERATION OF THE HUMAN RIGHTS ACT

4.1 INTRODUCTION

This chapter examines the approach to 'incorporation' of the Convention contained in the Human Rights Act, before considering the effect of the Act in litigation generally and in litigation concerning public authorities specifically.

A vital feature of the Human Rights Act is the 'interpretative obligation' in s. 3, which requires a fresh approach to statutory interpretation. Since the Act came into force its most frequent use has been an interpretative one. The 1998 Act requires domestic courts and tribunals to interpret statutory provisions and the common law so as to be compatible with Convention rights wherever possible, and regardless of other (perhaps more literal) interpretations or precedents to the contrary. This affects all cases, civil or criminal, public or private, against private legal persons or public authorities where a Convention right is at stake, regardless of whether the issue is one of statutory construction, declaration of the common law, or involves the exercise of a judicial discretion.

The 1998 Act further requires domestic courts and tribunals to take account of the decisions of the Strasbourg institutions. As already discussed, this means that the Convention can potentially be relevant in a large number of cases in which both parties are private persons. As Lord Cooke of Thorndon said during the parliamentary debates, '. . . the common law approach to statutory interpretation will never be the same again' (Hansard HL, 3 November 1997, col. 1273). Earlier (col. 1272) Lord Cooke had said:

[Section 3] will require a very different approach to interpretation from that to which the English courts are accustomed. Traditionally, the search has been for the true meaning: now it will be for a possible meaning that would prevent the making of a declaration of incompatibility.

The White Paper, *Rights Brought Home*, intended that the new rule of statutory interpretation would go 'far beyond the present rule' (para. 2.7).

Section 3(1) places a duty on the courts to read and give effect to primary legislation so that it complies with the Convention 'so far as it is possible to do so'. The Government rejected amendments proposed during the passage of the Human Rights Bill to reduce this to 'so far as it is *reasonable* to do so' precisely because it wished to preserve the strong obligation to find all 'possible' interpretations of a provision which were compatible with the Convention. The duty under s. 3 requires the courts to seek compatibility in all circumstances and, where necessary, to 'read in' the protections into the legislation, or to 'blue-pencil' particular words where they lead to an incompatibility.

Constitutional human rights protections are not to be construed in the same way as other statutes. Clayton and Tomlinson, *The Law of Human Rights* (Oxford: Oxford University Press, 2000), distinguish three overlapping approaches from the jurisprudence of the Privy Council which are variously adopted when interpreting constitutional instruments. The first, 'generous' approach involves the development of new principles of construction. These must be different from those developed in ordinary statutes, so as to avoid ' "the austerity of tabulated legalism". They must be suitable to give to individuals the full measure of the fundamental rights and freedoms referred to' (*Ministry of Home Affairs v Fisher* [1980] AC 319; see also *Attorney-General of Gambia v Momodou Jobe* [1984] AC 689; *Attorney-General of Hong Kong v Lee Kwong-kut* [1993] AC 951; *Vasquez v The Queen* [1994] 1 WLR 1304; *Flicklinger v Hong Kong* [1991] 1 NZLR 439).

In *Attorney-General of Trinidad and Tobago v Whiteman* [1991] 2 AC 240, the Privy Council held that a second 'broad and purposive' approach should be adopted in relation to constitutional instruments as:

> the language of a Constitution falls to be construed, not in a narrow and legalistic way, but broadly and purposively, so as to give effect to its spirit, and this is particularly true of those provisions which are concerned with the protection of human rights.

That the Human Rights Act 1998 is a constitutional instrument has been confirmed now in a number of decisions of the higher courts, including by Laws LJ in *Thoburn v Sunderland County Council* [2002] EWHC 195 Admin.

Lastly, under the 'realistic approach' identified by Clayton and Tomlinson, courts need to look for 'the substance and reality of what was involved and should not be over-concerned with what are no more than technicalities' (*Huntley v Attorney-General for Jamaica* [1995] 2 AC 1).

The House of Lords has accepted that in interpreting such legislation the courts need to consider authorities from other jurisdictions (*R v Khan* [1997] AC 558). The

New Zealand courts have also followed the same approach and have given their Bill of Rights an importance stemming from a broad and purposive approach to interpretation (*Ministry of Transport v Noort* [1992] 3 NZLR 260; *R v Goodwin (No. 1)* [1993] 2 NZLR 153).

These approaches to interpretation of constitutional instruments are very similar to the one adopted by the Commission and Court in Strasbourg to provide for effective, not merely theoretical, guarantees of protection for human rights (see Chapter 2, at 2.2 above).

4.2 THE HUMAN RIGHTS ACT MECHANISM

The key to the mechanism adopted by the Human Rights Act is the interplay between ss. 6, 3, 4, and 2, which—though they preserve parliamentary sovereignty—have fundamentally altered both the manner in which courts can scrutinize legislation and the ways in which judges must interpret common law. As Lord Hope said in *R v DPP ex parte Kebilene* [1999] 3 WLR 972:

> It is now plain that the incorporation of the European Convention on Human Rights into our domestic law will subject the entire legal system to a fundamental process of review and, where necessary, reform by the judiciary.

4.2.1 Section 6

Section 6(1) makes it unlawful for a public authority to act in a way which is incompatible with a Convention right. Courts and tribunals are defined as public authorities (s. 6(3)(a)) and they have their own primary duty to act compatibly with the Convention. Parliamentary sovereignty is preserved by s. 6(2). This limits the s. 6(1) duty in circumstances where the court or tribunal could not have acted differently as a result of a statutory obligation which cannot be read or given effect to in a way which is compatible with the Convention rights, notwithstanding the obligation in s. 3 to do so if possible. This clever device places courts and tribunals themselves under a primary obligation to give effect to Convention rights except where they are prevented from doing so by statute.

The obligation to interpret the law so as to accord with the Convention wherever possible applies to all cases. The consequence is that Convention questions are pivotal in cases where courts or tribunals are deciding the scope of a statutory provision (even one which regulates the behaviour of one private individual to another); where they are determining what the common law is (in so far as this is within their jurisdiction); or when they are exercising a judicial discretion.

So, for example, a court or tribunal will be under an obligation to give effect to Article 8 of the Convention in deciding whether a failure to respect an employee's private life constitutes a breach of a duty of trust and confidence implied into contract by the common law. Courts considering the scope of the tort of breach of confidence have to consider whether it creates a positive right to respect for private life (see *Campbell v MGN Limited* [2002] EWCA Civ 1373), and so on.

4.2.2 Section 3

Section 3(1) of the Act explains how courts will approach their interpretative obligation in relation to primary and secondary legislation. It provides that courts and tribunals *must* read primary and subordinate legislation and give it effect in a way which is compatible with Convention rights 'so far as it is possible to do so'. This obligation applies to both primary and secondary legislation whenever it was enacted, that is, whether before or after the enactment of the Human Rights Act 1998.

As was pointed out in the White Paper, this interpretative obligation goes far beyond the pre-incorporation use of the Convention in statutory interpretation. During the Third Reading of the Human Rights Bill, the then Lord Chancellor said that 'in 99% of all cases that will arise, there will be no need for judicial declarations of incompatibility' (Hansard HL Deb., 5 February 1998, col. 840) because of the intended impact of s. 3. In the first House of Lords judgment on the Convention, *R v DPP ex parte Kebilene* [2000] 2 AC 326, s. 3 was described as a 'strong' interpretative obligation (see Lord Steyn at para. 831 and Lord Cooke at para. 837).

As explained in Chapter 1, before the 1998 Act courts were permitted to (but did not have to) use the Convention as an interpretative tool where the supposed intention of an Act of Parliament was ambiguous. Now, the courts are under an express statutory duty to interpret legislation so as to accord with the purpose of the Convention if this is at all possible, even if this results in a strained rather than a literal meaning being selected from a range of possible interpretations. Courts may comply with this interpretative obligation by 'reading in' additional words so as to give effect to the presumed intended effect of the Convention, or by 'reading down' so as to apply a narrow interpretation of the legislation and enable the court to render it compatible with Convention rights.

This more purposive approach to statutory construction had already begun to permeate English judicial reasoning before the 1998 Act came into force, because a purposive approach is required in relation to European Community law. The obligation of domestic courts to comply with the objects and purposes of the underlying Community law provisions has been emphasized in many decisions in the European Court of Justice. It is exemplified in *Marleasing SA v La Comercial Internacional de Alimentacion SA* (case C-106/89) [1990] ECR I-4135, in which it was held that where national courts have to interpret national law in a field governed by Community law, they must interpret that law in the light of the wording *and purpose* of the Community legislation, so far as it is possible for them to do so.

An example of the way in which this interpretative obligation was used in the United Kingdom in the field of European Community law is *Litster v Forth Dry Dock and Engineering Co. Ltd* [1990] 1 AC 546, in which the House of Lords had to consider the construction of the Transfer of Undertakings (Protection of Employment) Regulations 1981 (SI 1981/1794). The Regulations were intended to implement the Acquired Rights Directive (77/187/EEC), the purpose of which was to protect the workers in an undertaking when its ownership was transferred. But the Regulations only protected those who were employed in the business 'immediately before' the time of the transfer. The House of Lords enquired into the purpose of the underlying Directive, and interpreted the Regulations so as to accord with that purpose by 'reading in' additional words to protect workers if they were employed 'immediately before' the time of transfer, 'or would have been so employed if [they] had not been unfairly dismissed [by reason of the transfer]'.

Since the Human Rights Act has been in force, the courts have grappled with the effect and limits of this new rule of construction. To date, the leading cases are three decisions of the House of Lords. *R v A (No. 2)* [2002] 1 AC 45, concerned the rape shield enacted in s. 41 of the Youth Justice and Criminal Evidence Act 1999, which restricts cross-examination of a rape victim about her sexual conduct. The House of Lords unanimously held that s. 41 had to be read subject to s. 3 and was subject to the implied provision that evidence and questioning required to ensure a fair trial under Article 6 should not automatically be treated as inadmissible. Lord Steyn (paras 44–45, 67–68) extensively analysed the obligation under s. 3 and stressed that it will sometimes be necessary to adopt an interpretation which is linguistically strained both by reading down the express language of the statute and by the implication of provisions. He held that a declaration of incompatibility was 'a measure of last resort' and must be avoided unless a clear limitation on Convention rights is stated and it is plainly impossible to read it compatibly under s. 3.

However, Lord Hope (para. 108) took a more cautious approach and held that, although s. 3 was 'quite unlike any previous rule of statutory interpretation', it was:

> only a rule of interpretation. It does not entitle the judges to act as legislators. As Lord Woolf CJ said in *Poplar Housing Association v Donoghue* [2001] QB 48, s. 3 does not entitle the court to legislate; its task is still one of interpretation. The compatibility is to be achieved only so far as this is possible. Plainly this will not be possible if the legislation contains provisions which expressly contradict the meaning which the enactment would have to be given to make it compatible.

This approach, which emphasizes the importance of identifying and respecting the intention of Parliament, was followed by the majority in the second House of Lords case of *R v Lambert* [2001] 3 WLR 206. Once again, Lord Hope (para. 79) set out that s. 3 needed to be used in a way that respected the will of the legislature and preserved the integrity of statute law. In *Lambert*, s. 3 was applied to construe the words 'if he proves' in s. 28(3) of the Misuse of Drugs Act 1971 to mean 'if he gives sufficient evidence', thus ensuring that the legal burden on the defendant was only an evidential burden and compatible with the right to a fair trial under Article 6.

The limits of s. 3 as an interpretative obligation were examined by the House of Lords in *Re S (Care Order: Implementation of Care Plan)* [2002] 2 AC 291. Lord

Nicholls held that s. 3 is a 'powerful tool' but its reach is not unlimited. He considered that the Court of Appeal's attempt to construe the Children Act 1989 as compatible with the Convention went beyond s. 3 when it led to a result which was directly contrary to one of the key principles of the Children Act (that the courts had no power to intervene in the way local authorities carried out their responsibilities to children under care orders). It seems that s. 3 cannot be invoked if the Convention compliant interpretation is contrary to express statutory provision as 'a meaning which departs substantially from a fundamental feature of an Act of Parliament is likely to have crossed the boundary between interpretation and amendment' (para. 40).

However, as Clayton has rightly stressed ('The Limits of What's "Possible": Statutory Construction under the Human Rights Act' [2002] EHRLR 559), these limitations should apply only in specific circumstances and should not undermine the constitutional purpose of the Human Rights Act to protect Convention rights—otherwise the parliamentary intention in enacting the 1998 Act would be undermined by the courts.

Section 3 has been the subject of much academic debate proposing a variety of different opinions. Detailed follow-up reading can be found in: Clayton and Tomlinson, *The Law of Human Rights* (Oxford: Oxford University Press, 2000), Chapter 4; Fenwick, 'The Interpretative Obligation under Section 3 of the Human Rights Act 1998' [2001] SL Rev 8; Gearty, 'Reconciling Parliamentary Democracy and Human Rights' (2002) 118 LQR 248; Rose and Weir, 'Interpretation and Incompatibility: Striking the Balance under the Human Rights Act', in Cooper and Jowell (eds), *Delivering Rights? How the Human Rights Act is Working and For Whom* (London: Hart Publishing, 2003).

4.2.3 Interplay of Sections 3 and 4

The dividing line between interpreting and legislating under s. 3 of the 1998 Act has an important impact upon the power conferred on higher courts to make 'statements of incompatibility' under s. 4. Section 4 states that, where legislation cannot be read compatibly with the Convention, courts are empowered to make a declaration of incompatibility (see 6.3). Logically, if courts find it impossible to construe primary legislation compatibly with the Convention under s. 3 then they should declare it incompatible under s. 4. So, for example, in *Mendoza v Ghaidan* [2002] EWCA Civ 1533, the Court of Appeal used its power under s. 3 of the 1998 Act to interpret the words 'living together as husband and wife' to mean *as if* they were living together as husband and wife, thus allowing the inclusion of all non-marital relationships under the protection of the Rent Act 1977. This avoided the need to make a declaration of incompatibility between the Rent Act 1977 and the non-discrimination protection contained in Article 14 of the Convention. However, in *R (Hooper) v Secretary of State for Work and Pensions* [2002] EWHC Admin 191, the provisions of the Social Security (Contributions and Benefits) Act 1992 relating to 'widows' could not be read under s. 3 to include 'widowers'. As a result, the court held that the discriminatory provisions (on the grounds of sex within Article 14 read with Article 8) were incompatible with the Convention and the court made a declaration of incompatibility under s. 4 of the Human Rights Act. (This part of the decision was upheld by the Court of Appeal in June 2003, [2003] EWCA Civ 813.)

4.2.4 Section 2

Section 2 of the Act introduced new 'relevant considerations' which courts must take into account when seeking to interpret domestic law in compliance with the Convention. The 1998 Act does not permit courts to decide these questions in accordance only with domestic precedent or their own instincts. Section 2 provides that a court or tribunal determining a question which has arisen under any Act in connection with a Convention right *must* take account of any judgment, decision, declaration, or advisory opinion of the European Court of Human Rights, opinion or decision of the Commission, or decision of the Committee of Ministers, whenever made or given, so far as, in the opinion of the court or tribunal, it is relevant to the proceedings in which that question has arisen. The decisions of the different Strasbourg organs carry different weights and decisions of the Court sitting as a Grand Chamber will take precedence over admissibility decisions from the Commission on the same issue of law (see Chapter 10, 'Researching Human Rights Jurisprudence').

The obligation to have regard to Strasbourg case law when considering a Convention question is explicable by reference to the White Paper, which intends that, by enactment of the Human Rights Act 1998, 'the [Convention] rights will be brought much more fully into the jurisprudence of the courts throughout the United Kingdom and their interpretation . . . far more subtly and powerfully woven into our law'. As a result, it will very rarely be appropriate for the English courts to adopt a standard of protection which is lower than that set in the Strasbourg case law (*R v Botmeh* [2001] 1 WLR 531).

As a United Kingdom court must give effect to the Convention wherever possible, it is also obliged to have regard to the Strasbourg case law so that it has in mind the appropriate principles in deciding what it must give effect to. The House of Lords, in *R (Anderson) v Secretary of State for the Home Department* [2002] UKHL 46, emphasized that the duty under s. 2 meant that courts must take into account any relevant judgments of the Strasbourg court and that the House of Lords would not, without good reason, depart from the principles laid down in a carefully considered judgment of the court sitting as a Grand Chamber (see Lord Bingham, at para. 18). In this case, reviewing the Home Secretary's controversial role in fixing tariffs for mandatory life prisoners, the Strasbourg decision in *Stafford v United Kingdom* (2002) 35 EHRR 32, was the decisive factor in overturning the Court of Appeal's judgment and making a declaration of incompatibility.

Nonetheless, Strasbourg case law is only relevant, not binding upon domestic courts. Over time, domestic courts may in some cases develop their own standards of interpretation of the Convention. Since the Convention is a 'living instrument', the interpretation of which changes from time to time, earlier decisions on the basis of particular Strasbourg case law may need to be reconsidered if, in the meantime, the Court has arrived at a different interpretation of a particular provision. The duty is to take the case law into account whenever a Convention issue arises, not to follow it. For example, though Strasbourg has not treated gay relationships as family relationships, in *Fitzpatrick v Sterling Housing Association* [1999] 3 WLR 1113, the House of Lords found that as a matter of English law, a stable gay relationship is a family one. This decision was drawn upon by the Court of Appeal in a case which recognized the rights of co-habiting same-sex couples (see *Mendoza v Ghaidan*, at 4.2.3 above).

An interpretation of a Convention right which offers less protection than the European Court of Human Rights would afford leaves the United Kingdom open to an unfavourable judgment against it in Strasbourg. The effect of s. 2, with the right of individual petition to Strasbourg, is that the Strasbourg jurisprudence is a long-stop or bottom line for human rights protection, but not the last word. It is a floor, not a ceiling.

4.2.5 Interplay of Sections 2 and 3

Sections 2 and 3 of the Act taken together have two principal effects. First, because the Convention must be given effect wherever possible, and because Strasbourg case law must be taken into account, the Strasbourg method of judicial reasoning is gradually entering English legal practice. The Court of Appeal has held that in the light of s. 2 of the 1998 Act, the court's task is 'to draw out the broad principles which animate the Convention' (*Aston Cantlow Parochial Church Council v Wallbank* [2001] EWCA Civ 713). This involves an explicit balancing of the rights of individuals against the rights and freedoms of others and the general public interest. Judges and legal representatives have begun to structure their arguments in the systematic way that is done in Strasbourg, namely, to identify the broad *prima facie* right that may have been infringed, and then to consider limitations to it. Where there is potentially a Convention question in play, the domestic court or tribunal first has to identify the right in question, including the positive aspects of the right (that is, the obligations of the court, as a public body, to take positive steps to protect the right). Then it must identify the alleged interference with the right and look to see whether it is prescribed by law. It then has to decide what objectives are said to be served by the interference, and whether the interference is necessary in a democratic society for the purposes of achieving those objectives.

Secondly, ss.2 and 3 read together mean that the doctrine of precedent has been abrogated to the extent that is necessary to give effect to Convention rights. Strasbourg case law has consistently held that the Convention is 'a living instrument which . . . must be interpreted in the light of present-day conditions' (*Tyrer v United Kingdom* (1978) 2 EHRR 1, at para. 31). The s. 3 rule of construction applies to past as well as to future legislation, and in interpreting legislation 'the courts will not be bound by previous interpretations. They will be able to build a new body of case law, taking into account Convention rights' (White Paper (Cm 3782), para. 2.8.).

Nonetheless, where a higher court has ruled on an issue of interpretation under the Human Rights Act, the normal doctrine of precedent will apply in the absence of a change of circumstances such as to enable the 'living instrument' doctrine to be used to argue that the previous case has been superseded. In *R (Williamson) v Secretary of State for Education and Employment* [2002] EWCA Civ 1820, Buxton LJ said (at para. 41) that if the House of Lords had previously considered a Convention issue fully then the Court of Appeal would be 'bound by any decision within the normal hierarchy of domestic authority as to the meaning of an Article of the Convention, in the same way as it is bound by such a decision as to the meaning of purely domestic law'. However, he also recognized (at para. 43) that when the House of Lords dealt with a Convention issue only briefly, the decision could not be relied upon if the 'general trend of Convention authority pointed in a different direction'.

Strasbourg case law (which a domestic court must take into account) requires *effective* protection of the Convention rights: '. . . the Convention is intended to guarantee not rights that are theoretical or illusory but rights that are practical and effective' (*Artico v Italy* (1980) 3 EHRR 1, para. 33; *Airey v Ireland* (1979) 2 EHRR 305). Accordingly, to comply with their obligation under s. 3(1) of the 1998 Act, United Kingdom courts have to interpret statutory provisions so as to give real and effective protection to the rights that the Convention was intended to safeguard. However, by reason of s. 3(2)(b) and (c), this interpretative obligation does not permit courts to 'strike down' primary legislation if it is simply incapable of interpretation so as to conform with the Convention. Judges (in the higher courts) are obliged to consider making 'declarations of incompatibility' in cases where they are unable to interpret legislation consistently with the Convention and this, coupled (in the case of legislation which post-dates the Act) with ministerial statements of compatibility, is a powerful incentive to judges to find consistent interpretations.

4.2.6 Section 19

The interpretative obligation applies to legislation whether passed before or after the Human Rights Act 1998. In respect of legislation which post-dates the Act, the task of compliant interpretation should be made easier by reference to the statement which s. 19 of the Act requires a minister to make spelling out whether he or she intends the legislation to comply with the Convention. Where such a statement has been made, whether or not in Parliament, the courts could use it as evidence of parliamentary intention—as they presently do with statements made by persons introducing legislation under the principle in *Pepper v Hart* [1993] AC 59. As Lord

Irvine of Lairg, the then Lord Chancellor, said in the Tom Sargant Memorial Lecture, 16 December 1997, in relation to future legislation:

> . . . it should be clear from the Parliamentary history, and in particular the Ministerial statement of compatibility which will be required by the Act, that Parliament did not intend to cut across a Convention right. Ministerial statements of compatibility will inevitably be a strong spur to the courts to find means of construing statutes compatibly with the Convention.

In assessing whether a particular provision complies with the Act and the Convention, those advising the Government have thus far not sought positive guarantees for Convention rights within the text of the statute before giving a 's. 19' statement. Instead, they have assumed that all those public authorities that have to implement the provision will act in compliance with the Convention if they have the power to do so. So for instance, a Bill that gave wide discretion to the police to act in ways which would clearly violate the Convention would still be assessed as complying with the Convention because the discretion would be constrained by the Human Rights Act. At the present time Lord Hope's view (expressed in *R v A (No. 2)* [2002] 1 AC 45)—that s. 19 statements of compatibility are no more than expressions of opinion by the minister; they are not binding on the court; nor do they have any persuasive authority—is unfortunately accurate. This does not mean that the courts cannot go on to try to construe the legislation compatibly with the Convention under s. 3, but it may make the likelihood of a declaration of incompatibility under s. 4 more likely (and thus Parliament could then legislate to ensure that the provisions do not offend against human rights). For a critique of the initial operation of s. 19 see Wadham, 'The Human Rights Act: One Year On' [2001] EHRLR 620.

4.3 EXCEPTIONS AND SPECIAL CASES

The Human Rights Act 1998 is principally a constitutional instrument of general application. However, one important omission from the Schedule to the Act (Article 13) and two specific provisions (ss. 12 and 13) about particular interest groups (the press and religious organizations) require brief explanation.

4.3.1 Article 13

Article 13 imposes a duty on the state to provide the opportunity to test at a national level whether a Convention right has been violated. It guarantees in general terms that there is a suitable national avenue of redress which is capable of providing a remedy in an appropriate case. However, it does not mean that states have to ensure that a *particular* result is secured. So, for example, the right will be breached where the victim has no right of recourse in the domestic courts (see *Halford v United Kingdom* (1997) 24 EHRR 523), or where primary legislation excludes any such challenge. Article 13 is not a free-standing right (that is, a claim cannot be founded on the Article alone and must be brought in connection with an alleged breach of another Convention right), but it is not necessary to show a breach of another Convention right before the court can consider its application—it is enough to show that the complaint in relation to the other right is 'arguable' but cannot be argued because there is no means for this to be done before a national court (*Boyle and Rice v United Kingdom* (1988) 10 EHRR 425). The question of whether a right is 'arguable' is broadly the same as the question of whether a complaint is 'admissible' under the Convention (see 9.4, for full details of the requirements).

Although Article 13 is not one of the rights included in the Schedule to the 1998 Act, during the parliamentary debates on the Bill, the then Lord Chancellor said that the Act itself gives effect to Articles 1 and 13 by securing the rights and freedoms of the Convention. In other words, Article 13 is given effect by establishing a scheme under which Convention rights can be raised and remedied before UK courts. Under s. 2(1) of the 1998 Act courts 'must take into account' the case law of the Convention organs and so 'the courts may have regard to Article 13. In particular, they may wish to do so when considering the very ample provisions of section 8(1) [remedies]'(Hansard, HL Deb., 18 November 1997, col. 477).

4.3.2 The Churches and the Press

During the passage of the Human Rights Bill, the churches and the press were particularly concerned to ensure that particular liberties which they perceived as important would still be protected. Fears were expressed on behalf of the Church of England, for example, that the Act might lead to questions about whether they could refuse to marry gay couples, or could dismiss church school teachers who had lost their faith. Sections of the press were concerned that the judiciary might interpret Article 8 of the Convention (right to respect for private and family life) in a way which unacceptably limited the freedom of the press (see 4.4.1, and 4.4.2 for a discussion of what some commentators have called the 'emerging right to privacy' under the 1998 Act). Sections 12 and 13 of the 1998 Act were added as late amendments to meet these concerns.

4.3.3 Section 12

The object of s. 12 is to emphasize that the courts must pay due regard to Article 10 and the right to freedom of expression contained in the Article. Section 12 has a number of components. First, it prevents 'gagging injunctions' being granted *ex parte* except in the rarest of circumstances. It provides that if a court is considering whether to grant any relief which might affect the exercise of the Convention right to freedom of expression, there is a presumption against the grant of such relief. 'No such relief is to be granted' unless the court is satisfied that the person seeking the relief has taken all practicable steps to notify the defendant, or there are compelling reasons why the defendant should not be notified (s.12(1) and (2)). Secondly, the merits of the claimant's case must be tested before any such restraint is made. Section 12(3) provides that no relief is to be granted so as to restrain publication before trial unless the court is satisfied that the applicant is likely to establish that publication should not be allowed. Thirdly, s. 12(4) provides that the court must have 'particular regard' to the right to freedom of expression, and that where the proceedings relate to material which the respondent claims is, or which appears to the court to be, journalistic, literary, or artistic material, the court must have regard to the extent to which the material has, or is about to become available to the public, or it is, or would be, in the public interest for the material to be published. It must also have regard to any relevant privacy code such as the code issued by the Press Complaints Commission.

Article 10 in itself requires 'particular regard' to be given to the right to freedom of expression; but the court has to take account of Strasbourg principles when reaching its decisions, and form its own view on the difficult balance between Article 8 and Article 10 on the facts of a particular case. Strasbourg jurisprudence is very strongly in favour of freedom of expression. There is little Strasbourg authority on how conflicts between respect for private life and freedoms of expression should be resolved (see *Winer v United Kingdom* (1986) 48 DR 154). Domestically, in *Cream Holdings v Banerjee* [2003] EWCA Civ 103, the majority of the Court of Appeal held that there was a 'presumptive equality' between the right to freedom of expression and other Convention rights such as Article 8. However, the media's right to freedom of expression is of a higher order when the societal interests set out in Article 10(2) are under consideration. For example, when a court is examining a claim involving political discussion and the competing interest is the 'right of an individual to his good reputation' set out in Article 10(2), the right to freedom of expression has a 'presumptive priority'. (This is a rapidly evolving area of law, and for an account of the current situation see Tomlinson and Rogers, 'Privacy Injunctions: Reviewing the Approach' (2003) 153 NLJ 818.)

4.3.4 Section 13

Section 13 provides that if the court's determination of any question under the Act might affect the exercise by a religious organization, whether as an organization or by its members collectively, of the Convention right to freedom of thought, conscience, and religion, it must have particular regard to the importance of that right. This is something that is inherent in the structure of Article 9 of the Convention, which is where that guarantee is to be found. Since the whole scheme of the Convention is to give particular regard to a *prima facie* right, permitting derogations from it only if they are necessary, proportionate, and so on, the effect of this section is really to add political comfort to religious interests rather than to add anything in terms of practical effect.

Fuller discussions of the scope and content of the Articles 8, 9, and 10 of the Convention can be found in Chapter 8.

4.4 THE EFFECT OF THE CONVENTION IN ANY LITIGATION

4.4.1 Private Parties and the Human Rights Act: 'Vertical' or 'Horizontal' Effect?

This chapter is concerned with the uses of the Human Rights Act in *all* litigation, whether the parties are public or private. This does not mean that the Convention is 'directly effective' against private litigants. In litigation concerning purely private bodies, there is no new cause of action, but in all cases, whatever the nature of the parties, under s. 6(3) of the 1998 Act, the courts are under a statutory duty to interpret the law (including the common law) so as to accord with the Convention wherever possible. This means that, for example, in interpreting a statutory right not to be unfairly dismissed, or the common law of trespass, a court or tribunal is required, if possible, to interpret the law in a way which gives a result compatible with the Convention. The debate about the nature and extent of this 'horizontal' obligation (that is, between private individuals as opposed to between the state and the individual as in the rest of the 'vertical' obligations under the Act) has given rise to a variety of academic and judicial opinion.

The Convention itself is an instrument of international law. Its unusual feature as a matter of international law is the right of individual petition to the European Court of Human Rights in Strasbourg. The rights created under the Convention are enforceable in Strasbourg against the state rather than against individuals. Someone who takes a case to Strasbourg takes it against the Government, alleging that it has infringed or failed to take steps to protect some Convention right; even if the failure is a failure to provide protection for the applicant from an infringement of his or her rights by a private third party (see 'Positive Obligations' at 2.3.2 above).

The White Paper introducing the Human Rights Bill was called *Rights Brought Home*, and some commentators take the view that it is those international law rights which have been brought home: in other words, that the 1998 Act is primarily a 'vertically effective' provision that will affect cases between individuals and state or public authorities rather than, in most cases, disputes between private parties. At committee stage in the House of Lords (see Hansard HL, 24 November 1997, col. 781), Lord Wilberforce said that ministerial statements made it 'perfectly clear . . . that the Bill is aimed entirely at public authorities and not at private individuals'.

Other commentators take the view that the Act effectively incorporates the Convention into domestic law. They argue that as s. 6(3) of the Act makes the courts 'public authorities' which are bound to act in accordance with the Convention in all cases, even between private individuals, the Government has effected 'full' incorporation of the Convention, with horizontal effect, so that the distinction which the Act draws between public bodies, quasi-public (or 'hybrid') authorities, and private bodies is an artificial one. This view is taken by, for example, Sir William Wade QC,

'The United Kingdom's Bill of Rights', in *Constitutional Reforms in the United Kingdom: Practice and Principles* (London: Hart Publishing, 1998).

We consider that the first view is too narrow an approach to the impact of the 1998 Act, because of the way in which the courts are obliged to use the Convention in determining cases, whereas the second overlooks some of the subtleties and difficulties in using the Convention against a private body. We agree with the broad position advanced by Murray Hunt ('The "Horizontal Effect" of the Human Rights Act' [1998] PL 423). The Convention must be used to interpret all law before the courts, but falls short of being directly horizontal as the 1998 Act does not *directly* confer any new private causes of action on individuals when their Convention rights have been violated by a private party.

Since the Human Rights Act came into force in October 2000, the case law has confirmed this view that the Articles of the Convention in sch. 1 to the Act are indirectly rather than directly enforceable against private persons: that is, it is not possible for one private individual to sue another private legal person for a tort of 'breach of the Convention'.

The Convention is enforceable against a private legal person, but only in the following ways:

(a) Where the effect of a statutory provision is in question in a dispute between private individuals, the courts are under an obligation to interpret the legislation so as to accord with the Convention (under s. 3 in conjunction with s. 6(3) of the 1998 Act). For example, in *Wilson v First County Trust (No. 2)* [2001] EWCA Civ 633, both parties were 'private' individuals. This did not prevent the Court of Appeal deciding that the bar against enforcing a credit agreement breached the pawnbroker's right of access to a court under Article 6 of the Convention and the right to property under Article 1 of Protocol 1. As a result, the first declaration of incompatibility between the 1998 Act and the Consumer Credit Act 1974 was made. (Although the House of Lords reversed the Court of Appeal's declaration of incompatibility on the technical grounds that the interpretative obligation in s. 3 did not apply on the facts of this case the general principle that the provisions of the 1998 Act have an effect on cases involving private parties still applies (see [2003] UKHL 40).

(b) Where there is a judicial discretion to be exercised, s. 6 requires it to be exercised so as to give effect to a Convention right (for example, in relation to the admission of evidence obtained in breach of a Convention right—see 'European Convention Rights in the United Kingdom before the 1998 Act' at 1.1.2 above).

(c) Where the courts are dealing with cases involving the common law they are under an obligation to develop the common law to be compatible with Convention rights (by virtue of s. 6(3)). The 'horizontal' effects of the 1998 Act in private litigation have been most marked in this area.

Where the rights in question touch upon positive obligations under Articles 2, 3, 8, 10, or 11, the court is itself under a positive obligation to afford protection to individuals from having their rights violated by other private individuals. For example, in *Venables and Thompson v Newsgroup Newspapers and Associated Newspapers Ltd* [2001] 2 WLR 1038, the two children who had been convicted of the murder of James Bulger were granted the continuation of injunctions preventing publication of further information about them as the Court of Appeal was under a positive obligation to secure their right to life (Article 2) and right to respect for private life (Article 8).

Before the 1998 Act came into force many commentators, including the authors, speculated that the judiciary would develop a right to privacy. In *Douglas v Hello!* [2001] QB 967, a celebrity couple claimed a right to respect for their private life under Article 8 of the Convention. Despite the pre-1998 Act position that the English law did not recognize a right to privacy as such, the Court of Appeal agreed that the claimants had a 'powerfully arguable case' that they had a 'right of privacy which English law will today recognise and, where appropriate, protect' (Sedley LJ, at paras 124–6). (See 4.4.2 below.)

This is a complex area and the commentators have widely differing views on the issues above. See, for example, Leigh, 'Horizontal Rights, the Human Rights Act and Privacy: Lessons from the Commonwealth' (1999) 48 ICLQ 57; Oliver, 'The Human Rights Act and the Public Law/Private Law Divide' [2000] EHRLR 343; Hare, 'Vertically Challenged: Private Parties, Privacy and the Human Rights Act' [2001] EHRLR 526; and Hunt, 'The "Horizontal Effect" of the Human Rights Act: Moving Beyond the Public-Private Distinction', in Jowell and Cooper (eds), *Understanding Human Rights Principles* (London: Hart Publishing, 2001).

4.4.2 An Enhanced Element for the Common Law

Courts and tribunals are included within the definition of a public authority under s. 6(3)(a) of the 1998 Act and they act unlawfully if they fail to develop the law—both statute and common law—in a way which is compatible with Convention rights. This applies even where the litigation is taking place between private individuals (see 4.4.1 above). Notably, the 1998 Act does not protect the common law from the effects of the Convention in the same way as it does primary legislation.

Although the common law recognized some fundamental rights, and the Convention could be used in some circumstances to give clarity to English law, since the 1998 Act came into force there has been a substantial impact on the common law. Some commentators, such as Lord Irvine ('The Impact of the Human Rights Act' [2003] PL 308), have argued that the common law has been 'reinvigorated' by the 1998 Act. In *Marcic v Thames Water* [2002] EWCA Civ 64, the first instance court found that the common law of nuisance was inadequate to provide a property owner with a remedy against a statutory sewerage undertaker after his house had been repeatedly flooded with sewage water. However, the court filled the gap with a remedy derived from the Protocol 1, Article 1 Convention right of the owner's right to peaceful enjoyment of his property. (The Court of Appeal agreed

with the conclusion under the Convention but found that the common law was sufficient to provide the same remedy—the case is under appeal to the House of Lords
and clear guidance may be forthcoming.) *Marcic* is good illustration of how the
rights and principles of the Convention have begun to permeate English legal
culture.

The effects of the Convention on evolving the common law have most clearly
been seen in a series of cases concerning the privacy of public figures. As noted
above, before the 1998 Act came into force many commentators, including the
authors, speculated that the judiciary would develop a right to privacy. In some cases
an 'enhanced' action for breach of confidence has been used as the basis for this
development (see *A v B and C* [2002] EWCA Civ 337 and *Campbell v MGN Limited*
[2002] EWCA Civ 1373). However, as a result of *Douglas v Hello!* [2001] QB 967
(see 4.4.1 above), some commentators have argued that a separate tort of invasion of
privacy is developing under the impetus of the 1998 Act (see Tomlinson (ed.),
Privacy and the Media: The Developing Law (London: Matrix, 2002)). This debate
will undoubtedly be affected by the 2003 Report of the House of Commons Culture,
Media, and Sport Select Committee, entitled 'Privacy and Media Intrusion', which
called for the enactment of a privacy law to recognize and codify the developments
in the common law brought about, at least in part, by the Human Rights Act (see
www.parliament.co.uk/selcom for the full report).

4.4.3 Summary of the General Effect of the 1998 Act on Interpretation

To summarize the interpretative obligation: in determining cases between private
individuals, as well as those between an individual and the state, a United Kingdom
court (as a public authority) is obliged to act in a way which is compatible with the
Convention, by interpreting statute and common law consistently with it wherever
possible, and by exercising judicial discretion compatibly with it. But the interpretative obligation does not create free-standing new rights. A litigant, A, who wishes to
use a Convention argument in a case brought against a private opponent B, needs to
find an existing private law argument on which to hang the Convention argument, or
focus the action on a public body, C, which has failed to protect A's rights from
being violated by B. For example, it may be possible on appropriate facts, for an
individual to sue the Press Complaints Commission for failure to provide a proper
remedy for breach of Article 8 of the Convention by a newspaper.

The initial case law under the 1998 Act indicates that Convention standards will
continue to infiltrate, influence, and even create new common law rights over time.
Whereas once Convention arguments were at best factors in ascertaining the scope
of the common law or exercises of judicial discretion, now the Human Rights Act
1998 is in force, a United Kingdom court is obliged to give effect to Convention
rights when performing its public functions, that is trying or administering cases—
even cases where both parties are private individuals.

Further, since courts and tribunals are public authorities they must exercise their judicial discretion so as to accord with the Convention whenever it is possible to do so. This obligation applies to all cases, whether the court is applying the common law or exercising an inherent judicial discretion (that is, in 'pure' s. 6(1) cases), or where it is interpreting statutes or exercising its own statutory powers (that is, under s. 6(1), (2), or 3). The requirement to have regard to Strasbourg case law falls, as a matter of statutory duty, on every court and tribunal from magistrates' court, social security appeal tribunal, or employment tribunal to the House of Lords. It goes far beyond the use of the Convention made by United Kingdom courts in the past when courts were permitted, but not required, to refer to Strasbourg case law, which was (consequently) often ignored.

4.5 THE SPECIAL POSITION OF PUBLIC AUTHORITIES

Public authorities are in a special position under the Human Rights Act 1998, because the Convention rights scheduled to the Act can be directly enforced against them. The reason for this is that s. 6 of the Act created a new statutory duty which requires public authorities to act compatibly with the Convention, and s. 7 created new causes of actions through which these 'vertically effective' rights can be enforced. Individuals are able to rely upon Convention rights against public authorities and any body exercising 'functions of a public nature' in respect of those functions (see s. 6(3)(b) and (5) of the Human Rights Act 1998).

The Convention is not 'directly effective' against private parties. In litigation concerning private bodies, there is no new cause of action under the 1998 Act. However, the impact of s. 6 has been wider than may have been intended, because s. 6(3) expressly includes courts and tribunals in the definition of 'public authority' and therefore in all cases, whatever the nature of the parties, the courts are under a statutory duty to interpret the law (including the common law) so as to accord with the Convention wherever possible. The debate about the nature and extent of this 'horizontal' obligation (that is, between private individuals as opposed to between the state and the individual as in the rest of the 'vertical' obligations under the Act) is discussed in more detail at 4.4.1 above.

4.5.1 Direct Enforcement of Convention Rights

Section 6(1) of the Act makes it unlawful for a public authority to act in a way which is incompatible with a Convention right. 'Act' includes failure to act: see s. 6(6). This general obligation is very wide, and means that in the exercise of any power or duty, any public body must act in such a way as to give effect to the Convention.

This means more than that the public authority must avoid violating Convention rights itself. It must also act in a way that gives effect to its positive obligations under the Convention (see 2.3.2). For example, a local authority faced with a family complaining of racial harassment by gangs of thugs on a council estate must not merely refrain from racially harassing the family itself. In order to comply with its positive obligations under the Convention, the s. 6(1) duty requires the local authority to take such positive steps as are necessary to protect the family's right to respect for their private or family life and home without discrimination on grounds of race (under Articles 8 and 14 of the Convention).

Section 6(1) is limited only in so far as is necessary to preserve the concept of parliamentary sovereignty. First, s. 6(2)(a) provides that s. 6(1) does not apply if the public authority *could not* have acted differently as a result of one or more provisions of primary legislation. Section 6(2)(b) provides that s. 6(1) does not apply if the authority was acting to give effect to or to enforce one or more provisions made under primary legislation which cannot be read or given effect in a way which is compatible with the Convention rights. In practice, s. 6(2) is rarely applied. Most powers or duties *can* be read in a way which is compatible with the Convention: and if public authorities do not themselves comply with s. 6(1) by reading their powers and duties in a Convention-compliant way, the courts (as public authorities themselves) are under their own duties to find a reading of the legislation which permits the public authority to comply with the Convention if at all possible (ss. 3 and 6(1) of the Act—see Chapter 3).

The second limit on the effect of s. 6(1) is that Parliament in its legislative capacity is not a 'public authority' (s. 6(3)) and so is not bound by s. 6(1). Though the 'act' of a public authority which can be challenged includes an omission, it does not include a failure to introduce proposals for legislation or a remedial order (s. 6(6)). This means that it is not possible for an individual to sue the executive for failing to introduce legislation which is necessary to give effect to a Convention right, or the legislature for failing to pass it. If the violation of a Convention right is contained in primary legislation incapable of consistent interpretation, the only remedy is to seek a declaration of incompatibility or to take the case to Strasbourg.

Section 6(1) can be enforced using s. 7 of the Act. Section 7(1) provides that a person who is or would be a victim of an act unlawful by virtue of s. 6(1) can rely on Convention rights:

(a) to bring proceedings against the authority under the Human Rights Act 'in the appropriate court or tribunal'; or

(b) to rely upon the Convention right or rights concerned 'in any legal proceedings'.

This means that the 1998 Act creates:

(a) a new cause of action for breach of statutory duty where a public authority has not acted compatibly with the Convention;

(b) a new head of illegality in judicial review proceedings;

(c) a defence in any proceedings which a public authority might itself bring against an individual which are themselves contrary to the Convention or founded on a breach of the Convention.

For example, a person might argue that a social services authority is in breach of statutory duty because it has violated Article 8 of the Convention (the right to respect for private and family life) in failing to give access to his or her file (*Gaskin v UK* (1990) 12 EHRR 36). Or it could be argued that a decision to refuse to allow a journalist access to a prisoner was *ultra vires* because rules contravened Article 10 of the Convention and the primary legislation did not require them to be read or given effect in that form, so founding a judicial review (*R v Secretary of State for the Home Department ex parte Simms* [2002] 2 AC 115). Or a defendant in criminal proceedings might raise a violation of the Convention by the prosecution in his or her defence (*R v Secretary of State for the Home Department ex parte Kebilene* [2000] 2 AC 326).

Section 6(1) creates new positive causes of action for acts or omissions that have taken place on or after 2 October 2000, when the Act came into force. However, it can provide a defence to proceedings brought by the public authority whenever the act or omission complained of took place—whether before or after the Act was in force. For example, a prosecution that relies on evidence gathered in violation of Article 8 in 1999 could be challenged by a defendant on that basis at a trial taking place after 2 October 2000. But a decision taken on 1 October 2000 by a public authority cannot be challenged by way of judicial review, or on the basis that it was a breach of statutory duty under s. 6(1).

The reason for this curious feature is that s. 22(4) of the Act (which came into force before 2 October 2000) provides that s. 7(1)(b) (reliance on the Convention in legal proceedings) applies to proceedings *brought by or at the instigation of a public authority* whenever the act in question took place, but otherwise only to acts taking place after the coming into force of that section.

The retrospectivity (or otherwise) of the 1998 Act has led to a series of confusing decisions. In *R v Lambert* [2001] 3 WLR 206, the House of Lords held that the 1998 Act did not apply retrospectively to the summing-up of a criminal trial heard before 2 October 2000, and that s. 22(4) does not apply to an appeal in relation to court decisions taken before the 1998 Act came into force. Lord Hope distinguished a breach of Convention rights by the act of a court (such as summing-up in a criminal trial) from an alleged breach of Convention rights by a prosecuting authority. In relation to this second situation, retrospective reliance on Convention rights under s. 7(1)(b) is permitted by s. 22(4) at each stage of an appeal (including an appeal to the House of Lords). In *R v Kansal (No. 2)* [2001] 3 WLR 1562, the House of Lords reconsidered its decision in *Lambert*, and although the majority took the view that it had been wrongly decided on the question of retrospective effect, it was held that there was no compelling reason to depart from the decision. The effect of the judgment in *Kansal* is that criminal convictions arrived at in breach of the United Kingdom's international obligations before October 2000 cannot be reconsidered by the criminal courts (see also the House of Lords decision in *R v Lyons* [2002] 3 WLR 1562). In civil law cases between individuals, the House of Lords has held that the interpretative obligation in s. 3 does not apply to acts, agreements, or transactions made before the 1998 Act came into force. In *Wilson v First County Trust* [2003] UKHL 40, the events in question occurred, and the cause of action arose, before the Human Rights Act came into force on 2 October 2000. The House of Lords held that Parliament could not have intended s. 3(1) to operate in such a way as to 'transform' individual parties' interests under pre-existing legislation, as such a change in interpretation would unfairly and capriciously alter the parties' agreed obligations. This technical area is discussed in more detail in Clayton and Tomlinson, *The Law of Human Rights* (Oxford: Oxford University Press, 2000) and supplements.

4.5.2 What is a Public Authority?

For the purposes of the Human Rights Act 1998 it is very important to determine whether a body or person involved in a breach of Convention rights is a 'public authority'; and in respect of which of its functions. If a body is a public authority then it is a body against which the Act creates new *direct* remedies for breach of s. 6(1) of the Act, either by judicial review or for breach of the statutory duty created by s. 6 of the Act to act in conformity with the Convention (unless there is a statutory excuse). This complex area has been the subject of conflicting case law since the 1998 Act came into force, and students and practitioners should be aware that it is a constantly evolving area of jurisprudence.

It is important to draw a distinction between 'pure' public authorities and quasi-public or 'hybrid' bodies of the kind identified in s. 6(3)(b), because pure public bodies are under a duty to act in conformity with the Convention whether exercising functions governed by public law (for example, assessment to tax) or functions governed by private law (for example, making employment contracts); whereas hybrid authorities will have to comply with s. 6(1) (which requires them to act in conformity with the Convention) in relation to their public functions, not their private law relationships (s. 6(5)). The effect of this is that there will be a direct cause of action available against hybrid bodies for acting in breach of the Convention, and hence unlawfully, when the act under challenge is of a public nature, but not when they are acting within the scope of their *private* law activities. Thus, the first issue is whether a body is a pure public authority, a hybrid authority of a s. 6(3)(b) kind, or a private body. Where a body is only a hybrid authority, the second issue is whether the particular action complained of is public or private.

The term 'public authority' is not defined positively in the 1998 Act, save to say that the term *includes* a court or tribunal (s. 6(3)(a)) and any person certain of whose functions are functions of a public nature (s. 6(3)(b)), but does not include either House of Parliament (save the House of Lords when acting in a judicial capacity), or a person exercising functions in connection with proceedings in Parliament (s. 6(3) and (4)). The concept of a public authority includes all bodies which are obviously public in nature, such as Government departments, local authorities, police officers, and immigration officials. Subject to the qualification in s. 6(2), all of these bodies will act unlawfully if they act inconsistently with the Convention, and this is the case whether such bodies are acting in a public or a private capacity.

However, as has been observed in the pre-1998 Act case law concerning judicial review (for example, *R v Panel on Take-overs and Mergers ex parte Datafin plc* [1987] QB 815), it is not always easy to categorize a body as either 'public' or 'private'. Section 6(3)(b) includes within the definition of 'public authority' any person 'certain of whose functions are functions of a public nature', but this is limited by s. 6(5) which provides that: 'In relation to a particular act, a person is not a public authority by virtue only of subsection (3)(b) if the nature of the act is private.'

During the parliamentary debates, the then Lord Chancellor gave as an example of a s. 6(3)(b) body Railtrack, which (he said) is a public authority when it exercises public functions in its role of safety regulator, but which acts privately in its role as property developer. Doctors would be public authorities in relation to their NHS functions, but not in relation to their private patients, and so on. This means that a new cause of action for acting in breach of the Convention can arise in relation to a hybrid body only in contexts where its functions would be amenable to judicial review and not, for example, in private law-type employment cases. For example, in general, employment law questions are questions of private law (*R v East Berkshire Health Authority ex parte Walsh* [1985] QB 152). However, they may be questions of public law if they relate to policy questions (*R v Crown Prosecution Service ex parte Hogg* [1994] COD 237). Thus, an employee of a hybrid body is not able to claim breach of s. 6 of the Act in an 'ordinary' employment situation, because that would be private law, and the decisions which the hybrid body took as an employer would be taken in its private capacity. But the situation might be different if the issue related to some question concerning public functions, for example, being disciplined for whistle-blowing in relation to Railtrack's activities as a public authority. In such a case, it could be argued that Railtrack would be under a s. 6(1) duty.

The pre-1998 Act judicial review cases established that the statutory source of the power to undertake a function was an important indicator, as well as the nature of the function, of whether a body was a public authority open to judicial review. In pre-1998 Act judicial review cases it was not sufficient merely for the body to be acting in the public interest. This meant that there were often cases which fell into a 'protection gap' where the courts could not afford protection to claimants. For example, Moses J expressed regret in the pre-1998 Act case of *R v Servite Houses ex parte Goldsmith* [2001] LGR 55, that precedent prevented him from holding a charitable housing association to be a public authority.

The Government intended the meaning of 'public authority' in the Human Rights Act to be widely construed. During debates on the Bill in Parliament, Jack Straw stressed that the main purpose of the Human Rights Act would be to protect the individual against abuse by the state (rather than to protect one individual against the actions of another), but made it clear that:

We wanted a realistic and modern definition of the state so as to provide a correspondingly wide protection against the abuse of human rights. Accordingly, liability under the Bill would go beyond the narrow category of central and local government and the police—the organisations that represent a minimalist view of what constitutes the state. (Hansard HC, 17 June 1998, coll. 405– 408)

Together with the principle that human rights instruments should be given a gener- ous interpretation (Lord Hope in *R v DPP ex parte Kebilene* [2000] 2 AC 326), it was hoped that the Human Rights Act would give the judicial review case law on the 'public/private divide' a fresh impetus to reflect contemporary realities and afford proper protection to human rights. It was hoped that the reach of the Human Rights Act 1998 would rectify these gaps, through courts interpreting the concept of a hybrid authority widely, and bringing more bodies under a legal obligation not to breach Convention rights. Following the implementation of the Human Rights Act, the test as to whether a body is a 'public authority' should relate to the substance and nature of the act, not just to the form and legal personality of an organization or indi- vidual. Although the 1998 Act defines public authorities broadly as going beyond the organs of the state, the extent to which the definition encompasses private orga- nizations performing public functions delegated by the state has proved controver- sial in the courts, and the initial decisions on s. 6 have adopted a relatively confined interpretation of the Act's application to private sector bodies.

In one of the first cases on the issue, Lord Woolf held that the definitions of public authority and public function under s. 6 should be given a generous interpre- tation (*Poplar Housing and Regeneration Community Association Ltd v Donoghue* [2001] EWCA Civ 595 at [para. 58]). The Court of Appeal considered the question of whether the Poplar Housing Association, a registered social landlord, was a public authority under the 1998 Act in relation to one of its tenants. However, the Court held that because a body performed an activity which otherwise the Government or a public body would be under a duty to perform, it did not mean that such performance was *necessarily* a public function:

. . . what can make an act, which would otherwise be private, public, is a feature or a combination of features which impose a public character or stamp on the act. Statutory authority for what is done can at least help to mark the act as being public; so can the extent of control over the function exercised by another body which is a public authority. The more closely the acts that could be of a private nature are enmeshed in the activities of a public body, the more likely they are to be public. (at [para. 65])

Lord Woolf held that the facts of each particular case would be crucial, and that on the situation before him in this 'borderline' case that it was capable of being a 'public authority'. In *R (A) v Partnerships in Care Ltd* [2002] 1 WLR 2610, the deci- sion of managers of a private psychiatric hospital to alter the care and treatment of a patient was an act of a public nature, susceptible to judicial review, and the hospital managers were, by virtue of the statutory regime and regulations under the Registered Homes Act 1984 and the Mental Health Act 1983, a public authority for the purposes of the 1998 Act. An example of a hybrid body falling on the other side of the 'borderline' is *Aston Cantlow Parochial Church Council v Wallbank* [2003] UKHL 37. The House of Lords held that a Parochial Church Council (PCC) could be a hybrid public authority under s. 6(3)(b) because it performs certain functions of a public nature, such as conducting marriage and burial ceremonies for the local community. However, it was held (with Lord Scott dissenting) that the PCC was carrying out a private rather than a public function when enforcing a lay rector's liability for chancel repairs. Contrary to the decision of the Court of Appeal, their Lordships held that the PCC was not under an obligation to act in a manner compatible with Convention rights.

These cases did not discuss the Government's expressed intention that the Human Rights Act should be available to challenge decisions the substance of which was a public function, rather than matters which were strictly 'governmental'. The test for amenability to judicial review and the Human Rights Act test for public authority are not identical. Judicial review includes a claim to review 'the lawfulness of . . . a decision, action or failure to act', but only in relation to 'the exercise of a public function'.

In contrast, s. 6(3)(b) applies to bodies performing 'functions of a public *nature*' as a means of characterizing the *nature* of the functions performed by the body in question, not the nature of the body, or of the legal dispute. During the passage of the Bill, Jack Straw (then Home Secretary) explained this choice of words as follows:

> . . . as we are dealing with public functions and with an evolving situation, we believe that the test must relate to the substance and nature of the act, not to the form and legal personality. (Hansard HC, 17 June 1998, coll. 409–410)

Markus has considered the differences between the two tests in 'Leonard Cheshire Foundation: What is a Public Function?' [2003] EHRLR 92.

In these early cases the courts, in our view, have missed the opportunity to establish a clear, principled approach to the meanings of 'public authority' and 'public functions'. The present state of the law is the heavily criticized decision of *R (Heather) v Leonard Cheshire Foundation* [2002] EWCA Civ 366. In that case, several long-stay patients in a home run by the Leonard Cheshire Foundation applied for judicial review of the Foundation's decision to close the home, claiming a breach of Article 8 (right to respect for their home). The Court of Appeal upheld the lower court's decision that the Leonard Cheshire Foundation was not a public authority for the purposes of the Act despite the fact that it was in receipt of public funding, was regulated by the state, and, if it had not provided care, such care would have to be provided by the state. The reasoning provided was that 'public' in s. 6(3)(c) of the Act was used in the sense of 'governmental'. This does not appear to reflect the intention of the drafters of the 1998 Act of a generous interpretation of 'public functions'. The House of Lords refused permission to appeal in this important case at the end of 2002, which caused some disquiet among human rights commentators. The Parliamentary Joint Committee on Human Rights (JCHR) launched an inquiry into the meaning of 'public authority' under the 1998 Act and started collecting evidence in May 2003 (see www.liberty-human-rights.org.uk for Liberty's submission). This is an area of human rights law in which further evolution is likely.

The consequence of the current conservative approach to s. 6 is that privatized companies or bodies which undertake 'contracted out' work which would have ordinarily been governmental activities, may not be subject to duties under the 1998 Act. In the most recent cases, this has meant that these bodies (and the public authorities who contracted out the work) escape liability for any violation of Convention rights despite the fact that individuals involved often have no choice but to accept the regime of private care offered by their local authority. This ignores the reality of increased reliance on private contractors by local authorities to carry out statutory duties. In time, such an interpretation may place the United Kingdom in violation of Article 13 of the Convention, because affected individuals in certain circumstances will have no effective remedy for breaches of Convention rights. In our view, Laws LJ in *Smart v Sheffield City Council* [2002] EWCA Civ 4, was correct when he said:

> The courts should give section 6 a generous interpretation. Any limitation upon the liabilities of public authorities for interfering in Convention rights should take place through striking a fair balance between the relevant interests, at least where *prima facie* interferences with rights are capable of being justified by reference to necessity and proportionality, rather than liability being excluded by defining such bodies out of the scope of the s. 6 duty.

Lord Woolf (in *Poplar Housing and Regeneration Community Association Ltd v Donoghue*, above) has suggested that a novel way to rectify this protection gap in the context of publicly-provided services would be through the law of contract—that is, by requiring private bodies to enter into contractual obligations to respect the Convention rights of those they deal with, when they enter into arrangements to provide services for governmental bodies. The service users could then use the Contracts (Rights of Third Parties) Act 1999 to enforce contractual clauses to respect their Convention rights. (See also Carss-Frisk, 'Public Authorities: The Developing Definition' [2002] EHRLR 319.) It is not clear how effective this approach might prove in practice, and it would appear that the purpose of the wide definition of 'public authority' in s. 6 was intended to avoid the procedural complexities which would necessarily arise from the development of some form of 'third party' procedure.

For a detailed examination of the cases in this developing area and a variety of opinions see Oliver, 'The Frontiers of the State: Public Authorities and Public Functions under the Human Rights Act' [2000] PL 476; Craig, 'Contracting Out, the Human Rights Act and the Scope of Judicial Review' (2002) 118 LQR 551; and Markus, 'What is a Public Power? The Court's Approach to the Public Authority Definition under the Human Rights Act', in Cooper and Jowell (eds), *Delivering Rights? How the Human Rights Act is Working and for Whom* (London: Hart Publishing, 2003).

4.5.3 The Standard of Review

In claims brought against public authorities, it is often not disputed that the issue in question concerns a Convention right. (For example, all decisions in the fields of public housing, or family law, will engage the protection of Article 8.) Frequently, too, it is clear that the public body has a source of legal power to take the action in question. Whether the impugned decision violates the Convention depends on whether the limitations on an individual's rights in question are proportionate.

A detailed discussion of the principles of the Strasbourg doctrine of proportionality and its impact on English law is contained in Chapter 2 (see pp. 35–39 above). The test of whether an infringement of a *prima facie* right is 'necessary in a democratic society', and hence does not violate the Convention, has been interpreted by the Strasbourg Court as meaning that the infringement is proportionate to the end to be achieved.

As discussed, the proportionality concept has been extensively developed by Strasbourg case law. It involves a more rigorous standard of judicial scrutiny than that required by the common law doctrine of 'irrationality', which did not sit easily with the habit of reasoning acquired by United Kingdom judges. At first, under the 1998 Act, domestic courts were reluctant to adopt the more rigorous Strasbourg proportionality review in cases involving fundamental human rights (see, for example, *R (Mahmood) v Secretary of State for the Home Department* [2001] 1 WLR 840, *R (Isiko) v Secretary of State for the Home Department* [2001] HRLR 295, *R (Samaroo) v Secretary of State for the Home Department* [2001] EWCA Civ 1139). However, the House of Lords underlined the 'material difference', between the Convention principle of proportionality and the old test of *Wednesbury* unreasonableness, in the important case of *R (Daly) v Secretary of State for the Home Department* [2001] UKHL 26. Lord Steyn said that:

(a) proportionality may require the reviewing court to assess the actual balance which the decision-maker has reached, not merely whether it is within the range of rational or reasonable decisions;

(b) the proportionality doctrine may go further than the traditional grounds of review as it may require attention to be directed to the relative weight accorded to the interests and considerations;

(c) even the domestic 'heightened scrutiny' test developed in *R v Ministry of Defence ex parte Smith* [1996] QB 517 to deal with human rights cases cannot necessarily be approximated with the proportionality test employed by Strasbourg (see *Smith and Grady v United Kingdom* (1999) 29 EHRR 493).

However, Lord Steyn emphasized that proportionality does not mean a shift to a merits review. The intensity of the review will depend on the subject matter in hand, even in cases involving Convention rights. What this means in practice is the subject of an ongoing, and important, constitutional debate.

The distinction between this new, intense review and a merits review is a fine one and the courts are, perhaps understandably, nervous that they may be seen to overstep the limits of their constitutional powers by seeming to make decisions which are beyond the proper remit of their expertise and authority. This debate has played out in a number of important cases (see, for example, *R (Wilkinson) v Responsible Medical Officer Broadmoor Hospital* [2002] 1WLR 419 and *R (ProLife Alliance) v BBC* [2003] UKHL 23).

Although the proportionality test has been firmly settled on, there are still questions about the contexts in which it is appropriate, and the scope and extent of 'judicial deference' to other public authorities in determining what is 'proportionate'. These questions affect the intensity of the proportionality review which the courts will undertake.

Judicial Deference to Decisions of Public Authorities

The question of when it is appropriate (and when it is not) for the courts and judges to defer to decisions made by other constitutional bodies such as the legislative, executive, or administrative branches has been a contentious one since the 1998 Act came into force. The intense legal, academic, and political debates stimulated by the concept of 'judicial deference' go to the heart of the provisions contained in the Human Rights Act. If the courts 'defer' to the views and acts of public authorities so much that they fail to form their own assessment of the proportionality, and hence the legality, of their actions this has the potential to undermine the purpose of the 1998 Act itself. However, if judges are overly active and attempt to replace the primary decisions of bodies selected for their expertise, they run the risk of making decisions which have been afforded to bodies accountable in other ways. They may then be criticized for inappropriately offending against the doctrine of separation of powers, or even for interfering in political decisions. The balance between judicial activism and restraint has been one of the most important challenges that the Human Rights Act has faced in its early years.

Since the 1998 Act came into force, two distinct views have emerged from the courts and commentators about the extent to which the judiciary should defer to Parliament and other bodies exercising public functions. The first group argues that the doctrine of proportionality imposes on the judges the assessment of whether an infringement of a Convention right is proportionate, and hence lawful, and allows little or no 'discretionary area of judgment' to the primary decision-maker (see Leigh, 'Taking Rights Proportionately: Judicial Review, the Human Rights Act and Strasbourg' [2002] PL 265). The second group argues that expert matters of judgment in balancing private and public interest are matters for the decision of the democratically elected legislature and those exercising power on its behalf as matters of public interest. Thus, the courts should in principle bow to these assessments (see Atrill, 'Keeping the Executive in the Picture: a Reply to Professor Leigh' [2003] PL 41). These commentators argue that the judiciary is institutionally incompetent to deal with the complex process of policy adjudication and the socio-economic issues such as resource allocation that arise in some cases involving human rights issues.

These two schools of thought are not necessarily irreconcilable: see the interesting analysis of Elias J in *R (Williamson) v Secretary of State for Education and Employment* [2001] EWHC Admin 960 (not displaced by the Court of Appeal [2002] EWCA Civ 1820). However, this judicial 'third way' does require the domestic courts to require other constitutional actors to take human rights issues seriously themselves, and be prepared to justify and defend the proportionality of decisions which they have reached, not merely to plead that the judges should not replace their decisions. It is important to emphasize that the concept of deference in a domestic context is not synonymous with the Strasbourg doctrine of margin of appreciation (see 2.5.2 above). During the passage of the Human Rights Bill, writers such as Pannick (in 'Principles of Interpretation of Convention Rights under the Human Rights Act and the Discretionary Area of Judgment' [1998] PL 545) argued that courts should respect the executive's expertise and special knowledge and Parliament's democratic credentials, and recognize a 'discretionary area of judgment' when reviewing the actions of public authorities. In *R v DPP ex parte Kebilene* [2000] 2 AC 326, Lord Hope confirmed that the margin of appreciation doctrine was not available to national courts but that in difficult cases involving the rights of individuals and society as a whole:

> . . . in some circumstances it will be appropriate for the courts to recognise that there is an area of judgment within which the judiciary will defer, on democratic grounds, to the considered opinion of the elected body or person whose act or decision is said to be incompatible with the Convention.

Lord Hope stated that the circumstances in which this 'area of judgment' might be found by the courts could include the adjudication of qualified rights (for example, Articles 8 to 11), or where cases raised issues of social and economic policy. It is less likely to be found where the right in question is unqualified, or where the rights are of constitutional importance and within the traditional jurisdiction of the courts. For example, the due process and fair trial rights encapsulated in Articles 5 and 6 fall firmly into the courts' area of expertise, and therefore judicial deference to decision-makers will barely exist; whereas cases involving national security would afford greater deference to the executive. A number of cases have grappled with the issue of 'deference' (see, for example, *Brown v Stott* [2001] 2 WLR 817, *R (Pretty) v Director of Public Prosecutions* [2001] UKHL 61). In these cases, deference on its own is not used as a justification for rejecting a claim under the 1998 Act but is used to reinforce the court's judgment. So, for example, it is held by courts that deference is appropriate because a decision-maker is democratically accountable for his decision (as *per* Lord Phillips MR in *Farrakhan v Secretary of State for the Home Department* [2002] EWCA Civ 606), or that 'in deference to the legislature, courts should not easily be persuaded to condemn what has been done, especially where it has been done in primary legislation after careful evaluation and against a background of increasing public concern about crime' (as *per* Kennedy LJ in *R (Pearson and Martinez) v Secretary of State for the Home Department* [2001] EWHC Admin 239).

It is right that courts should not seek to become primary judgment makers and replace their assessment of a situation for that of the original decision-maker. However, attempts to identify spheres of activity in which it is inappropriate for the courts to intervene are not conducive to legal certainty: issues of national security and rights to a fair trial, for example, frequently overlap. Rather, courts should subject the decision-maker's analysis to rigorous scrutiny, and inquire whether the decision-maker can objectively justify a conclusion that there is a pressing social need which merits the limitation of the Convention right in question. As the Court of Appeal recognized in *International Transport Roth GmbH v Secretary of State for the Home Department* [2002] 3 WLR 344, if courts refuse to engage in broad areas of social policy and national security this could undermine their ability to protect some fundamental rights. Simon Brown LJ rightly pointed out that 'the court's role under the Human Rights Act is as the guardian of human rights. It cannot abdicate this responsibility.'

If courts do abdicate that role they, in effect, cede to the executive the interpretation of proportionality, which is an issue of law. As Lord Hoffman pointed out (in *R (Prolife Alliance) v British Broadcasting Corporation* [2003] UKHL 23):

> Although the word 'deference' is now very popular in describing the relationship between the judicial and the other branches of government, I do not think that its overtones of servility, or perhaps gracious concession, are appropriate to describe what is happening. In a society based upon the rule of law and the separation of powers, it is necessary to decide which branch of government has in any particular instance the decision-making power and what the legal limits of that power are. That is a question of law and must therefore be decided by the courts.

Affording the legislature a degree of deference under the most stringent part of the proportionality test is appropriate—granting deference to the views of decision-makers even before any form of limitation analysis is undertaken (as in cases such as *R (Mahmood) v Secretary of State for the Home Department* [2001] 1 WLR 840, and *Carson v Secretary of State for Work & Pensions* [2003] EWCA Civ 797) is not. Increasingly, commentators are focusing on the nature and degree of analysis and evidence which courts should be demanding from decision-makers as the price of judicial 'deference' to their assessment of a proportionality issue.

Murray Hunt ('Sovereignty's Blight: Why Contemporary Public Law Needs the Concept of "Due Deference" ', in Bamforth and Leyland (eds), *Public Law in a Multi-Layered Constitution* (London: Hart Publishing, 2003)) argues that:

> deference from the courts must be *earned* by the primary decision maker by openly demonstrating the justifications for the decisions they have reached and by demonstrating the reasons why their decision is worthy of crucial respect.

Hunt argues that 'due deference' should not be conceptualized in terms of a spatial 'area' in which the courts should not venture according to the broad subject matter under consideration (for example, national security or social and economic policy) but in terms of the degree of scrutiny or deference that the courts will exercise according to the specific facts of each case. Convention rights often raise difficult questions which normally courts are reluctant to deal with, but these are precisely the situations where rigorous scrutiny is required to ensure that the rights in question are adequately protected. Hunt gives the example of cases involving immigration and national security which have been deemed to be within the executive's 'area of discretion'. Instead of carefully examining the various possible reasons as to why a degree of 'deference' is necessary on the facts of the case (and thereby ensuring that any potential violations of an individual's rights are carefully examined), courts often decline to venture into this 'area' to consider the matter at all. This approach to 'deference' leads the court to adopt an overly-submissive approach to the acts of public authorities. If domestic courts do not sufficiently examine the reasons advanced for the limitation of Convention rights by refusing to adjudicate on broad areas such as 'national security', it is likely that the standard of review will not meet the test laid down in *Smith and Grady v United Kingdom* (1999) 29 EHRR 493.

Edwards (in 'Judicial Deference under the Human Rights Act' (2002) 65 MLR 859) also argues that the adoption of a rigorous, principled approach to deference requires detailed reasoning from judges and, supporting this process, detailed evidence from the decision-maker or public authority concerned that the restrictions on rights or freedoms are both necessary and justified.

We agree that, to fulfil their constitutional function, the courts need to develop a clear approach to adjudicating upon proportionality. They need to develop criteria illustrating the factors which courts should take into account when deciding on the degree of deference appropriate in the circumstances. Hunt argues that relevant factors could include the relative expertise of the decision-maker in the subject matter in question (for example, does the primary decision-maker possess some expertise in the particular subject matter, such as scientific, technical, or academic matters, which are central to the issue to be decided and which a reviewing court does not possess?); the relative institutional competence of the primary decision-maker to determine the type of issue in question (for example, is the court's adjudicative process equipped to conduct the type of decision-making which preceded the initial decision?); and the degree of democratic accountability of the original decision-maker and the extent to which other mechanisms of accountability may be available. The mere fact that a decision has been taken by a democratically accountable person or body should never in itself be determinative, but in a democratic society a reviewing court should give careful consideration to whether other avenues of accountability are available and more appropriate.

Resolving this question of 'judicial deference' is one of the key tasks facing domestic courts dealing with human rights questions. If it is not properly resolved, it has the potential to undermine the intention at the heart of the 1998 Act to 'bring rights home'.

For further examination of this evolving area see Ewing, 'The Human Rights Act and Parliamentary Democracy' (1999) MLR 79; Craig, 'The Courts, the Human Rights Act and Judicial Review' (2001) 117 LQR 589; Elliott, 'The Human Rights Act 1998 and the Standard of Substantive Review' (2001) 60 CLJ 301; Jowell, 'Due Deference under the Human Rights Act', in Jowell and Cooper (eds), *Delivering Rights? How the Human Rights Act is Working and for Whom* (London: Hart Publishing, 2003); and Klug, 'Judicial Deference Under the Human Rights Act 1998' [2003] EHRLR 125.

5

BRINGING A CLAIM UNDER THE HUMAN RIGHTS ACT

5.1 INTRODUCTION

The creation of new causes of action against public authorities has brought with it new procedural problems. The procedures for bringing claims against public authorities are not straightforward.

One issue is the question of limitation periods for bringing proceedings directly under s. 7(1)(a) (which are contained in s. 7(5) of the Act), and the way in which these interact with other relevant limitation periods. Though the importance of this issue will inevitably diminish as the Act becomes better-established, it will remain a central issue in a number of cases for some time.

The questions of standing and third party interventions are important, in particular to the evolution of 'public interest' litigation, because s. 7(7) requires English courts to apply Strasbourg case law on who is a victim, not simply to 'have regard' to it. The limitations which these cases impose may restrict the circumstances in which important public interest questions are tried. There are also jurisdictional questions as to where proceedings involving s. 6(1) should be brought.

These are the subject matter of this chapter. For more details of these issues, reference should be made to the rules made under the 1998 Act (some of which are included at Appendix 2). Analysis of some of the practical considerations involved in using the 1998 Act in judicial review proceedings can be found in Steyn and Wolfe, 'Judicial Review & the Human Rights Act: Some Practical Considerations' [1999] EHRLR 614.

5.2 LIMITATION PERIODS: ARE THERE TIME LIMITS FOR BRINGING A CLAIM UNDER THE 1998 ACT?

Section 7(5) of the 1998 Act creates a primary limitation period of one year for cases against public bodies alleging a breach of a Convention right, beginning with the date that the act complained of took place. This can be extended, where the court considers it equitable in all the circumstances. The normal one-year limitation period is also subject to any more restrictive rule which imposes a stricter time limit in relation to the proceeding in question (for example, the three-month time limit for bringing proceedings by way of judicial review contained in Part 54 of the Civil Procedure Rules). In *R (Burkett) v Hammersmith and Fulham London Borough Council* [2002] UKHL 23, the House of Lords, said that the court may extend time limits in judicial review proceedings only if there is a good reason for doing so.

The one-year time limit applies only to claims which directly allege breach of the Convention by a public authority, that is, only where there is a cause of action created by s. 7(1)(a) of the Act. There is no limit to the interpretative obligation in s. 7(1)(b). This could cause difficulties in cases where proceedings under the Act overlap with other proceedings with a longer limitation period.

5.3 STANDING AND INTERVENTIONS: WHO MAY BRING PROCEEDINGS UNDER THE 1998 ACT?

Any legal or natural person can use the 1998 Act. This includes companies, as to restrict the benefit of the 1998 Act to natural persons would probably infringe the provisions of Articles 6 and 14 (right to a fair trial in respect of civil rights and obligations, and right not to be discriminated against in application of the Convention rights).

By virtue of s. 7(1) and (3), however, the Act can be used to bring proceedings only by a person who is, or would be, a victim of the violation, even if he or she would otherwise have standing to be a party to judicial review proceedings on the broader test of 'standing' employed under Part 54 of the Civil Procedure Rules.

These restrictive provisions on standing to challenge breaches of Convention rights were heavily criticized during the parliamentary and extra-parliamentary debates that accompanied the passage of the Human Rights Bill. In support of the restriction it was argued that, for any violation with real effects, a public interest group would be able to find a 'victim' to act as applicant, so that the standing provision would avoid challenges which were purely academic. It was also said that the courts would be likely to accept '*amicus*' briefs from interested groups, as in *R v Khan* [1997] AC 558, when the House of Lords considered a written submission on the wider implications of the case prepared by Liberty. Nevertheless, the 'victim' provision means that it will be necessary to determine whether a particular litigant is a 'victim' in order to decide whether they can use the Human Rights Act; and if the litigant is *not* a victim, but still has standing, the court will have to decide the extent to which the litigant can nevertheless raise Convention arguments under the pre-Act conditions. It seems likely that, applying this test of who is a 'victim', local authorities will probably not be able to use the Human Rights Act (*Austria Municipalities v Austria* (1974) 17 Yearbook 338).

The position may be mitigated by the relaxed rule on third party interventions and '*amicus*' briefs which had already evolved before the 1998 Act came into force (see *R v Department of Health ex parte Source Informatics* [2000] 2 WLR 940, in which there were four intervenors raising human rights arguments).

5.3.1 Victims

The concept of victim, in s. 7(7) of the Act, is taken from Article 34 of the Convention as amended by Protocol 11. (Before the amendment the provision was in Article 25, to which the earlier case law refers.) Only a person who would have standing as a victim to bring proceedings in the European Court of Human Rights (ECtHR) is counted as a victim for the purposes of s. 7. Section 7(7) requires domestic courts to give effect to Strasbourg case law on who is a 'victim'. Unlike other Strasbourg decisions, which need only be 'taken into account' under s. 2 of the Act, this case law is binding. The ECtHR and the European Commission on Human Rights (ECmHR) insist that a person has standing as a victim only if actually and directly affected by the act or the omission that is the subject of the complaint. There is no role for individual 'public defenders' of human rights to be recognized (see *Klass v Germany* (1978) 2 EHRR 214).

However, in Strasbourg case law it is not necessary for standing that the applicant has actually suffered the consequences of the alleged breach, provided there is a risk of their being directly affected by it (*Klass v Germany*; *Marckx v Belgium* (1979) 2 EHRR 330). For example, a gay man living in Northern Ireland was allowed to complain (successfully) about the criminalization of all homosexual conduct in private between consenting males, even though he had not yet been prosecuted under the law (*Dudgeon v United Kingdom* (1981) 4 EHRR 149; and *Norris v Ireland* (1988) 13 EHRR 186). The risk of being affected must be a real threat, not a theoretical possibility (see *Campbell and Cosans v United Kingdom* (1982) 4 EHRR 293). Examples include cases in which challenges were made to legislation discriminating against children born out of wedlock, who were held to be victims of that legislation (*Marckx v Belgium* (1979) 2 EHRR 330), and a case where a litigant successfully persuaded the Court that she was a victim of the ban on divorce in Ireland because of the consequences for certain family relationships (*Johnston v Ireland* (1986) 9 EHRR 203).

The most liberal interpretation of 'victim' was in *Open Door and Dublin Well Woman v Ireland* (1992) 15 EHRR 244, where it was held that two abortion advice centres and two counsellors who *offered* abortion advice and women of childbearing age wishing to *receive* it, all had standing to challenge an injunction which was held to breach Article 10. However, in *Leigh v United Kingdom* (1984) 38 DR 74, the ECmHR refused to consider an applicant a victim because he was not directly affected by the alleged breach. In that case, three applicants, a journalist and two newspapers, complained that there had been a violation of their right under Article 10 to receive and impart information. This arose out of *Home Office v Harman* [1983] 1 AC 280, in which the House of Lords had held that a lawyer had acted in contempt of court when she allowed the first applicant to inspect confidential documents disclosed on discovery after they had been read out in court. The applicants each claimed to be a victim, arguing that their sources of information for journalistic coverage had been adversely affected by the decision. The Commission said that these applicants were interpreting the concept of 'victim' so broadly that it could encompass every newspaper or journalist in the United Kingdom who might conceivably be affected by the decision of the House of Lords. It held that, to be a victim, the form of detriment must be of a less indirect and remote nature.

5.3.2 Standing

In many—perhaps most—cases there is no problem for a litigant in establishing standing to use the 1998 Act. There could be no doubt, for example, that a person who wants to use Article 5 of the Convention (the right to liberty) in the context of a refusal of bail in a criminal trial is a victim of the alleged contravention.

But the victim provisions could cause problems in the context of judicial review proceedings. Section 7(3) of the 1998 Act explicitly applies the 'victim' requirement to standing in such cases. Judicial review proceedings do not involve just the two parties before the court: they relate to a public concern about the decisions of public authorities. In recent years, the High Court has taken a realistic approach to this and permitted 'public interest' organizations, perhaps not themselves 'suffering' from an unlawful or unreasonable action, to bring proceedings in appropriate cases (for example, *R v Sefton Metropolitan Borough Council ex parte Help the Aged* [1997] 4 All ER 532; *R v Lord Chancellor ex parte Child Poverty Action Group* [1998] 2 All ER 755). The provision in s. 7(3) of the Act—that in cases under the Act, a claimant is to be taken to have a sufficient interest to challenge an allegedly unlawful act by way of judicial review only if the claimant is, or would be, a victim of it—constitutes a very significant restriction on the way in which the judges have interpreted the concept of standing in recent years (see, for an example of the generous approach to standing, *R v Secretary of State for Social Security ex parte Joint Council for the Welfare of Immigrants* [1997] 1 WLR 275).

The distinction between victims and bodies with standing could lead to conceptual and practical difficulties in deciding whether the public interest group is itself a victim or group of victims. The consequence of this unattractive distinction is that courts have to grapple with two definitions of 'sufficient interest' in judicial review proceedings: one (as defined in the general case law under Part 54 of the Civil Procedure Rules) for the purposes of deciding whether to grant permission; and another (as statutorily defined in s. 7(3)) for determining whether the 1998 Act can be used. This has been heavily criticized by Miles (see 'Standing under the Human Rights Act 1998: Theories of Rights Enforcement and the Nature of Public Law Adjudication' (2000) 59 CLJ 133) as hindering the positive steps taken in recent public-interest litigation towards a more comprehensive 'sufficient interest' test.

Two types of public-interest litigation have been recognized (see Cane, 'Standing up for the Public' [1995] PL 276). In some cases a public-interest group is really an association of interested individuals and may be regarded as a group of persons each of whom may be regarded as a victim. (An example of such a group which might have associational standing would be Stonewall, a gay rights group.) It remains to be seen whether under the 1998 Act, courts will interpret s. 7(3) as preventing such a group from asserting 'sufficient interest' to bring a human rights challenge. There seems to be no reason why they should, particularly in light of s. 11 of the 1998 Act which preserves existing rights. The other sort of public-interest group which has standing to bring judicial review proceedings is a 'representative' group which may have special expertise. Amnesty International is an example in this category. These groups consist of people who may not themselves suffer in consequence of an allegedly illegal act, but who act on behalf of those who do. They are often well-placed to identify and to bring the proceedings in the public interest, because of particular expertise in a field. Sometimes they bring actions where no individual could get legal aid because no individual would suffer a sufficiently large loss to pass the legal aid test or could be expected to bring the case personally (see, for example, *R v Secretary of State for Social Services ex parte Child Poverty Action Group* [1990] 2 QB 540). This sort of 'representative' body seems plainly to be prevented from arguing Convention points in a judicial review by the terms of s. 7(3), save in so far as it could do so irrespective of the Human Rights Act.

It could be difficult to determine whether a public-interest group is a group of persons who are victims under s. 7(3), or a representative association. For example, what is an expert environmental group which also has members affected by environmental decisions, such as Greenpeace or Friends of the Earth: is it an associational group of victims, or a representative body? In *R v Inspectorate of Pollution ex parte Greenpeace Ltd (No. 2)* [1994] 4 All ER 329, the applicant convinced the court that it was a proper person to be heard using both types of standing. If a public-interest group is considered to be a representative group, and so not a victim, it will have standing to challenge actions by way of judicial review under the common law of human rights if it would have been considered to have 'sufficient interest' before the passing of the 1998 Act. The Act is not intended to remove existing rights, and it is unlikely that Administrative Court judges will use the s. 7(3) definition of 'victim' to draw back from the liberal approach they have adopted to standing in general.

The consequence is still, however, that a public-interest group which cannot claim to be a victim will not be able to found a claim or application for judicial review straightforwardly on s. 7(1)(a) and s. 6(1) of the Act. As a result, important breaches of Convention rights may go unremedied because it is not possible to find a nominal applicant.

5.3.3 Third Party Interventions

The restrictive provisions of s. 7(3) and (7) have been partially mitigated by public-interest groups, supporting individuals who can establish their claim to be victims, acting as third party intervenors in relevant cases.

As Hannett ('Third Party Intervention: In the Public Interest?' [2003] PL 128) has documented, support for the increased use of such interventions has been wide-ranging. For example, a working party set up by JUSTICE and the Public Law Project in 1996 endorsed the use of third party interventions (see *A Matter of Public Interest: Reforming the Law and Practice on Intervention in Public Interest Cases* (1996)). During the parliamentary debates on the Bill, the then Lord Chancellor expressly stated that there was nothing in the Bill, and s. 7(3) in particular, 'which would prevent pressure groups—interest groups—from assisting and providing representation for victims who wish to bring cases forward' and that 'interest groups will plainly be able to provide assistance to victims who bring cases under the Bill, including . . . the filing of *amicus* briefs' (Hansard, HL Deb, 5 February 1998, col. 810). Finally, the practice received tentative endorsement from the House of Lords in *Re Northern Ireland Human Rights Commission* [2002] UKHL 25.

Third party interventions can provide considerable benefits to courts and litigants. They can draw to the court's attention the wider significance of a point in a way that an individual litigant may be unable to do. They may provide supporting statistical or other evidence. They can help the court to determine whether an interference with a Convention right is 'necessary in a democratic society' or 'proportionate' by drawing to the court's attention the wider social significance or effects of a particular outcome. The technique of placing written submissions or witness statements before the court was adopted, to good effect, in the case of *R v Lord Chancellor ex parte Witham* [1998] QB 575, in which the court used affidavit evidence filed by the Public Law Project to establish that Article 3 of the Supreme Court Fees (Amendment) Order 1996 had the effect of denying the constitutional right of access to the courts to people on low incomes in a variety of categories, without parliamentary authority, and was accordingly *ultra vires*.

The 1998 Act does not give an express right to intervene, except to the Crown, but the House of Lords and the Court of Appeal have shown themselves increasingly willing to allow third party interventions under the normal rules of court (for example, Part 54 of the Civil Procedure Rules and Practice Direction 36 of the House of Lords *Practice Directions Applicable to Civil Appeals* (June 2001 Edition)). Hannett (above) has documented this phenomenon with statistics from the House of Lords illustrating that in 2000 there were five petitions for leave to intervene (with one granted for full oral and written submissions and four for written submissions alone) rising to 14 petitions in 2002 (with eight being granted full oral and written submissions and four for written submissions alone). Recent examples of such interventions include *Sepet v Secretary of State for the Home Department* [2003] UKHL, where the United Nations High Commissioner for Refugees' petition to intervene in an immigration appeal concerning whether 'conscientious objectors' could be protected under the ambit of the UN-sponsored Geneva Convention on Refugees was granted; and *Horvath v Secretary of State for the Home Department* [2001] AC 489, where the Refugee Legal Centre was able to present written submissions in the House of Lords case involving the similarities and differences between the 'sufficiency of protection' cases under refugee law and those under Article 3 of the Convention (the right not to be subject to torture, or inhuman or degrading treatment).

Commentators have criticized public interest interventions as being merely one strategy of a political campaign for some organizations, leading to these groups having a disproportionate, potentially undemocratic influence on the judicial adjudication process (for further discussion of these themes see Harlow, 'Public Law and Popular Justice' [2002] MLR 1). However, we believe that the benefits of third party interventions in providing a diversity of expert information to assist the court in the adjudication process fulfil a valuable role—particularly in the context of the 1998 Act, where experience from other countries and details of other international human rights standards may be of great use.

5.4 THE APPROPRIATE FORUM FOR AN ARGUMENT UNDER THE 1998 ACT

The 1998 Act was intended to 'bring rights home' (see the Government White Paper in Appendix 3), so that whatever remedy can be secured in Strasbourg should be available in national courts. The 1998 Act seeks to achieve this objective by enabling the domestic courts, at all levels, to award the remedies that could be awarded by the ECtHR in any proceedings, by ensuring that the Convention is an intrinsic part of all aspects of the legal system. Thus the 1998 Act provides that all courts and tribunals are able to consider arguments brought under the Convention. It also aims to minimize disruption to existing court and tribunal procedures.

The Act does not provide any sort of reference procedure whereby an argument about a Convention point must be sent to a special court for adjudication. Convention arguments are available in every public forum in which legal rights are determined, from the magistrates' court to the House of Lords (even though only the higher courts have the power to make a declaration of incompatibility or to award damages—see Chapter 6). Section 7 of the Act refers to bringing proceedings against a public authority 'in the appropriate court or tribunal' (s. 7(1)(a)) and to relying on Convention rights 'in any legal proceedings' (s. 7(1)(b)), including as a defence. The ambit of the phrase 'legal proceedings' is not clear, and there may be litigation in future about what constitutes a 'legal proceeding'. For example, is a complaint to a statutory ombudsman a legal proceeding? In most cases, the debate is not important because the body conducting the proceeding is itself a public authority and so under a duty to interpret the law in line with the Convention (see Chapter 3). But questions may arise in relation to non-statutory self-regulatory organizations, especially those apparently subject to contract rather than judicial review, such as the insurance ombudsman or the Jockey Club (see *R v Disciplinary Committee of the Jockey Club ex parte Aga Khan* [1993] 1 WLR 909).

The 'appropriate court or tribunal' is determined by rules issued under the 1998 Act (s. 7(2) and (9)) (see Appendix 2) but, broadly, claims go to the court or tribunal most accustomed to dealing with claims analogous to the subject matter in question. For example, the Criminal Appeals (Amendment) Rules 2000 (SI 2000/2036) deal with the treatment of human rights issues in the criminal courts; the Civil Procedure (Amendment No. 4) Rules 2000 (SI 2000/2092) deal with the procedure to be adopted in the Administrative Court; and the Family Proceedings (Amendment) Rules 2000 (SI 2000/2267) deal with the treatment of human rights issues in the family courts. The House of Lords *Practice Directions and Standing Orders Applicable to Civil Appeals* (dated June 2001) and *Practice Directions and Standing Orders Applicable to Criminal Appeals* (dated June 2001) make provision for the procedure under the 1998 Act.

Some illustrative examples of an appropriate forum are as follows. In a false imprisonment claim, a person who wishes to claim damages for breach of Article 3 (freedom from torture or inhuman or degrading treatment) or Article 5 (the right to liberty and security of the person) could bring a claim for breach of statutory duty under s. 6(1) of the Human Rights Act 1998 in the High Court. Alternatively, the breach could be the basis for a habeas corpus or judicial review application. A demonstrator who is prosecuted for obstruction of the highway or obstruction of a police officer may be able to invoke the right to peaceful assembly in Article 11 as a defence in the Crown Court or a magistrates' court. Article 5 arguments can also be used, for example, to argue for the release of a person before the Mental Health Review Tribunal. A taxpayer who wishes to contend that a tax demand based on withdrawal of an extra-statutory concession is insufficiently precise and hence contrary to Protocol 1, Article 1, might be heard before the Special Commissioners of the Inland Revenue.

It should be remembered, however, that the lower courts and tribunals do not have the power under s. 4(5) of the 1998 Act to issue a declaration of incompatibility. In *Whittaker v Watson (t/a P & M Watson Haulage)* [2002] ICR 1244, the Employment Appeal Tribunal (EAT) held that it did not have jurisdiction to rule on the compatibility of legislation with the Convention. The tribunal remarked that it was odd that the President could hear submissions as to compatibility sitting alone, but could not to rule on them in the EAT. Lindsay J then suggested that, in such cases, it would be helpful for the President to deal with the appeal on paper, either adjourning or dismissing the appeal as appropriate, and giving leave to appeal to a higher court with the power to award a declaration of incompatibility. Where proceedings are brought in the county court and a question of making a declaration of incompatibility has arisen, Part 33 of the Civil Procedure Rules requires the court to consider transferring the proceedings to the High Court. Practice Direction 30 states that a transfer should be made only if there is a real prospect that a declaration of incompatibility will be issued.

This cumbersome (and potentially time-consuming) solution to the problem of jurisdiction might have been avoided if the Government had adopted a 'residual reference' procedure akin to a reference to the European Court of Justice, for cases where an inferior court or tribunal dealing with a Human Rights Act considered that there might be a case for a declaration of incompatibility which would be beyond its jurisdiction to award. Under such a procedure the declaration could have been made by the High Court but as part of the main proceedings.

In civil proceedings generally, Practice Direction 16 (of the Civil Procedure Rules) sets out the requirements in relation to the contents of a statement of case where a party is seeking to rely on any provision of, or right arising under, the 1998 Act, or seeks a remedy available under the Act. This provides that in his or her statement of case, the party alleging a breach of Convention rights must:

(a) give precise details of the Convention right which it is alleged has been infringed and details of the alleged infringement;

(b) specify the relief sought;

(c) state whether the relief sought includes a declaration of incompatibility pursuant to s. 4 of the Act and, if so, give precise details of the legislative provision which is alleged to be incompatible and details of the alleged incompatibility;

(d) state whether the relief sought includes damages in respect of a judicial act (to which s. 9(3) applies) and, if so, the judicial act complained of and the court or tribunal which is alleged to have made it; and

(e) give details of any finding of unlawfulness by another court or tribunal upon which the claim is based.

Where a declaration of incompatibility is sought, the Crown must be formally notified so that it can be joined as a party to the proceedings (see Civil Procedure Rules, Part 19 and the accompanying Practice Direction). This formal notice should always be given by the court, as it is in the best position to assess whether there is a likelihood of a declaration of incompatibility being made. Additionally, unless the Crown has been given 21 days' formal notice (or other such period as the court directs) the court may not make a declaration of incompatibility. (For further details see *Poplar Housing and Regeneration Community Association v Donoghue* [2002] QB 48; and Thomas and Kellar, 'Joining the Crown in Civil Proceedings under the Human Rights Act 1998' [2001] JR 135.)

This is a complex area and reference to the detailed procedures to be followed should be sought out from comprehensive practitioner works such as Clayton and Tomlinson, *The Law of Human Rights* (Oxford: Oxford University Press, 2000), and the annually issued updating supplements, or the Civil Procedure Rules themselves (accessible via www.dca.gov.uk).

6

HUMAN RIGHTS ACT REMEDIES FOR BREACHES OF CONVENTION RIGHTS

6.1 INTRODUCTION

The Human Rights Act has already had a substantial impact on the law of remedies. It creates both a new cause of action, including a right to damages, under s. 8 *and* gives courts the power to grant 'declarations of incompatibility' under s. 4. Courts also retain existing remedies that fall within the jurisdiction of the relevant court, so remedies which can be awarded under s. 8(1) will be familiar. For example, in the civil courts: damages; declarations; injunctions; and/or a mandatory, quashing, or prohibiting order under judicial review proceedings governed by Part 54 of the Civil Procedure Rules. The editors of *Archbold* (Sweet & Maxwell, 2003) have suggested that the remedies available to a defendant in criminal proceedings who establishes a violation of his or her Convention rights might include: an order withdrawing the issue of a summons; a motion to quash an indictment; a stay of the criminal proceedings; the dismissal of the prosecution; excluding the admission of evidence (or an order requiring the inclusion of evidence); and an order of the Court of Appeal quashing a conviction.

Before considering the provisions of s. 8 it is important to stress that the 1998 Act does not incorporate Article 13 of the Convention, that is, the duty to afford an effective remedy for the violation of Convention rights. The rationale for the Government's decision was that the Human Rights Act itself constituted compliance with Article 13 (see 4.3.1 above for a discussion of the exclusion of Article 13 from the 1998 Act). However, s. 8 is deliberately drafted in wide terms, and the then Lord Chancellor stressed during the debates on the Bill that:

> I cannot conceive of any state of affairs in which an English court, having held an act to be unlawful because of its infringement of a Convention right, would under [section] 8(1) be disabled from giving an effective remedy. (Hansard, HL Debs, 18 November 1997, col. 479)

Lord Hope, in *Brown v Stott* [2001] 1 WLR 817, also suggested that Article 13 was omitted from the Act because ss. 7 to 9 were intended to lay down an appropriate remedial structure for giving effect to Convention rights. In addition, s. 2 may incorporate Article 13, in an interpretative context at least, by requiring a court considering any question arising 'in connection with' a Convention right to take into account Convention jurisprudence, in which Article 13 has a significant place.

6.2 SECTION 8—DAMAGES

Section 8(1) of the Human Rights Act 1998 authorizes a court which has found that an act or proposed act of a public authority is unlawful, to grant 'such relief or remedy, or make such order, within its powers as it considers just and appropriate'. This creates a new cause of action which can be used to found a claim for relief, including damages, against public authority. Courts and tribunals of limited jurisdiction cannot award a remedy if it is outside their statutory power to do so. For example, an employment tribunal is not able to order an injunction to prevent a discriminatory dismissal going ahead (because it has no statutory power to do so), even though this might be necessary to afford just satisfaction of a Convention right.

There has been some debate over whether ss. 7 and 8 of the 1998 Act create a 'constitutional tort' of infringing Convention rights (see Lester and Pannick, 'The Impact of the Human Rights Act on Private Law: The Knight's Move' (2000) 116 LQR 380), or whether these provisions give rise to a public law remedy (see Clayton and Tomlinson, *The Law of Human Rights* (Oxford: Oxford University Press, 2000), para. 21.21). This academic debate is of importance as the classification of the newly created remedies may influence the courts' approach to the type and level of damages that they award under the 1998 Act. Perhaps the least controversial description is provided by the Law Commission in *Damages Under the Human Rights Act* (Law Com No. 266 (2000)):

> . . . sections 6 and 7 of the HRA create a new cause of action, which is in effect a form of action for breach of statutory duty, but with the difference that the remedy is discretionary rather than of right. (para. 4.20)

It is instructive to note that the language used in s. 8(1) is similar to s. 6 of the Hong Kong Bill of Rights Ordinance 1991, which itself is an expanded version of s. 24(1) of the Canadian Charter of Fundamental Rights and Freedoms 1982. This means that the case law from those and other jurisdictions is likely to be taken into account by English courts in developing the principles as to what remedies should be afforded in respect of particular breaches, or acts which constitute proposed breaches, of the Convention. (For details of how to find this jurisprudence see Chapter 10, 'Researching Human Rights Jurisprudence'.)

Section 8(2) permits a court to make an award of damages under the Act where it has the power to award compensation (even if it is not otherwise called 'damages'). This in principle includes statutory tribunals such as employment tribunals.

The principles on which damages in respect of a breach of a Convention right may be awarded are set out in s. 8(3) and (4). Section 8(3) provides that damages are to be awarded only where they are necessary to afford 'just satisfaction' to the victim, taking account of all the circumstances of the case, including any other remedy granted by the court or any other court, and the consequences of any decision (of that or any other court) in respect of the breach.

Section 8(4) provides that a court or tribunal deciding whether to award damages and how much to award must take into account the principles applied by the European Court of Human Rights (ECtHR) in relation to the award of compensation under Article 41 of the Convention. However, it is difficult to identify a concrete set of principles from the case law on Article 41, and it is likely that the domestic courts will have to develop the Strasbourg case law substantially. The following general principles have been used by the ECtHR when determining awards under Article 41 (and have been broadly affirmed by Silber J in *R v Secretary of State for Home Department ex parte N* [2003] EWHC 207 (Admin)):

(a) Compensation is discretionary and will be awarded only if 'necessary', and this is decided on the circumstances of the case as a whole. It is not uncommon for the Strasbourg Court to decline to award compensation on the basis that a declaration of unlawful conduct is sufficient remedy for an applicant. Equally, the ECtHR does refuse to award just satisfaction to applicants, such as terrorist suspects, that it considers 'undeserving' (see *McCann v United Kingdom* (1995) 21 EHRR 97).

(b) There must be a 'causal link' between the compensation sought and the breach of the applicant's Convention rights.

(c) The principle of compensation is '*restitutio in integrum*', that is, that the applicant is, so far as possible, put back into the situation in which he or she would have been but for the violation of his or her Convention rights (*Kingsley v United Kingdom* (2002) 35 EHRR 10). Exemplary damages are not recoverable.

The ECtHR measures 'just satisfaction' under three heads: pecuniary loss, non-pecuniary loss, and costs and expenses:

(a) *Pecuniary loss.* Where applicants have claimed for things such as loss of earnings and career prospects under Article 6(1), the ECtHR has rarely held that a procedural failing has caused pecuniary loss and refuses to speculate on what the outcome of proceedings would have been had the violation not occurred. However, domestic courts may follow the reasoning of *Barbera, Messegue and Jabardo v Spain* (1988) 11 EHRR 360, where the ECtHR held that there had been a loss of opportunity (to prove innocence) as a result of a procedural failing.

(b) *Non-pecuniary loss.* The ECtHR has awarded non-pecuniary damages in respect of pain, suffering and physical or mental injury—particularly in relation to allegations of excessive length of proceedings under Article 6.

(c) *Costs and expenses.* The test applied by the ECtHR is whether the costs were actually and necessarily incurred in order to prevent, or obtain redress for, the breach of the Convention, and were reasonable as to quantum.

The Law Commission (see the Report above) has also highlighted that the ECtHR: has never awarded punitive damages; does award damages for pure economic loss irrespective of whether the state has acted intentionally or negligently; and regularly awards damages to compensate parents whose right to respect for family life has been infringed when state action has led them to lose contact with their children. The quantum of awards granted by the Strasbourg Court is generally cautious, particularly for 'non-pecuniary' damage such as in cases of unlawful detention. For example, in *Johnson v United Kingdom* (1999) 27 EHRR 296, the Strasbourg Court awarded damages of £10,000 for a wrongful detention in a maximum security psychiatric hospital lasting three and a half years; whereas in *R v Governor of Brockhill Prison ex parte Evans (No.2)* [1999] QB 1043, the Court of Appeal awarded damages of £5,000 for 59 days' unlawful detention following a miscalculation of the applicant's prison release date.

The Law Commission Report expressed the view that damages for tort are the most relevant domestic analogy to damages under s. 8 of the Act, and suggests that courts could treat the rules in tort as the *prima facie* measure to be applied—unless the results are inconsistent with Strasbourg case law under Article 41. But even if they are inconsistent, the level of awards under s. 8 of the Human Rights Act 1998 should not be used to detract from the level of damages which an applicant would have obtained in a like action before the enactment of the Convention, such as for false imprisonment. Section 11 of the Act provides that a person may rely on a Convention right without prejudice to any other right or freedom conferred on him or her by or under any (other) law having effect in the United Kingdom.

In *R (Bernard) v London Borough of Enfield* [2002] EWHC Admin 2282, Sullivan J awarded £10,000 damages for a violation of Article 8 rights. The court appeared to take up the Law Commission's recommendations and held that any s. 8 award for non-pecuniary losses should be broadly comparable to tortious awards and *not* be set at a minimal level as that would diminish respect for the policy underlying the 1998 Act. *R (Mambakasa) v Secretary of State for the Home Department* [2003] EWHC Admin 319, suggested the opposite—that the correct analogy for just satisfaction should not be the tortious awards for psychiatric damage but the awards made by the Parliamentary Ombudsman for distress caused by maladministration (which are usually less). In our view the approach suggested by the Law Commission and taken up by Sullivan J is the correct one, but this is an area that is likely to be the focus of much judicial discussion and rapid change until the law is more firmly resolved.

In *Mambakasa*, the claimant unsuccessfully argued that psychiatric damage arising from a delay in granting entry clearance in an asylum and family reunion case gave rise to a violation of Article 8 of the Convention. However, in *R (N) v Secretary of State for the Home Department* [2003] EWHC Admin 207, the court held that an asylum seeker was entitled to damages under the Human Rights Act where the Home Office's administrative inactivity and omissions when processing his claim led to psychiatric injury and financial loss. When assessing whether to make an award of damages in these situations, courts will seek to establish whether the claimant's Convention rights have been unjustifiably violated by the public authority in question, whether there was a causal link between the breach of Convention rights and the harm suffered, and lastly, whether the victim has already been afforded 'just satisfaction' or not.

In general, it is not possible to make a claim for damages against a court that has breached the Convention, even though it is a public authority. Where a first-instance court acts unlawfully, s. 9 of the Act requires proceedings in respect of its decision to be brought on appeal from the decision or by way of judicial review. This prevents collateral claims for damages against, for example, a court which it is argued has breached Article 8 of the Convention in determining a family law claim. However, there is provision in s. 9(3) and (4) of the Act for awards of damages against the Crown where any judicial body has been guilty of a breach of Article 5 in, for example, cases of false imprisonment following a bail application. To claim this remedy, the 'appropriate person', if not already a party to the proceedings, must be joined. The appropriate person (defined in s. 9(5) of the Act) is the minister responsible for the court concerned, or a person or government department nominated by him or her. In the important case of *R (KB) v Mental Health Review Tribunal* [2003] EWHC Admin 193, the claimants were awarded 'modest' damages after they had established breaches of Article 5(4) rights arising from the failure of the MHRT to deal speedily with their applications for a review of their detention. The guidelines that courts should adopt when dealing with claims of this type were suggested by Stanley Burnton J and will probably be cited extensively in subsequent cases.

There is *no* remedy of right in damages where the breach of the Convention is caused by an Act of Parliament. It is still not clear how the Human Rights Act 1998 intends 'just satisfaction' to be afforded in cases where the breach of the Convention is a consequence of a statutory provision, and where a court has made a declaration of incompatibility under s. 4, given the failure to incorporate Article 13. It is possible that *ex gratia* payments of compensation under s. 10 are intended to be the appropriate remedy (see, for example, the discussion at page 103 below of the case of *R(H) v Mental Health Review Tribunal* [2001] EWCA Civ 415 and the payment scheme established by the government following a declaration of incompatibility).

This is an area of law which changes rapidly, and reference should be made to up-to-date discussions and analysis in practitioner texts such as Clayton and Tomlinson (see Chapter 10), or Scorey and Eicke, *Human Rights Damages* (London: Sweet & Maxwell, 2001).

6.3 SECTION 4—DECLARATIONS OF INCOMPATIBILITY

If a court cannot interpret primary legislation in such a way as is compatible with the Convention then, although it must give primacy to the statute, the higher courts also have the further option of making a 'declaration of incompatibility' (s. 4(2)). Thus, if a court is unable to construe a statute in a way that is compatible with the Convention, the Human Rights Act gives it the power to expose the problem by making a declaration that there has been a violation of Convention rights.

6.3.1 The Effect of Declarations of Incompatibility

A declaration of incompatibility is intended to have two effects. First, making a declaration creates public interest and so puts pressure on the Government to change the law. Secondly, the courts try to avoid making such declarations and they strive to find meanings for statutory provisions which conform with the Convention. The making of a declaration of incompatibility is intended to be a rare event as, wherever possible, the strong interpretative obligation in s. 3 of the 1998 Act allows the courts to construe legislation compatibly with Convention rights. This was confirmed by Lord Steyn in *R v A (No. 2)* [2001] UKHL 25, at para. 44, where he stated: 'A declaration of incompatibility is a measure of last resort. It must be avoided unless it is plainly impossible to do so.'

The power to make declarations of incompatibility is available only in the higher courts. These include the High Court, the Court of Appeal, and the House of Lords but not the various tribunals which sit in place of the High Court and from which appeals lie to the Court of Appeal (for example, the Employment Appeal Tribunal and the Immigration Appeal Tribunal). Although the Convention can be argued in the lower courts because of the effect of ss. 3, 6, and 7, and the lower courts must interpret primary legislation, as far as possible, to make it compatible with the Convention, declarations of incompatibility are *not* available in county courts, tribunals, the Crown Court, or magistrates' courts.

If a lower court cannot interpret legislation in a way which conforms with the Convention then it must follow the legislation and not the Convention. However, to arrive at that point the court has to come to a view of the effect of the Convention in the instant case. In the reasons for its decision (for example, a case stated by magistrates for the purposes of an appeal) it will logically, nevertheless, have to set out its view that the legislation is incompatible with the Convention in order for the litigant to make sense of the decision. The lower court's opinion that the provision does not comply with the Convention will not trigger the 'remedial order' provisions in s. 10, but could create the pressure for action to remedy the law. Although a higher court can make a declaration of incompatibility it will not be able to set aside a statute, because of s. 3(2)(c). However, s. 10 (see 6.4 below) provides a 'fast-track' procedure

S. 4(6)

for the amendment of legislation which has been declared incompatible, to bring it into line with human rights principles.

Part 16 (and the accompanying Practice Direction) of the Civil Procedure Rules (CPR) sets out the requirements for a statement of case where the 1998 Act is relied upon in private law claims. Although at the time of writing there is no explicit reference to the procedure to be adopted when a declaration of incompatibility is sought in judicial review proceedings, Part 54 of the CPR should be used to bring a claim alleging that a public authority has acted unlawfully in relation to its Convention obligations under the 1998 Act. (For a detailed explanation of the current procedures that should be adopted see Singh, 'The Declaration of Incompatibility' [2002] JR 237.)

The Act states that a declaration of incompatibility 'is not binding on the parties to the proceedings in which it is made' (s. 4(6)(b)). It is understood that this provision is designed to allow the Government to take a different position from that of the court should the case be argued in the ECtHR. Of course it is already implicit that the making of a declaration of incompatibility does not result in the conclusion of the proceedings being resolved in favour of the litigant whose rights were violated.

Although there have been many challenges to legislation since the 1998 Act came into force, declarations of incompatibility have been made in only a handful of cases, including:

(a) *R (Alconbury Developments Ltd) v Secretary of State for Transport, the Environment and the Regions* [2001] UKHL 23, where the House of Lords reversed the Divisional Court's declaration that the Secretary of State's role in various provisions of planning, highways, and compulsory purchase legislation was incompatible with Article 6(1).

(b) *R (H) v Mental Health Review Tribunal* [2001] EWCA Civ 415, where the Court of Appeal declared parts of the Mental Health Act 1983 incompatible with Article 5(1) and (4) of the Convention as they placed the burden of proof on the patient to show that the conditions for detention were no longer satisfied. As a result of this decision the Mental Health Act 1983 (Remedial) Order 2001 (SI 2001/3712) was introduced using the fast-track procedure. In addition the Government accepted that those patients affected should be appropriately compensated and an *ex gratia* payment scheme has been set up to consider each case on its individual merits (in accordance with the principles set out in s. 8(4) of the 1998 Act).

(c) *Wilson v First County Trust Ltd (No. 2)* [2001] EWCA Civ 633, where the Court of Appeal made a declaration in this private law case (s. 4(2) of the 1998 Act is applicable in 'any proceedings') that s. 127(3) of the Consumer Credit Act 1974 was incompatible with Article 6 and Article 1 of Protocol 1 to the Convention, though this declaration was reversed on appeal by the House of Lords ([2003] UKHL 40).

(d) *R (Wilkinson) v Inland Revenue Commissioners* [2002] EWHC Admin 182, where provisions of the Income and Corporation Taxes Act 1988 were held to be discriminatory on the grounds of sex and incompatible with Article 14 read with Article 1 of Protocol 1 to the Convention.

(e) *R (Hooper) v Secretary of State for Work and Pensions* [2002] EWHC Admin 191, where provisions of the Social Security (Contributions and Benefits) Act 1992 (before they were amended) were also discriminatory on the grounds of sex and incompatible with Article 14 read with Article 8.

(f) *R (International Roth GmbH) v Secretary of State for the Home Department* [2002] EWCA Civ 158, where the Court of Appeal declared the penalties imposed on carriers entering the United Kingdom who were found to have illegal entrants in their vehicles under Part II of the Immigration and Asylum Act 1999 were a disproportionate interference with Article 1 of Protocol 1. The Government has enacted sch. 8 to the Immigration and Nationality Act 2002 to address the breach.

(g) *A and others v Secretary of State for the Home Department* (unreported, 30 July 2002), where the Special Immigration Appeals Commission (SIAC) declared the detention of suspected international terrorists under s. 23 of the Anti-Terrorism, Crime and Security Act 2001 to be incompatible with Article 14 of the Convention as it discriminated on the grounds of nationality. The case is currently under appeal from the Court of Appeal to the House of Lords.

(h) *R v Secretary of State for the Home Department ex parte Anderson* [2002] UKHL 46, where, after the Strasbourg ruling in *Stafford v United Kingdom* (2002) 35 EHRR 32, the House of Lords found that the involvement of the Home Secretary, as a member of the executive, in fixing the tariff term of imprisonment for those convicted of murder was incompatible with Article 6(1).

(i) *R v Secretary of State for the Home Department ex parte D* [2002] EWHC Admin 2805, where it was held that a discretionary life prisoner who was detained under the provisions of the Mental Health Act 1983 had a legal right of access to a court to determine the lawfulness of the detention and direct the prisoner's release under Article 5(4).

(j) *Matthews v Ministry of Defence* [2003] UKHL 4, where the House of Lords did *not* uphold the Divisional Court's original finding that the bar to personal injury claims by ex-servicemen under the Crown Proceedings Act 1947 amounted to a substantive, rather than procedural, bar and was therefore incompatible with Article 6 of the Convention.

(k) *Bellinger v Bellinger* [2003] UKHL 21, where the House of Lords held that s. 11(c) of the Matrimonial Causes Act 1973 was incompatible with Articles 8 and 12 of the Convention as it denied a post-operative transsexual wishing to have her marriage legally recognized her right to respect for family and private life. The declaration of incompatibility was made following the Strasbourg Court's decision in *Goodwin v United Kingdom* (2002) 35 EHRR 18 and the Government's announcement in December 2002 that it would bring forward primary legislation to remedy the breach.

This is not a definitive list and will grow rapidly as the courts continue to grapple with the issues raised by the Convention and the 1998 Act. Students and practitioners should refer to Chapter 10 to understand how to keep up to date with the latest developments.

6.3.2 Notice Provisions

In any case where a court is considering whether to make a declaration of incompatibility, the Crown is entitled to notice of this in accordance with rules of court (s. 5). In some cases the parties will be aware in advance that this is likely and notice can be given. In other cases the Crown will already be a party. However, sometimes the conflict between the Convention and statute will arise in the context of the proceedings themselves. In such circumstances the case will need to be adjourned for notice to be given. The procedure to be followed in these cases is set out in Part 19, and the accompanying Practice Direction, of the CPR. (See also Thomas and Kellar, 'Joining the Crown in Civil Proceedings under the Human Rights Act 1998' [2001] JR 135.)

Once notice has been given, a minister of the Crown (or a person nominated by the minister) has a right to be joined as a party to the proceedings. The Crown is also given a particular right of appeal, with leave, to the House of Lords against any declaration of incompatibility made in criminal proceedings (s. 5(4)).

6.3.3 Costs

One serious issue is the question of how costs are awarded in such cases. In previous editions, we argued that where a declaration of incompatibility is made by the court, costs should not be awarded against the unsuccessful litigant. During the passage of the Human Rights Bill, at committee stage in the House of Lords, an amendment to ensure that the Crown at least bore its own expenses was debated. The Government rejected the proposal, preferring to allow the courts to use their current discretion as to how costs are dealt with. It was suggested that factors for the court to consider included whether the case put forward by the person seeking the declaration had merit and whether or not there was any wider public interest in the matter. Also relevant were the means of the parties and, of course, the outcome of the application for a declaration. This unresolved issue has a potentially 'chilling' effect on the protection of Convention rights, as litigants are reluctant to take test cases under the 1998 Act if they may obtain a declaration of incompatibility but still face a substantial adverse costs order.

6.4 SECTION 10—'FAST-TRACK' PROCEDURE

The fast-track procedure in s. 10 and sch. 2 for amending legislation that is found to be incompatible with the Convention can be started either:

(a) following a declaration of incompatibility made under s. 4; or

(b) where the Government decides, following a decision of the ECtHR, that a provision of legislation is incompatible with a Convention right. The European Court's decision has to be in a case against the United Kingdom, but ministers could also start the procedure following a Court decision concerning another country. It is not necessary that the judgment of the Court is in favour of the applicant.

As it was envisaged in the original draft of the Act, the fast-track procedure would have made it easy for the executive to correct breaches of human rights and could have made it politically embarrassing not to do so. However, late on in the parliamentary debates, s. 10 was amended. This came about as a result of pressure from MPs concerned about excessive use of 'Henry VIII' clauses, that is, provisions empowering the executive to legislate without reference to Parliament (so called after a statute of the reign of Henry VIII which gave the Crown power to repeal Acts of Parliament). As a result, remedial orders can be made only where there are 'compelling reasons' to do so, and normally by positive resolution procedure (sch. 2). The consequence of this amendment could be that a breach of human rights may go uncorrected for want of parliamentary time, or because it relates to an unpopular group or a controversial cause—precisely the domination of majority over minority interests which human rights law is designed to prevent. The amendment therefore had the unfortunate effect of weakening the structure of the Act.

6.4.1 Remedial Orders

Section 10 empowers a minister to make a 'remedial order' embodied in a statutory instrument (s. 20(1)) that amends legislation so as to remove its incompatibility with the Convention. The Act provides two procedures for making a remedial order: a standard procedure in sch. 2, para. 2(a), and an emergency procedure in sch. 2, para. 2(b).

A remedial order can be fairly wide in scope and can have retrospective effect, and can 'make different provision for different cases'. This retrospective effect is limited by sch. 2, para. 1(3), which states that, 'No person is to be guilty of an offence solely as a result of the retrospective effect of a remedial order'. It must be assumed that the power to change the law retrospectively could be used to backdate a change to the date of the domestic court's decision on incompatibility or the judgment of the ECtHR.

The standard procedure of sch. 2, para. 2(a) is a 'positive resolution procedure'. The minister must first, by sch. 2, para. 3, lay before Parliament a document containing a draft of the proposed order together with what is called the 'required information', which is (sch. 2, para. 5):

(a) an explanation of the incompatibility which the proposed order seeks to remove, including particulars of the court declaration, finding, or order which caused the minister to propose a remedial order; and

(b) a statement of the reasons for proceeding under s. 10 and for making an order in the terms proposed.

This document must be before Parliament for at least 60 days, during which representations about the draft order may be made to the minister, either by Parliament in the form of a report or resolution, or by any other person. The minister can amend the draft in the light of these representations. Whether or not the draft is amended it must be laid before Parliament again, this time accompanied by a summary of any representations that have been made and details of any changes made as a result. The order does not come into effect unless it is approved by a resolution of each House within 60 days after it is laid for the second time.

Under the emergency procedure of sch. 2, para. 2(b), the minister may make the order before laying it before Parliament, but must state in the order that it appears to him or her that, because of the urgency of the matter, it is necessary to make it without prior parliamentary approval. However, after making an order under this emergency procedure the minister must, under sch. 2, para. 4, lay the order before Parliament, with the required information, for 60 days, during which representations may be made, as under the standard procedure. The minister can amend the order in the light of the representations, but, whether it is amended or not, the order must be laid before Parliament again, with a summary of representations and details of amendments, and it will cease to have effect 120 days after it was made unless it is approved by a resolution of each House. Following the Court of Appeal's decision in *R (H) v Mental Health Review Tribunal* [2001] EWCA Civ 415, the Secretary of State introduced the Mental Health Act 1983 (Remedial) Order 2001 (SI 2001/3712) using this urgent procedure. This route was probably used because the problem involved fundamental rights to personal liberty and, if not rectified quickly, would have created confusion as the tribunal system would be unsure as to what burden of proof they should be applying.

The power given by s. 10 to amend legislation applies to both primary and secondary legislation. This provision allows campaigners, lobbyists, and lawyers to make representations to Government to amend primary legislation following any case in the Court in Strasbourg that raises questions about legislation. The Government is not, of course, bound to act by way of either primary or secondary legislation, even following a declaration of incompatibility. However, if it does not do so, it would be a virtual certainty that the victim could then seek just satisfaction in the ECtHR. This would then impose an obligation on the Government as a matter of international law to remedy its violation.

In *R v Lyons* [2002] UKHL 44, the House of Lords refused to quash the defendants' convictions for theft, false accounting, and conspiracy—even though the defendants had successfully argued their case in the ECtHR (in *Saunders v United Kingdom* (1997) 23 EHRR 313). The ECtHR held that where evidence which had been obtained under compulsion in a statutory inquiry into allegations of fraud was subsequently used in criminal proceedings, there was a breach of the right against self-incrimination contained in Article 6 of the Convention. When the case came before the House of Lords, their Lordships decided that as the Convention was merely an unenforceable international treaty at the time of the original convictions, the decision of the ECtHR was not binding in domestic law. We suggest that the general international law obligation on the Government to adhere to judgments of the ECtHR is likely to limit any future application of this unique decision.

7

THE INTERACTION BETWEEN CONVENTION PRINCIPLES AND EUROPEAN UNION LAW

7.1 INTRODUCTION

This chapter concerns the ways in which Convention arguments are considered in cases within the scope of European Community (EC) (and European Union (EU)) law. This is not the place for a wide discussion of the history or present state of development of human rights in the law of the EU. Sources of more detailed analysis of these subjects are given in Chapter 10, 'Researching Human Rights Jurisprudence'. However, no lawyer dealing with an argument of EC law (or of application of the law of the EU by United Kingdom authorities) can afford to ignore Convention arguments. This is because:

(a) EC law and EU law are informed by Convention principles (see 7.2 below);

(b) EC law and EU law are part of the law of the United Kingdom. In the EC's fields of competence, s. 2 of the European Communities Act 1972 and Article 5 of the Treaty of European Union require UK courts to give EC law rights effect in the United Kingdom, either through laws which transpose directives into UK law, or through the doctrine of direct effect, or by reference to the interpretative *Marleasing* principle (see 7.3 below);

(c) ss. 3 and 6 of the Human Rights Act 1998 require UK courts to give effect to Convention principles wherever possible, and this includes cases where they are interpreting questions of EC law or EU law;

(d) the European Court of Human Rights has been prepared to consider the compatibility with the Convention of actions of member states which have been taken in order to comply with obligations under EC law or EU law (see 7.3 below);

(e) there may be circumstances in which there are tactical or procedural advantages in using the Convention through EC/EU law, or in using Convention arguments in determining the scope of EC/EU obligations (see 7.3 below).

This chapter outlines the developing doctrine of fundamental rights in EC and EU case law, and then examines how EC/EU and Convention principles will overlap in practice.

7.2 THE DEVELOPING DOCTRINE OF FUNDAMENTAL RIGHTS IN EC AND EU LAW

The EU is not itself a signatory to the European Convention on Human Rights ('the Convention'). However, all the EU's member states are also signatories to the Convention, and there is undoubtedly a developing doctrine of 'fundamental rights' in EC law. The Treaty of European Union (TEU) itself now provides that such rights are directly enforceable in the European Court of Justice. Article 6 (ex F) of the TEU reads:

> The Union is founded on the principles of liberty, democracy, respect for human rights and fundamental freedoms, and the rule of law, principles of which are common to the Member States.

> The Union shall respect fundamental rights, as guaranteed by [the Convention] and as they result from the constitutional traditions common to the Member States, as general principles of Community law.

The growing importance of fundamental rights jurisprudence is explained by the expanding scope of EC/EU competence. The Communities began their lives as largely economic bodies, but they have gradually acquired competence over many areas—for example, free movement of persons, discrimination, asylum—which raise particularly human rights-sensitive issues. Talk of human rights within the EC and EU can only develop as these areas acquire further political importance at an EU level. It has also been heightened following the adoption of powers for the EU to legislate against discrimination on grounds of sex, racial or ethnic origin, religion or belief, disability, age, or sexual orientation, under Article 13 EC and the directives published under it (2000/43—the Anti-race Discrimination Directive, and 2000/78—the Framework Employment Directive), and by the adoption in December 2000 of the EU's Charter of Fundamental Rights.

The European Convention on Human Rights is an important source of EC/EU law of fundamental rights. In an Advisory Opinion, 2/94 [1996] ECR 1759, the European Court of Justice (ECJ) held (at para. 33) that although the EC did not have competence to sign the Convention:

. . . it is well settled that fundamental rights form an integral part of the general principles of law whose observance the Court ensures. For that purpose, the Court draws inspiration from the constitutional traditions common to the Member States and from the guidelines supplied by international treaties for the protection of human rights on which the Member States have collaborated or of which they are signatories.

(See, among other cases, *Roquette Frères* [2002] ECR I-9011, para. 25, and *Booker Acquaculture Ltd v Secretary of State for Scotland* (case C20/00), 10 July 2003.)

The ECJ has gone further, and recognized the 'special significance' of the Convention as a source of principles of EC law: see, for example, *Rutili v Ministre de l'Interieur* [1975] ECR 1219, and *ERT* [1991] ECR I-2925). The ECJ has used Convention standards both to interpret the scope of rights guaranteed by EC/EU law, and in deciding the extent of derogations that are permitted from it. An example of the former is *P v S* [1996] ECR I-2143 (especially the opinion of Advocate General Tesauro and paras 17–22 of the judgment), in which the ECJ used Convention principles to conclude that the EC Equal Treatment Directive excluded discrimination against transsexuals.

The ECJ has applied its fundamental rights jurisprudence to member states applying Community law as well as the EC/EU's own institutions. It has held that member states implementing Community rules or applying national rules within the scope of Community law must do so in a way compatible with fundamental rights that derive in particular from the Convention. See, for example, *Booker Acquaculture v The Scottish Ministers* (case C20/00), 10 July 2003. For example, in *ERT* (above), at paras 41–45, restrictions on television licences were considered by reference to Article 10 of the Convention. In his opinion in *Konstantinidis v Stadt Altensteig-Standesamt* [1993] ECR I-1191, Advocate General Jacobs said that a Community national could 'oppose any violation of his fundamental rights' when exercising Community free movement rights in another member state, and this has recently been reflected by the judgment of the ECJ in *Carpenter v Secretary of State for the Home Department* (case C-60/00), 11 July 2002. In the *Carpenter* case it was held that the decision to deport the applicant interfered with her husband's free movement rights and that the UK could invoke reasons of public interest to justify the national measure which did this only if it was compatible with fundamental rights. Having regard to the case law of the ECtHR, the decision to deport the applicant did not strike a fair balance between the right of Mr Carpenter to respect for his family life and the maintenance of public order.

Two further examples from the United Kingdom are illustrative. In *Johnston v Chief Constable of the Royal Ulster Constabulary* (case 222/84) [1986] ECR 1651, the UK sought to defend a provision which stopped female police officers from carrying handguns in Northern Ireland. It served public interest immunity certificates to prevent the reasons for this being presented in court. The ECJ used Articles 6 and 13 of the Convention as principles which 'must be taken into consideration in Community law' to hold that Article 6 of the EC's Equal Treatment Directive, EC/76/207, prevented a member state from derogating from the right to equal treatment in this way without legal scrutiny. And in *R v Kent Kirk* (case 63/83) [1984] ECR 2689, the ECJ held that a UK statutory instrument applying a retroactive provision in an EC regulation was unlawful because it violated Article 7 of the Convention.

It is still unclear how far the ECJ regards the standards in the Convention as a minimum below which the EC may not fall, or merely as 'inspiration' or 'guidelines' (*National Panasonic (United Kingdom) Ltd v Commission* [1980] ECR 2033; *Commission v Germany* [1989] ECR 1263; *Kremzow v Austria* [1997] ECR I-2629; *Martinez Sala* [1998] ECR I-2691; *Bickel & Franz* (case C-274/96) [1998] ECR I-7637). And it would probably be going too far to say that Convention standards are actually part of EC law. There have been a number of cases in which the ECJ has decided issues without reference to important decisions of the ECtHR—for example, *Hoechst v Commission* [1989] ECR 2859, para. 18, which held that no case law under Article 8 ECHR extended to business premises, in apparent ignorance of *Niemietz v Germany* [1993] 16 EHRR 97. In *Emesa Sugar (Free Zone) NV v Aruba* (case C-17/98) [2000] ECR I-665, the ECJ reviewed its own procedures by reference to Article 6 ECHR, distinguished the case law of the ECtHR in ways which have surprised some commentators, and held that there was no violation of the right to a fair trial.

It remains the case that EC/EU fundamental rights and Convention rights may not be identical, and that the ECtHR is not, at present, prepared to consider the conformity of the actions of EC/EU bodies themselves with Convention standards, even if creatively addressed as an application against all EU member states (see *Guerin Automobiles v 15 Members of the EU* (App. No. 5157/99), declared inadmissible 4 July 2000). Nonetheless, Convention standards are probably the most important source for establishing the 'common traditions' of the members of the EC/EU. In effect, the ECJ applies the Convention directly, by requiring rules of national law within the scope of Community competence, and Community law, to be reviewed for conformity with Convention principles, because these are generally recognized principles of law which underlie the constitutional traditions of all the member states of the EC/EU.

The provisions of the EU's Charter of Fundamental Rights state that they endeavour to promote harmony between the two systems, and though the Charter does not resolve all the issues which may arise as to how this to be achieved, it is likely to emphasize the importance of Convention standards in EC/EU law.

There remain important constitutional and international law questions to be addressed. Though the ECtHR will not address the conformity of EC/EU actions with the Convention, it is quite prepared to declare that EC/EU member states have violated Convention rights whilst acting so as to give effect to EC/EU obligations (see the discussion of *Cantoni* and *Matthews* at 7.4 below).

The importance of Convention principles in the context of EC/EU law is therefore likely to develop, both as a result of political changes at EU level and because of a heightened awareness of them in the UK as a result of the enactment of the Human Rights Act 1998.

7.3 THE EUROPEAN CHARTER OF FUNDAMENTAL RIGHTS

The Charter is an EU instrument—it is wholly distinct from the European Convention on Human Rights, though clearly informed by it. It is addressed to the EU and its institutions, and member states when they are implementing Union law, and requires states to promote the rights contained in it. It is not yet a legally binding instrument. However, it has been referred to at a political level and in at least one Advocate General's opinion (in *Booker Acquaculture Ltd v Secretary of State for Scotland* (case C-20/00), 10 July 2003). It was drafted 'as if' it were to have full legal effect (COM (2000) 644), but its legal status will not be resolved until the EU's Intergovernmental Conference in 2004. It is set out at Appendix 7 of this book.

The preamble to the Charter refers to the common and indivisible universal values upon which the EU was founded, as well as to the diversity of cultures, traditions, and identities in Europe. The substance of the Charter is divided into six chapters: I Dignity, II Freedoms, III Equality, IV Solidarity, V Citizens' Rights, and VI Justice. The final Chapter, VII, contains general clauses which relate to the scope and applicability of the Charter, the bodies to which it is addressed, and its relationship to other legal instruments, including the European Convention on Human Rights.

The relationship between the Convention and other international human rights instruments is addressed in Articles 52(3) and 53 of the Charter. Article 52(3) provides:

> Insofar as this Charter contains rights which correspond to rights guaranteed by the Convention for the Protection of Human Rights and Fundamental Freedoms, the meaning and scope of those rights shall be the same as those laid down by the said Convention. This provision shall not prevent Union law providing more extensive protection.

Though this provision does not fully explain the relationship between the ECtHR and the ECJ, it seems likely that it is intended that the ECJ should defer to the ECtHR on Convention issues. The relationship between the ECtHR, the ECJ, and national constitutional courts, however, will clearly remain a matter of controversy for some time.

7.4 THE INTERACTION OF THE CONVENTION WITH EC/EU LAW IN THE UK COURTS

The obligation of UK courts to apply EC/EU law on fundamental rights applies only in areas of EC/EU competence. The UK's judges do not always agree as to what this means, as can be seen by comparing the judgments in *R v Ministry of Agriculture, Fisheries and Food ex parte Hamble Fisheries (Offshore) Ltd* [1995] 1 CMLR 553 and *R v Ministry of Agriculture, Fisheries and Food ex parte First City Trading Ltd*

[1997] 1 CMLR 250, though ultimately, the scope of EU competence is a matter for the ECJ itself: see *ERT* (at 7.2 above).

Whilst EC/EU law has an impact on domestic law only within fields of European Union competence, the Human Rights Act 1998 can be used directly to challenge any Government action which has an impact on Convention rights. It might be thought, therefore, that EC/EU law has nothing to add to Convention principles in giving effect to fundamental rights in UK courts, and (conversely) that Convention principles add nothing to questions of EC/EU law. However, such an approach would be misconceived.

First, many cases which involve EC/EU law rights concern the balance to be struck between a right contained in EC/EU law and the state's power to protect a competing public interest (for example, public order or public safety). In such a case, a public authority might argue that the public interest exception to the underlying EC/EU law right is engaged. Whether this is in fact the case involves a decision as to whether the proposed restriction on the underlying right can be justified in the public interest. The scope of the state's power to restrict the underlying EC/EU law right may be limited by having regard to case law of the ECtHR. For example, in the *Carpenter* case described at 7.2 above, the scope of the exception to free movement rights contained in Article 49 EC was limited by the ECJ, 'in the light of the fundamental right to respect for family life' as it had been interpreted by the ECtHR.

Secondly, there is Convention case law which means that the state may be obliged to extend rights which do not apparently exist in EC/EU law so as to give effect to the Convention in certain ways which would be by no means obvious by reference to EC/EU law principles alone. In other words, EC/EU law does not permit national authorities acting in a field covered by it to act in a manner contrary to fundamental rights as understood and protected in member states: see the opinion of Advocate General Gulmann in *R v MAFF ex parte Bostock* [1994] ECR I-955, at para. 33.

The ECtHR has also been clear that the fact that a member state may be acting so as to give effect to an obligation imposed upon it by EC/EU law will not justify a breach of the Convention, if one exists. So, in *Cantoni v France* (RJD 1996-V 1614), the ECtHR held that a national legislative provision based on a Community directive did not remove the provision from the scope of the Convention or the member state from its responsibility to ensure that offences imposed by implementing measures complied with Article 7 of the Convention. And in *Matthews v United Kingdom* (1999) 28 EHRR 361, the applicant, a resident of Gibraltar, successfully challenged the failure to afford her a vote in EU elections, even though she did not reside in a territory which was defined as part of the UK for the purposes of European parliamentary elections. The ECtHR nonetheless found a breach of Article 3 of Protocol 1 by the UK.

Thirdly, even after the incorporation of the Convention into domestic law, there may be cases in areas covered by EC/EU law rights in which the Convention will be more effective if it is used in conjunction with EC/EU law than on its own through the Human Rights Act 1998. The most obvious is where the provision complained of is contained in a statute that falls within the sphere of EC/EU competence. Section 2 of the European Communities Act 1972 and Article 5 TEU afford EU law supremacy over other provisions of domestic law—it can override even statutory provisions where it is directly effective. EC/EU law can be given effect in the United Kingdom without further enactment both through the principle of direct effect and the interpretative *Marleasing* principle (*Collins v Imtrat Handelsgesellschaft mbH* (cases C-92 & 326/92) [1993] ECR I-5145).

This makes EC/EU law in some respects more powerful than the Human Rights Act 1998, which explicitly prevents the courts from using the Convention to 'strike down' incompatible primary legislation (contrast *Marshall v Southampton and South West Hampshire Area Health Authority (Teaching)* (case 152/84) [1986] QB 401 and the European Communities Act 1972, s. 2, with the Human Rights Act 1998, s. 3(2)(b) and (c)).

In spheres of EC/EU competence, it may therefore be more beneficial to use the Convention through EU law rather than through the Human Rights Act 1998 alone where the challenge is to primary legislation. Whereas the Act alone would permit the court only to declare the domestic legislation incompatible with the Convention (see s. 4), if primary domestic legislation contravenes directly effective EU legislation, the national court is required to disapply the primary domestic legislation. So if a court or tribunal could be persuaded that a provision of EU law must be interpreted in accordance with the Convention, and where EU law is directly effective, the Convention standard will become part of domestic law even to the extent of overriding inconsistent domestic provisions (for example, *Marshall v Southampton and South West Hampshire Area Health Authority (Teaching) (No. 2)* (case C-271/91) [1993] ICR 893).

There are other tactical areas in which the interaction of EC/EU and Convention law may be considered. For example, s. 7 of the Human Rights Act 1998 gives only 'victims' of acts standing to sue (see Chapter 5, at 5.3). The English courts have arguably adopted a more generous attitude to representative standing in some cases involving EC/EU law: for example, *R v Secretary of State for the Environment ex parte Friends of the Earth* [1996] Env LR 198. So, in cases engaging EU law, it is arguable that this restrictive approach to standing would not apply, and so a 'representative' applicant may be able to argue Convention points which would not be available under the Human Rights Act 1998 alone.

Another example is that there may be a difference between an 'emanation of the state' as defined in EC/EU law and a 'public authority' for Convention purposes. There may, or may not, be a distinction between:

(a) the test used in judicial review proceedings (see, e.g., *R v Panel on Takeovers and Mergers ex parte Datafin plc* [1987] QB 815), in which questions as to the *sources* of power as well as the functions are potentially relevant;

(b) the test used in EU law, in which a body is held to be an emanation of the state, regardless of its legal form, if it has been made responsible pursuant to a measure adopted by the state for providing a public service, or where it has been given special powers (see *Foster v British Gas plc* (case C-188/89) [1990] ECR I-3313); and

(c) the definition of 'public authority' in the Human Rights Act 1998, s. 6 (see 4.5.2 above).

If an argument falls within both Convention and EU law, more beneficial remedies might be available than could be obtained under the Human Rights Act alone. The Human Rights Act expressly excludes the possibility of obtaining damages against the state for a failure to legislate (see 6.2 above). However, EC/EU law provides that damages must in principle be available if the Government has failed properly to transpose a measure of EC/EU law into domestic law (see *Francovich v Italy* [1991] ECR I-5357).

Lastly, the interaction between EC/EU law and the Convention may lead to difficult questions as to whether it is appropriate to seek a reference to the ECJ. Curiously, in areas of EU competence, the ECJ rather than (or as well as) the ECtHR may provide guidance to the interpretation of relevant Convention provisions. *Campbell v Secretary of State for the Home Department* (see 7.2 above) is one example of such a case. In another, *R v Hertfordshire County Council ex parte Green Environmental Industries Ltd and another* [2000] All ER 773, the question arose whether a local authority could require a company to give answers to requests for information under s. 71(2) of the Environmental Protection Act (EPA) 1990 without giving an undertaking that the information gathered would not be used to prosecute. The 1990 Act was passed to give effect to the European Waste Framework Directive, Council Directive (EEC) 91/156, a measure of EU law. The company argued that s. 71(2) of the EPA 1990 must be interpreted in accordance with EU law, including general principles of human rights, and this included the privilege against self-incrimination contained in Article 6(1) of the Convention as an aspect of EU law. The House of Lords felt able to resolve the case before it without dealing with Article 6(1), because the question before it did not involve a trial. However, Lord Cooke observed (at 784 E–F) that had it been necessary to determine whether Article 6(1) would have ruled out the admission of prosecution evidence obtained in consequence of the answers given, he would have made a reference to the ECJ.

The conclusion is that EC/EU law, the Convention, and domestic law cannot be compartmentalized into discrete boxes. The interaction between them must be absorbed and considered in any relevant case.

8

CONVENTION RIGHTS AND THE HUMAN RIGHTS ACT

8.1 INTRODUCTION

This chapter summarizes the content of the rights protected under the European Convention for the Protection of Human Rights and Fundamental Freedoms ('the Convention'). It is intended as an introduction to the substantive rights incorporated by the Human Rights Act 1998. While the emphasis is on the incorporated rights, consideration is also given to Article 13 and various non-incorporated Protocols.

For each Article, an overview is given of the jurisprudence of the European Court of Human Rights, accompanied by reference to consistent domestic cases where appropriate. We have included a brief discussion of the approach to the Articles in the domestic courts, providing some non-exhaustive examples of areas in which the Articles have arisen and indicating any major inconsistencies with Strasbourg decisions. Detailed considerations of human rights jurisprudence can be found in the texts highlighted in Chapter 10, 'Researching Human Rights Jurisprudence'.

Article 1 is simply the duty on the states that have ratified the Convention to 'secure to everyone within their jurisdiction the rights and freedoms' protected by the Convention. As the Human Rights Act is a piece of domestic legislation, this Article is not incorporated into domestic law (see further 9.4.3 below).

When inviting a court to consider Convention jurisprudence under s. 2 of the Human Rights Act, it is important to be aware that the decisions are context specific. For example, cases concerning Article 3 in the context of medical treatment may require different policy judgments to those the courts have reached in difficult cases involving terrorists.

In this chapter, 'ECtHR' means the European Court of Human Rights and 'ECmHR' means the European Commission of Human Rights. Citations are either from the most commonly available sets of law reports, or (where a judgment is not yet available in these publications) consist of the Strasbourg case's application number or the domestic case's neutral citation. For details of how to source the relevant case law see Chapter 10.

8.2 ARTICLE 2: RIGHT TO LIFE

1. Everyone's right to life shall be protected by law. No one shall be deprived of his life intentionally save in the execution of a sentence of a court following his conviction of a crime for which this penalty is provided by law.

2. Deprivation of life shall not be regarded as inflicted in contravention of this Article when it results from the use of force which is no more than absolutely necessary:
    (a) in defence of any person from unlawful violence;
    (b) in order to effect a lawful arrest or to prevent the escape of a person lawfully detained;
    (c) in action lawfully taken for the purpose of quelling a riot or insurrection.

Article 2 has, not surprisingly, been described by the ECtHR as 'one of the most fundamental provisions in the Convention' (*McCann v United Kingdom* (1995) 21 EHRR 97, at para. 197). With very limited exceptions, it cannot be subject to derogation under Article 15. The Article is comprehensive, imposing a substantive obligation to protect the right to life, a substantive prohibition on the taking of life, and a procedural obligation to investigate the taking of life. As is the case with the Convention more generally, the Article 2 right applies only post-natally (*Paton v United Kingdom* (1980) 19 DR 244). Although Article 2 does not prohibit the use of a death penalty which has been properly authorized, the abolition of the death penalty is required by Protocol 6, which is incorporated by the Act, and also by the new Protocol 13.

It was argued in *R (Pretty) v Director of Public Prosecutions* [2001] UKHL 61 and *Pretty v United Kingdom* (2002) 35 EHRR 1 that Article 2 extends beyond the right to life and protects the more comprehensive right to self-determination in relation to issues of life and death. However, this argument was rejected by both the ECtHR and the House of Lords, which held that Article 2 does not confer a right to die.

Article 2 is relevant to many aspects of state power, including the use of lethal force by the state through the police and armed forces to combat terrorism, fight crime, and quell civil unrest. In keeping with the importance of this provision (the right to life) in a democratic society, the courts must, in making their assessment, subject deprivations of life to the most careful scrutiny (*McCann*, at para. 150).

8.2.1 Obligation to Protect the Right to Life

The first sentence of Article 2 imposes a positive duty on states to protect the right to life. This duty obliges states 'to take appropriate steps to safeguard the lives of those within [their] jurisdiction' (*Osman v United Kingdom* (2000) 29 EHRR 245, at para. 115). Primarily, these steps will take the form of effective criminal legislation supported by law enforcement machinery. However, the ECtHR has affirmed that, in certain circumstances, the state will be obliged 'to take preventive operational measures to protect an individual whose life is at risk from the criminal acts of another individual' (*Osman*, at para. 115) or from suicide (*Keenan v United Kingdom* (2001) 3 EHRR 913). This obligation is enhanced in respect of individuals who are in state custody, given their particularly vulnerable position (*Keenan*, at para. 90). The Court of Appeal decision *R (Middleton) v West Somerset Coroner, R (Amin) v Secretary of State for the Home Department* [2002] EWCA Civ 390, confirms that the domestic courts will mirror the Strasbourg approach to the protective obligation.

The broad scope of the Article 2 positive obligation is demonstrated by the decision, *Oneryildiz v Turkey* [2002] ECHR 48939/99. In this case, the state's negligence in relation to environmental and safety conditions at a rubbish tip was found to violate Article 2. Accordingly, Article 2 may well be relevant in cases of extreme environmental damage.

Despite its broad scope, Article 2 does not extend to an absolute positive obligation on the state to protect the right to life in all circumstances. In order for the obligation to be engaged, the state authorities must have known or ought to have known that there was a real and immediate risk to life yet failed to take measures within the scope of their power which, judged reasonably, might have been expected to avoid that risk (*Osman*). In *Osman* (at para. 116), the ECtHR noted that in limiting the scope of the protective obligation:

> [a]nother relevant consideration is the need to ensure that the police exercise their powers to control and prevent crime in a manner which fully respects the due process and other guarantees which legitimately place restraints on the scope of their action to investigate crime and bring offenders to justice, including the guarantees contained in Articles 5 and 8 of the Convention.

The Grand Chamber of the ECtHR recently considered the allegation that a system of alternative measures to imprisonment may violate the state's protective obligation (*Mastromatteo v Italy* [2002] ECHR 37703/97). The applicant's son had been murdered by an individual who had been granted prison leave for the final stages of his sentence. Such social reintegration measures were held to pursue a legitimate objective and not to pose a real and immediate risk to life.

8.2.2 Prohibition on Taking Life

In addition to the protective obligation, Article 2 expressly prohibits the state from intentionally taking life. It is possible that, in exceptional circumstances, intentional non-fatal physical ill-treatment may violate the prohibition (*Ilhan v Turkey* (2002) 34 EHRR 36, at para. 76). Unintentional taking of life is implicitly prohibited in a situation where it is permitted to use force under Article 2(2) but the force used is more than absolutely necessary and results in death (*McShane v United Kingdom* (2002) 35 EHRR 23, at para. 93).

8.2.3 Procedural Obligation

The protection of the substantive rights requires that there should be an effective official investigation into deaths resulting from the use of force (*McCann*, at para. 161; *Middleton*, at 519). In *McCann*, the ECmHR described this investigative obligation as the 'procedural aspect' of Article 2. This obligation is engaged in situations where death has resulted from state use of force, and also where death has resulted from a state's failure to protect the right to life (see, for example, *Edwards v United Kingdom* (2002) 35 EHRR 487 and *Middleton*).

While the form of the investigation is flexible, there are a number of features that will generally be necessary to guarantee the effectiveness of an investigation (*Edwards*, at paras 69–73; see also *Jordan v United Kingdom* (2001) 31 EHRR 6). These features include independence, promptness, and an element of public scrutiny.

Although the degree of public scrutiny may vary from case to case, it is necessary in all cases for the victim's next of kin to be involved to the extent required to safeguard their legitimate interests (*Edwards*, at para. 73). In all cases, the authorities must engage the investigative mechanism on their own initiative rather than waiting for the next of kin to take action (*Edwards*, at para. 69). Further requisite features are an ability to establish cause of death, to determine if the force was or was not justified, and to identify and punish those responsible for the death (*Edwards*, at paras 70–71). Accordingly, civil proceedings will not constitute an effective investigation (*McShane*, at para.125). See generally Friedman, Christian, and Thomas, *Inquests: A Practitioners Guide* (London: LAG, 2002).

In *McShane*, the applicant's husband was killed when a security forces' vehicle struck a hoarding under which he had fallen during a disturbance in Belfast. The applicant complained that there was no effective investigation into her husband's death, as required by Article 2. Although there was a police investigation and inquest proceedings were scheduled to commence, the ECtHR held that a number of deficiencies rendered both inconsistent with the investigative obligation. A central deficiency of the police investigation was the involvement of police officers indirectly connected with the security operation. That involvement was held to cast doubts on the independence of the investigation. A series of delays in both the investigation and inquest proceedings, including a delay of over five months in questioning the driver of the vehicle, demonstrated a lack of the requisite promptness.

Compliance with the procedural obligation is closely related to the Article 13 right to an effective remedy. However, violation of Article 2, stemming from non-compliance with the procedural obligation, will not necessarily constitute a violation of Article 13 (*McShane*). Article 13 is discussed in further detail at 8.13 below.

8.2.4 Exceptions to the Right to Life

The second paragraph of the Article details the exceptions to the right to life. All these situations involve curbing violence or the control of prisoners or criminals—generally, maintaining law and order. 'No more force than is absolutely necessary' is the crucial test for these exceptions. The ECmHR examined the phrase 'absolutely necessary' in *Stewart v United Kingdom* (1984) 38 DR 162. In this case a 13-year-old boy was accidentally killed by a plastic bullet fired into a crowd by the army while trying to quell a riot. The ECmHR held that this was not a violation of Article 2 as the force fell within the category of 'absolutely necessary'. It stated that force is 'absolutely necessary' if it is 'strictly proportionate to the achievement of the permitted purpose'. The ECmHR explained further:

> In assessing whether the use of force is strictly proportionate, regard must be had to the nature of the aim pursued, the dangers to life and limb inherent in the situation and the degree of risk that the force employed might result in the loss of life. The Commission's examination must have due regard to all the relevant circumstances.

The ECmHR found that the exceptions included in Article 2(2) indicate that this provision extends to, but is not concerned exclusively with, intentional killing. It stated that Article 2, when read as a whole, indicates that para. (2):

> does not primarily define situations where it is permitted intentionally to kill an individual, but defines the situations where it is permitted to 'use force' which may result, as an unintended outcome of the use of force, in the deprivation of life.

The leading case on the use of lethal force is *McCann v United Kingdom* (1995) 21 EHRR 97, in which three Provisional IRA members were shot and killed by Special Air Service soldiers in Gibraltar in 1988. The ECtHR held, by a slim 10:9 vote, that there had been a violation of Article 2. In making its decision the ECtHR took into consideration 'not only the actions of the organs of the state who actually administer the force but also the surrounding circumstances including such matters as the planning and control of the actions under examination'. This idea of 'planning and control' is important. The ECtHR held that the state must give appropriate training, instructions, and briefing to its agents who are faced with a situation where the use of lethal force is possible. The state must also exercise 'strict control' over any operations that may involve use of lethal force.

A contrasting case to *McCann* is *Andronicou v Cyprus* (1997) 25 EHRR 491. This involved a hostage situation where the police mistakenly believed that a gunman had more ammunition and weapons than he actually possessed. The gunman and his hostage were killed by shots fired by the police. The ECtHR sought to determine whether the force administered in this situation was 'strictly proportionate' to the achievement of the aims set out in Article 2(a), (b), and (c). It decided that the degree of force used was proportionate to the dangerous hostage situation. As in *McCann*, the ECtHR looked also to the planning and control of the actions under examination. It found that the police actions were designed and carried out to minimize the risk to the lives of the gunman and his hostage. Even though the police were mistaken about the gunman's weapons, the ECtHR ruled that they had good reason to believe as they did, and were pursuing the legitimate aims of Article 2(2). Therefore, no violation of Article 2 was found in this case.

8.2.5 Human Rights Act Decisions

Article 2 has been considered by the domestic courts on a number of occasions. The provision has been raised in relation to a wide range of subject areas, including assisted suicide (see the discussion at 8.2 above regarding *Pretty v Director of Public Prosecutions*), immigration (for example, *R (R) v Chief Immigration Officer* (2000) *The Times*, 29 November), witness protection and safety (for example, *R (F) v Chief Constable of Norfolk Police* [2002] EWHC Admin 1738 and *R (A and Others) v Lord Saville of Newdigate and Others* [2001] EWCA Civ 2048), and the scope of the law of confidentiality where secrecy is necessary to protect life (for example, *Venables v News Group Newspapers Ltd* [2001] 2 WLR 1038).

Medical law has been a particularly prominent area in which the right to life has been raised before domestic courts. The courts have held that Article 2 does not impose a continuing obligation to maintain life in the case of permanent vegetative state patients (see, for example, *NHS Trust A v M* [2001] 2 WLR 942). It has also been found that an operation to separate conjoined twins, which will result in the death of one, is not inconsistent with Article 2, since the purpose of the operation would be to save the life of one twin rather than to take the life of the other (*In re A (Conjoined Twins)* [2001] 2 WLR 480).

While the substantive obligations have been approached in conformity with decisions of the ECtHR, the Court of Appeal has arguably taken a different approach to the content of the procedural obligation. In *R (Middleton) v West Somerset Coroner, R (Amin) v Secretary of State for the Home Department* [2002] EWCA Civ 390, the Court of Appeal held that publicity and family participation are not necessarily fixed requirements which must be distinctly and separately fulfilled in every case where the investigative duty is triggered. While the Court stated that this finding was not inconsistent with Strasbourg case law, the decision is difficult to reconcile with *Edwards*. However, the Court indicated that a degree of inconsistency would not necessarily place domestic law in breach of Article 2, since the adjectival nature of the investigative duty permits a domestic discretion in defining the content of that duty. This case is currently pending before the House of Lords, and it is hoped that their judgment will clarify the nature of the Article 2 procedural obligation in domestic law.

R (Green) v Police Complaints Authority and Others [2002] EWCA Civ 389 is a further indication of the narrow approach being taken by the Court of Appeal to the investigative obligation. There, the Court held that when investigating a complaint of a breach of Article 2 by a police officer, the Police Complaints Authority is not obliged to disclose witness statements to the complainant. See also *R (Wright and Bennett) v Home Office* [2001] EWHC Admin 520 regarding the investigative obligation.

8.3 ARTICLE 3: PROHIBITION OF TORTURE

No one shall be subjected to torture or to inhuman or degrading treatment or punishment

Article 3 concerns freedom from torture, inhuman treatment, degrading treatment, inhuman punishment, and degrading punishment. This Article places a negative duty on the state not to inflict the proscribed suffering on human beings, as well as a positive duty to ensure that these forms of suffering are not endured. Article 3, like Article 2, is one of the most fundamental provisions of the Convention (*Pretty v United Kingdom* (2002) 35 EHRR 1). The importance of the Article is reflected in its absolute and non-derogable status. Furthermore, the ECtHR has emphasized that Article 3 applies irrespective of the conduct of an applicant (*Chahal v United*

Kingdom (1996) 23 EHRR 413). In *Ireland v United Kingdom* (1978) 2 EHRR 25, the ECtHR considered the types of treatment that are prohibited by Article 3. It characterized the activities prohibited by Article 3 as follows:

(a) *Torture*: deliberate inhuman treatment causing very serious and cruel suffering.

(b) *Inhuman treatment*: treatment that causes intense physical and mental suffering.

(c) *Degrading treatment*: treatment that arouses in the victim a feeling of fear, anguish and inferiority capable of humiliating and debasing the victim and possibly breaking his or her physical or moral resistance.

As a threshold standard, treatment must attain 'a minimum level of severity'. In the *Ireland* decision, the ECtHR described the determination of this 'minimum level' as 'relative' and set out some criteria, such as the duration of the treatment, its physical or mental effects, and, in some circumstances, the sex, age, and state of health of the victim (at para. 162). These factors are relevant in two contexts: when determining whether the suffering caused is sufficient to amount to inhuman or degrading treatment or punishment; and when distinguishing between these lesser kinds of ill-treatment and torture. As the Convention is a living instrument, acts that have previously been classed as inhuman treatment, for example, could well be classed differently in the future (*Selmouni v France* (2000) 29 EHRR 403).

8.3.1 Torture

Torture is an aggravated form of inhuman or degrading treatment or punishment. Accordingly, classification of treatment as torture implies suffering of a particular intensity and cruelty (*Ireland v United Kingdom* (1978) 2 EHRR 25). In addition, the treatment will usually have a purpose such as obtaining information or a confession, or inflicting punishment (*The Greek Case* (1969) 11 YB 501).

In *Aydin v Turkey* (1997) 25 EHRR 251, the complainant had been raped, blindfolded, beaten, stripped, and sprayed with high pressure water while in the custody of the Turkish security forces. This treatment was held to amount to torture. The ECtHR commented that a finding of torture would have been made even in the absence of rape. The accumulation of similarly violent and humiliating treatment was classified as torture in *Selmouni v France* (2000) 29 EHRR 403, where the complainant had been urinated on, threatened with a blowtorch, and severely beaten by the police.

In *Denmark v Greece* (1969) 12 YB 1, the ECmHR held that torture had occurred. The ECmHR's finding was confirmed by the Committee of Ministers. The Athens security police were found to have used a system of torture and ill-treatment against political detainees. The ECmHR referred to non-physical as well as physical torture, describing 'the infliction of mental suffering by creating a state of anguish and stress by means other than bodily assault'. From this and the judgment in *Ireland v United Kingdom* (above), commentators have surmised that mental anguish alone may constitute torture if it reaches a certain level of severity. The ECmHR has mentioned mock executions, threats of death, and threats of reprisal against a detainee's family as evidence of non-physical torture without concluding that any of these equalled torture in fact.

8.3.2 Inhuman Treatment or Punishment

The ECtHR has taken a fairly robust approach to the meaning of inhuman treatment or punishment, giving substantial weight to the vulnerability of the complainant and the attitude of those inflicting the treatment (*Tomasi v France* (1992) 14 EHRR 1). Such an approach is demonstrated by *Dulas v Turkey* [2001] ECHR 25801/94, where the ECtHR considered the destruction of an elderly woman's home and property by security forces. This destruction was held to constitute inhuman treatment as it was carried out while she watched, and deprived her of means of shelter and support, which obliged her to leave the village and community where she had lived all her life.

Inhuman treatment or punishment will often be found to coexist with degrading treatment or punishment. For example, in *Keenan v United Kingdom* (2001) 3 EHRR 913, defects in the medical care provided to a mentally-ill person known to be a suicide risk were found to have contributed to the imposition of inhuman and degrading treatment and punishment. An additional contributory factor was the imposition of serious disciplinary punishment, which the ECtHR considered might well have threatened his physical and moral resistance. For a contrasting decision, see *Kudla v Poland* (2002) 35 EHRR 11.

8.3.3 Degrading Treatment or Punishment

The assessment of whether treatment or punishment is degrading depends on all the circumstances, with particular importance being placed on the nature and context of the treatment or punishment and the method and manner of its execution (*Tyrer v United Kingdom* (1978) 2 EHRR 1). As judicial punishment inevitably entails a degree of humiliation, degrading punishment must involve a degree of humiliation or debasement that exceeds that which is usual in punishment (*Tyrer*). Unlike torture, it is not necessary that there be any specific intention or purpose such as intent to debase, although an aim to humiliate or debase will be highly relevant (*Peers v Greece* (2001) 33 EHRR 51).

In *Ireland v United Kingdom* (1978) 2 EHRR 25, the ECtHR examined five techniques used by the British Government to interrogate prisoners allegedly involved in terrorism. These techniques included forcing them to stand against a wall in an uncomfortable position, hooding, subjecting them to loud, continuous noise, and depriving them of food, drinks, and sleep. Although not rising to the level of torture, the ECtHR determined that these practices constituted degrading treatment and, therefore, violated Article 3 (at paras 167–8).

Detention conditions have been held to constitute degrading treatment in several cases (for example, *Peers v Greece* (above) and *Price v United Kingdom* (2002) 34 EHRR 53). In *Price*, the ECtHR held that the detention of a severely disabled person in conditions where she was dangerously cold, risked developing sores because her bed was too hard or unreachable, and was unable to go to the toilet or keep clean without the greatest of difficulty, constituted degrading treatment contrary to Article 3, despite the absence of any intention to subject the complainant to degrading treatment. In a separate opinion in *Price*, Judge Bratza, joined by Judge Costa, stated that in the circumstances, the primary responsibility for the violation lay with the judicial authorities who had decided to sentence the complainant to imprisonment without ensuring that there were adequate facilities for detaining her and that her special needs could be met while in detention. The view that Article 3 may be breached through a lack of planning may have wider ramifications in relation to issues such as the treatment of those detained because of their mental health and any failure to provide appropriate palliative care in hospitals.

Race discrimination may constitute degrading treatment. In *East African Asians v United Kingdom* (1973) 3 EHRR 76, the applicants were British passport holders and had been refused permission to take up residence in the United Kingdom. The ECmHR considered that:

> the racial discrimination, to which the applicants have been publicly subjected by the application of . . . immigration legislation, constitutes an interference with their human dignity which . . . amounted to 'degrading treatment' in the sense of Article 3 of the Convention.

8.3.4 State Responsibility

Both Strasbourg bodies have ruled that the state is responsible for the actions of its agents under Article 3. In *Cyprus v Turkey* (1976) 4 EHRR 482, the ECmHR found the state responsible for rapes committed by its soldiers. It held that satisfactory actions had not been taken to prevent these attacks and that disciplinary measures after the conduct were insufficient. To similar effect, the ECtHR commented in *Ireland v United Kingdom* (1978) 2 EHRR 25 that the higher authorities of a state are strictly liable for the conduct of their subordinates: 'they are under a duty to impose their will on subordinates and cannot shelter behind their inability to ensure that it is respected.'

8.3.5 Positive Obligation

As well as refraining from inflicting torture, Article 3 places states under a positive obligation to prevent the proscribed treatment. Accordingly, states have a positive obligation to ensure that individuals within their jurisdiction are not subjected to torture or other forms of ill-treatment, including ill-treatment administered by a private individual (for example, *Mahmut Kaya v Turkey* (1999) 28 EHRR 1 and *Z and Others v United Kingdom* (2002) 34 EHRR 3). However, the obligation does not extend to the provision of a lawful opportunity for assisted suicide in circumstances of significant physical and mental suffering (*Pretty v United Kingdom* (2002) 35 EHRR 1).

This positive obligation manifests itself in the principle that a state may not extradite an individual to a country where there are substantial grounds for believing that there is a real risk that he or she would be subjected to torture or ill-treatment (*Soering v United Kingdom* (1989) 11 EHRR 439). In *Chahal v United Kingdom* (1997) 23 EHRR 413, the ECtHR held that a deportation of a person to a country where there was a real risk that he could be tortured could offend Article 3, because of the positive obligation within the Article to prevent torture. The ECtHR made the same ruling in *D v United Kingdom* (1997) 24 EHRR 423, although the reasoning was based on the lack of treatment the receiving country would be able to provide for the applicant, who was in the advanced stages of AIDS and had no family in the receiving state. In *Soering v United Kingdom*, the ECtHR took the view that extradition to the United States, where the applicant was likely to receive the death sentence for murder, would contravene Article 3. While the death penalty *per se* is not prohibited by Article 3, the conditions of detention, the length of time between sentencing and execution, and the personal circumstances of the individual may amount to a violation of Article 3.

Another case involving the state's positive obligations was *A v United Kingdom* (1999) 27 EHRR 611, in which A had been hit by his stepfather with a stick. The stepfather was charged with assault occasioning actual bodily harm. The stepfather contended that the assault amounted to reasonable punishment, which is a defence to a charge of assault of a child by a parent, and he was acquitted. The ECtHR decided there was a violation of Article 3 because the law failed to give adequate safeguards in insufficiently defining what constituted 'reasonable punishment' (see also *Tyrer v United Kingdom* (1978) 2 EHRR 1, *Campbell v United Kingdom* (1982) 4 EHRR 293, and *Costello-Roberts v United Kingdom* (1993) 19 EHRR 112).

8.3.6 Investigative Obligation

As in the case of Article 2, the ECtHR has held that the combined effect of Articles 1 and 3 is to require an effective official investigation into credible allegations of serious ill-treatment by state agents (*Assenov v Bulgaria* (1998) 28 EHRR 652). This investigation, as with that under Article 2, should be capable of leading to the identification and punishment of those responsible for the violation of Article 3.

8.3.7 Human Rights Act Decisions

Like Article 2, Article 3 has been raised before the domestic courts on a number of occasions and in a diverse range of contexts. Thus far, the approach of the domestic courts has been largely consistent with that of the ECtHR.

Article 3 has featured prominently in a number of challenges to decisions to remove individuals from the United Kingdom. In *R (R) v Chief Immigration Officer* (2000) *The Times*, 29 November, it was unsuccessfully argued that deportation to Colombia of a person who was HIV positive violated Article 3. The Court held that adequate treatment would be available in Colombia. This decision indicates that *D v United Kingdom* (see 8.3.5 above) has been regarded as an exceptional case in the domestic case law. See also *X v Secretary of State for the Home Department* [2001] 1 WLR 740 and *McPherson v Secretary of State* [2001] EWCA Civ 1955.

Criminal sentences have been another particularly active field of Article 3 complaints. In *R v Offen* [2001] 1 WLR 253, the Court of Appeal accepted that the imposition of an automatic life sentence, in circumstances where the defendant posed no significant risk to the public, could constitute inhuman and degrading treatment. See also *R v Kelly* [2001] EWCA Crim 1751. The same sentencing provision was unsuccessfully challenged in *R v Drew* [2001] Crim LR 224, where it was argued that sentencing a mentally disordered offender to life imprisonment was inhuman and degrading. In the absence of any evidence that an offender sentenced to life imprisonment would not receive appropriate medical treatment, no issue was held to arise under Article 3. This decision suggests that the domestic courts will follow *Keenan v United Kingdom* (2001) 3 EHRR 913 (see 8.3.2 above).

Conditions of detention came under challenge in *R (Russell and Wharrie) v Secretary of State* [2000] 1 WLR 2027. The Court indicated that a failure to provide prisoners with adequate food 'may well' breach Article 3.

R v H [2001] EWCA Crim 1024 demonstrates that jury directions on the defence of reasonable chastisement have now been modified to comply with *A v United Kingdom* (see 8.3.5 above).

In a recent decision, the Court of Appeal held that in the absence of other sources of support, to withdraw financial support from destitute asylum seekers who lack the means of obtaining adequate accommodation or for meeting their essential needs would be a violation of Article 3 if there was a real risk that destitution leading to injury to health would occur (*R (Q and others) v Secretary of State for the Home Department* [2003] EWCA Civ 364).

8.4 ARTICLE 4: PROHIBITION OF SLAVERY AND FORCED LABOUR

1. No one shall be held in slavery or servitude.

2. No one shall be required to perform forced or compulsory labour.

3. For the purpose of this Article the term 'forced or compulsory labour' shall not include:

    (a) any work required to be done in the ordinary course of detention imposed according to the provisions of Article 5 of this Convention or during conditional release from such detention;

(b) any service of a military character or, in case of conscientious objectors in countries where they are recognized, service exacted instead of compulsory military service;

(c) any service exacted in case of an emergency or calamity threatening the life or well-being of the community;

(d) any work or service which forms part of normal civic obligations.

Article 4 concerns the twin issues of slavery or servitude and forced or compulsory labour. The Article 4(1) prohibition on slavery and servitude is another of the rights from which no derogation is allowed under Article 15. However, the Article 4(2) prohibition on forced or compulsory labour is both derogable under Article 15 and subject to the exceptions listed in Article 4(3). Relatively few Article 4 complaints have been heard by the ECtHR or ECmHR, and none has been upheld. Of those complaints that have been made, only a very small number have been against the United Kingdom.

8.4.1 Slavery and Servitude

Slavery has not been defined by the ECtHR or ECmHR. However, drawing on historical notions of slavery, a claim of ownership of the person is an integral element (see, for example, Article 1 of the Slavery Convention 1926). Servitude differs from slavery in that no ownership of the person is claimed. The ECmHR suggested, in *Van Droogenbroeck* (Case B 44 (1980) Com Rep, para. 79), that:

... in addition to the obligation to provide another with certain services the concept of servitude includes the obligation on the part of the 'serf' to live on another's property and the impossibility of changing his condition.

The ECtHR's judgment in the *Van Droogenbroeck* case (*Van Droogenbroeck v Belgium* (1982) 4 EHRR 443) provides further guidance as to the meaning of servitude. There, the ECtHR found that a sentence of two years in prison, followed by 10 years 'at the Government's disposal' did not amount to 'that particularly serious form of deprivation of liberty' that constitutes servitude (at paras 58–9). It went on to rule that this sentence 'did not go beyond what is "ordinary" in this context since it was calculated to assist him in reintegrating himself into society'.

8.4.2 Forced or Compulsory Labour

The ECtHR and ECmHR have taken a generous approach to the concept of labour. Rather than being limited to physical labour, Article 4(2) is applicable to all forms of work (see, for example, *Van der Mussele v Belgium* (1983) 6 EHRR 163). In order for labour to be forced or compulsory, the work must be performed involuntarily and the requirement to do the work must be unjust or oppressive, or the work itself involve avoidable hardship (*X v Federal Republic of Germany* (1974) 17 YB 148, drawing on the International Labour Organization Convention of 1930). There is clearly scope for overlap between the concepts of forced labour and servitude.

The complaints deemed admissible under Article 4(2) have usually fallen into the categories of treatment of prisoners, or professionals being compelled to provide their services free to the community. In *Van der Mussele v Belgium*, a barrister tried to extend the boundaries of Article 4 when he claimed that being made to do pro bono legal work for indigent defendants violated the Article 4 prohibition of forced labour. The key question became whether the applicant had 'offered himself voluntarily' when he was taken on as a trainee barrister. The ECtHR asked whether the labour imposed 'a burden which was so excessive or disproportionate to the advantages attached to the future exercise of the profession that the service could not be treated as having been voluntarily accepted'. Ruling against the barrister, the ECtHR relied on the fact that he had entered the profession of his own will, knowing that pro bono work was expected of him.

8.4.3 Human Rights Act Decisions

We are not aware of any cases under the Human Rights Act in which Article 4 has been raised.

8.5 ARTICLE 5: RIGHT TO LIBERTY AND SECURITY

    1.   Everyone has the right to liberty and security of person. No one shall be deprived of his liberty save in the following cases and in accordance with a procedure prescribed by law:
- (a)   the lawful detention of a person after conviction by a competent court;
- (b)   the lawful arrest or detention of a person for non-compliance with the lawful order of a court or in order to secure the fulfilment of any obligation prescribed by law;
- (c)   the lawful arrest or detention of a person effected for the purpose of bringing him before the competent legal authority on a reasonable suspicion of having committed an offence or when it is reasonably considered necessary to prevent his committing an offence or fleeing after having done so;
- (d)   the detention of a minor by lawful order for the purpose of educational supervision or his lawful detention for the purpose of bringing him before the competent legal authority;
- (e)   the lawful detention of persons for the prevention of the spreading of infectious diseases, of persons of unsound mind, alcoholics or drug addicts or vagrants;
- (f)   the lawful arrest or detention of a person to prevent his effecting an unauthorised entry into the country or of a person against whom action is being taken with a view to deportation or extradition.

    2.   Everyone who is arrested shall be informed promptly, in a language which he understands, of the reasons for his arrest and of any charge against him.

    3.   Everyone arrested or detained in accordance with the provisions of paragraph 1(c) of this Article shall be brought promptly before a judge or other officer authorised by law

to exercise judicial power and shall be entitled to trial within a reasonable time or to release pending trial. Release may be conditioned by guarantees to appear for trial.

4.   Everyone who is deprived of his liberty by arrest or detention shall be entitled to take proceedings by which the lawfulness of his detention shall be decided speedily by a court and his release ordered if the detention is not lawful.

5.   Everyone who has been the victim of arrest or detention in contravention of the provisions of this Article shall have an enforceable right to compensation.

Article 5 protects the 'right to liberty and security of person'. This is a combined right, with the right to security of person having no separate meaning from the right to liberty. Accordingly the phrase, 'right to liberty and security of person', should be read as a whole, with 'security of person' being understood in the context of physical liberty (*East African Asians v United Kingdom* (1973) 3 EHRR 76). The specific concern of the right is to ensure that no one is deprived of his or her liberty in an 'arbitrary fashion' (*Engel v Netherlands* (1976) 1 EHRR 647, at para. 58). In addition to protecting the basic right to liberty, Article 5 provides persons who are deprived of their liberty with a number of procedural rights, which are detailed in paras (2)–(5).

The Article 5 rights are not absolute and can be derogated from under Article 15. Indeed, following the attacks in the USA on 11 September 2001, the United Kingdom lodged a derogation from Article 5(1) with the Council of Europe. The purpose of the derogation was to enable the detention of suspected international terrorists under the provisions of the specially enacted Anti-Terrorism, Crime and Security Act 2001. This legislation enables non-United Kingdom nationals, who are suspected to be international terrorists, to be detained without charge or trial in circumstances where they cannot be removed from the United Kingdom. The lawfulness of the derogation was upheld by the Court of Appeal in *A and others v Secretary of State for the Home Department* [2002] EWCA Civ 1502. This derogation is discussed further at 8.15.2 below.

8.5.1 Deprivation of Liberty

Article 5 is not engaged by every restriction on an individual's liberty. The provision is concerned with actual deprivation of liberty rather than with mere restrictions on liberty or movement (*Engel v Netherlands* (1976) 1 EHRR 647, at para. 58). As the ECtHR noted in *H.M. v Switzerland* [2002] ECHR 39187/98, restrictions on freedom of movement are the concern of Article 2 of Protocol 4 (which is not a Convention right for the purposes of the Human Rights Act). However, it will not always be easy to distinguish between a deprivation of and a restriction on liberty, since the difference is one of degree rather than of nature or substance (*Ashingdane v United Kingdom* (1985) 7 EHRR 528, at para. 41). Factors such as the type, duration, effects, and manner of implementation of the impugned conduct will provide guidance as to whether a situation falls within Article 5 or within Article 2 of Protocol 4.

8.5.2 Exceptions to the Right to Liberty

Article 5(1) sets out an exhaustive list of exceptions to the prohibition on deprivation of liberty. The list in paras (a)–(f) is to be given a narrow interpretation (*Winterwerp v Netherlands* (1979) 2 EHRR 387) and the excepted forms of detention must be both lawful and in accordance with a procedure prescribed by law. In *Amuur v France* (1996) 22 EHRR 533, the ECtHR stated (at para. 50) that:

> Where the 'lawfulness' of detention is in issue, including the question whether 'a procedure prescribed by law' has been followed, the Convention refers essentially to national law and lays down the obligation to conform to the substantive and procedural rules of national law, but it requires in addition that any deprivation of liberty should be in keeping with the purpose of Article 5, namely to protect the individual from arbitrariness.

Article 5(1)(a)

Article 5(1)(a) permits 'the lawful detention of a person after conviction by a competent court'. A competent court under this Article is one with jurisdiction to try the case and, presumably, one that complies with the provisions of Article 6 (*X v Austria* (1987) 11 EHRR 112). This Article is concerned only with the fact of detention and not with the conditions of the detention. In order for a detention to be 'lawful' there must be a court judgment that justifies the confinement, as well as lawful procedures followed to effect the detention. Strasbourg has held that Article 5(1)(a) does not permit the ECtHR to review convictions or sentences imposed by a domestic court, though any such decision would have to comply with Article 6.

Article 5(1)(b)

Article 5(1)(b) sanctions the detention of a person who has failed to observe a court order or obligation. This includes failure to pay a court fine and refusal to submit to a court-ordered medical examination. The obligations may include military service or the filing of tax returns. The ECtHR has held that the order or obligation must be clear, the person detained must usually be given an opportunity to comply with the order or obligation, and the detention must be the only reasonable way to secure the fulfilment of the order or obligation.

In *McVeigh v United Kingdom* (1981) 25 DR 15, the obligation was to submit to 'further examination' upon entering Great Britain. Three men were detained for 45 hours under suspicion of terrorist activities, but were released and not charged with any crimes. The ECmHR ruled that in 'limited circumstances of a pressing nature' Article 5(1)(b) could be extended to cover periods of detention necessary to fulfil an obligation. It went on to state, at p. 42:

> In considering whether such circumstances exist, account must be taken . . . of the nature of the obligation. It is necessary to consider whether its fulfilment is [a] matter of immediate necessity and whether the circumstances are such that no other means of securing fulfilment is reasonably practicable. A balance must be drawn between the importance in a democratic society of securing the immediate fulfilment of the obligation in question, and

the importance of the right to liberty. The duration of the period of detention is also a relevant factor in drawing such a balance.

Article 5(1)(c)

Article 5(1)(c) concerns the arrest or detention of suspects while involved in the administration of criminal justice. Arrest is lawful only if it is based on a reasonable suspicion that a person has committed a crime, or when it is reasonably considered necessary to prevent a person from committing a crime or from fleeing after committing one. The test of reasonable suspicion is an objective one; an honestly held suspicion is insufficient (*Fox v United Kingdom* (1990) 13 EHRR 157). The applicants had been arrested under the Northern Ireland (Emergency Provisions) Act 1978, which, at that time, required only that the arresting official 'genuinely and honestly' suspected the person arrested to be a terrorist. The ECtHR found a violation of Article 5(1)(c) on the basis that 'genuine and honest' suspicion was a lower standard than reasonable suspicion and was, therefore, not acceptable under the Convention. In the ECtHR's view, 'reasonable suspicion supposes the existence of facts or information which would satisfy an objective observer that the person concerned may have committed the offence' (para. 32).

In *Murray v United Kingdom* (1994) 19 EHRR 193, another terrorist case, the ECtHR was less robust in its defence of Article 5(1)(c), but the principles in the case are context-specific and may not apply in non-terrorist cases.

An arrest is legal under Article 5(1)(c) only if the purpose is to bring the detainee before a competent legal authority. The fact that the suspect may not ultimately be brought before a court or charged with a crime does not undermine the arrest since 'the existence of such a purpose must be considered independently of its achievement' (*Brogan v United Kingdom* (1988) 11 EHRR 117).

Article 5(1)(d)

Article 5(1)(d) covers the detention of minors. The accepted European classification of a 'minor' is a person under the age of 18. This exception is designed primarily to cover education and the detention of children for purposes such as placement in care or secure accommodation.

Article 5(1)(e)

Article 5(1)(e) permits the detention of those with infectious diseases, persons of unsound mind, alcoholics, drug addicts, and vagrants. These people are specified because 'they have to be considered as occasionally dangerous for public safety' and 'their own interests may necessitate their detention' (*Guzzardi v Italy* (1980) 3 EHRR 333). In our view, a high standard of justification would be necessary to render such detention proportionate. The mere fact of being, for example, a drug addict will be unlikely to justify detention under Article 5(1)(e) without some other factor (such as objective reason to believe that the person in question would harm himself or herself or others). This view is supported by the ECtHR's decision in

Johnson v United Kingdom (1999) 27 EHRR 296, where it held that three elements will be necessary to justify the detention of persons of unsound mind:

(a) the individual must be reliably shown to be of unsound mind;

(b) the mental disorder must be of a kind or degree warranting compulsory confinement;

(c) the mental disorder must be persisting.

In *Johnson*, the applicant was a patient detained at a mental hospital who was found by the Mental Health Tribunal to be no longer suffering from a mental disorder. He was conditionally discharged, but no hostel accommodation could be found for him and he had to remain in hospital. Once it was shown that the preconditions justifying the applicant's detention had ceased to exist, the ECtHR accepted that there might be a delay in allowing the unconditional discharge of the patient into the community. However, the ECtHR also stressed that appropriate safeguards should be in place so as to ensure that any deferment of discharge was not unreasonably delayed. It therefore found that the interference with the applicant's right to liberty under Article 5(1) could not be justified by the exception in relation to persons of unsound mind under Article 5(1)(e).

The combination of the requirement of 'lawfulness' under Article 5(1)(e) and the obligation on the state to allow judicial review of detention under Article 5(4) has led to a number of decisions against measures in states, including the United Kingdom, relating to the detention of psychiatric patients (for example, *X v United Kingdom* (1980) Series B 41).

Article 5(1)(f)

Article 5(1)(f) provides wide grounds for deprivation of liberty. In *Zamir v United Kingdom* (1983) 40 DR 42, it was held that, in a deportation context, the lawfulness of the detention depends only on whether the intention behind the detention was the deportation of the detainee. The ECtHR will not examine the merits of the decision to deport, with the scope of its review being limited 'to examining whether there is a legal basis for the detention and whether the decision of the courts on the question of lawfulness could be described as arbitrary in light of the facts of the case'. The ECmHR expanded the scope of Strasbourg review in *Lynas v Switzerland* (1976) 6 DR 141, where it held that detention can cease to be lawful if the extradition or deportation proceedings are not carried out diligently or amount to an abuse of power (see also *Chahal v United Kingdom* (1997) 23 EHRR 413). The *Chahal* decision introduced a further limit on state power under Article 5(1)(f) by finding that detention is justified only if actual deportation proceedings are in progress.

8.5.3 Procedural Safeguards

Article 5(2)

Under Article 5(2), everyone arrested has the right to be informed in a language which he or she understands of the reasons for the arrest and of any charge against him or her. The purpose of this obligation is to enable the arrested person to challenge the lawfulness of the detention (*X v United Kingdom* (1982) 4 EHRR 188). Reasons need not be in writing and formal notification may not be necessary if the reasons are made clear during the arrest. However, in *Ireland v United Kingdom* (1978) 2 EHRR 28, the ECtHR held that it was not enough to tell an arrested person that he or she was being held pursuant to the provisions of emergency legislation.

Article 5(3)

Article 5(3) requires that anyone arrested shall be brought promptly before a judge or other officer authorized by law to exercise judicial power. The aim of this requirement is to impose a limit on the length of detention authorized by Article 5(1)(c) and thereby ensure that the prosecuting authorities do not unreasonably prolong provisional detention (*Wemhoff v Germany* (1968) 1 EHRR 25 and *Neumeister v Austria* (1968) 1 EHRR 91).

Determining the reasonableness of a period of detention is a matter of fact and degree. In *Wemhoff v Germany*, the ECtHR developed a two-part test. First, the ECtHR will review whether the reasons advanced by the state for continued detention are relevant and sufficient, that is, whether the domestic determination that the public interest outweighs the right to liberty in any given case can be sustained. Applying this part of the test, the ECtHR has recognized that the argument that a suspect might flee loses practicality as time passes, since it is likely that periods in detention on remand would be deducted from any period of imprisonment imposed on conviction (*Neumeister v Austria* (1968) 1 EHRR 91, at para. 6). Secondly, even if the first limb is satisfied, the ECmHR and ECtHR will go on to consider whether the proceedings have been unduly prolonged by avoidable delay. Periods of detention that have been held to contravene Article 5(3) include detention without charge for four days and six hours (*Brogan v United Kingdom* (1988) 11 EHRR 117) and detention in police custody for 14 days (*Aksoy v Turkey* (1996) 23 EHRR 553).

The presumption is that bail should be granted, and denial of bail must be justified by relevant and sufficient reasons. Reasons that are justified include:

(a) a risk that the accused will fail to appear at the trial (*Stögmüller v Austria* (1969) 1 EHRR 155);

(b) a risk that the accused may interfere with the course of justice (*Wemhoff v Germany*, above);

(c) a risk of further offences (*Toth v Austria* (1991) 14 EHRR 551); and

(d) the preservation of public order (*Letellier v France* (1991) 14 EHRR 83).

In any of these situations, the reason advanced must be justified by the facts in the particular case. In the case of *Caballero v United Kingdom* (2000) 30 EHRR 643, the denial of bail under s. 25 of the Criminal Justice and Public Order Act 1994 was held to be a breach of Article 5(3). This section has now been amended to be Convention and Human Rights Act compliant.

Article 5(4)

Under Article 5(4), anyone under any form of detention must be able to challenge the lawfulness of that detention. Review must be by a court and must be speedy. The 'court' does not necessarily have to be a classic court of law, which is formally part of the state's judicial machinery. However, the body must 'exhibit the necessary judicial procedures and safeguards appropriate to the kind of deprivation of liberty in question, including most importantly independence of the executive and of the parties' (*Benjamin and Wilson v United Kingdom* (2003) 36 EHRR 1, at para. 33). In addition, as the ECtHR emphasized in *Benjamin and Wilson*, the body must have the ability to decide the lawfulness of the detention and to order release if detention is found to be unlawful.

The ECtHR has deliberately refrained from stating timeframes that will or will not be considered speedy; the issue of 'speedily' cannot be assessed in the abstract. Accordingly, the approach of the ECtHR is to examine the particular facts of the case before it and to consider whether, in those specific circumstances, there was a failure to proceed with reasonable speed. However, by way of example, in *Zamir v United Kingdom* (1983) 40 DR 42 the ECmHR held that seven weeks between applying for habeas corpus and the actual hearing violated Article 5(4).

In cases of prolonged detention, this right has ongoing effect and the Article requires the availability of a process to enable the lawfulness of the detention to be reviewed at reasonable intervals (*Bezicheri v Italy* (1989) 12 EHRR 210). There has been a series of key cases where the ECtHR has held that Article 5(4) requires a regular review of the lawfulness of continuing detention, particularly where the circumstances of the detention change over time. Thus, the lawfulness of detention in psychiatric hospitals (*X v United Kingdom* (1980) Series B 41); during post-tariff mandatory life imprisonment, where the Home Secretary has a power of veto over Parole Board decisions (*Stafford v United Kingdom* (2002) 35 EHRR 32); during the discretionary period of discretionary life sentences (*Weeks v United Kingdom* (1987) 10 EHRR 293 and *Thynne v United Kingdom* (1990) 13 EHRR 666); and of young people convicted of murder and detained (*Hussain v United Kingdom* (1996) 22 EHRR 1 and *T and V v United Kingdom* (1999) 30 EHRR 121) has been challenged successfully. These cases have had at their core the fact that the legality of the detention was based on the extent to which the person would be dangerous if released. The assessment of this changed over time, and thus so did the justification and therefore legality of the detention

The ECtHR held in *Winterwerp v Netherlands* (1979) 2 EHRR 387 that the judicial proceedings referred to in Article 5(4) need not always be attended by the same guarantees as those required by Article 6(1) for civil or criminal litigation. However, in the more recent decision of *Schops v Germany* [2002] ECHR 25116/94, the ECtHR stated that proceedings under Article 5(4) should, to the largest extent possible in the context of an ongoing investigation, meet the basic requirements of a fair trial.

8.5.4 Right to Compensation

Article 5(5) guarantees a right to compensation if a person has been detained in violation of Article 5. This provision requires a binding award of compensation that can be enforced by the courts (see, for example, *Brogan v United Kingdom* (1988) 11 EHRR 117, *Fox v United Kingdom* (1990) 13 EHRR 157, *Caballero v United Kingdom* (2000) 30 EHRR 643, and *Curley v United Kingdom* (2001) 31 EHRR 14).

After the requirements of this provision were brought to the Government's attention, it amended the Human Rights Bill so as to make an exception to the general rule that damages could not be obtained against a court; damages can now be obtained where a court has permitted an unlawful detention (Human Rights Act 1998, s. 9(3)–(5)).

8.5.5 Human Rights Act Decisions

Article 5 has had a significant domestic impact in the fields of criminal, sentencing, mental health, and immigration law.

In the area of criminal law, a report on the impact of the Human Rights Act on bail procedures has been published by the Law Commission (*Bail and the Human Rights Act 1998*, Law Com 269). The House of Lords had an opportunity to consider Article 5 in the context of criminal charges in *R (Wardle) v Leeds Crown Court* [2001] 2 WLR 865, where custody time limit provisions were unsuccessfully challenged.

There have been a number of challenges to mandatory sentences under Article 5. In *R v Offen* [2001] 1 WLR 253, for example, the Convention compliance of s. 2 of the Crime (Sentences) Act 1997 (now s. 109 of the Powers of the Criminal Courts (Sentencing) Act 2000) came under challenge. This provision requires courts to impose an automatic life sentence on a person convicted of a serious offence for the second time, unless there are 'exceptional circumstances', which justify its not doing so. The Court of Appeal considered that in the way s. 2 had previously been interpreted, it could result in offenders being sentenced to life imprisonment when there was no objective justification for that sentence, risking violation of Articles 5 and 3. The Court applied s. 3 of the Human Rights Act to reach a revised, Convention compliant interpretation of s. 2.

Mandatory life sentences (the only sentence available for murder) have been another point of challenge in the sentencing field. In *R v Lichniak* [2002] UKHL 47, the House of Lords held that mandatory life sentences were not inconsistent with Article 5. However, the Secretary of State's role in fixing tariffs in the context of mandatory life sentences was successfully challenged in *R (Anderson and Taylor) v Secretary of State for the Home Department* [2002] UKHL 46. In Anderson, the House of Lords declared that s. 29 of the Crime (Sentences) Act 1997, which permits the Secretary of State a role in fixing tariffs in the context of mandatory life sentences, is incompatible with Article 6(1) of the Convention. Although the decision is based on Article 6 rather than on Article 5, it has the practical effect of achieving domestic compliance with recent Strasbourg principles, including those articulated in *Stafford v United Kingdom* (2002) 35 EHRR 32 (see 8.5.3 above).

One of the few declarations of incompatibility and remedial orders have been made in relation to Article 5. In *R (H) v Mental Health Review Tribunal* [2001] EWCA Civ 415, the Court of Appeal declared that ss. 72(1) and 73(1) of the Mental Health Act 1983 were incompatible with Article 5(1) and (4). The effect of these provisions was that where a restricted patient applied to a Mental Health Review Tribunal for discharge from detention in hospital, the burden of proof was placed on the patient to prove that the criteria justifying his or her detention no longer existed. A remedial order was subsequently made (the Mental Health Act 1983 (Remedial) Order 2001).

Other key decisions in the mental health area include *R (C) v London and South West Region Mental Health Review Tribunal* [2001] EWCA Civ 1110 and *R (von Bradenburg) v East London and City Mental Health NHS Trust* [2001] EWCA Civ 239. In the latter case, the Court of Appeal held that the Mental Health Review Tribunal, which has the power to order compulsory admission to hospital, possesses sufficient judicial attributes to comply with Article 5(4). Leave to appeal to the House of Lords has been granted.

The House of Lords decision, *R (Saadi and Others) v Secretary of State for the Home Department* [2002] UKHL 41, concerned the temporary detention of asylum seekers for the purposes of expediting consideration of asylum applications. It was held that such detention comes within Article 5(1)(f) and is both proportionate and reasonable.

As indicated above, the Court of Appeal's decision on the United Kingdom's Article 5 derogation (*A and others v Secretary of State for the Home Department* [2002] EWCA Civ 1502) is discussed at 8.15.2.

8.6 ARTICLE 6: RIGHT TO A FAIR TRIAL

1.   In the determination of his civil rights and obligations or of any criminal charge against him, everyone is entitled to a fair and public hearing within a reasonable time by an independent and impartial tribunal established by law. Judgment shall be pronounced publicly but the press and public may be excluded from all or part of the trial in the interests of morals, public order or national security in a democratic society, where the interests of juveniles or the protection of the private life of the parties so require, or to the extent strictly necessary in the opinion of the court in special circumstances where publicity would prejudice the interests of justice.

2.   Everyone charged with a criminal offence shall be presumed innocent until proved guilty according to law.

3.   Everyone charged with a criminal offence has the following minimum rights:
  (a)   to be informed promptly, in a language which he understands and in detail, of the nature and cause of the accusation against him;

(b) to have adequate time and facilities for the preparation of his defence;
(c) to defend himself in person or through legal assistance of his own choosing or, if he has not sufficient means to pay for legal assistance, to be given it free when the interests of justice so require;
(d) to examine or have examined witnesses against him and to obtain the attendance and examination of witnesses on his behalf under the same conditions as witnesses against him;
(e) to have the free assistance of an interpreter if he cannot understand or speak the language used in court.

Article 6 concerns the right to a fair trial. This right has 'a position of pre-eminence in the Convention' (Harris, O'Boyle, and Warbrick, *Law of the European Convention on Human Rights* (London: Butterworths, 1995), at 164; 2nd edn forthcoming (London: Butterworths, 2003)). Its central position is reflected in the fact that there have been more applications to Strasbourg concerning Article 6 than any other Article in the Convention.

8.6.1 Article 6(1)

Article 6(1) is complex and contains several different elements. However, at its core is the concern that individuals should have a fair hearing and a right of access to the courts. This right is applicable only in the context of the determination of civil rights and obligations or of a criminal charge. Accordingly, the meaning of the undefined phrases, 'civil rights and obligations' and 'criminal charge', controls the sphere of application of the right of access. Also open to interpretation are the component subrights, such as the right to a 'public' hearing. The ECtHR has emphasized that given the prominent place of Article 6(1) in a democratic society, there can be no justification for taking a restrictive approach when interpreting its various elements (*Moreira de Azevedo v Portugal* (1990) 13 EHRR 721, at para. 66).

The Article 6(1) right is absolute. However, the constituent rights are not absolute and may be limited in accordance with the general principles of limitation under the Convention (see 2.4). However, a central consideration in any limitation of the constituent rights is whether the essence of the overarching right to a fair hearing is preserved (see, for example, *Heaney and McGuinness v Ireland* (2001) 33 EHRR 12).

8.6.2 Determination

Article 6(1) is applicable only to the 'determination' of civil rights or criminal charges. In general, determination in the civil context involves a decision on the merits; while in the criminal context, a final decision as to guilt or innocence is necessary. Accordingly, a merely investigative procedure will not attract the protection of Article 6(1) (*Fayed v United Kingdom* (1994) 18 EHRR 393). The issue of whether decisions on procedural costs amount to a 'determination' has come before the ECtHR on several occasions. The ECtHR's recent approach has been to view costs proceedings as a continuation of the substantive litigation and accordingly as part of a 'determination' of civil rights and obligations (for example, *Robins v United Kingdom* (1998) 26 EHRR 527 and *Ziegler v Switzerland* [2002] ECHR 33499/96).

8.6.3 Criminal Charge

The interpretation of 'criminal charge' involves consideration of the meaning of both 'criminal' and 'charge'. A person will face a 'charge', for the purposes of Article 6(1), when his or her situation has been 'substantially affected' (*Heaney and McGuinness v Ireland* (2001) 33 EHRR 12 and *Quinn v Ireland* [2000] ECHR 36887/97). While the meaning of 'charge' is relatively uncomplicated, the meaning of 'criminal' has proved more complex, particularly in light of the potentially fine distinction between disciplinary and criminal charges (for example, *Engel v Netherlands* (1976) 1 EHRR 647). When deciding whether an act is a 'criminal' offence for the purposes of the Convention, the primary criteria are: domestic classification; nature of the offence; and severity of the penalty incurred (*Engel v Netherlands*). If a national court classifies an act as a criminal offence, the ECtHR and ECmHR will not challenge this determination; but if an act is classified as non-criminal in domestic law, this fact is relevant although not definitive (for example, *Lauko v Slovenia* (2001) 33 EHRR 40). Even loss of liberty as a punishment is not conclusive. In *Engel v Netherlands*, the fact that Engel faced a penalty of two days' 'strict arrest', for offences against military discipline, was not enough to categorize the offence as criminal. Deciding which side of the line a case will fall is not always easy. In *McFeeley v United Kingdom* (1981) 3 EHRR 161, the ECmHR considered whether Article 6 applied to decisions by prison governors dealing with disciplinary adjudications, and concluded that although the results imposed could be severe, the process had not reached the required level to make it a trial of a criminal offence. However, this decision should be contrasted with the more recent judgment of *Ezeh and Connors v United Kingdom* (2002) 35 EHRR 28, which held that prison disciplinary proceedings could amount to a determination under Article 6.

8.6.4 Civil Right

The Article 6(1) right to a fair and public hearing is also enjoyed by an individual in the determination of his or her civil rights and obligations. In many respects, this is a wide phrase: issues arising in contract, commercial law, insurance law, succession, family law, and real and personal property are generally regarded as matters to which Article 6 applies. Even a pending negligence claim is likely to amount to a civil right for the purposes of Article 6, since such a claim can be a possession for the purposes of Protocol 1, Article 1 (*Pressos Compañia Naviera SA v Belgium* (1995) 21 EHRR 301, though the ECtHR declared it unnecessary to deal with the Article 6 issue in that case). It should be noted, however, that tax disputes do not involve civil rights or obligations, for the purposes of Article 6(1) (*Ferrazzini v Italy* (2002) 34 EHRR 1068).

However, despite the generous approach to the phrase, it is sometimes difficult to decide whether a case concerns what the Strasbourg institutions would regard as a 'civil right'. The concept is an autonomous one: the classification is not necessarily the same as that in the domestic law of the country concerned (for example, *James v United Kingdom* (1986) 8 EHRR 123).

'Pure' public law rights are generally not regarded as 'civil rights'. This means that, for example, the 'due process' guarantees in Article 6 do not apply to such issues as the categorization of prisoners (*Brady v United Kingdom* (1979) 3 EHRR 297), or decisions involving the entry or removal of immigrants (*Uppal v United Kingdom* (1980) 3 EHRR 391). Nor, it would appear, is the right to discretionary benefits a civil right. However, the limitation has been much reduced in recent years, with the Strasbourg institutions increasingly willing to find a 'civil right' within, or alongside, a public law right. So, for example, in *Gaygasuz v Austria* (1996) 23 EHRR 365, an emergency assistance benefit with contributory elements was property within the scope of Protocol 1, Article 1, and therefore was a 'civil right' for the purposes of considering a breach of Article 14. Planning determinations also affect property rights. Education decisions will affect civil rights under Protocol 1, Article 2. Thus, cases which English lawyers might think of as 'public law' cases may yet involve determinations of civil rights.

Another distinction peculiar to English lawyers' eyes is that matters concerning public employment are not generally considered to concern 'civil rights' by the Strasbourg institutions (see *Koseck v Germany* (1986) 9 EHRR 328 and *Neigel v France* (2000) 30 EHRR 310). This leads to results such as in *Balfour v United Kingdom* (App. No. 30976/96), 2 July 1997, ECmHR, in which a former diplomat was unable to use Article 6 to challenge the use of public interest immunity certificates to exclude evidence from his case alleging unfair dismissal. See also *Huber v France* (1998) 26 EHRR 457, which suggested in blanket terms that rights relating to a civil service pension were not 'civil' even though they also had a pecuniary element. In *Pellegrin v France* (2001) 31 EHRR 651, the ECtHR stated that only decisions concerning those with functions relating to the 'specific activities' of the public service would be outside the protection provided by Article 6. Accordingly, it will be necessary to consider whether the nature of an employee's duties and responsibilities involves 'direct or indirect participation in the exercise of the powers conferred by public law and duties designed to safeguard the general interests of the state or of other public authorities' (at para. 66).

The *Pellegrin* decision appears to conflict with the ECtHR's earlier decision in *Vogt v Germany* (1995) 21 EHRR 205, where it was held that a civil servant's complaint relating to dismissal from civil service employment *could* amount to a civil right, in the context of freedom of expression. However, as *Pellegrin* is a decision of the Grand Chamber, specifically designed to remove the uncertainty about the applicability of Article 6(1) to public employment, the new 'functional' criterion approach should supersede earlier case law on the subject. Disciplinary proceedings which determine a right to practise a profession do concern civil rights and so must conform to Article 6(1) of the Convention (see *König v Germany* (1978) 2 EHRR 170 and *Wickramsinghe v United Kingdom* (App. No. 31503/96), 9 December 1997, ECmHR (General Medical Council disciplinary hearing)).

In the determination of civil rights, only the protection of Article 6(1) is enjoyed. However, when an individual faces a criminal charge, he or she enjoys the general protection of Article 6(1) and also the specific rights guaranteed under Article 6(2) and (3).

8.6.5 Fair Hearing

Article 6(1) sets the overall standard to be applied in determining whether a trial has been fair. The more detailed provisions in Article 6(2) and (3) apply only to criminal charges, but the right to a fair hearing in relation to civil and criminal proceedings has been widely interpreted, and even guarantees which are specifically protected in relation to criminal trials under Article 6(3) (such as legal aid) may be implied in relation to civil trials too, if they constitute a necessary part of the general right to a fair hearing (*Airey v Ireland* (1979) 2 EHRR 305). The ECtHR has held that

> In a democratic society . . . the right to a fair administration of justice holds such a promi-
> nent place that the restrictive interpretation of Article 6(1) [advanced by the state in that
> case] would not correspond to the aim and purpose of that provision. (*Delcourt v Belgium*
> (1970) 1 EHRR 355, at para. 25)

The right to a fair hearing requires, among other things, that a litigant:

(a) has real and effective access to a court;
(b) has notice of the time and place of the proceedings;
(c) has a real opportunity to present the case sought to be made; and
(d) is given a reasoned decision.

In *Neumeister v Austria* (1968) 1 EHRR 91, the concept of 'equality of arms' was introduced. This requires that there be a fair balance between the opportunities afforded the parties involved in litigation. The requirement can be breached merely by procedural inequality, without the need for quantifiable unfairness (*Fischer v Austria* [2002] ECHR 33382/96). A defence witness should be examined under the same conditions as a witness for the prosecution. Each party should be afforded the opportunity to cross-examine the other's evidence and findings. Both parties should certainly have the right to be represented by counsel, as well as the right to appear in person. In addition, both parties should be informed of the other's submissions and any written material provided to the court, and be given an opportunity to reply (*Fischer*). In *Dombo Beheer BV v Netherlands* (1993) 18 EHRR 213, the ECtHR stated, at para. 33:

The Court agrees with the Commission that as regards [civil] litigation involving opposing private interests, 'equality of arms' implies that each party must be afforded a reasonable opportunity to present his case—including his evidence—under conditions that do not place him at a substantial disadvantage vis-à-vis his opponent.

Equality of arms does not extend to an automatic entitlement to legal aid in the civil context (*McVicar v United Kingdom* (2002) 35 EHRR 22). However, requirements of fairness may demand that legal assistance be provided in certain situations (*P, C, and S v United Kingdom* (2002) 35 EHRR 31). For example, in *Airey v Ireland* (1979) 2 EHRR 305, the ECtHR considered whether the right of access to domestic courts included the existence of civil legal aid. The ECtHR stated:

To hold that so far-reaching an obligation exists would . . . sit ill with the facts that the Convention contains no provision on legal aid for those disputes. . . . However, despite the absence of . . . a clause for civil litigation, Article 6(1) may sometimes compel the state to provide for the assistance of a lawyer when such assistance proves indispensable for an effective access to the court, either because legal representation is rendered compulsory, as is done by the domestic law of certain contracting states . . . or by reason of the complexity of the procedure of the case.

On the facts of that case, which concerned an emotionally and legally complex matrimonial dispute, with important issues of child custody at stake, it was held that the guarantee of real and effective access to a court and the concept of 'equality of arms' did require a lawyer to be provided free of charge to Mrs Airey by the Irish state.

Issues of evidence are obviously crucial to the concept of a fair trial. The ECtHR has taken the view that decisions about evidence are largely a matter for the domestic courts, but in *Edwards v United Kingdom* (1992) 15 EHRR 417, for instance, disclosure by the prosecution was seen as a crucial precondition of a fair trial. The ECtHR remains concerned about the extent to which the rules of evidence affect the right to a fair trial. This was particularly evident in the judgment in *McGinley and Egan v United Kingdom* (1999) 27 EHRR 1. In that case the applicants, who had been present during nuclear weapons tests on Christmas Island during 1957, claimed that they had been deprived of the right to a fair hearing when they sought to challenge a decision that their leukaemia was not due to exposure to radiation. They were unable to prove this because state documents that may have shown a link between their health problems and exposure to radiation were withheld. The ECtHR held that in these particular circumstances they had failed to avail themselves of the relevant rules in Scottish civil procedure to apply for disclosure of relevant documents. However, on the general point it held that if the Government had prevented the applicants from gaining access to documents in its possession, which would have helped them to ground a case, it would have denied them a fair hearing in contravention of Article 6(1).

In *Rowe and Davis v United Kingdom* (2000) 30 EHRR 1, the ECtHR found a violation of Article 6(1) where the prosecution failed to place relevant documents before the trial judge or invite him to rule on disclosure. However, in *Jasper v United Kingdom* and *Fitt v United Kingdom* (2000) 30 EHRR 1, it was held by a 9:8 majority that there was no breach of Article 6(1) where public interest immunity (PII) procedures were adopted. The ECtHR ruled that the entitlement to disclosure of relevant evidence is not an absolute right and that competing interests of national security, protecting witnesses at risk of reprisal, and preserving the secrecy of police methods of investigating crime have to be balanced against the accused's rights. Given the narrow majority of this view and the ruling in *Rowe and Davis v United Kingdom*, it is likely that this position will be reargued now in the domestic courts.

The right to silence is relevant to the issue of a fair trial, as well as to the presumption of innocence under Article 6(2) (see 8.6.10 below). While the right to silence and the privilege against self-incrimination are central to the notion of a fair procedure, they are not absolute (*Condron v United Kingdom* (2001) 31 EHRR 1). Accordingly, it may be permissible for a trial judge to leave a jury with the option of drawing an adverse inference from an accused's silence. See also *Beckles v United Kingdom* (2003) 36 EHRR 13 and *Heaney and McGuinness v Ireland* (2001) 33 EHRR 12.

It is a basic requirement that judgments of courts and tribunals should adequately state the reasons on which they are based. The extent of this duty may vary according to the nature of the decision and the circumstances of the case (*Ruiz Torija v Spain* (1995) 19 EHRR 553). However, it does not require that a detailed answer be given to every argument (*Van de Hurk v Netherlands* (1994) 18 EHRR 481).

8.6.6 Public Hearings

Although Article 6(1) requires a public hearing, it provides for circumstances where the press and public may be excluded from the proceedings. These include situations where the interests of morals, public order, or national security may be compromised; where the interests of juveniles or the protection of the private life of the parties require; or in situations where publicity could prejudice the interests of justice. In *Diennet v France* (1995) 21 EHRR 554, the ECtHR held that the right of a public hearing extended to the disciplinary hearing of a doctor before the French Medical Association. The presumption in favour of private hearings in cases under the Children Act 1989 was upheld in *B v United Kingdom* (2002) 34 EHRR 19.

The judgment is also to be pronounced publicly. Unlike the limitations that apply to a public trial, the right to public pronouncement of the judgment is unqualified. However, this right does not necessarily require that the judgment be read in open court, provided the outcome is publicly availability (*Pretto v Italy* (1983) 6 EHRR 182). Accordingly, in *B v United Kingdom*, the ECtHR held that lack of public pronouncement of residence decisions under the Children Act did not contravene Article 6(1). It is significant in this regard that anyone who can establish an interest in the case is entitled to read or obtain a copy of the decision of first instance courts in child residence cases. Furthermore, there is routine publication of the judgments of the Court of Appeal and of first instance courts in cases of special interest.

8.6.7 Hearing Within a Reasonable Time

Article 6(1) calls for the hearing to be held within a 'reasonable time'. Unlike Article 5(3), which applies only to individuals under arrest, this provision applies to civil and criminal cases and whether an accused is being held or is on bail. What constitutes a reasonable time will depend on the circumstances. However, particularly relevant factors include the complexity of the case, the applicant's conduct and that of the competent authorities, and the importance of what was at stake for the applicant (*Gast and Popp v Germany* (2001) 33 EHRR 37). The advanced age of the applicant may also be relevant (*GOC v Poland* (App. No. 48001/99), 23 October 2001, ECtHR).

In the criminal context the ECmHR has stated that time begins to run from the point 'at which the situation of the person concerned has been substantially affected as a result of a suspicion against him' (*X v Austria* (1967) 24 CD 8, at 18). This approach has been adopted by the ECtHR and applies even if no charges have been levelled at that point (*Eckle v Germany* (1982) 5 EHRR 1). In *Neumeister v Austria* (1968) 1 EHRR 91, the accused was investigated on 21 January 1960, charged on 23 February 1961, and indicted on 17 March 1964. The ECtHR chose the date he was charged as the starting point for the period covered by Article 6(1). On the other hand, in a judgment handed down by the ECtHR on the same day, *Wemhoff v Germany* (1968) 1 EHRR 55, the accused was determined to have been 'substantially affected' only when he was arrested.

In civil cases, the period to be taken into consideration begins at the point at which proceedings are instituted (*Scopelliti v Italy* (1993) 17 EHRR 493). In *Darnell v United Kingdom* (1993) 18 EHRR 205, the applicant was dismissed from his post with an area health authority in 1984. There then followed several judicial review applications, an industrial tribunal hearing, and an Employment Appeal Tribunal appeal, which was finally dismissed in 1993. The ECtHR and ECmHR found that the total period taken for the trial of the matter to be concluded was unreasonable. This case also illustrates the ECtHR's approach when dealing with the period taken up by appeals, which is to include all the time taken to resolve the matter, including appeals. See also *Somjee v United Kingdom* (2003) 36 EHRR 16.

8.6.8 Impartiality

Article 6(1) requires an 'independent and impartial tribunal established by law'. The ECtHR has been as concerned with actual impartiality as it has been with the appearance of impartiality. For instance, in *Langborger v Sweden* (1989) 12 EHRR 416, the ECtHR ruled that Article 6(1) was violated by the membership of a housing tribunal that had the 'possible appearance of lacking impartiality'. In *McGonnell v United Kingdom* (2000) 30 EHRR 289, it was held that there was a breach of Article 6(1) where the Bailiff, who presided over the Royal Court of Guernsey in legal proceedings concerning the applicant's planning appeal, had also sat as the Deputy Bailiff over the States of Deliberation when the earlier, detailed development plan had been adopted. However, in this case the ECtHR did not go as far as fully endorsing the doctrine of separation of powers.

Similar issues have been raised in cases concerning disciplinary proceedings—in particular those of court martial procedures. In *Hood v United Kingdom* (2000) 29 EHRR 365, the applicant was tried and convicted under the Army Act 1955 by court martial on charges of absence without leave and desertion. Under the provisions of the Act, the convening officer was responsible for convening the court martial and appointing its members and the prosecuting officer. Applying *Findlay v United Kingdom* (1997) 24 EHRR 221, the ECtHR observed that a court martial convened pursuant to the Act did not meet the requirements of independence and impartiality set by Article 6, particularly in view of the central part played in the prosecution by the convening officer, who was closely linked to the prosecuting authorities, was superior in rank to members of the court martial, and had the power to dissolve the court martial and refuse to confirm its decision.

The court martial proceedings at issue in *Hood* and *Findlay* were amended by the Armed Forces Act 1996. However, the revised procedure was the subject of challenge, again on the basis of lack of independence and impartiality, in *Morris v United Kingdom* (2002) 34 EHRR 52. The ECtHR held that while the changes introduced by the 1996 Act went 'a long way' to addressing the problems identified in the earlier decisions, the court martial procedure still did not comply with Article 6(1). Of particular concern was the risk of outside pressure being placed on two junior serving officers who had sat on the applicant's court martial. See the discussion of *Morris* in *R v Spear* [2002] UKHL 31, at 8.6.14 below.

In *Pullar v United Kingdom* (1996) 22 EHRR 391, the ECtHR found that there was no violation of the applicant's right to a fair trial when the jury which convicted him included an employee of a key prosecution witness. The ECtHR held that the appeal court's reliance on the juror's unchallenged written statement of his impartiality was sufficient for the purposes of Article 6(1).

The ECtHR found a violation of Article 6 in *Sander v United Kingdom* (2001) 31 EHRR 44. In the applicant's domestic case, issues of racial prejudice were raised after a letter was received by the judge from a jury member complaining that two fellow jurors were making racist remarks and jokes. A second letter from the whole jury refuting the allegations in the first was received, and finally a third, from one of the alleged jokers, was received denying any racial bias. The Strasbourg Court held that racial bias does not disappear overnight and that as a result the jury should have been discharged. It ruled that the judge's redirection of the jury to stress the importance of avoiding racial prejudice was inadequate. See the domestic consideration of *Sander* in *R v Qureshi* [2001] EWCA Crim 1807.

In *Kingsley v United Kingdom* (2002) 35 EHRR 10, the ECtHR noted that even where an adjudicatory body determining disputes over civil rights and obligations is not impartial and independent, there will be no breach of Article 6(1) if the proceedings before that body are subject to subsequent control by an independent and impartial judicial body, with ability to quash the impugned decision.

8.6.9 Access to Justice

The right to real and effective access to a court is a fundamental aspect of Article 6, though it is not without limitations: it is a crucial but not absolute right. In *Golder v United Kingdom* (1975) 1 EHRR 524, Article 6 was violated when a prisoner was denied access to a lawyer whom he wished to consult for the purpose of bringing defamation proceedings against a prison warder. In *Ashingdane v United Kingdom* (1985) 7 EHRR 528, however, the ECtHR found that the restriction in the Mental Health Act 1959 on the right of a psychiatric patient to sue the hospital which cared for him was not absolute and was justified. See also *Stubbings v United Kingdom* (1996) 23 EHRR 213, in which it was held that a statutory limitation period for bringing an action did not breach Article 6 or Article 14. There is no right to bring private prosecutions unless a successful subsequent civil claim is closely linked to the private prosecution (*Helmers v Sweden* (1993) 15 EHRR 285).

An illustration of the type of limitation which may be placed on access to a court is the case of *Fayed v United Kingdom* (1994) 18 EHRR 393, which was an application made by the Fayed brothers arising out of an investigation of their affairs by inspectors appointed by the Department of Trade and Industry. One of their complaints was that, in breach of Article 6(1) of the Convention, English law denied them access to a court to have determined whether there was any justification for the attack on their reputations contained in the inspectors' report. It was accepted that any defamation proceedings would have been met by a successful defence of privilege. The ECtHR concluded that the system of investigation and reporting under the Companies Act 1985 pursued the public interest in the proper conduct of the affairs of public companies whose owners benefit from limited liability, and the objective of according the inspectors freedom to report 'with courage and frankness' was legitimate and proportionate.

Article 6(1) has also been used to challenge prosecutorial prohibitions. For example, in *Osman v United Kingdom* (2000) 29 EHRR 245, the applicants claimed that the English rule of immunity that prevented them from pursuing a negligence action against the police breached their right of access to the courts under Article 6. Their claim was upheld, with the majority of the ECtHR of the opinion that Article 6(1) was applicable to the case on the basis that the exclusionary rule against actions in negligence against the police did not work as a blanket ban; that the courts could conduct their assessment as to the applicability of the rule in *Hill v Chief Constable of West Yorkshire Police* [1989] AC 53 on a case-by-case basis. Therefore the applicants had been denied access to the court for the assertion of their 'civil rights' under Article 6(1). Judge Jambrek urged the ECtHR to take on a more extensive interpretation of 'civil rights and obligations': the ECtHR should need to be satisfied only that a right existed under the domestic law—in this case, a right derived from the general tort of negligence or the duty of care owed by the police to the plaintiff. The only condition for the ECtHR's recognition of a right as a 'civil right', thereby guaranteeing an applicant the right of access to a domestic court, would be that the right at issue is recognized in the national legal system as an individual right within the sphere of general individual freedom. The decision in *Osman* has been heavily criticized by commentators (see, for example, Gearty, 'Osman Unravels' (2002) 65 MLR 87) and the ECtHR has retreated slightly from its position in cases such as *Z v United Kingdom* (2002) 34 EHRR 3, *Al-Adsani v United Kingdom* (2002) 12 BHRC 89, *McElhinney v Ireland* (2002) 34 EHRR 13, and *Fogarty v United Kingdom* (2002) 34 EHRR 302. The concept of access to justice contained in Article 6(1), and elucidated in cases such as *Fayed* and *Osman*, means that civil claims should be capable of being submitted to a judge for adjudication. However, a state's ability to remove whole ranges of civil claims from the jurisdiction of the courts, or confer immunities on groups of people, is often in tension with this concept. The scope of this area of Article 6 has not yet been definitively resolved by the ECtHR, and will continue to be the subject of intense judicial and academic debate in the future.

8.6.10 Presumption of Innocence

Article 6(2) provides for the presumption of innocence of the defendant in criminal trials (*Funke v France* (1993) 16 EHRR 297). This presumption is applicable only to the offence with which the accused is charged and does not extend to allegations made during the sentencing process (*Phillips v United Kingdom* (App. No. 41087/98), 5 July 2001, ECtHR). The principle assumes that the prosecution will need to produce evidence of guilt in the trial (*Barberà v Spain* (1988) 11 EHRR 360). In *Minelli v Switzerland* (1983) 5 EHRR 554, the ECtHR concluded that presumption of innocence means that the defendant has the right to be heard in his or her own defence. However, domestic laws which place the onus on the defendant to prove certain elements of his or her defence do not necessarily violate this provision (*Lingens v Austria* (1981) 26 DR 171). Equally, the provision does not necessarily prevent presumptions of law or fact from being in favour of the prosecution and against the defendant. However, these presumptions must be 'within reasonable limits' (*Salabiaku v France* (1988) 13 EHRR 379).

In *Murray v United Kingdom* (1996) 22 EHRR 29, the ECtHR considered whether the drawing of adverse inferences from exercising the right to silence was a violation of Article 6 and held that on the facts of the case the drawing of inferences did not interfere with the applicant's right to a fair trial. Murray was arrested under the Prevention of Terrorism (Temporary Provisions) Act 1989 and taken to the police station. While being interviewed he stated repeatedly that he had 'nothing to say'. He was able to see his solicitor only after 48 hours, and in subsequent interviews he stated that he had 'been advised by my solicitor not to answer any of your questions'. During several interviews that lasted for 21 hours and 39 minutes over two days, these statements were the only ones made by the applicant. Murray also refused to give any evidence at trial and no witnesses were called on his behalf. The ECtHR, at para. 45, made it clear that:

> there can be no doubt that the right to remain silent under police questioning and the privilege against self-incrimination are generally recognised international standards which lie at the heart of the notion of a fair procedure under Article 6. By providing the accused with protection against improper compulsion by the authorities these immunities contribute to avoiding miscarriages of justice and to securing the aims of Article 6.

The ECmHR and ECtHR accepted that a jury, which did not have to give reasons, might not be so careful about the weight to be given to the adverse inference. *Murray* was a case where guilt was decided by a judge who had to give reasons.

In *Condron v United Kingdom* (2001) 31 EHRR 1, the Strasbourg authorities held that allowing a jury to draw an adverse influence from 'no comment' police interviews after caution was a violation of Article 6. The applicants in this case were heroin addicts charged with supplying heroin. Their solicitor had advised them not to answer police questions as he thought they were unfit to be questioned. At trial both defendants gave evidence and first-time explanations for aspects of the prosecution case. The domestic Court of Appeal held that the summing-up was defective but the conviction was 'safe'. The Strasbourg Court did not agree though, and held that the test was 'fairness' not 'safety' and found a violation of Article 6. However, the ECtHR declined to rule on further defence submissions that adverse inferences can be drawn only after proof of a *prima facie* case and cannot be the main basis for a conviction. See also *Beckles v United Kingdom* (2003) 36 EHRR 13 and Judicial Studies Board Directions.

In *Saunders v United Kingdom* (1996) 23 EHRR 313, the ECtHR found a violation of Article 6(1) when the applicant complained that he was denied a fair hearing because of the use at his criminal trial of statements obtained from him by Department of Trade and Industry inspectors in exercise of their statutory powers under the Companies Act 1985 to compel him to answer questions and provide information. For domestic discussion of *Saunders*, see *R v Dimsey* [2001] UKHL 46.

8.6.11 Further Specific Rights in Criminal Cases

Article 6(3) stipulates specific safeguards, which apply to criminal trials. They are particular examples of the overall right to a fair trial (*Artico v Italy* (1980) 3 EHRR 1; *Edwards v United Kingdom* (1992) 15 EHRR 417) and constitute the minimum rights to be afforded a defendant in a criminal trial.

Article 6(3)(a)

Article 6(3)(a) guarantees prompt, intelligible notification of charges. The right to know the case against the accused is seen as essential to preparing an informed defence. It requires that a defendant be notified in a language that he or she understands (*Brozicek v Italy* (1989) 12 EHRR 371). In addition, it requires that the charges be formulated with adequate precision (*Mattoccia v Italy* (2003) 36 EHRR 47).

Article 6(3)(b)

Article 6(3)(b) requires that the accused be given adequate time and facilities to mount a defence. This principle is obviously relative, but the ECmHR has created some guidelines in holding it to be 'the right of the accused to have at his disposal, for the purpose of exonerating himself or to obtain a reduction in his sentence, all relevant elements that have been or could be collected by the competent authorities' (*Jespers v Belgium* (1981) 27 DR 61). See also *Can v Austria* (1985) 8 EHRR 121.

Article 6(3)(c)

Article 6(3)(c) gives the right to representation and legal aid. This section gives way to three principles:

   (a) the right to defend oneself;

   (b) the right to legal assistance of one's choosing; and

   (c) the right to free legal assistance if one is indigent and if the interests of justice so require.

These principles apply to the pre-trial stages as well as to the trial itself (*Imbrioscia v Switzerland* (1993) 17 EHRR 441). In *Imbrioscia*, the ECtHR was asked to consider whether the defendant was entitled to have a lawyer present at pre-trial questioning. It held that Article 6(3) may be relevant to the pre-trial stages if and so far as the fairness of the trial is likely to be seriously prejudiced by an initial failure to comply with its provisions. Harris, O'Boyle, and Warbrick's view of the case (in *The Law of the European Convention on Human Rights* (London: Butterworths, 1995), 257; 2nd edn forthcoming (London: Butterworths, 2003)) is that:

> What emerges . . . is that Article 6(3)(c) does not require a state to take the initiative to invite an accused's lawyer to be present during questioning in the course of the investigation. However, although the Court does not say this in so many words, it would appear from the tenor of its judgment that if the accused or his lawyer requests the latter's attendance, this must be allowed if, as is likely, there is a risk the information obtained will prejudice the accused person's defence.

In *Murray v United Kingdom* (1996) 22 EHRR 29 the ECtHR held that the exclusion of a lawyer from the police station when the individual was being questioned, in the circumstances of the restriction of the right to silence and the threat of an adverse inference being drawn from silence, constituted a violation of Article 6. See also *Magee v United Kingdom* (2001) 31 EHRR 822.

    The ECtHR considered whether unavailability of full legal aid for a committal hearing in a poll tax case constituted a violation of Article 6 in *Benham v United*

Kingdom (1996) 22 EHRR 293. In answering this question, the ECtHR stated that regard must be had to the severity of the penalty at stake and the complexity of the case. In general, the ECtHR held that, '[w]here deprivation of liberty is at stake, the interests of justice in principle call for legal representation'. In the specific case before it, the ECtHR went on to decide, at para. 64, that:

> In view of the severity of the penalty risked by the applicant and the complexity of the applicable law, the Court considers that the interests of justice demand that, in order to receive a fair hearing, the applicant ought to have benefited from free legal representation during the proceedings before the magistrates. In conclusion, there has been a violation of Article 6(1) and (3)(c) of the Convention taken together.

In *Granger v United Kingdom* (1990) 12 EHRR 469, the ECtHR found that the defendant should have received free legal assistance 'in the interests of justice'. The defendant was denied legal aid during an appeal in respect of a five-year sentence. Granger appeared for himself against a QC and a junior counsel for the Crown. The ECtHR found a violation of Article 6(3)(c), citing the defendant's obvious lack of understanding regarding the intricacies of the law in the face of the professional prosecution.

The right to be provided with legal representation means the right to be provided with genuine and effective representation, not the mere presence of a lawyer (see *Artico v Italy* (1980) 3 EHRR 1).

This right is not restricted, of course, to the provision of legal aid. In *S v Switzerland* (1991) 14 EHRR 670, the police had set up a special unit to investigate a protest group concerned with arms dealing and nuclear power. The police shadowed the members, tapped telephones, and regularly emptied their dustbins. One of those subsequently arrested was held in custody and when his lawyer came to see him, the interview was supervised by police officers. In addition, letters written by him to his lawyer were intercepted and later used for graphological reports. The argument that the surveillance of the lawyer was necessary to prevent collusion was rejected by the ECtHR, which said that '[f]ree communication between a lawyer and his detained client is a fundamental right which is essential in a democratic society, above all in the most serious of cases'. See also *Brennan v United Kingdom* (2002) 34 EHRR 18.

Article 6(3)(d)
Article 6(3)(d) ensures the right to the attendance of witnesses and their examination. This is in line with the above-mentioned 'equality of arms' principle and applies to both the accusatorial and inquisitorial systems of criminal law. Article 6(3)(d) has been raised in relation to proceedings involving sexual offences, where witnesses may not be available for questioning in person. In *S.N. v Sweden* (App. No. 34209/96), 2 July 2002, ECtHR, the ECtHR held that playing a videotaped interview and reading a record of an interview with a child, alleged to be the victim of sexual abuse, was sufficient to have enabled the complainant to challenge the

statements and the child's credibility. See *P.S. v Germany* (2003) 36 EHRR 61, for a contrasting decision.

Article 6(3)(e)
Article 6(3)(e) guarantees the right to an interpreter in the defendant's native language if he or she does not speak the language of the tribunal. In *Zana v Turkey* (1997) 27 EHRR 566, Z refused to answer allegations against him in criminal proceedings in respect of statements he had made supporting an armed group, the Workers' Party of Kurdistan. The reason for his refusal was that he would not speak Turkish and wished to proceed in Kurdish, his mother tongue. The ECtHR held that his subsequent conviction amounted to a breach of his right to a fair trial.

8.6.12 Evidence in Criminal Proceedings

Evidence is in general a matter for the domestic courts and Article 6 does not require any particular rules of evidence provided the trial as a whole is fair (*Edwards v United Kingdom* (1992) 15 EHRR 417). However, the use of particular evidence, such as that obtained by maltreatment, may make the trial unfair. Similarly, the use of hearsay evidence without the opportunity of this evidence being tested may also create unfairness (*Kostovski v Netherlands* (1989) 12 EHRR 434; *Unterpertinger v Austria* (1986) 13 EHRR 175). The ECtHR has also considered the use of evidence from anonymous witnesses (*Kostovski v Netherlands* (1989) 12 EHRR 434; *Windisch v Austria* (1990) 13 EHRR 281; *Doorson v Netherlands* (1996) 22 EHRR 330; *Van Mechelen v Netherlands* (1997) 25 EHRR 647); entrapment (*Teixeira de Castro v Portugal* (1999) 28 EHRR 101); witnesses giving evidence behind screens (*X v United Kingdom* (1992) 15 EHRR CD 113); accomplices (*X v United Kingdom* (1976) 4 DR 115); undercover agents (*X v Germany* (1987) 11 EHRR 84); undercover police officers (*Van Mechelen v Netherlands* (1998) 25 EHRR 647); and pleas of guilt from co-defendants (*M.H. v United Kingdom* [1997] EHRLR 279).

8.6.13 Disclosure in Criminal Proceedings

It is arguable that the denial of disclosure to the defence of material that the prosecution has in its possession, and which they could use if they chose, inevitably creates unfairness. In *Kaufman v Belgium* (1986) 50 DR 98, the ECmHR decided that 'everyone who is a party to . . . proceedings should have a reasonable opportunity of presenting his case to the court under conditions which do not place him at a substantial disadvantage vis-à-vis his opponent'.

Whether there is any actual unfairness and, therefore, whether the ECtHR will find a violation in any particular case, will depend on the importance of the material to the defence. The ECmHR and the ECtHR have already recognized that the right to a fair trial requires the prosecution to disclose all relevant evidence to the defence (*Jespers v Belgium* (1981) 27 DR 61; *Edwards v United Kingdom* (1992) 15 EHRR

417). In *Bendenoun v France* (1994) 18 EHRR 54, the ECtHR decided that this principle applies whether or not the prosecution intends to rely on the documents and whether or not the defence decides to use them.

A practice that may interfere with the Article 6 right to a fair trial is the restricted disclosure now available from the prosecution in the United Kingdom as a result of the Criminal Procedure and Investigations Act 1996 (see the discussion of *Rowe and Davis v United Kingdom* (2000) 30 EHRR 1 and *McGinley and Egan v United Kingdom* (1999) 27 EHRR 1 at 8.6.3 above).

In *Jespers v Belgium* (1981) 27 DR 61, the ECmHR held that the 'equality of arms' principle imposes on prosecution and investigating authorities an obligation to disclose any material in their possession. This also applies to any material to which they *could* gain access which may assist the accused in exonerating himself. Such a duty is necessary to redress the inequality of resources between the prosecution and defence. This principle extends to material that might undermine the credibility of a prosecution witness. In *Jespers v Belgium* the ECmHR stated, at 87–8:

> ... the prosecution has at its disposal, to back the accusation, facilities deriving from its powers of investigation supported by judicial and police machinery with considerable technical resources and means of coercion. It is in order to establish equality, as far as possible, between the prosecution and the defence that national legislation in most countries entrusts the preliminary investigation to a member of the judiciary or, if it entrusts the investigation to the public prosecutor's department, instructs the latter to gather evidence in favour of the accused as well as against him.
>
> ... everyone charged with a criminal offence should enjoy ... the opportunity to acquaint himself, for the purpose of preparing his defence, with the results of investigations carried out throughout the proceedings ... a right to access to the prosecution file ... can be inferred from Article 6, para. 3(b) ...
>
> In short, Article 6, para. 3(b), recognises the right of the accused to have at his disposal, for the purposes of exonerating himself or of obtaining a reduction in his sentence, all relevant elements that have been or could be collected by the competent authorities.

Also, in *Edwards v United Kingdom* (1992) 15 EHRR 417, the ECtHR stated, at para. 36, that it:

> ... considers that it is a requirement of fairness under Article 6(1), indeed one which is recognised under English law, that the prosecution authorities disclose to the defence all material evidence for or against the accused and that the failure to do so in the present case gave rise to a defect in the trial process.

Article 6 is at the centre of Strasbourg jurisprudence, but the ECmHR and the ECtHR tread a fine line in deciding how far to monitor the internal workings of the varying legal systems of the signatory states, including the differences between adversarial and inquisitorial criminal justice systems. They are prepared to intervene where they regard the procedure adopted as violating the essence of a fair trial, but they have thus far pursued a policy of not questioning a national court with regard to the merits of a case based on the facts presented.

8.6.14 Human Rights Act Decisions

Article 6 has quickly established itself as the most frequently invoked Convention right in the domestic courts. Its domestic incorporation has engendered prolific litigation across a wide range of criminal and civil matters. This is not surprising given the United Kingdom's poor record for Article 6 compliance at Strasbourg.

In *R v A (No. 2)* [2001] UKHL 251, the House of Lords outlined its general approach to the Article 6 rights. As in Strasbourg jurisprudence, the guarantee of a fair trial is conceived as absolute, while a degree of balancing is permitted in relation to what the concept of a fair trial actually entails. Explaining this approach, Lord Steyn stated (at para. 38):

> It is well established that the guarantee of a fair trial under Article 6 is absolute: a conviction obtained in breach of it cannot stand . . . The only balancing permitted is in respect of what the concept of a fair trial entails: here account may be taken of the familiar triangulation of interests of the accused, the victim and society. In this context proportionality has a role to play.

See also *Brown v Stott* [2001] 2 WLR 817 at 836, where Lord Bingham observed that:

> The jurisprudence of the European Court very clearly establishes that while the overall fairness of a criminal trial cannot be compromised, the constituent rights comprised, whether expressed or implicitly, within Article 6 are not themselves absolute. Limited qualification of these rights is acceptable if reasonably directed by national authorities towards a clear and proper public objective and if representing no greater qualification than the situation calls for.

Further discussion of limitations on Article 6 and other Convention rights can be found in Chapter 2, at 2.4.

Article 6(1)
The threshold issues of 'criminal charge' and 'civil rights and obligations' have been considered by the courts on several occasions. In *R (Husain) v Asylum Support Adjudicator* [2001] EWHC Admin 852, the court held that discretionary benefits are not 'civil rights' for the purposes of Article 6(1). This restrictive interpretation appears to be consistent with Strasbourg jurisprudence. However, a more generous approach has also been taken and it appears that determinations of the Regulation of Investigatory Powers Tribunal will be classified as determinations of 'civil rights' (App. Nos IPT/01/62 and IPT/01/77, 23 January 2003). For an example of the courts' approach to 'criminal charge', see *R (Carroll) v Secretary of State for the Home Department* [2001] EWCA Civ 1224.

The right to silence has been acknowledged as an element of the right to a fair trial. The Court of Appeal decision, *R v Kearns* [2002] EWCA Crim 748, provides a helpful overview of domestic and European case law in this area. See also Judicial Studies Board Directions.

The decision of *Mousaka v Golden Seagull Maritime Inc.* [2002] 1 WLR 395 indicates that the domestic courts will follow the Strasbourg approach to assessing whether a reasoned judgment has been given.

The House of Lords took a robust approach to the right to a hearing within a 'reasonable time' in *Magill v Porter* [2001] UKHL 67. It was held that this right is an independent element of Article 6(1), which should not be subsumed by general considerations of the right to a fair trial. Furthermore, breach of the right is not dependent upon evidence of prejudice having been caused by the delay. See also *A-G's Reference (No. 2 of 2001)* [2001] EWCA Crim 1568 and *R v HM Advocate* (Privy Council, 28 November 2002).

The right to a hearing by an 'independent and impartial' tribunal has been invoked in several cases. Helpful guidance as to when a judge should disqualify himself or herself on the grounds of bias is provided by the Court of Appeal decision, *Locabail (UK) Ltd v Bayfield Properties Ltd and Another* [2000] 2 WLR 870. The revised court martial procedure, held to contravene Article 6(1) in *Morris v United Kingdom* (2002) 34 EHRR 52, was assessed by the House of Lords in *R v Spear* [2002] UKHL 31. Surprisingly, the House of Lords reached a different conclusion to the ECtHR, primarily on the basis that the Strasbourg body did not have all the relevant information about safeguards against impartiality or lack of independence. This right was also the subject of consideration by the House of Lords in *R (Alconbury Developments Ltd) v Secretary of State for the Environment, Transport and the Regions* [2001] UKHL 23. There, the court adopted a similar position to that taken by the ECtHR in *Kingsley v United Kingdom* (2002) 35 EHRR 10. See also *London Borough of Tower Hamlets v Begum* [2002] EWCA Civ 239, *Magill v Porter* [2001] UKHL 67, and *International Transport Roth GmbH v Home Secretary* [2002] EWCA Civ 158. In *Matthews v Ministry of Defence* [2003] UKHL 4, the House of Lords considered the Strasbourg cases on access to justice when deciding whether primary domestic legislation which prevented an ex-serviceman from bringing a personal injury claim against the Ministry of Defence, was Convention compliant. Their Lordships held that the legislative provision in question was a substantive bar to bringing any claim and the protection of Article 6(1), which applies to procedural limitations, was not engaged.

Article 6(2)

In *R (Kebilene) v DPP* [2000] 2 AC 326, certain members of the House of Lords indicated, in *obiter* comments, that reverse onus provisions may not violate Article 6(2). However, the use of s. 3 of the Human Rights Act to translate an apparently legal burden into an evidential burden in *R v Lambert* [2001] UKHL 37, indicates that at least in certain circumstances, the domestic courts will hold that the placement of a legal burden on an accused contravenes Article 6(2). See also *Lynch v DPP* [2001] EWHC Admin 882.

The House of Lords has followed *Phillips v United Kingdom* (App. No. 41087/98), 5 July 2001, ECtHR, in two cases concerning confiscation orders under the Drug Trafficking Act 1994 (*R v Rezvi* [2002] UKHL 1 and *R v Benjafield* [2002] UKHL 2).

Article 6(3)

Article 6(3) has not been as active a source of litigation as Article 6(1) and (2). However, the Court of Appeal decisions, *R v Oates* [2002] EWCA Crim 1071 and *R v Thakrar* [2001] EWCA Crim 1096, provide an example of the domestic approach to complaints under this head.

8.7 ARTICLE 7: NO PUNISHMENT WITHOUT LAWFUL AUTHORITY

1.   No one shall be held guilty of any criminal offence on account of any act or omission which did not constitute a criminal offence under national or international law at the time when it was committed. Nor shall a heavier penalty be imposed than the one that was applicable at the time the criminal offence was committed.

2.   This Article shall not prejudice the trial and punishment of any person for any act or omission which, at the time when it was committed, was criminal according to the general principles of law recognised by civilised nations.

Article 7 guards against retrospective criminal laws and forbids a heavier penalty being imposed than that which was in effect at the time of the commission of the crime. The ECtHR has held that it follows from these prohibitions that any criminal offence must be clearly defined in law, enabling individuals to know what acts and omissions will attract criminal liability (*Kokkinakis v Greece* (1993) 17 EHRR 397). The principles of Article 7(1) apply to both national legislation and the actions of criminal courts. They are subject to the narrow exception detailed in Article 7(2).

In *Welch v United Kingdom* (1995) 20 EHRR 247, the applicant was arrested on drug charges in November 1986. In January 1987, a law concerning the seizure of any proceeds gained as a result of the drug trade came into effect. The applicant argued that if this new law were applied to him, it would constitute retrospective criminal legislation and offend Article 7. On the other hand, the United Kingdom argued that the confiscation of these proceeds, as well as imprisonment as punishment for their non-payment, did not constitute penalties for the purpose of Article 7. The ECtHR disagreed with the United Kingdom and ruled that the retrospective application of the confiscation order was a penalty and offended Article 7. It found (at para. 34) that Welch faced more 'far-reaching detriment' as a result of the Government seizure than he would have at the time he perpetrated the crimes.

However, in the case of *SW v United Kingdom* (1995) 21 EHRR 363, it was held that the change in the direction of the common law with regard to rape within marriage was sufficiently foreseeable to mean that Article 7 was not violated when a man was convicted for raping his wife.

In *Streletz, Kessler and Krenz v Germany* (2001) 33 EHRR 31, three former senior East German officials alleged that their convictions for the deaths of people trying to cross the intra-German border violated Article 7. The ECtHR held that the complainants could not rely on the state's border-policing policy as rendering their actions lawful at the time of commission since the policy 'flagrantly infringe[d] human rights and above all the right to life' and accordingly could not be described as 'law'.

8.7.1 Human Rights Act Decisions

There have been relatively few domestic cases concerning Article 7. In *R v Alden and Wright* [2001] EWCA Crim 296, the Court of Appeal held that an increase in sentencing guidelines is not inconsistent with Article 7, provided the sentence does not exceed the maximum applicable at the time of commission of the offence.

A fairly narrow approach to the meaning of 'penalty' was displayed in *Gough v Chief Constable of Derbyshire* [2002] EWCA Civ 351, where the Court of Appeal upheld a High Court finding that orders banning attendance at football matches do not constitute penalties. In another decision concerning the meaning of 'penalty', the High Court held that extradition proceedings do not involve a penalty, even though the decision to extradite might well be detrimental to the individual (*Re Marais* [2001] EWHC Admin 1051).

The requirement of legal certainty was considered in *R v Muhamad* [2002] EWCA Crim 1856. There, the appellant had argued that a strict liability offence was inconsistent with the general requirement for sufficiently clear criminal provisions. The Court rejected the argument, holding that only legal uncertainty, rather than factual uncertainty, contravenes Article 7.

8.8 ARTICLE 8: RIGHT TO RESPECT FOR PRIVATE AND FAMILY LIFE

> 1.   Everyone has the right to respect for his private and family life, his home and his correspondence.
>
> 2.   There shall be no interference by a public authority with the exercise of this right except such as is in accordance with the law and is necessary in a democratic society in the interests of national security, public safety or the economic well-being of the country, for the prevention of disorder or crime, for the protection of health or morals, or for the protection of the rights and freedoms of others.

Article 8 protects the right to respect for a person's private and family life, home, and correspondence. The essential object of this right is to protect the individual against arbitrary action by the public authorities (*Kroon v Netherlands* (1994) 19 EHRR 263). Article 8 has been used in a wide range of contexts: from phone-tapping to the use of medical records in court; from the rights of children whose parents are deported to the right to have records altered, to the rights of transsexuals to have their status recognized on official records; from the right to protection from aircraft noise to the right to practise one's sexuality. In the majority of the diverse case law, the central issue has been the meaning of 'private life', 'family life', 'home', and 'correspondence'.

The ECtHR has held that the right to respect for private life contains both positive and negative aspects—not just that the state should refrain from interference, but also that it has an obligation to provide for an effective respect for private life. In *Stjerna v Finland* (1994) 24 EHRR 194, the ECtHR stated that:

> the boundaries between the State's positive and negative obligations under Article 8 do not lend themselves to precise definition. . . . In both contexts regard must be had to the fair balance that has to be struck between the competing interests of the individual and of the community as a whole.

See Feldman, 'The developing scope of Article 8 of the European Convention on Human Rights' (1997) 3 EHRLR 265 for further discussion of the general scope of Article 8.

8.8.1 Limitations on the Right to Respect for Private and Family Life

Article 8 is a qualified right, with a number of purposes for which it may be justifiable to restrict the Article 8(1) right being listed in Article 8(2). For example, the right may be limited in order to protect the rights of others through preservation of the environment (*Chapman v United Kingdom* (2001) 33 EHRR 18). However, Article 8(2) does not mean that *any* interference with a person's private life, which is intended for one of the specified purposes, can be justified. Interference by the state with a person's private and family life, home, or correspondence must be justified by one of the exceptions detailed in Article 8(2) and must meet the general requirements of justification, which are discussed in detail in Chapter 2. Only these exceptions, along with the restrictions in Article 17, are allowed.

Peck v United Kingdom (2003) 36 EHRR 41 is a recent example of a case in which an infringement of Article 8(1) was found to be unjustifiable, even though a legitimate objective had been pursued. The case concerned the disclosure by a council of CCTV footage, featuring a suicidal man, to the media. This disclosure constituted a disproportionate interference with Article 8(1) as it was not accompanied by safeguards sufficient to ensure respect for Mr Peck's private life. Possible safeguards included obtaining Mr Peck's consent prior to disclosure, masking the images of Mr Peck, or ensuring that the media masked those images.

8.8.2 Private Life

The ECtHR has taken a consistently broad approach to the meaning of 'private life'. Such an approach is typified by comments of the ECtHR in *Niemietz v Germany*

(1992) 16 EHRR 97, a decision in which the concept of private life was held to cover the right to develop one's own personality as well as one's right to create relationships with others. The ECtHR held, at para. 29, that in defining 'private life' for the purposes of Article 8:

> ... it would be too restrictive to limit the notion to an 'inner circle' in which the individual may live his own personal life as he chooses and to exclude therefrom entirely the outside world not encompassed within that circle. Respect for private life must also comprise to a certain degree the right to establish and develop relationships with human beings.

The broad approach to private life is seen in the ECtHR's acceptance that intrusions into the public sphere through environmental damage may interfere with an individual's private life. There are a number of cases in which this has been accepted. In *Rayner v United Kingdom* (1986) 47 DR 5, for example, the ECmHR considered a complaint about the amount of air traffic over the applicant's home. The ECmHR agreed that this complaint fell within the ambit of Article 8 even though it involved 'indirect intrusions which are unavoidable consequences of measures not directed against private individuals', but ultimately decided that the interference was justified under Article 8(2).

Aircraft noise was again the subject of complaint in *Hatton v United Kingdom* (2002) 34 EHRR 1, in the specific context of night noise. The ECtHR initially accepted the argument that an increase in the noise levels at the applicants' homes, resulting from aircraft using Heathrow airport at night, was an unjustifiable interference with their Article 8 rights; in implementing a review on night flight restrictions, the state had failed to strike a fair balance between the United Kingdom's economic well-being and the applicants' effective enjoyment of their right to respect for their homes and their private and family lives. However, this decision was reviewed by the Grand Chamber, which came to a different conclusion and held that there was no violation of Article 8. It was held that, under Article 8(2), it was legitimate for the Government to have taken into consideration the economic interests of the airline operators and other enterprises. The Grand Chamber accepted the United Kingdom's evidence pointing to the economic benefit of night flights to the general economy, and found that the authorities were afforded a margin of appreciation when striking a balance between the competing interests ((App. No. 36022/97), 8 July 2003, ECtHR).

Lopez Ostra v Spain (1994) 20 EHRR 277 is a further decision concerning private life and environmental damage. There, it was held that permitting a waste treatment plant to operate in breach of a licence condition may affect the right of enjoyment of people's homes and so affect their right to private and family life even if it did not adversely affect their health.

However, it would seem that on the present state of the law, Article 8 may not require the Government to take positive steps to allow private life to take place in public spaces: see *Botta v Italy* (1998) 26 EHRR 241, where it was held that Articles 8 and 14 did not require the state to make access to a beach available to disabled persons. The situation may be different if the space is owned by a public authority. See also *Guerra v Italy* (1998) 26 EHRR 357.

It is clear that sexuality is an element of private life for the purposes of Article 8. Indeed, in *Dudgeon v United Kingdom* (1981) 4 EHRR 149, the ECtHR considered a person's sexual life to be 'a most intimate aspect' of his or her private life. This case and other, more recent decisions, such as *ADT v United Kingdom* (2001) 31 EHRR 33, indicate that an individual's sexual activities fall within the meaning of 'private life' irrespective of sexual orientation.

The ECtHR held in *Smith and Grady v United Kingdom* (2000) 29 EHRR 548 that investigations conducted by the Ministry of Defence into the sexual orientation of members of the services, together with their consequent discharge from the armed forces, constituted 'especially grave' interferences with their private lives. The ECtHR rejected the Government's argument that such a policy was justified to preserve the morale of the fighting forces, saying that the Ministry of Defence could not ignore widespread and developing views in other contracting states in favour of the admission of homosexuals into the armed forces of those states. This decision has been followed in the recent cases of *Perkins and R v United Kingdom* (App. Nos 43208/98 and 44875/98), 22 October 2002, ECtHR, and *Beck, Copp and Bazeley v United Kingdom* (App. Nos 48535/99, 48536/99, and 48537/99), 22 October 2002, ECtHR.

Article 8 has been held to protect the right of a transsexual to have his or her changed sex recognized by the state. In *B v France* (1992) 16 EHRR 1, the ECtHR held that the French Government violated the Article when it refused to allow a change to the applicant's birth certificate. Though the ECtHR took a different view in a number of cases from the United Kingdom in the 1980s and 1990s (*Rees v United Kingdom* (1986) 9 EHRR 56, *Cossey v United Kingdom* (1990) 13 EHRR 622, and *Sheffield v United Kingdom* (1999) 27 EHRR 163), it no longer takes the view that it is within the margin of appreciation for a state to refuse to recognize a change of gender. In the landmark case of *Goodwin v United Kingdom* (2002) 35 EHRR 447, it was held that the United Kingdom had failed to comply with a positive obligation to ensure the right of the applicant, a post-operative male to female transsexual, to respect for her private life, in particular through the lack of legal recognition given to her gender reassignment.

The right to a private life under Article 8 also includes the right not to have private information disclosed to third parties. This includes the unnecessary disclosure of confidential medical data in legal proceedings (*Z v Finland* (1998) 25 EHRR 371) and the unauthorized passing on of medical information from a hospital to authorities in the process of verifying a claim for social insurance and disability benefit (*MS v Sweden* (1999) 28 EHRR 313). In both cases a breach of Article 8 was found to have taken place, but in each case the breach was held to be justified on the particular facts of the case. In slightly different circumstances a violation could be found.

'Private life' can extend to the office context. For example, in *Halford v United*

Kingdom (1997) 24 EHRR 523, it was held that the bugging of private telephone calls made to an office telephone could constitute a violation of the right to respect for private life (see also *Niemietz v Germany* (1992) 16 EHRR 97).

8.8.3 Family Life

Article 8 case law has seen an evolution in what is considered 'family' (see Liddy, 'The concept of family life under the European Convention on Human Rights' [1998] EHRLR 15). Family life is now considered to extend beyond formal relationships and legitimate arrangements. In *Marckx v Belgium* (1979) 2 EHRR 330, the ECtHR found legislation that discriminated against children born outside of wedlock to be in violation of Article 8. Illustrating its flexible approach, the ECtHR has held that 'the mutual enjoyment by parent and child of each other's company constitutes a fundamental element of family life' (*B v United Kingdom* (1988) 10 EHRR 87).

In *K v United Kingdom* (1986) 50 DR 199, the ECmHR provided guidance as to the meaning of family life when it stated that '[t]he question of the existence or non-existence of "family life" is essentially a question of fact depending upon the real existence in practice of close personal ties'. In *Kroon v Netherlands* (1994) 19 EHRR 263, the ECtHR determined that, as a rule, living together may be a requirement for a relationship under Article 8, but exceptionally other factors may also serve to demonstrate that a relationship has sufficient constancy to create de facto 'family ties'. Generally, the ECtHR and ECmHR consider a family to constitute a male and female and their children. Homosexual and transsexual unions are not protected under the Article's family life principle, although those relationships may be protected under the private life principle (*S v United Kingdom* (1986) 47 DR 274 and *X v United Kingdom* (1997) 24 EHRR 143). In *X v United Kingdom*, it was held that the right to a family life did not protect life with a transsexual partner, and the failure to register a female-to-male transsexual as the father of his female partner's child did not constitute a breach of Article 8. However, in light of the ECtHR's progressive stance in *Goodwin* and the status of the Convention as a living instrument, this may be an area in which the ECtHR modifies its conservative position in the near future.

The right to family life is likely to be disrupted by immigration controls and procedures. However, the Strasbourg institutions have taken the view that if the family can go elsewhere to re-establish itself then the immigration procedures do not violate that right. Similarly, there may be no violation if the disruption is of the applicant's own making because he has breached immigration controls (*X v United Kingdom* (1987) 11 EHRR 48). A contrasting decision was reached in the recent case of *Amrollahi v Denmark* (App. No. 56811/00), 11 July 2002, ECtHR, where deportation of the complainant to Iran was held to violate Article 8, despite the basis of that deportation being a drug trafficking conviction.

The rights of parents to a private family life may be infringed if they are not allowed sufficient involvement in decisions taken by public authorities in fostering arrangements, taking children into care, or denying parents access to their children once in care. In *W, B v United Kingdom* (1987) 10 EHRR 29 and *R v United Kingdom* (1988) 10 EHRR 74, the ECtHR found a violation of Article 8 because parents were denied proper access to their children held in care and were given insufficient involvement in the local authority's decision-making process. Likewise, when the state intervenes by removing children into care, Article 8 requires that the natural parents be properly involved in the decision-making process, and that full account is taken of their views and wishes (*Johansen v Norway* (1996) 23 EHRR 33). See also *T.P and K.M. v United Kingdom* (2002) 34 EHRR 2.

8.8.4 Home

In *Gillow v United Kingdom* (1986) 11 EHRR 335, the ECtHR held that the notion of 'home' could extend to the place where one intends to live. The applicants in this case were absent from their house in Guernsey for 18 years because the husband's job caused him to travel. The Government refused the couple a new residence permit when they finally returned, arguing that this was not their home. The ECmHR and ECtHR held that, in this case, there was a right to 're-establish home life'. In *Buckley v United Kingdom* (1996) 23 EHRR 101, the ECtHR defined 'home' as a continuous residence with no intention to establish home elsewhere.

The concepts of home life and private life may overlap. In *Niemietz v Germany* (1992) 16 EHRR 97, the ECtHR extended the notion of 'privacy' to include some places of work. The case involved a search by the police of a lawyer's office. The ECtHR held that the Article protected his office space. The lawyer's office was protected because the ECtHR accepted that one's private life was carried on both at 'home' and, at times, elsewhere, including the office.

In *McLeod v United Kingdom* (1999) 27 EHRR 493, the ECtHR held that the powers of the police to enter private premises to prevent a breach of the peace were justified under Article 8(2). However, the ECtHR found that the police action, though justified, had been disproportionate in this situation since they entered the applicant's home when little or no risk of disorder existed. Thus, in operational terms, an action of a public authority may not survive ECtHR scrutiny even though the policy satisfies the legitimate aim test. Civil search powers in the course of executing an *Anton Piller* order (now a search order) have also been held to be justified under the 'rights of others' and 'economic well-being of the country' exceptions to Article 8 (see *Chappel v United Kingdom* (1990) 12 EHRR 1).

So far, however, the Article's notion of respect for home has not been extended to the right to have a particular home (*Buckley v United Kingdom* (1997) 23 EHRR 101 and *Chapman v United Kingdom* (2001) 33 EHRR 18).

8.8.5 Correspondence

The right to respect for one's correspondence is a right to uninterrupted and uncensored communication with others. In the telephone-tapping case, *Malone v United*

Kingdom (1984) 7 EHRR 14, the ECtHR found that the British Government violated Article 8 when it intercepted the phone calls of the applicant, an antique dealer convicted of receiving stolen goods. The ECtHR reasoned that, because the Government did not have statutory procedures for monitoring the phone calls of private citizens, it was not acting in accordance with the law. The ECtHR said, at para. 79:

> In view of the attendant obscurity and uncertainty as to the state of the law in this essential respect, . . . the law of England and Wales does not indicate with reasonable clarity the scope and manner of exercise of the relevant discretion conferred on the public authorities. To that extent, the minimum degree of legal protection to which citizens are entitled under the rule of law in a democratic society is lacking.

The ECtHR considered the same issue in *Halford v United Kingdom* (1997) 24 EHRR 523, where the applicant, a former Assistant Chief Constable, complained that calls which she had made from her office and home telephones were intercepted by the police in order to gather information for use against her in sex discrimination proceedings. The ECmHR found no proof that the applicant's home telephone was being monitored, but the ECtHR held that Article 8 was violated with respect to the calls made from the applicant's office because there was no legal regulation of the monitoring. The Regulation of Investigatory Powers Act 2000 is an important measure in ensuring that the use of covert listening devices now complies with the requirements of Article 8(2).

Some considerable case law is dedicated to prisoners' rights under Article 8. The ECtHR and ECmHR recognize that the restrictions inherent in imprisonment violate the rights under Article 8(1), but that these restrictions can sometimes be justified under Article 8(2) (see, for example, *Faulkner v United Kingdom* (2002) 35 EHRR 27). As regards prisoner correspondence, the ECtHR has held that a prisoner has the right to communicate with his or her lawyer with almost no interference. In *Golder v United Kingdom* (1975) 1 EHRR 524, the ECtHR held that there was no justification in restricting the applicant's correspondence with his lawyer. While the prison may interfere with non-legal correspondence, the ECtHR in *Silver v United Kingdom* (1983) 5 EHRR 347 stated that Strasbourg will investigate these interferences to make sure that they are justified under Article 8(2).

8.8.6 Human Rights Act Decisions

As anticipated in the 2nd edition of this book, Article 8 has provided fertile ground for imaginative litigation. The Article has been raised in a vast number of contexts and has proved influential in many areas. Areas of impact include:

(a) media law (e.g., *Venables v News Group Newspapers* [2001] 2 WLR 1038, *Douglas v Hello! Ltd* [2001] QB 967 (and [2003] EWHC 786), and *Naomi Campbell v Mirror Group Newspapers* [2002] EWCA Civ 1373);

(b) housing law (e.g., *Poplar Housing and Regeneration Community Association Ltd v Donoghue* [2001] EWCA Civ 595);

(c) immigration and asylum law (e.g., *R (Q and others) v Secretary of State for the Home Department* [2003] EWCA Civ 364 (see discussion at 8.3.7) and *R (Isiko) v Secretary of State for the Home Department* [2001] 1 FLR 930);

(d) employment law (e.g., *De Keyser v Wilson* [2001] IRLR 234);

(e) data protection (e.g., *Norman Baker MP v Secretary of State for the Home Department* [2001] UKHRR 1275);

(f) criminal law (e.g., *R v P* [2001] 2 WLR 463);

(g) prison law (e.g., *R (Daly) v Secretary of State for the Home Department* [2001] UKHL 26 and *R (Mellor) v Secretary of State for the Home Department* [2001] EWCA Civ 472);

(h) family law (e.g., *Re S, Re W* [2002] UKHL 10 and *R (Ann Stevens) v Plymouth City Council* [2002] EWCA Civ 388);

(i) planning law (e.g., *R (Ward) v London Borough of Hillingdon* [2001] EWHC Admin 91); and

(j) other environmental issues (e.g., *Marcic v Thames Water Utilities Ltd* [2002] EWCA Civ 65).

Privacy and the Media

One area in which Article 8 has had a particularly large impact is privacy intrusion by the media, as predicted in the 2nd edition of this guide. Now empowered with Article 8, the domestic courts have developed existing law to provide enhanced privacy protection in the circumstances of media intrusion, primarily through expanding the action of breach of confidence (see, for example, *Douglas v Hello! Ltd* [2003] EWHC 786 (Ch)). However, as the Court of Appeal decision, *Naomi Campbell v Mirror Group Newspapers* [2002] EWCA Civ 1373, indicates, breach of confidence will not be used to suppress all media disclosures about the private lives of celebrities. It remains to be seen whether the courts will recognize a domestic right to privacy as a means of giving effect to Article 8, rather than expanding existing law (see the comments of Sedley LJ in the Court of Appeal in *Douglas* [2001] QB 967, at 1001).

The Court of Appeal decision, *A v B* [2002] EWCA Civ 337, provides helpful guidance as to balancing the potentially conflicting rights to privacy and freedom of expression. At issue was an interim injunction, which prevented a newspaper from publishing details of a professional footballer's extramarital affairs. The Lord Chief Justice commented on Articles 8 and 10 at para. 6 as follows:

> The manner in which the two articles operate is entirely different. Article 8 operates so as to extend the areas in which an action for breach of confidence can provide protection for privacy. It requires a generous approach to the situations in which privacy is to be

protected. Article 10 operates in the opposite direction. This is because it protects freedom of expression and to achieve this it is necessary to restrict the area in which remedies are available for breaches of confidence. There is a tension between the two articles which requires the court to hold the balance between the conflicting interests they are designed to protect. This is not an easy task but it can be achieved by the courts if, when holding the balance, they attach proper weight to the important rights both articles are designed to protect. Each article is qualified expressly in a way which allows the interests under the other article to be taken into account.

The judgment sets out the principles that the courts should apply when faced with the task of balancing conflicting rights in injunction applications at paras 11–12.

This is an area which will undoubtedly be affected by the 2003 Report of the House of Commons' Culture, Media and Sport Select Committee, entitled *Privacy and Media Intrusion*, which called for the enactment of a privacy law to recognize and codify the developments in the common law brought about, at least in part, by the Human Rights Act (see www.parliament.co.uk/selcom for the full report).

For further discussion of privacy and the media, see Tomlinson (ed.), *Privacy and the Media: The Developing Law* (London: Matrix, 2002) and Tambini and Heywood (eds), *Ruled by Recluses? Privacy and the Media* (London: Institute for Public Policy Research, 2002). See also Singh and Strachan, 'The Right to Privacy in English Law' (2002) 2 EHRLR 129.

Article 8(2)
The Court of Appeal decision, *R (Marper) v Chief Constable of South Yorkshire* [2002] EWCA Civ 1275, examined the police retention of fingerprints and samples containing DNA taken during the course of a criminal investigation from individuals who ultimately were neither prosecuted nor convicted. The Court accepted that the retention was inconsistent with Article 8(1) but held that it was nevertheless justifiable under Article 8(2). This finding may have implications for the retention of fingerprints and DNA in other circumstances, such as the voluntary provision of samples. At the time of writing, an application for leave to appeal to the House of Lords is pending.

By contrast, Article 8(2) was unsuccessfully invoked in *R (Robertson) v Wakefield Metropolitan Council* [2001] EWHC Admin 915. The case concerned the refusal of the Electoral Registration Officer to agree to Mr Robertson's request that his name and address on the electoral register should not be supplied to commercial organizations. This practice of supplying information to commercial organizations was found to engage Article 8, and although it pursued a legitimate objective, the lack of any right of objection was held to be a disproportionate way of pursuing that objective. The case also raised issues under Article 3 of Protocol 1 (see 8.21.1 below).

See also *R (P) v Secretary of State for the Home Department* [2001] 1 WLR 2002.

8.9 ARTICLE 9: FREEDOM OF THOUGHT, CONSCIENCE, AND RELIGION

1. Everyone has the right to freedom of thought, conscience and religion; this right includes freedom to change his religion or belief and freedom, either alone or in community with others and in public or private, to manifest his religion or belief, in worship, teaching, practice and observance.

2. Freedom to manifest one's religion or beliefs shall be subject only to such limitations as are prescribed by law and are necessary in a democratic society in the interests of public safety, for the protection of public order, health or morals, or for the protection of the rights and freedoms of others.

Article 9 protects the rights to hold religious and non-religious beliefs, to change those beliefs, and to manifest them in 'worship, teaching, practice and observance', whether alone or with others, in public or in private. The right to hold and change beliefs is absolute. However, the right to manifest one's religion or beliefs can be limited under Article 9(2).

8.9.1 Freedom of Thought, Conscience, and Religion

In emphasizing the importance of freedom of thought, conscience, and religion, the ECtHR has stated that:

As enshrined in Article 9 . . . freedom of thought, conscience and religion is one of the foundations of a 'democratic society' within the meaning of the Convention. It is, in its religious dimension, one of the most vital elements that go to make up the identity of believers and their conception of life, but it is also a precious asset for atheists, agnostics, sceptics and the unconcerned. The pluralism indissociable from a democratic society, which has been dearly won over the centuries, depends on it. (*Kokkinakis v Greece* (1993) 17 EHRR 397, at para. 31)

While Article 9 protects a broad range of beliefs, including both religious and non-religious, it is not unlimited in its scope. In order to attract the protection of the Article, the thoughts or beliefs must be of a 'certain level of cogency, seriousness, cohesion and importance' (*Campbell and Cosans v United Kingdom* (1982) 4 EHRR 293, at para. 36).

8.9.2 Manifestation of One's Religion or Beliefs

The right to manifest one's religion or beliefs complements the primary right of freedom of thought, conscience, and religion. This right relates to acts that are an expression of a religion or belief and not to those that are merely influenced or motivated by it (*Arrowsmith v United Kingdom* (1978) 19 DR 5). It has been raised before the ECtHR in a number of contexts, including employment (for example, *X v United*

Kingdom (1981) 22 DR 27) and prisoners' rights (for example, *X v United Kingdom* (1976) 5 DR 100).

While recognizing the broad relevance of the right, the Court has arguably taken a rather restrictive approach to it. For example, in *Jewish Liturgical Association Cha'are Shalom Ve Tesedek v France* (App. No. 27417/95), 27 June 2000, ECtHR, the Court held that the right will not be violated if some form of obstacle renders manifestation more difficult, provided the obstacle does not make manifestation impossible. It is arguable that a similarly restrictive approach was taken in *Stedman v United Kingdom* [1997] EHRLR 545. There, the ECmHR dismissed a complaint that an employee's dismissal for refusing to work on Sundays violated her right to manifest her religion. The Commission considered that the applicant was dismissed for failing to agree to work on certain days, rather than because of her religious beliefs. This decision can be seen as prioritizing contractual obligations over *prima facie* rights, and additionally as taking an undeveloped approach to notions of indirect discrimination, though see now *Thlimmenos v Greece* (2001) 31 EHRR 411 at 8.14.2.

The ECtHR has consistently emphasized that in societies where several religions coexist it may be necessary to limit the right in order to reconcile the interests of the various groups and to ensure that all beliefs are respected (*Kokkinakis v Greece* (1993) 17 EHRR 397, at para. 33). This approach was applied in *Dahlab v Switzerland* (App. No. 42393/98), 15 February 2001, ECtHR, which involved a complaint by a teacher that a prohibition on wearing the Islamic veil at work violated her right to freedom of religion. The ECtHR held that the prohibition came within the state's margin of appreciation since it was designed to ensure the religious neutrality of the public education service in a society with diverse religious views. This aim was considered to contribute to the protection of the rights of others, order, and public safety.

Article 9(2) has frequently been applied by the ECtHR to remedy *prima facie* violations of Article 9(1). Indeed, the Strasbourg case law places considerable weight on Article 9(2), and is relatively narrow when it seeks to balance the right to religious expression and the contractual rights of others, specifically employers.

In *X v United Kingdom* (1981) 22 DR 27 (which arose from *Ahmed v Inner London Education Authority* [1978] QB 36), the ECmHR held that the decision of the Inner London Education Authority not to release a Muslim schoolteacher to attend mosque on Friday afternoons did not violate Article 9, because he had not disclosed this need at interview or during the first six years of employment. The ECmHR accepted that the education authority had reached a fair balance between the applicant's religious requirements and its own need to organize the school timetable efficiently. Therefore, the United Kingdom's failure to provide a remedy for his dismissal fell within Article 9(2).

However, not all invocations of Article 9(2) are successful. For example, in *Kokkinakis* (above), the ECtHR considered the actions of two Jehovah's Witnesses who engaged in door-to-door evangelism. The couple were convicted of the crime of proselytism and fined. The ECtHR recognized that attempting to convert others was a manifestation of belief capable of protection under Article 9(1). It decided that the limitation on this right was prescribed by law, and that the law itself had a legitimate aim, namely the protection of the rights and freedoms of others. However, it held that the decision to prosecute was 'not justified by a pressing need' because no regard had been given to whether the couple had used improper means to evangelize; hence there was a violation of Article 9.

8.9.3 Human Rights Act Decisions

The domestic courts have been required to consider what constitutes manifestation of a religion or belief on a number of occasions. In *R (Williamson) v Secretary of State for Education and Employment* [2001] EWHC Admin 960, the High Court held that teachers and parents in a private Christian school who wished to impose corporal punishment upon pupils were not manifesting a religion or belief. Elias J noted that not every action that is motivated by or is in accordance with a belief constitutes a manifestation of that belief. The Court of Appeal ([2002] EWCA Civ 1926) upheld the decision. For further discussion of the first instance decision, see Mountfield, 'Spare the Rod and Spoil the Child: A Philosophical Conviction?' [2002] *Education Law Journal* 9.

A similarly restrictive approach to Article 9(1) was applied by the House of Lords in *Pretty v United Kingdom* [2001] UKHL 61, where it was held that Article 9 was never intended to give individuals a right to perform any acts in pursuance of whatever beliefs they might hold. The difference in breadth between freedom of thought and the right to manifest one's belief was demonstrated by the court's finding that while an individual is free to hold and express a belief in the virtue of assisted suicide, such a belief cannot found a requirement that an individual who assists another to commit suicide be absolved from the legal consequences of engaging in such proscribed conduct.

Article 9(2) was the subject of consideration by the Court of Appeal in *R v Taylor* [2001] EWCA Crim 2263. The Court held that while the legal prohibition on the supply of cannabis did *prima facie* interfere with the right of a member of the Rastafarian religion to manifest his religion, it was a justifiable limitation on the right under Article 9(2). In this regard, a distinction had to be drawn between legislation which prohibited conduct specifically because it related to or was motivated by religious belief, and legislation which was of general application but prohibited conduct which happened to be encouraged or required by religious belief.

During the parliamentary debates on the Human Rights Bill, members of certain churches became concerned that the effect of Article 9 would be to prevent them from selecting employees in a manner consistent with the ethos and beliefs of their organization. The solution adopted by the Government is contained in s. 13 of the Act. This section provides that if the court's determination of any question under the Act might affect the exercise by a religious organization (whether as an organization, or by its members collectively) of the Convention right to freedom of thought, conscience, and religion, the court must have 'particular regard' to the importance of that right. For further discussion of s. 13, see Chapter 4, at 4.3.

Section 13 is really no more than an exhortation to apply the balance inherent in Article 9 properly. It might, however, affect the outcome in a case about discrimination with respect to dismissal, such as *O'Neill v Governors of St Thomas More Roman Catholic Voluntarily Aided Upper School* [1997] ICR 33, where it was held that to dismiss a teacher in a Catholic school by reason of pregnancy was sex discrimination. The governors argued that it was not the fact of pregnancy *per se* which caused the dismissal, but rather that the dismissal was motivated by the particular circumstances of the pregnancy (that is, the mother being unmarried and the father of the child being the local Catholic priest) which affected the religious character of the school. It was held that these factors could not be separated from the fact of the pregnancy. The existence of s. 13 may produce a different outcome, should a similar case come before the courts now that the 1998 Act is in force.

8.10 ARTICLE 10: FREEDOM OF EXPRESSION

1. Everyone has the right to freedom of expression. This right shall include freedom to hold opinions and to receive and impart information and ideas without interference by public authority and regardless of frontiers. This Article shall not prevent States from requiring the licensing of broadcasting, television or cinema enterprises.

2. The exercise of these freedoms, since it carries with it duties and responsibilities, may be subject to such formalities, conditions, restrictions or penalties as are prescribed by law and are necessary in a democratic society, in the interests of national security, territorial integrity or public safety, for the prevention of disorder or crime, for the protection of health or morals, for the protection of the reputation or rights of others, for preventing the disclosure of information received in confidence, or for maintaining the authority and impartiality of the judiciary.

Both the European and domestic courts have recognized the fundamental importance of freedom of expression in democratic societies (see, for example, *Handyside v United Kingdom* (1976) 1 EHRR 737, at para. 49 and *McCartan Turkington Breen v Times Newspapers Ltd* [2001] 2 AC 277, at 297). In *Handyside v United Kingdom* (at para. 49) the ECtHR described the Article 10 right as follows:

Freedom of expression constitutes one of the essential foundations of . . . a [democratic] society, one of the basic conditions for its progress and for the development of every man. Subject to para. 2 of Article 10, it is applicable not only to 'information' or 'ideas' that are favourably received or regarded as inoffensive or as a matter of indifference, but also to those that offend, shock or disturb the state or any sector of the population. Such are the demands of that pluralism, tolerance and broadmindedness without which there is no 'democratic society'.

The right to freedom of expression concerns the freedom to hold ideas, and to receive opinions and information, as well as the right to express them. However, while the right to receive information encompasses a right to be provided with information (*Open Door and Dublin Well Woman v Ireland* (1992) 15 EHRR 244), it does not create a general right to freedom of information (*Leander v Sweden* (1987) 9 EHRR 433). At present, any right to freedom of information arises only as a consequential requirement of protecting another right (see, for example, *Gaskin v United Kingdom* (1989) 12 EHRR 36, which considered a right to access to a social services file in connection with Article 8).

Article 10(1) protects both the substance of the ideas and information conveyed and the form in which they are conveyed (*Oberschlick v Austria* (1997) 25 EHRR 357, at para. 57). The concept of 'expression' covers words, pictures, images, and actions intended to express an idea or to present information (*Stevens v United Kingdom* (1986) 46 DR 245). Forms of expression that have been held to attract the protection of Article 10 include:

(a) political (such as distribution of political leaflets before an election: *Bowman v United Kingdom* (1998) 26 EHRR 1);

(b) journalistic (such as refusal to disclose journalistic sources: *Goodwin v United Kingdom* (1996) 22 EHRR 123);

(c) artistic (for example, *Müller v Switzerland* (1988) 13 EHRR 212 and *Wingrove v United Kingdom* (1996) 24 EHRR 1); and

(d) commercial (for example, *Barthold v Germany* (1985) 7 EHRR 383 (vets' advertising) and *Colman v United Kingdom* (1993) 18 EHRR 119 (doctors' advertising)).

In practice, the ECtHR gives rather stronger protection to political and journalistic expression than to other forms of expression, though the ECtHR has expressly disavowed any theoretical basis for this distinction (*Thorgeirson v Iceland* (1992) 14 EHRR 843, at para. 64). Though the ECtHR has never gone so far as the US Supreme Court in *New York Times v Sullivan* (1964) 376 US 254, which requires proof of malice in defamation cases brought by public figures, it affords considerable protection to those who criticize politicians and other public figures, such as judges, whether or not the views they express are facts or based on opinion, and whether or not they are politely or elegantly expressed, unless they are 'gratuitous personal attacks' (*Oberschlick v Austria* (1997) 25 EHRR 357; *De Haes v Belgium* (1997) 25 EHRR 1). The ECtHR is interested in protecting the elements of a free press, such as the rights of journalists to protect their sources as well as the actual expression of views (*Goodwin v United Kingdom* (1996) 22 EHRR 123).

However, in other areas, the ECtHR is more likely to give greater weight to the rights and freedoms of others. For example, in *Otto-Preminger Institute v Austria* (1994) 19 EHRR 34, the ECtHR decided that it was within the state's margin of appreciation to decide to seize a film which satirized God, Jesus, and Mary in a predominantly Catholic country, because it could be said to be 'necessary in a democratic society'. A similar conclusion was reached in *Wingrove v United Kingdom*

(1996) 24 EHRR 1, in which the British Board of Film Classification refused a certificate for a video called *Visions of Ecstasy*.

The balance between the importance of the right to freedom of expression to a democratic system overall and the rights and the freedoms of others has caused the ECtHR great difficulty. This is partly because the right to freedom of expression can often conflict with competing social interests such as the right to a fair trial (*Sunday Times v United Kingdom* (1979) 2 EHRR 245), the protection of the democratic process (*Bowman v United Kingdom* (1998) 26 EHRR 1), the privacy of others (*Lingens v Austria* (1986) 8 EHRR 103), and the right to respect for thought, conscience, and religion (*Otto-Preminger Institute v Austria* (1994) 19 EHRR 34). The issue of balance was considered by the Grand Chamber in its review of *Refah Partisi v Turkey* (App. Nos 41340/98 and 41342/98, 13 February 2003), a controversial decision concerning the absolute banning of a major political party, on the basis that this was necessary to protect the democratic foundations of the state (see further discussion at 8.11.5 below).

8.10.1 Exceptions to the Right to Freedom of Expression

Article 10 contains substantial internal limits on the right to freedom of expression. Article 10(1) specifically provides that it does not prevent states from requiring the licensing of broadcasting, television, or cinema enterprises, and a significant list of exceptions is specified in Article 10(2). This list of exceptions is longer and more specific than in relation to other Articles, and the second paragraph specifically states that the exercise of the freedoms in Article 10(1) 'carries with it duties and responsibilities'.

When the right is limited pursuant to the licensing exception in Article 10(2), it is not necessary that any of the objectives in Article 10(2) be pursued. However, the interference must still be compatible with the broad requirements of the second paragraph (*Informationsverein Lentia v Austria* (1994) 17 EHRR 93).

Despite the seemingly broad reach of Article 10(2), it is evident from the case law that the ECtHR will require a strong justification for interfering with the right to freedom of expression. Indeed, the ECtHR has made it clear that there is limited scope under Article 10(2) for restrictions on political speech, or on debate on questions of public interest (*Wingrove v United Kingdom* (1996) 24 EHRR 1, at para. 58; but see also *McVicar v United Kingdom* (2002) 35 EHRR 22 and *Refah Partisi v Turkey* (2002) 35 EHRR 3 and the Grand Chamber decision of 13 February 2003).

When considering if an interference is justified, the ECtHR follows the approach outlined in Chapter 2. The common law is in principle sufficient to meet the requirement that an interference is 'prescribed by law' if it is 'adequately accessible' and 'formulated with sufficient precision' (*Sunday Times v United Kingdom* (1979) 2 EHRR 245). In *Hashman and Harrup v United Kingdom* (2000) 30 EHRR 241, the ECtHR decided that the imposition of binding-over orders on hunt saboteurs for behaviour that was not unlawful but that was *contra bonos mores* was insufficiently precise to be justified as a limitation on the applicants' right to protest against hunting with hounds. This case also engaged Article 11 issues, reflecting the frequent role that Article 10 plays as one of the central means of securing enjoyment of the Article 11 freedoms (see also *Rekvenyi v Hungary* (2000) 30 EHRR 519, at para. 58).

The ECtHR will also examine whether the restriction can be 'justified as being necessary in a democratic society'. This involves it in considering the facts and circumstances prevailing before it. So, for example, it upheld injunctions to restrain the publication of Peter Wright's *Spycatcher* before it was published in other countries, and held that risk of material prejudicial to MI5 justified the injunctions (*Observer v United Kingdom* (1991) 14 EHRR 153), whereas it took a different view after the book was available in other jurisdictions and the justification no longer stood. See also *Goodwin v United Kingdom* (1996) 22 EHRR 123, in which the ECtHR recognized that fining a journalist who refused to disclose his sources for contempt of court was 'prescribed by law' and 'pursued a legitimate aim', but was nonetheless disproportionate in the circumstances, and *Tolstoy Miloslavsky v United Kingdom* (1995) 20 EHRR 442, in which a level of libel damages which at the time was not open to review by the Court of Appeal and, at £1.5 million, was so high as to stifle freedom of speech, was not necessary in a democratic society and hence breached Article 10.

However, in other cases concerning freedom of expression, the ECtHR felt it appropriate to draw back from pronouncing on the proportionality issue, holding that the decision reached by the national court had been within its 'margin of appreciation' (for example, *Handyside v United Kingdom* (1976) 1 EHRR 737). The breadth of the margin afforded to states will vary according to the subject matter involved. For example, in *VGT Verein Gegen Tierfabriken v Switzerland* (2002) 34 EHRR 4, the ECtHR stated that the margin of appreciation acquires particular importance in relation to commercial matters, but is reduced in scope when the expression at issue concerns an individual's participation in a debate that affects the general interest. In all cases, the ECtHR exercises strict supervision of the margin of appreciation because of the crucial importance of the Article 10 right (*United Christian Broadcasters Ltd v United Kingdom* (App. No. 44802/98), 7 November 2000, ECtHR).

8.10.2 Human Rights Act Decisions

The right to freedom of expression has been recognized at common law for many years (see, for example, *Cassell & Co. Ltd v Broome* [1972] AC 1027 and *R v Shayler* [2002] UKHL 11). This common law recognition has been held by the House of Lords to be consistent with Article 10 (*Derbyshire County Council v Times Newspapers Ltd* [1993] AC 534, at 551). Against this background, the courts have stated that the central impact of the Human Rights Act in this area is to strengthen protection of freedom of expression (*Reynolds v Times Newspapers Ltd and others* [1999] 4 All ER 609, at 621).

Despite judicial assertions that freedom of expression receives the same protection at common law as under the Convention, Article 10 has been raised in a number of cases. Defamation law has been a particularly active area, with the Convention compliance of various elements coming under challenge. In the vast majority of cases, such as *Loutchansky v Times Newspapers Ltd* [2001] EWCA Civ 1805, the existing law has been found to comply with Article 10 (but see *O'Shea v MGN Ltd* [2001] EMLR 943).

Media law has been another prominent area of Article 10 challenge (for example, *Ashworth Hospital Authority v MGN Ltd* [2002] UKHL 29). This area has seen the relationship between freedom of expression and the right to respect for private life come under consideration on several occasions (for example, *Douglas v Hello! Ltd* [2001] QB 967). The relationship between Article 10 and the right to privacy is discussed at pp. 164–165 above.

Other areas of activity include criminal law (for example, *R v Perrin* [2002] EWCA Crim 747) and public inquiries (for example, *Persey, Jackson, Hindmarsh and Others v Secretary of State for Environment, Food and Rural Affairs* [2002] EWCA Admin 371). The *Persey* case involved a challenge to the Secretary of State's decision to hold three inquiries into the foot and mouth outbreak in private. The Court held that there is no legal presumption of openness with regard to all forms of public inquiry and that Article 10 is not automatically engaged by a decision to hold a public inquiry in private.

Article 10(2)

The role of Article 10(2) was considered by the House of Lords in *R v Shayler* [2002] UKHL 11, where it was argued that the Official Secrets Act 1989 was inconsistent with Article 10. While the House of Lords accepted that the legislation interfered with freedom of expression, it observed that Article 10(1) is qualified by Article 10(2) and held that, in all the circumstances, the restrictions imposed by the Official Secrets Act were proportionate and pursued a legitimate aim. In reaching this conclusion, their Lordships noted that Convention jurisprudence recognizes the need to preserve the secrecy of information relating to intelligence and military operations in order to counter terrorism, criminal activity, hostile activity, and subversion.

Article 10(2) was again used to remedy a *prima facie* breach of Article 10(1) in *R (Farrakhan) v Secretary of State for the Home Department* [2002] EWCA Civ 606. In this decision, the Court of Appeal accorded a 'particularly wide margin of discretion' to the Secretary of State. The effect of such a wide margin appeared to be a less than rigorous enforcement of the requirement that interferences with freedom of expression be 'convincingly established'. Such an approach is arguably inconsistent with the ECtHR's insistence that the margin of appreciation be strictly supervised. The domestic approach to the margin of appreciation is discussed further in Chapter 2.

The domestic approach to Article 10(2) in the particular context of political speech was addressed by the Court of Appeal in *ProLife Alliance v British Broadcasting Corporation* [2002] EWCA Civ 297. This case concerned a refusal to broadcast a party election broadcast that graphically depicted the abortion process. The Court of Appeal held that it was only in very rare circumstances that a party election broadcast could properly be rejected by broadcasters on the grounds of taste and decency. In this situation, the broadcast should not have been rejected as the broadcasters had failed to give sufficient weight to the pressing imperative of free political expression. The BBC's appeal against this decision to the House of Lords ([2003] UKHL 23) was upheld (by a majority, with Lord Scott dissenting). Their Lordships decided that the BBC and other broadcasters were entitled to refuse to broadcast the party election broadcast by the ProLife Alliance on the ground that it was offensive to public feeling.

The legitimacy, under both Article 10(2) and Article 11, of the proscription of political organizations under s. 3 of the Terrorism Act 2000 was also the subject of cases before the Proscribed Organizations Appeal Commission (see *R (Ahmed) v Secretary of State for the Home Department, R (People's Mojahedin Organization of Iran) v Secretary of State for the Home Department, R (Kurdistan Workers' Party) v Secretary of State for the Home Department* [2002] EWHC Admin 644).

Section 12 of the Human Rights Act 1998
In contrast to decisions such as *Farrakhan* (see p. 173 above), case law concerning s. 12 of the Human Rights Act clearly indicates that freedom of expression has been strengthened domestically. In *Imutran v Uncaged Campaigns* [2001] 2 All ER 385, for example, s. 12 was held to create a slightly higher threshold for the granting of an injunction. The 'horizontal' applicability of Article 10, flowing from s. 12(4), is a further example of the strengthened protection (see *Douglas v Hello! Ltd*, at 133). Section 12 is discussed in greater detail at 4.3.

8.11 ARTICLE 11: FREEDOM OF ASSEMBLY AND ASSOCIATION

1.   Everyone has the right to freedom of peaceful assembly and to freedom of association with others, including the right to form and to join trade unions for the protection of his interests.

2.   No restrictions shall be placed upon the exercise of these rights other than such as are prescribed by law and are necessary in a democratic society in the interests of national security or public safety, for the prevention of disorder or crime, for the protection of health or morals or for the protection of the rights and freedoms of others. This Article shall not prevent the imposition of lawful restrictions on the exercise of these rights by members of the armed forces, of the police or of the administration of the state.

Article 11 protects the rights to freedom of peaceful assembly and freedom of association with others. These rights include the right to form and to join trade unions for the protection of a person's interests. The Article confers these rights on both individuals and trade unions (*Schmidt v Sweden* (1976) 1 EHRR 632). Rights under Article 11 are qualified in two ways: first, because a court or tribunal will often be required to balance competing rights under Article 11 with rights under other Articles of the Convention; and, secondly, because of the qualifications in Article 11(2).

8.11.1 Positive Obligation

In addition to imposing a negative obligation on the authorities not to interfere unjustifiably with the protected rights, Article 11 contains a positive obligation on states to secure the effective enjoyment of the rights (*Wilson and Palmer v United Kingdom* (2002) 35 EHRR 20). In *Plattform 'Arzte für das Leben' v Austria* (1988) 13 EHRR 204, it was held that the state had a duty to protect the participants in a peaceful demonstration from disruption by a violent counter-demonstration. The ECtHR held, at para. 32, that:

> Genuine, effective freedom of peaceful assembly cannot . . . be reduced to a mere duty on the part of the state not to interfere: a purely negative conception would not be compatible with the object and purpose of Article 11. . . . Article 11 sometimes requires positive measures to be taken, even in the sphere of relations between individuals, if need be.

In the context of freedom of association, the ECtHR has held that the Convention safeguards upon the freedom for individual trade unionists to protect their interests by trade union action are rights that the state must 'both permit and make possible' (*National Union of Belgian Police v Belgium* (1975) 1 EHRR 578, at para. 39).

8.11.2 Freedom of Association

The right to freedom of association protects the right to join or form 'associations' (such as political parties), as well as the right to join trade unions. Although not expressly mentioned, Article 11(1) also protects the negative right not to join an association (*Cheall v United Kingdom* (1985) 42 DR 178, at 185). Professional regulatory bodies set up by a state to regulate a profession, with compulsory membership within a profession, do not fall within this definition of an association (*Le Compte v Belgium* (1981) 4 EHRR 1). A bar association and an architects' association are not within the definition; but a taxi drivers' association has been held to fall within it (*Sigurdur A. Sigurjónsson v Iceland* (1993) 16 EHRR 462).

The 'closed shop' is not always a violation of Article 11. In *Young v United Kingdom* (1981) 4 EHRR 38, it was held that a closed shop was a violation of Article 11 because the refusal to join a union led to 'a threat of dismissal involving loss of livelihood' which was 'a most serious form of compulsion' and as such struck 'at the very substance of the freedom guaranteed by Article 11'. However, in *Sibson v United Kingdom* (1993) 17 EHRR 193, an employer exercised his contractual right to transfer an employee to a different depot after he resigned from one union to join another and others refused to work with him. The ECtHR held that moving him to a different depot did not 'strike at the very substance of the freedom of association guaranteed by Article 11' because there was no question of him losing his job.

Article 11 does not create a right to membership of a particular association in all circumstances. In *Cheall v United Kingdom* (1985) 42 DR 178, the ECmHR decided that generally an individual had no right to belong to a particular trade union. The decision to expel Mr Cheall was analysed as the decision of a private body exercising its rights under Article 11 not to associate with him. However, the ECmHR made the point that the right of the trade union to choose its members is not absolute:

> . . . for the right to join a union to be effective the state must protect the individual against any abuse of a dominant position by trade unions. . . . Such abuse might occur, for example, where exclusion or expulsion was not in accordance with union rules or where the rules were wholly unreasonable or arbitrary or where the consequences of exclusion or expulsion resulted in exceptional hardship such as job loss because of a closed shop.

8.11.3 Freedom of Assembly

In relation to freedom of assembly, Article 11 applies only to peaceful gatherings; it does not encompass 'a demonstration where the organisers and participants have violent intentions which result in public disorder' (*G v Germany* (1989) 60 DR 256). However, a just balance must be achieved. In *Ezelin v France* (1991) 14 EHRR 362, a demonstrator who was a lawyer by profession refused to leave when a march disintegrated into violence, and refused to answer questions at a subsequent inquiry. The French Court of Appeal, exercising its disciplinary function over lawyers, reprimanded him for 'breach of discretion', though his actions were not unlawful. The ECtHR regarded this as disproportionate to the state's need to prevent disorder. It held that a 'just balance' must not discourage people from making their beliefs known in a peaceful way.

8.11.4 Right to Form and Join Trade Unions

The ECtHR has emphasized that while Article 11 includes trade union freedom as a specific aspect of freedom of association, it does not secure any particular treatment of trade union members by the state. Rather, it protects the broader freedom of trade unions to protect the occupational interests of their members. Accordingly, Article 11 does not protect a specific right to strike, or impose an obligation on employers to engage in collective bargaining. (*Schmidt v Sweden* (1976) 1 EHRR 632).

The right to join a trade union for the protection of one's interests was the subject of recent scrutiny by the ECtHR in *Wilson and Palmer v United Kingdom* (2002) 35 EHRR 20. This case concerned a complaint by a number of employees and trade unions regarding a requirement to sign a personal contract relinquishing certain trade union rights, or remain under a collective bargaining agreement and accept a lower pay rise. The ECtHR found that the requirement, which was permitted by English law, amounted to a disincentive or restraint on the use of union membership by employees to protect their interests. It enabled an employer effectively to under-mine or frustrate a trade union's ability to strive for the protection of its members' interests. Accordingly, the state was held to have violated Article 11 by failing to secure enjoyment of the protected rights through permitting employers to use finan-cial incentives to induce employees to surrender important union rights.

In *Sanchez Navajas v Spain* (App. No. 57442/00), 21 June 2001, ECtHR, the Court considered that it could infer from Article 11, read in the light of Article 28 of the European Social Charter, that workers' representatives should have access to appropriate facilities to enable them to perform their trade union functions rapidly and effectively.

8.11.5 Article 11(2)

Article 11(2) permits states to place limitations on the exercise of the Article 11(1) rights by members of the armed forces, police, or members of the administration of the state. In *Council of Civil Service Unions v United Kingdom* (1987) 50 DR 228 (the GCHQ case) the ECmHR took the view that that staff at GCHQ were 'members of the administration of the State' and that therefore there was no breach of the Convention in the decision of the British Government to prohibit them from membership of trade unions. By contrast, in *Vogt v Germany* (1995) 21 EHRR 205, the ECmHR found that German schoolteachers were not 'members of the adminis-tration of the State', and the ECtHR held that this part of Article 11(2) 'should be interpreted narrowly in the light of the post held by the official concerned'.

Article 11(2) was considered by the Grand Chamber in its review of *Refah Partisi v Turkey* (App. Nos 41340/98 and 41342/98, 13 February 2003). The majority of the ECtHR found that a ban on the Refah Partisi political party was justified under Article 11(2) since a state is justified in preventing implementation of a political programme that is inconsistent with Convention norms and which, if given effect, might jeopardize civil peace and a country's democratic regime. The Grand Chamber upheld this unanimously.

8.11.6 Human Rights Act Decisions

Article 11 has been the subject of relatively few complaints before the domestic courts. The provision was raised in a trade union context in *National Union of Rail, Maritime and Transport Workers v London Underground Ltd* [2001] EWCA Civ 211. There, the Court of Appeal affirmed the approach of the ECtHR in *Schmidt v Sweden* (see 8.11.4 above) to the right to form and join trade unions.

Freedom of association was raised in a rather different context in *RSPCA v Attorney General and Others* [2002] 1 WLR 448, where the RSPCA sought guid-ance as to whether it could adopt a membership policy that excluded individuals who wished to change its policy on hunting. The Court found that the freedom of associa-tion of the RSPCA itself 'embraces the freedom to exclude from the association those whose membership it honestly believes to be damaging the interests of the Society'. The exclusionary policy would not therefore violate Article 11.

8.12 ARTICLE 12: RIGHT TO MARRY

Men and women of marriageable age have the right to marry and to found a family, according to the national laws governing the exercise of this right

Article 12 protects the right to marry and to found a family. These are qualified rights as the state is expressly given wide berth to regulate the exercise of the rights.

While bearing a superficial resemblance to Article 8, Article 12 is a distinct provision and is of much narrower scope. The ECtHR affirmed the distinction between Articles 8 and 12 in *P, C and S v United Kingdom* (2002) 35 EHRR 31, holding that complaints regarding inteference with family life between a parent and child cannot be raised under Article 12.

Until recently, Article 12 provided only a right to marry a person who was biologically of the opposite sex (see, for example, *Cossey v United Kingdom* (1990) 13 EHRR 622). However, in the striking decision *Goodwin v United Kingdom* (2002) 35 EHRR 447, the ECtHR held that:

While it is for the Contracting State to determine *inter alia* the conditions under which a person claiming legal recognition as a transsexual establishes that gender reassignment has been properly effected or under which past marriages cease to be valid and the formalities applicable to future marriages . . . the Court finds no justification for barring the transsexual from enjoying the right to marry under any circumstances.

It remains to be seen whether this more expansive approach to Article 12 will lead to recognition of a right to same-sex marriage.

In *Hamer v United Kingdom* (1979) 24 DR 5 and *Draper v United Kingdom* (1980) 24 DR 72, the ECmHR ruled that prohibiting prisoners from marrying interfered with their Article 12 rights and served no legitimate state objective. Accordingly, while the state has the power to regulate the exercise of the right to marry, any restrictions must not be arbitrary.

8.12.1 Human Rights Act Decisions

English case law regarding the right to marry is currently inconsistent with European jurisprudence; the domestic courts do not recognize the ability or right of a post-operative transsexual to marry (*Bellinger v Bellinger* [2001] EWCA Civ 1140). However, there is an opportunity to remedy the inconsistency as the *Bellinger* decision has been appealed to the House of Lords.

In *R (Mellor) v Secretary of State for the Home Department* [2001] EWCA Civ 472, the Court of Appeal held that Article 12 does not, in the absence of exceptional circumstances, guarantee prisoners the right to have a child using artificial insemination. In another case involving the right to found a family, the Court of Appeal held that, in the context of surrogacy, Article 12 does not provide a right to be supplied with a child (*Briody v St Helens and Knowsley Area Health Authority* [2001] EWCA Civ 1010). These decisions suggest that, at present, Article 12 as interpreted by the domestic courts primarily protects the right to have children by natural means.

8.13 ARTICLE 13: RIGHT TO AN EFFECTIVE REMEDY

Everyone whose rights and freedoms as set forth in this Convention are violated shall have an effective remedy before a national authority notwithstanding that the violation has been committed by persons acting in an official capacity.

Article 13 requires member states to provide a real and effective remedy in a domestic court for violations of the substantive rights enumerated in the Convention. This means that there must be domestic procedures for dealing with the substance of an 'arguable complaint', and for granting appropriate relief in cases of actual breach of the Convention. Accordingly, as the ECtHR stated in *Klass v Germany* (1978) 2 EHRR 214, the available remedy must 'involve the determination of the claim as well as the possibility of redress'.

The scope of the Article 13 obligation varies depending on the nature of the complaint. For example, in the case of a violation of Article 2, Article 13 will require, in addition to the payment of compensation where appropriate, an effective investigation capable of leading to the identification and punishment of those responsible for the deprivation of life, including effective access for the complainant to the investigation procedure (for example, *Keenan v United Kingdom* (2001) 3 EHRR 913 and *Edwards v United Kingdom* (2002) 35 EHRR 487). By contrast, compensation alone may be a sufficient remedy for breaches of other Articles. However, in all cases the requisite remedy must be 'effective' in both practice and law (*Aksoy v Turkey* (1996) 23 EHRR 553). The requirement of practical efficacy means that exercise of the remedy must not be unjustifiably hindered by the acts or omissions of state authorities (*Aksoy*).

The question will often be whether all the procedures, in the lower tribunals and the courts, taken together, amount to an 'effective remedy'. For example, *Silver v United Kingdom* (1983) 5 EHRR 347 concerned a complaint by a prisoner that his correspondence had been interfered with contrary to Article 8 and that no effective remedy was available in respect of that breach. The ECtHR took the view that neither the prison board of visitors, the Parliamentary Commissioner for Administration, the Home Secretary, nor subsequent judicial review of the Home Secretary's decisions was a sufficiently effective remedy to comply with Article 13.

Equally, in *Govell v United Kingdom* (App. No. 27237/95), 14 January 1998, ECmHR, it was held that the police complaints procedure was an inadequate remedy for the purposes of Article 13. This position was re-affirmed in the case of *Khan v*

United Kingdom (2000) 31 EHRR 45, where it was held that there was a violation of Article 13 (in conjunction with Article 8) on the basis that the Police Complaints Authority was not a sufficiently independent body for the purposes of the provision. As these decisions indicate, the body with the ability to provide the remedy must be independent of the body alleged to have breached the Convention obligation. See also *Taylor-Sabori v United Kingdom* (2003) 36 EHRR 17.

Much of the Strasbourg case law involving the United Kingdom is concerned with the extent to which judicial review proceedings, in which issues of fact can rarely be considered, can be treated as an effective remedy. The ECtHR's case law in this respect is variable. Whether judicial review is adequate as a remedy appears to depend on the context, and in particular, whether the ECtHR is satisfied that the domestic courts can afford a sufficient degree of review properly to examine the legality of the executive's actions.

In *Soering v United Kingdom* (1989) 11 EHRR 439, the ECtHR found judicial review to be an effective remedy for the purposes of Article 13. The applicant was threatened with extradition to the United States of America to face a charge of murder. The ECtHR held that the 'death-row phenomenon' (being kept on death row for long periods of time before a final decision is pronounced on execution) constituted torture or inhuman and degrading treatment. The fact that a United Kingdom court would have jurisdiction to set aside a decision to extradite for this reason convinced the ECtHR that this review constituted an effective remedy.

This meant that in *Vilvarajah v United Kingdom* (1991) 14 EHRR 248, in which the ECmHR had decided that an appeal on the merits *after* an applicant had left the United Kingdom was not an effective remedy for potential breaches of Article 3, the ECtHR declined to address the point because it had already decided that judicial review was an adequate remedy, and an individual would not be removed from the jurisdiction during that process. See also *Bensaid v United Kingdom* (2001) 33 EHRR 10.

However, in *Chahal v United Kingdom* (1997) 23 EHRR 413, the ECtHR held unanimously that there had been a violation of Article 13 in conjunction with Article 3. A Sikh separatist leader was detained in custody for deportation purposes in response to the Home Secretary's determination that he was a threat to national security. The ECtHR found that this deportation would be a violation of Article 3, as the applicant would face a real risk of being subjected to ill-treatment in the receiving country. Because neither the advisory panel nor the courts could review the Home Secretary's decision to deport the applicant, the ECtHR found that there were no effective remedies available to the applicant.

It seems, however, that *Chahal* may be confined to cases where national security issues have been invoked. In *D v United Kingdom* (1997) 24 EHRR 423, the applicant sought to rely on the decision in *Chahal* to persuade the ECtHR not to follow its conclusion in *Soering* and *Vilvarajah* that judicial review proceedings were an effective remedy in complaints raised under Article 3 in the context of deportation and extradition. D, who was dying of AIDS, challenged the Chief Immigration Officer's decision not to let him stay on compassionate grounds. He argued that judicial review proceedings were an insufficient remedy because the Court of Appeal did not seek to ask itself whether Article 3 would be breached by the deportation but merely asked whether the decision-maker had taken the matter into account. The Court, however, held that there was no reason to depart from the two earlier cases, because the ECtHR afforded 'anxious scrutiny' in cases involving a risk to life expectancy. The approach in this case been criticized (Blake, 'Judicial review of discretion in human rights cases' [1997] EHRLR 391). See also the discussion in Chapter 4 of 'Judicial Deference to Acts of Public Authorities'.

The ECtHR has also regarded judicial review and/or appeal from a tribunal of fact on a point of law as constituting an adequate remedy in other contexts than removal from the United Kingdom (for example, *Bryan v United Kingdom* (1995) 21 EHRR 342). However, where there is no system of regulating interferences with rights by private bodies, there will be a breach of Article 13 (*Halford v United Kingdom* (1997) 24 EHRR 523).

Judicial review was held not to be an effective remedy in *Smith and Grady v United Kingdom* (2000) 29 EHRR 548. The domestic courts themselves had expressed concerns when they were dealing with the case on judicial review. The remedial deficiency stemmed from the threshold at which the domestic courts could find the Ministry of Defence policy of excluding homosexuals from the armed forces irrational. The height of the threshold effectively prevented the domestic courts considering whether the interference answered a pressing social need, or was proportionate to the national security and public order aims pursued.

Again, in *Hatton v United Kingdom* (App. No. 36022/97, 8 July 2003) the Grand Chamber of the ECtHR held that judicial review did not satisfy the requirements of Article 13. The basis of the ECtHR's decision was that the scope of review by the domestic courts was insufficient since it was limited to the classic English public law concepts, such as irrationality, unlawfulness, and unreasonableness. Accordingly, judicial review did not allow for consideration of whether the subject of the primary complaint under Article 8 (an increase in night flights) was a justifiable limitation on the right to respect for the private and family lives of those who lived in the vicinity of Heathrow airport.

The United Kingdom has recently come under Article 13 scrutiny in relation to allegations of child abuse, triggering Article 3. In both *Z v United Kingdom* (2002) 34 EHRR 3 and *D.P. and J.C. v United Kingdom* (2003) 36 EHRR 14, the lack of any appropriate means of obtaining a determination of allegations that the local authority had failed to protect the applicants from ill-treatment during childhood was found to breach Article 13.

8.13.1 Human Rights Act Implications

Article 13 is not directly incorporated into domestic law by the Human Rights Act 1998. However, it may play an important role in the interpretation of incorporated rights since, by virtue of s. 2 of the Human Rights Act, Strasbourg case law must be taken into account when a United Kingdom court is considering a case 'in connection with' an incorporated right. Further discussion of Article 13 can be found in Chapter 4.

8.14 ARTICLE 14: PROHIBITION ON DISCRIMINATION

The enjoyment of the rights and freedoms set forth in this Convention shall be secured without discrimination on any ground such as sex, race, colour, language, religion, political or other opinion, national or social origin, association with a national minority, property, birth or other status.

Article 14 guarantees that everyone shall enjoy the Convention rights, without discrimination. In doing so, it reflects the international consensus regarding the inherent place of equality rights in a free and democratic society. However, limitations in the scope of the right and in the ECtHR's approach to complaints under the Article have given it only a limited prominence in Convention case law.

8.14.1 Scope of Article 14

Article 14 is not a general 'equal treatment' guarantee. Unlike other human rights instruments, such as Article 26 of the International Covenant on Civil and Political Rights of 1966, the Convention contains no generally applicable free-standing prohibition on discrimination. It requires only that the enjoyment of other Convention rights be secured without discrimination: in effect it is a guarantee of equality before the law of the Convention. This means that it can operate only within the ambit of another Convention right.

The application of Article 14 does not require a *breach* of another Article but merely that the facts of the case come within the scope (or ambit) of another Article (*Abdulaziz, Cabales and Balkandali v United Kingdom* (1985) 7 EHRR 471). A claim falls 'within the ambit' of a Convention right if it concerns the subject matter protected by that Article of the Convention.

In the *Belgian Linguistics Case (No. 2)* (1968) 1 EHRR 252, the ECtHR held that a failure to maintain a particular type of school was not itself a violation of Article 14, but a state which had set up such an establishment could not operate discriminatory entrance requirements for it because this would violate Article 14. Another example of the scope of Article 14 given in that case is access to a court. Article 6 does not require a right of appeal, but if one exists, it would violate Article 6 read with Article 14 if certain people were barred from appealing without a legitimate reason while others with the same cause of action could appeal. See also *Inze v Austria* (1987) 10 EHRR 394 and *Abdulaziz v United Kingdom* (above), at paras 65, 71, and 72. In *National Union of Belgian Police v Belgium* (1975) 1 EHRR 578, the ECtHR said, 'It is as though Article 14 formed an integral part of each of the articles laying down rights and freedoms whatever their nature'.

In many cases the ECtHR, once it has found a breach of the substantive right, has held that it is unnecessary to go on to consider whether there has also been a breach of Article 14. For example, in *Dudgeon v United Kingdom* (1981) 4 EHRR 149, which concerned the criminalization of all homosexual activity in Northern Ireland, the claim was brought under Article 8 (right to respect for private and family life) and Article 14; but having found a breach of Article 8, the ECtHR found it unnecessary to consider whether there was also discrimination on grounds of sexual orientation. Similarly, in *Smith and Grady v United Kingdom* (2000) 29 EHRR 548, a violation of Articles 8 and 14 was claimed following the applicants' discharge from the armed services on the grounds of their homosexuality. The ECtHR upheld the complaints under Article 8 and concluded that the claim under Article 14 had been subsumed under that finding of a violation.

The Council of Europe has now drawn up a new protocol, Protocol 12, which contains a general, free-standing prohibition on discrimination. The Protocol was opened for signature on 4 November 2000, but has not yet received the necessary 10 ratifications to enter into force. The United Kingdom has not ratified the Protocol and there is no indication that it will do so in the immediate future. For further discussion of the Protocol, see Moon, 'The Draft Discrimination Protocol to the European Convention on Human Rights: A progress report' [2000] EHRLR 49, and Choudhury 'Interpreting the Right to Equality' [2003] EHRLR 24.

Although it is not a free-standing provision, Article 14 is wider than some other human rights equality guarantees because the grounds on which discrimination is prohibited are very wide. The particular grounds of prohibited discrimination specified in Article 14 are only examples and the phrase 'or other status' has been broadly interpreted, with the ECtHR and ECmHR having held that marital status, sexual orientation, ownership of a particular breed of dog, trade union membership, military status, conscientious objection, poverty, and imprisonment are prohibited grounds of discrimination, in the absence of relevant and sufficient justification. The list of prohibited grounds of discrimination remains open.

8.14.2 The Meaning of Discrimination

Not all forms of differentiation amount to discrimination in Convention terms; different treatment of people 'placed in analogous situations' is the key aspect of prohibited differentiation (*Lithgow v United Kingdom* (1986) 8 EHRR 329). Expanding on the notion of discriminatory differentiation, the ECtHR has stated that the Article will be breached by different treatment of individuals in relevantly similar or analogous situations, without any objective or reasonable justification for the distinction (*Fredin v Sweden* (1991) 13 EHRR 784). However, the ECtHR has also emphasized that '[t]he right not to be discriminated against in the enjoyment of the rights guaranteed under the Convention is also violated when States without an objective and reasonable justification fail to treat differently persons whose situations are significantly different' (*Thlimmenos v Greece* (2000) 31 EHRR 411, at para. 44). This second aspect of discrimination is discussed below at 8.14.3, under 'Indirect Discrimination'.

In cases involving complaints of differential treatment, once a complainant has established that the ground for differentiation falls within the scope of Article 14, he or she must then establish that his or her situation can be considered otherwise to be relevantly similar or analogous to those who have been treated differently. The ECtHR has often decided cases alleging discriminatory treatment by determining that no Article 14 question is raised because the comparison is not truly with a person in an analogous situation. For example, in *Van der Mussele v Belgium* (1983) 6 EHRR 163, the ECtHR held that trainee barristers could not legitimately be compared with trainees in other professions because the differences between their situations were too great. This approach has the potential to weaken the protection offered by Article 14 since examination of the core complaint may be precluded by technical points concerning appropriate comparators.

Where it is established that people in factually similar circumstances are treated dissimilarly, a case of *prima facie* discrimination arises. However, *prima facie* discrimination can be remedied by the existence of an objective and reasonable justification, which must be established by the respondent state. In the *Belgian Linguistics Case (No. 2)* (1968) 1 EHRR 252, the ECtHR said, at para. 10:

> The existence of such a justification must be assessed in relation to the aims and effects of the measure under consideration, regard being had to the principles which normally prevail in democratic societies. A difference of treatment in the exercise of a right laid down in the Convention must not only pursue a legitimate aim: Article 14 is likewise violated when it is clearly established that there is no reasonable relationship of proportionality between the means employed and the aim sought to be realised.

The concepts of whether there has been different treatment of people in analogous situations, and whether discrimination is justified, have often been blurred in the Strasbourg case law.

In determining whether a *prima facie* discriminatory measure has a 'legitimate aim', the ECtHR affords states a 'margin of appreciation' (see, for example, *Inze v Austria* (1987) 10 EHRR 394 and *Gillow v United Kingdom* (1986) 11 EHRR 335). However, there are some grounds for distinguishing how people are treated, such as race or gender, which the ECtHR will not normally accept. In such cases, '[v]ery weighty reasons would have to be put forward before the Court could regard a difference of treatment based exclusively on the ground of sex as compatible with the Convention' (*Schmidt v Germany* (1994) 18 EHRR 513, at para. 24).

8.14.3 Indirect Discrimination

The concept of indirect discrimination was, until fairly recently, relatively undeveloped in the Strasbourg case law. The *Belgian Linguistics* decision (see 8.14.2 above) implies that the Convention is capable of covering both direct and indirect discrimination since the ECtHR suggested that justification of a measure would be required where the 'aims *and effects*' were *prima facie* discriminatory . However, decisions such as *Abdulaziz v United Kingdom* (1985) 7 EHRR 471 indicated that the Strasbourg bodies were reluctant to develop the concept. The subject of complaint in *Abdulaziz* was the UK Immigration Rules that disqualified people who had never met their intended partners from entering the country for the purposes of marriage. These rules had a far greater impact on would-be entrants from the Indian subcontinent, where arranged marriages are traditional, than on those from else-where. Although a minority of the ECmHR had concluded that the 'practical effect' of the rule was race discrimination, the ECtHR did not analyse the issue of indirect discrimination as an independent question, preferring to run it together with the question of justification.

However, the ECtHR has now taken the important step of recognizing that a measure which is applied equally to everyone but which has adverse effects on members of a particular group can discriminate. In *Thlimmenos v Greece* (2000) 31 EHRR 411, the ECtHR considered the ban imposed by a professional regula-tory body, on anyone with a criminal record. The applicant had such a record because he had objected, on religious and conscientious grounds, to performing military service. Though the blanket ban on those with any criminal record was not intended to discriminate, it nonetheless had an adverse effect on persons with his belief, which was disproportionate and could not be justified, and was there-fore held to be discriminatory on grounds of religion, contrary to Articles 9 and 14.

8.14.4 Human Rights Act Decisions

The domestic courts have sought to follow the Strasbourg approach to Article 14. In terms of scope, it is clear that the Article is confined to parasitic status (see, for example, *R (McLellan v Bracknell Forest Borough Council* [2001] EWCA Civ 1510). The Court of Appeal has also followed Strasbourg's open approach to prohib-ited grounds of discrimination and has indicated that it will apply the *ejusdem generis* principle of interpretation to the meaning of 'other status' (*Waite v London Borough of Hammersmith and Fulham* [2002] EWCA Civ 482).

However, there has (as in the Strasbourg case law) been a good deal of domestic confusion in deciding whether it should be said that two people are not in an analo-gous situation (so that no *prima facie* issue of discrimination arises), or whether there is indeed *prima facie* discrimination giving rise to the issue of justification. The differences in approach between different judges of the Court of Appeal in *R (Marper) v Chief Constable of South Yorkshire* [2002] EWCA Civ 1275 clearly demonstrate this confusion. The best domestic explanation of how Article 14 works, analytically, is that of Sedley LJ in *Aston Cantlow and Wilmcote with Billesley Parochial Church Council v Wallbank and Another* [2001] EWCA Civ 713, in which he said:

The treatment complained of is not that of Mr and Mrs Wallbank personally but that of lay impropriators generally, the Wallbanks included. It is therefore necessary to compare the situation of lay impropriators with that of a larger class of which they form part—a class of persons 'in an analogous or relevantly similar situation' (*Stubbings v United Kingdom* (1996) 23 EHRR 213, para. 70). This class has therefore to be identified by reference to shared material characteristics other than the impugned one. The material characteristic in the present case is in our view the ownership of freehold land either in England at large or in the parish of Aston Cantlow. Whichever is taken, the answer is the same: the law discriminates between the owners of land which was formerly glebe and of land which was. not by making the former but not the latter liable for chancel repairs.

However the House of Lords reversed this decision on other grounds (see [2003] UKHL 37). See also *Wandsworth London Borough Council v Michalak* [2002] EWCA Civ 271.

It appears from decisions such as *R (Carson) v Secretary of State for Work and Pensions* [2003] EWCA Civ 797, that the adherence to the comparative approach to discrimination may create the same problems domestically as have arisen in Strasbourg. See also *A and others v Secretary of State for the Home Department* [2002] EWCA Civ 1502.

The decision of *Aston Cantlow and Wilmcote with Billesley Parochial Church Council v Wallbank and Another* (above) affirms the *Belgian Linguistics* approach to the final question of justification. When assessing this question, the domestic courts have tended to adopt a deferential stance towards policy decisions and to afford the Government a broad discretionary area of judgment. This approach is evident in cases such as *SR v Nottingham Magistrates' Court* [2001] EWHC Admin 802, where the court was required to consider Government policy concerning detention facilities for juvenile defendants. However, some more recent decisions indicate a greater willingness to scrutinize matters of policy: see *Mendoza v Ahmad Raja Ghaidan* [2002] EWCA Civ 1533.

The Administrative Court has taken a bolder approach to indirect discrimination than has Strasbourg. In *R and Others v Manchester City Council* [2001] EWHC Admin 707, at para. 91, the court stated expressly that Article 14 extends both to direct and indirect discrimination.

8.15 ARTICLE 15: EXCEPTIONS IN TIME OF WAR

1. In time of war or other public emergency threatening the life of the nation any High Contracting Party may take measures derogating from its obligations under this Convention to the extent strictly required by the exigencies of the situation, provided that such measures are not inconsistent with its other obligations under international law.

2. No derogation from Article 2, except in respect of deaths resulting from lawful acts of war, or from Articles 3, 4 (paragraph 1) and 7 shall be made under this provision.

3.   Any High Contracting Party availing itself of this right of derogation shall keep the Secretary General of the Council of Europe fully informed of the measures which it has taken and the reasons therefor. It shall also inform the Secretary General of the Council of Europe when such measures have ceased to operate and the provisions of the Convention are again being fully executed.

Article 15 allows a government to derogate from certain of its Convention obligations during 'war or other public emergency threatening the life of the nation'. Such derogation can be only to the extent strictly required by the exigencies of the situation. The central object of Article 15 is to enable the derogating state to return to normality and respect all human rights as soon as possible, premised on the notion that it is sometimes necessary to limit human rights in order to protect them. This rationale is not without its critics and it has been stated that the question of derogations is an issue 'of the integrity of the Convention system of protection as a whole' (Judge Makarczyk, dissenting, in *Brannigan v United Kingdom* (1993) 17 EHRR 297).

The precondition to any derogation under Article 15 is the existence of war or a 'public emergency threatening the life of the nation'. The ECtHR has defined the latter as an '[e]xceptional situation of crisis or emergency that affects the whole population and constitutes a threat to the organised life of the community of which the state is composed' (*Lawless v Ireland* (1961) 1 EHRR 1).

As stated in Article 15(1) and above, derogation is permitted only 'to the extent strictly required by the exigencies of the situation'. The ECmHR, in *Ireland v United Kingdom* (1978) 2 EHRR 25, stated:

There must be a link between the facts of the emergency on the one hand and the measures chosen to deal with it on the other. Moreover, the obligations under the Convention do not entirely disappear. They can only be suspended or modified 'to the extent that is strictly required' as provided in Article 15.

While states are afforded a wide margin of appreciation in relation to this condition, the ECtHR still retains a supervisory role (*Ireland v United Kingdom*). Factors that are relevant to supervision of the margin include the nature of the rights affected by the derogation, the nature and duration of the emergency, and any safeguards against arbitrary state behaviour (*Brannigan*). The Court has insisted that general references to terrorism will not be sufficient evidence that a derogation is strictly required (*Demir v Turkey* (2001) 33 EHRR 43).

Article 15(2) specifies the Convention provisions from which no derogation is permitted. It is possible that in the future the ECtHR may extend the list of non-derogable rights by accepting the notion of consequential non-derogability. For example, in *Aksoy v Turkey* (1996) 23 EHRR 553, the Court observed that prompt judicial intervention (Article 5(3)) can lead to detection of ill-treatment, which is a non-derogable prohibition (Article 3).

Article 15(3) sets out the procedural requirements when derogating from a Convention obligation. Although not expressly stated, notification to the Council of Europe must be without delay (*Lawless*).

8.15.1 Derogations and the Human Rights Act

Section 1(2) of the Human Rights Act allows the Government to avoid the incorporation of the Convention to the extent that it has lodged a 'derogation' with the Council of Europe, as defined in s. 14. Thus, as a matter of international law, the Government, by lodging a derogation in Strasbourg, can, to the extent that the derogation is lawful under Article 15, avoid a particular obligation in particular circumstances. See, for instance, Chowdhury, *Rule of Law in a State of Emergency* (London: Pinter, 1989).

The United Kingdom has, in the past, used Article 15 in relation to Northern Ireland, and until February 2001 there was a derogation in force which allowed the police to detain people under the Prevention of Terrorism (Temporary Provisions) Act 1989 for up to seven days. The derogation followed *Brogan v United Kingdom* (1988) 11 EHRR 117, where the ECtHR had decided that periods of longer than four days' detention for interrogation without access to a judge violated the Article 5(3) requirement to bring the suspect before a judge 'promptly'. The lawfulness of the derogation was then subject to an unsuccessful challenge (*Brannigan v United Kingdom* (1993) 17 EHRR 539). The introduction of judicial authorization for extended detentions in the Terrorism Act 2000 allowed this derogation to be withdrawn.

Section 14 of the Act identifies 'designated derogations', which, under s. 16, are permitted to continue for up to five years. Section 14(5) allows the Secretary of State to amend sch. 3 to the Act to enable the continuation of the current derogation and to add any future derogations. The Act does not permit the United Kingdom to make a 'designated derogation' for the purposes of domestic law unless it reflects an actual derogation lodged with the Council of Europe. The effect of making a designated derogation is to exclude the Article in question from being a 'Convention right' for the purposes identified in that derogation (see s. 1(2)). Any derogation is likely to be specific and to refer to particular statutory powers.

8.15.2 The Current United Kingdom Derogation

After the events of 11 September 2001, Part 4 of the Anti-terrorism, Crime and Security Act 2001 brought in provisions to detain a specific category of people without trial, and this required a new derogation from Article 5 of the Convention. The Immigration Act 1971 already allowed for the deportation of non-UK citizens whose presence in the UK is 'not conducive to the public good' (including on grounds of national security). Immigrants may be detained (and have been detained for long periods) pending examination, appeal, and removal. The mischief that the 2001 Act was designed to deal with was the fact that some of these people are suspected of being terrorists but face torture in the only country to which they may be returned. Under Article 3 of the Convention (the prohibition on torture), these people are effectively irremovable from the UK. The 'solution' provided by the Act is to give the Home Secretary the power to detain this small group of people indefinitely. The new power to detain is based solely on the Home Secretary's assessment as to whether he has a reasonable belief that the person's presence in the United Kingdom is a risk to national security and that he suspects that the person is a terrorist. There is an appeal to the pre-existing Special Immigration Appeals Commission (SIAC), set up by the Act of the same name in 1997, following the decision in *Chahal v UK* (1996) 23 EHRR 413.

This new derogation seeks exemption from the prohibition on arbitrary detention—Article 5 states:

> . . . No one shall be deprived of his liberty save in the following cases and in accordance with a procedure prescribed by law:
>
> . . .
>
> (f) the lawful arrest or detention . . . of a person against whom action is being taken with a view to deportation or extradition.

Any such detention must ordinarily be limited in time because the provision requires active steps to be taken to deport or to extradite. As a result, any unlimited period of detention in the absence of such active steps would be unlawful under the Convention and therefore contrary to the Human Rights Act: 'If such proceedings are not pursued with due diligence, the detention will cease to be permissible' (*Chahal*, at para. 113).

At the time of writing, the lawfulness of this derogation is being challenged. The first basis of challenge is the argument that there is no emergency threatening the life of the nation. The second aspect of the challenge focuses on the condition that the provisions that violate Article 5 must be 'strictly required' by this emergency and designed, in this case, to avoid further terrorist incidents.

The first domestic challenge to the derogation was taken in the SIAC. A number of individuals were in December 2001 certified by the Secretary of State as being suspected international terrorists. The detainees in this case, supported by Liberty, which was granted leave to intervene, argued that their detention was in breach of Articles 3 (prohibition of torture), 5 (right to liberty and security), 6 (right to a fair trial), and 14 (prohibition of discrimination) taken together with Article 15. They argued in particular that the derogation was unlawful.

With the exception of Article 14, the SIAC found no breaches of the Convention. It accepted that there was a public emergency threatening the life of the nation and that the detention provisions 'were strictly required by the exigencies of the situation'. In relation to Article 14, the detainees contended that the fact that the Anti-terrorism, Crime and Security Act 2001 authorized detention of non-UK nationals, but not of UK nationals, constituted discrimination on the grounds of nationality. The SIAC agreed that there had been a breach of Article 14, stating that:

> A person who is irremovable cannot be detained or kept in detention simply because he lacks British nationality. In order to detain him there must be some other justification, such as that he is suspected of having committed a criminal offence. If there is to be an effective

derogation from the right to liberty enshrined in Article 5 in respect of suspected interna-tional terrorists—and we can see powerful arguments in favour of such a derogation—the derogation ought rationally to extend to all irremovable suspected international terrorists. It would properly be confined to the alien section of the population only if, as the Attorney General contends the threat stems exclusively or almost exclusively from that alien section.

But the evidence before us demonstrates beyond argument that the threat is not so confined. There are many British nationals already identified—mostly in detention abroad—who fall within the definition of 'suspected international terrorists' and it was clear from the submissions made to us that in the opinion of the respondent there are others at liberty in the United Kingdom who could be similarly defined. In those circumstances we fail to see how the derogation can be regarded as other than discriminatory on the grounds of national origin. (at paras 94–5, unreported SIAC judgment, 31 July 2002)

In the light of its findings, SIAC made the following Orders: an Order quashing the Derogation Order and an Order under s. 4 of the Human Rights Act declaring s. 23 of the Anti-terrorism, Crime and Security Act to be incompatible with Articles 5 and 14 of the Convention in so far as they permit the detention of suspected international terrorists in a way which discriminates on the ground of nationality (a declaration of incompatibility). The SIAC ruled out the possibility of derogating from the non-discrimination provisions in the Convention and in the ICCPR:

Merely scheduling such a derogation [from Article 14] would not assist, however, for in our judgment in any event there is not a reasonable relationship between the means employed and the aims sought to be pursued. (at para. 96)

However, the Court of Appeal gave judgment on 25 October 2002 overturning the SIAC finding on the discrimination point and ruling that the derogation was lawful (*A and others v Secretary of State for the Home Department* [2002] EWCA Civ 1502). At the time of writing the matter was being appealed to the House of Lords.

8.16 ARTICLE 16: RESTRICTIONS ON POLITICAL ACTIVITY OF ALIENS

Nothing in Articles 10, 11 and 14 shall be regarded as preventing the High Contracting Parties from imposing restrictions on the political activities of aliens.

On its face, Article 16 allows states considerable latitude to interfere with the politi-cal rights of aliens. However, the provision enjoys only limited support, and in January 1977 the Parliamentary Assembly of the Council of Europe recommended its removal. Although Article 16 remains in force, the Strasbourg authorities have emphasized that it should have little, if any, impact. In *Piermont v France* (1995) 20 EHRR 301, the ECmHR expressly recognized that the provision was outdated. It observed that:

. . . those who drafted [Article 16] were subscribing to a concept that was then prevalent in international law, under which a general, unlimited restriction of the political activities of aliens was thought legitimate.

The ECmHR then reiterated the status of the Convention as a living instrument, which should be interpreted in the light of present-day conditions and the evolution of modern society. Consonant with this interpretative direction, it has been suggested that the expression 'political activities' might apply only narrowly to the setting up and operation of political parties, expressions of opinion in connection with these parties, and voting in elections (see, for example, Harris, O'Boyle, and Warbrick, *Law of the European Convention on Human Rights* (London: Butterworths, 1995), at 510; 2nd edn forthcoming (London: Butterworths, 2003)).

The *Piermont* decision also indicates that Members of the European Parliament cannot be regarded as aliens within any jurisdiction in the European Union and, as a result of the rights of citizenship created by the Maastricht Treaty, this must be extended to all citizens of the EU.

8.16.1 Human Rights Act Decisions

The restrictive Strasbourg approach to Article 16 has been followed by the Court of Appeal. In *R (Farrakhan) v Secretary of State for the Home Department* [2002] EWCA Civ 606, the Court described the provision as 'something of an anachronism', indicating that it is unlikely to feature prominently, if at all, in domestic decisions.

8.17 ARTICLE 17: PROHIBITION OF ABUSE OF RIGHTS

Nothing in this Convention may be interpreted as implying for any state, group or person any right to engage in any activity or perform any act aimed at the destruction of any of the rights and freedoms set forth herein or at their limitation to a greater extent than is provided for in the Convention.

The primary purpose of Article 17 is to safeguard the provisions of the Convention from abuse at the hands of extremists. It may be invoked by persons against a government, or be used by a government to defend its actions against persons. It may not, however, be used to deny the rights and freedoms of people considered extremists by the state. For instance, in *Lawless v Ireland* (1961) 1 EHRR 1, the ECtHR held that Article 17 could not be used to deny IRA members the right to liberty or a fair trial.

Article 17 is potentially relevant to hate speech; for a discussion of this issue, see Cooper and Marshall Williams, 'Hate speech, holocaust denial and international human rights law' (1999) 6 EHRLR 593.

8.17.1 Human Rights Act Decisions

In *Douglas v Hello! Ltd* [2001] QB 967, Sedley LJ noted that it would be inconsistent with Article 17 and s. 3 of the Human Rights Act to read s. 12 of the Act as giving the right to freedom of expression presumptive priority over other rights. This confirms that Article 17 will be applied by the domestic courts to safeguard other Convention rights.

8.18 ARTICLE 18: LIMITATION ON USE OF RESTRICTIONS ON RIGHTS

> The restrictions permitted under this Convention to the said rights and freedoms shall not be applied for any purpose other than those for which they have been prescribed.

Aimed primarily at the ulterior motive, Article 18 is a parasitic provision. In *Kamma v Netherlands* (1974) 1 DR 4, the ECmHR described the Article thus:

> Article 18, like Article 14 of the Convention, does not have an autonomous role. It can only be applied in conjunction with other Articles of the Convention. There may, however, be a violation of Article 18 in connection with another Article, although there is no violation of that Article taken alone.

8.18.1 Human Rights Act Decisions

We are not aware of Article 18 having been raised before the domestic courts.

8.19 PROTOCOL 1, ARTICLE 1: PROTECTION OF PROPERTY

> Every natural or legal person is entitled to the peaceful enjoyment of his possessions. No one shall be deprived of his possessions except in the public interest and subject to the conditions provided for by law and by the general principles of international law.
>
> The preceding provisions shall not, however, in any way impair the right of a state to enforce such laws as it deems necessary to control the use of property in accordance with the general interest or to secure the payment of taxes or other contributions or penalties.

The extent to which, and the way in which, property interests should be protected by the Convention have always been controversial. Some argued that property was an economic interest rather than a civil/political right, and should not be protected in a human rights Convention. Others (including, when the Convention was drafted, the United Kingdom) were sensitive to the possibility of a court interfering with important political choices, such as the state's power to nationalize industries, to create redistributive socio-economic programmes, to tax, and to fine. These controversies explain why the initial Convention did not contain an Article protecting property interests; why the right protected is to 'peaceful enjoyment of possessions' rather than a right actually to possess; and why the ECtHR has afforded so wide a margin of appreciation to states in deciding whether it is in the public interest for such rights to be curtailed. See generally Kingston, 'Rich people have rights too? The status of property as a fundamental right', in Heffernan (ed.), *Human Rights: A European Perspective* (Dublin: Round Hall Press, 1994), Anderson 'Compensation for Interference with Property' (1999) 6 EHRLR 543, and Whale, 'Pawnbrokers and parishes: the protection of property under the Human Rights Act' [2002] EHRLR 67.

In *Sporrong v Sweden* (1982) 5 EHRR 35, the ECtHR analysed Protocol 1, Article 1, and interpreted it as containing three distinct rules. This interpretation of Protocol 1, Article 1 has been followed in subsequent cases, such as *Lithgow v United Kingdom* (1986) 8 EHRR 329, para. 106. In accordance with this interpretation, in order to show that Protocol 1, Article 1, has been violated, it must be shown that:

(a) the peaceful enjoyment of the applicant's possessions has been interfered with by the state (rule 1); or

(b) the applicant has been deprived of possessions by the state (rule 2); or

(c) the applicant's possessions have been subjected to control by the state (rule 3).

But interference, deprivation, or control will not violate Protocol 1, Article 1 if done 'in the public interest' or 'to enforce such laws [as the state] deems necessary to control the use of property in accordance with the general interest'.

8.19.1 Possessions

The ECtHR has interpreted the concept of 'possessions' broadly. In addition to physical items and land, 'possessions' have been held to include contractual rights (e.g., *Association of General Practitioners v Denmark* (1989) 62 DR 226), leases (e.g., *Mellacher v Austria* (1989) 12 EHRR 391), company shares (e.g., *Bramelid & Malmstrom v Sweden* (1982) 29 DR 64), patents (e.g., *Smith Kline and French Laboratories Ltd v The Netherlands* (1990) 66 DR 70), crystallized debts (e.g., *Agneesens v Belgium* (1998) 58 DR 63), the goodwill of a business (e.g., *Van Marle & Others v The Netherlands* (1986) 8 EHRR 483), liquor licences (e.g., *Tre Traktörer AB v Sweden* (1989) 13 EHRR 309), and a claim for compensation in tort (e.g., *Pressos Compañia Naviera SA v Belgium* (1995) 21 EHRR 301).

However, the position is rather more equivocal in relation to pecuniary rights gained by virtue of public law. In such cases the ECtHR will consider whether the right is nevertheless in the nature of a possession. The question of whether a pension or social security entitlement is a possession was considered by the ECmHR in early cases (*X v Netherlands* (1971) 38 CD 9; *Muller v Austria* (1975) 3 DR 25), which created a distinction between contributory and non-contributory schemes. A contributory scheme creates an individual share in the fund, and a claim to this type of benefit is a possession. What is not yet clear from the case law is whether that distinction still stands at all, or if it does, whether the fact of a benefit depending upon having contributed at all is sufficient to make it a 'pecuniary' benefit, so falling within the scope of Article 1 of Protocol 1. On the present state of the case law, it would seem that the fact of a benefit amounting to a pecuniary entitlement (rather than an administrative discretion) is sufficient to place it within the scope of Article 1 of Protocol 1, but there are, at the time of writing, a number of pending cases both in Strasbourg and in domestic courts on these issues.

In *Gaygusuz v Austria* (1996) 23 EHRR 365, it was held that an emergency assistance benefit, which was not itself contributory but which was nonetheless paid for through an unemployment insurance fund, fell within the scope of Article 1 of Protocol 1. The scope of this decision is uncertain. The right, if there is one, is to the amount provided for in the legislation: even if a right to benefits can be asserted under Article 1 of Protocol 1, it does not necessarily give an individual a right to a pension of a particular amount (see, for example, *Kuna v Germany* (App. No. 52449/99), 10 April 2001, ECtHR).

There is uncertainty as to the way in which the *Gaygusuz* judgment affects certain British social security benefits, some of which depend on the fact of having contributed but do not require any level of contributions before they have been earned. In *Willis v United Kingdom* (2002) 35 EHRR 21, the ECtHR was satisfied that certain social security benefits paid to widows but not widowers had a sufficient element of pecuniary entitlement as to fall within the scope of Article 1 of Protocol 1. The issue will be explored further in the context of disability and retirement benefits in *Hepple, Kimber and Others v United Kingdom* (forthcoming).

A series of recent Strasbourg admissibility decisions highlights the possibility that the distinction between contributory and non-contributory schemes may be abandoned in the near future. In *Matthews v United Kingdom* (App. No. 40302/98), 15 July 2002, ECtHR, for example, the Court stated that an allegation of discrimination on grounds of gender in relation to a non-contributory benefit (a bus pass) 'raises complex issues under Article 14 of the Convention and Article 1 of the First Protocol taken together'.

8.19.2 Deprivation of Possessions

In determining the level of permissible interference with peaceful enjoyment of possessions the ECtHR applies the 'fair balance' test. Any interference must achieve a fair balance between the demands of the general interests of the community and the protection of the fundamental rights of individuals. There must be a reasonable relationship of proportionality between the means employed and the aim pursued. The availability of an effective remedy and compensation is relevant in assessing whether a fair balance has been struck.

Sporrong v Sweden (1982) 5 EHRR 35 related to town planning in Stockholm. The applicants owned properties that were subject to lengthy expropriation permits and prohibitions on construction. The ECtHR held that there had been an interference with the applicants' rights of property by rendering the substance of ownership 'precarious and defeasible'. The prohibitions on construction were characterized as a 'control on the use' of the property within the third rule (see 8.19 above), while the expropriation permits were an interference within the first rule. The fair balance between the protection of the right of property and the requirements of the general interest had been upset by the prolonged extension of the permits and prohibitions. As the domestic law did not provide a means for the applicants to seek a reduction in the time limits for expropriation or to claim compensation, they had unnecessarily borne an individual and excessive burden. A violation of Protocol 1, Article 1 had thus occurred.

Again, in *Chassagnou v France* (2000) 29 EHRR 615, the ECtHR found that compelling small landowners, who were opposed to hunting, to transfer hunting rights over their land enabling others to hunt on it, did not strike a fair balance. Compensation, which involved a right to hunt on others' property, did not assist to achieve a fair balance since the compensation was not valuable to the landowners, who neither hunted nor accepted hunting.

Compensation

The basic approach to compensation was set out in *Holy Monasteries v Greece* (1994) 20 EHRR 1, where the ECtHR held (at para. 71):

> In this connection, the taking of property without payment of an amount reasonably related to its value will normally constitute a disproportionate interference and a total lack of compensation can be considered justifiable under Protocol 1, Article 1 only in exceptional circumstances. Article 1 does not, however, guarantee a right to full compensation in all circumstances, since legitimate objectives of 'public interest' may call for reimbursement of less than the full market value.

A similar approach was taken in *Gaganus v Turkey* (App. No. 39335/98), 5 June 2001, ECtHR, where the Court held that, in general, the amount of compensation in cases of expropriation in the public interest should bear a reasonable relationship to the value of the property. However, the ECtHR emphasized in *Lithgow v United Kingdom* (1986) 8 EHRR 329 that where a state considers that objectives of public interest justify reimbursement at less than the full market value, the ECtHR will respect the national legislature's judgment unless manifestly without reasonable foundation.

The Public Interest

In deciding whether a deprivation is in the public interest the ECtHR affords the state a wide margin of appreciation in deciding what public interest demands. The characterization of an objective of deprivation as being in the public interest is a question left almost exclusively to the determination of the state.

James v United Kingdom (1986) 8 EHRR 123 concerned the compulsory transfer of ownership of residential properties in central London to the tenants of those properties pursuant to the Leasehold Reform Act 1967, which was designed to protect long-term tenants' moral entitlement to their properties at the end of their leases. The property owners complained that the compulsory nature of, and the calculation of the price of, the transfers violated Protocol 1, Article 1. The ECtHR was unanimous in holding that compulsory transfer from one individual to another may be a legitimate means of promoting the public interest, even where the community at large has no direct enjoyment of the property taken. The objective of eliminating social injustice by leasehold reform is within the state's margin of appreciation. The means chosen to regulate the injustice was not disproportionate, nor was it unreasonable to restrict the right of enfranchisement to less valuable houses since they were perceived as cases of greatest hardship.

Conditions Provided by Law

The deprivation of property must be 'subject to the conditions provided for by law'. This means that there must exist a basis for the deprivation in domestic law which must be accessible and sufficiently certain, and which protects against arbitrariness (*Sunday Times v United Kingdom* (1979) 2 EHRR 245). In *James v United Kingdom* (1986) 8 EHRR 123, the ECtHR (at para. 67) held that the Leasehold Reform Act 1967 was not arbitrary simply because it provided compensation at less than full market value. In *Hentrich v France* (1994) 18 EHRR 440, however, a law creating a right of pre-emption over land to enable the Commissioner of Revenue to collect tax was held to violate Protocol 1, Article 1 because it 'operated arbitrarily and selectively and was scarcely foreseeable, and it was not attended by the basic procedural safeguards'. Other methods were available to the state to prevent tax evasion which were adequate.

8.19.3 Controls on the Use of Property

The third rule contained in Protocol 1, Article 1 recognizes that states are entitled to control the use of property where it is considered to be in the general interest to do so, or to secure the payment of taxes or other contributions or penalties.

Controls on the use of property have included laws requiring positive action by property owners, as in *Denev v Sweden* (1989) 59 DR 127, where environmental laws obliged a landowner to plant trees, as well as restrictions on their activities, such as planning controls, seizure of property for legal proceedings, and inheritance laws.

In a number of cases the ECtHR has considered housing laws that suspended or staggered the enforcement of eviction orders by residential property owners against their tenants. These laws have been held to constitute 'controls on the use of property'. The ECtHR stated in *Mellacher v Austria* (1989) 12 EHRR 391:

The second paragraph reserves to states the right to enact such laws as they deem necessary to control the use of property in accordance with the general interest. Such laws are especially common in the field of housing, which in our modern societies is a central concern of social and economic policies.

In order to implement such policies, the legislature must have a wide margin of appreciation both with regard to the existence of a problem of public concern warranting measures of control and as to the choice of the detailed rules for the implementation of such measures.

The need to strike a fair balance between the general interest and the rights of individual property owners pervades the whole of Protocol 1, Article 1, including its second paragraph. Thus in *Spadea v Italy* (1995) 21 EHRR 482, it was held that the applicants had been treated fairly by the laws suspending a tenant eviction order, whereas the applicant in *Scollo v Italy* (1995) 22 EHRR 514 had not. In both cases the suspensions of the eviction orders had the reasonable aim of preventing a large number of people all becoming homeless at the same time. The facts of each case meant that the application of the fair balance test produced different results.

Another example of laws that have been characterized as a 'control on the use of the property' are forfeiture laws. In *Handyside v United Kingdom* (1976) 1 EHRR 737, the ECtHR found no violation where books that had been held to have been obscene were destroyed by the state. Customs seizure of gold bullion owned by the applicants, which a third party had attempted to import illegally, was a permissible control on the use of property (*Allgemeine Gold- und Silberscheideanstalt v United Kingdom* (1986) 9 EHRR 1). *Air Canada v United Kingdom* (1995) 20 EHRR 150 concerned seizure by Customs authorities of the applicant's aircraft, in which a third party had smuggled cannabis, and which the applicant company had to pay £50,000 to retrieve. In all these cases the ECtHR applied the fair balance test, and in all of the cases the laws were considered proportionate.

The ability of the state to levy tax is specifically preserved in the second paragraph. The fair balance test generally applies to this control on the use of property only in so far as it will require procedural guarantees to establish the applicant's liability to make payments—the state can decide for itself as to levels of tax, and the means of assessment and collection.

In *Gasus Dosier- und Fördertechnik GmbH v Netherlands* (1995) 20 EHRR 403, the ECtHR said it 'will respect the legislature's assessment in [enforcing tax obligations] unless it is devoid of reasonable foundation'. In *National and Provincial Building Society v United Kingdom* (1997) 25 EHRR 127, the ECtHR upheld retrospective legislation designed to frustrate a claim that the applicants might have made to recover tax they had already paid. This was characterized as a control on the use of property, and was held to have been justified to prevent the applicants from exploiting a technical defect in laws that sought to change the method by which tax was assessed. By adopting retrospective measures to reaffirm their intention to collect the tax (after legislation had been invalidated by the domestic courts on technical grounds) the legislature 'did not upset the fair balance between the demands of the general interests of the community and the protection of the fundamental rights of the applicant society' (at 170).

The proportionality of confiscation orders under the Drug Trafficking Act 1994 was challenged in *Phillips v United Kingdom* (App. No. 41087/98), 5 July 2001, ECtHR. However, the ECtHR rejected the complaint that such confiscation orders were unreasonably extensive, holding that the interference was not disproportionate, given the important role such penalties play in efforts to combat drug trafficking. See the House of Lords decisions, *R v Rezvi* [2002] UKHL 1 and *R v Benjafield* [2002] UKHL 2, for consistent domestic findings on the issue of confiscation orders.

8.19.4 Human Rights Act Decisions

There has been fairly active domestic litigation involving Article 1 of Protocol 1. In a number of cases, there have been unsuccessful attempts to expand the meaning of 'possessions'. In *Legal & General Assurance Ltd v Kirk* [2001] EWCA Civ 1803, the focus of complaint was a rule that no individual with an industry debt of more than £1,000 could be employed in the insurance industry. It was argued that this rule, which precluded the complainant from gaining employment in the insurance industry, violated his proprietary right to seek a particular type of employment. The Court of Appeal held that a putative right to seek a particular type of employment is not a 'possession' and can be distinguished from a case in which a public authority has granted a licence to carry on a particular trade. See also *R (Amvac Chemical UK Ltd) v Secretary of State for the Environment, Food and Rural Affairs* [2001] EWHC Admin 1011, where the Court rejected an argument that an economic interest in product approvals under the Control of Pesticides Regulations 1986 held by third parties constituted a 'possession' for the purposes of Protocol 1, Article 1.

The extent, and the way, in which social security entitlements constitute pecuniary rights have featured in several cases. Arguments relating to the applicability of Protocol 1, Article 1 to a diverse range of social security benefits have been raised, but so far been dismissed by the Court of Appeal, in the cases of *Hooper v Secretary of State for Work and Pensions* [2003] EWCA Civ 813, and *R (Carson) v Secretary of State for Work and Pensions; R (Reynolds) v Secretary of State for Work and Pensions* [2003] EWCA Civ 797.

Marcic v Thames Water Utilities Ltd [2002] EWCA Civ 65 provides an example of the domestic approach to the fair balance test. The claimant argued that the repeated flooding of his garden, resulting from an inadequate sewerage system operated by the defendant, was incompatible with his right to the peaceful enjoyment of his possessions. The Court of Appeal upheld the finding of the Technology and Construction Court that the defendant had not demonstrated that the interference reflected a fair balance between the interests of the claimant and those of other members of the public. It was further held that the existence of a statutory complaints procedure under the Water Industry Act 1991 was no answer to the complaint. Leave to appeal has been granted by the House of Lords.

The Court of Appeal made an early declaration of incompatibility in *Wilson v First County Trust (No. 2)* [2002] QB 74. It was declared that s. 127(3) of the Consumer Credit Act 1974, which bars the courts from enforcing loan agreements where the agreement did not set out certain terms, was incompatible with Protocol 1, Article 1 and Article 6. The Court held that while the policy aim of s. 127(3) was legitimate, the inflexible prohibition on enforceability was a disproportionate means of achieving that objective. Leave has been granted to appeal to the House of Lords.

8.20 PROTOCOL 1, ARTICLE 2: NON-DENIAL OF THE RIGHT TO EDUCATION

No person shall be denied the right to education. In the exercise of any functions which it assumes in relation to education and to teaching, the state shall respect the right of parents to ensure such education and teaching in conformity with their own religious and philo-sophical convictions.

The existence and scope of 'a right to education' is one of the more controversial Convention questions. During the drafting of Protocol 1, many states expressed concern that the existence of such a right would impose onerous positive obligations upon governments. In an attempt to limit the impact of the right, the first sentence of Protocol 1, Article 2 was changed from its original positive form ('Every person has the right to education.') to the current negative expression ('No person shall be denied the right to education.'). Furthermore, following the conclusion of Protocol 1, several states, including the United Kingdom, entered reservations to the Article (see below at 8.20.3).

8.20.1 The Extent of the Right to Education

In the *Belgian Linguistics Case (No. 2)* (1968) 1 EHRR 252, the ECtHR held that despite the negative formulation, the first sentence of Protocol 1, Article 2 clearly enshrines a right. The content of that right was identified as follows:

(a) A right to an effective education.

(b) A right of access to existing educational institutions.

(c) A right to be educated in the national language or in one of the national languages.

(d) A right to obtain official recognition of completed studies.

The significance of the negative formulation was held to be that the Article does not require states to establish at their own expense, or to subsidize, education of any particular type or at any particular level. Since all member states at the time of sign-ing the Protocol possessed, and continued to possess, a general and official educa-tional system, there was no question of requiring each state to establish such a system. Rather, the Article obliged states to guarantee that individuals could take advantage of the existing means of instruction.

The focus of the right not to be denied an education is on primary and secondary education. It is recognized that the state may limit tertiary education to those who will benefit from it (*X v United Kingdom* (1980) 23 DR 228; *Glazewska v Sweden* (1985) 45 DR 300). The right is that of the student, which can be exercised by the parents on his or her behalf when he or she is young and by the student personally when he or she grows older.

The state may require parents to send their children to school or to educate them adequately at home (*Family H v United Kingdom* (1984) 37 DR 105). It may allow private education and schools, but is under no obligation to fund or subsidize these arrangements.

8.20.2 The Parental Right to Educate Children in Conformity with Religious and Philosophical Convictions

The second sentence of Protocol 1, Article 2 seeks to prevent the state from indulging in indoctrination of children through the education system, by providing to parents the right to have their religious and philosophical convictions respected. This applies to all educational systems, be they public or private, and to all functions the state exercises with respect to education, be they academic or administrative.

In *Campbell v United Kingdom* (1982) 4 EHRR 293, two parents challenged the existence of corporal punishment in state schools, on the basis that it was contrary to their philosophical beliefs. The ECtHR upheld their complaint. It held that the obligation to respect religious and philosophical convictions is not confined to the content of educational instruction but includes the organization and financing of public education, the supervision of the educational system in general, and questions of discipline.

The extent to which the religious and philosophical convictions of parents can influence the provision of education is limited, however, in a number of ways. First, the conviction itself must come within the limited definition set out in *Campbell v United Kingdom*. The parents must also show that the holding of the belief is the reason for their objection to what the state is doing, and that they have brought the reason for their objection to the attention of the authorities. Lastly, the state will not contravene Protocol 1, Article 2 if the education system conveys religious or philosophical knowledge in an objective, critical, and pluralistic manner.

In *Kjeldsen v Denmark* (1976) 1 EHRR 711, parents challenged a law which made sex education a compulsory component of the curriculum of state primary schools. The ECtHR held that the state was forbidden to pursue an aim of indoctrination that might be considered as not respecting parents' religious and philosophical convictions; this was the limit that could not be exceeded. The ECtHR looked at the nature of the sex education and concluded that it did not overstep the bounds of what a democratic state might regard as being in the public interest. The instruction was a way of objectively conveying information, with no attempt to indoctrinate towards a particular moral view. The law did not therefore offend the parents' religious and philosophical convictions to the extent forbidden by Protocol 1, Article 2. The ECtHR further held that if the parents wished to disassociate their children from the sex education programme, the alternatives of a highly subsidized private school system, where the law did not apply as strictly, or home education existed.

In the case of *Valsamis v Greece* (1996) 24 EHRR 294, the ECtHR applied the principles developed in *Kjeldsen v Denmark* and *Campbell v United Kingdom* to a challenge to Greek law which caused the one-day suspension of children of Jehovah's Witnesses for refusing to take part in a nationalistic military parade. The ECtHR found that no violation of Protocol 1, Article 2 arose.

Where a conflict arises between the child's right to education and respect for a parent's convictions, the former will prevail. Allowing parents the options of sending their children to a private school or educating them at home is sufficient to deal with the conflicts. As noted previously, there is no obligation on the state to subsidize the alternatives.

Protocol 1, Article 2 is subject to the prohibition on discrimination found in Article 14 of the Convention. This issue was raised in the *Belgian Linguistics Case (No. 2)* (1968) 1 EHRR 252, which concerned legislation that dictated the language of education in certain areas of Belgium. A school that failed to comply with the language rules could suffer penalties, which included denial of public support and non-recognition. The parents, who were French-speaking, argued that their children's right to education, their right to respect for their family life (Article 8), and the protection from discrimination had all been violated. The ECtHR ruled against them. Language was not within the concept of 'philosophical convictions' for the purposes of Protocol 1, Article 2. In relation to discrimination it held that Article 14 did not prohibit all difference in treatment, but that the principle of equality of treatment was violated only if the distinction had no objective and reasonable justification. Article 14 of the Convention and Protocol 1, Article 2 ensure that the right to education is secured without discrimination, and in the absence of any express terms the two provisions do not guarantee to everyone the right to be educated in the language of their choice.

8.20.3 The United Kingdom Reservation

The Human Rights Act 1998 creates the concept of 'designated reservations' (s. 15). A reservation to an international treaty is a device used by a signatory state to reserve particular policies or laws in order to exempt them from challenge under the instrument. Reservations can be made only at the time of ratification, though amendments to the Convention by a new protocol might allow a new reservation.

There is currently a reservation by the United Kingdom to the second sentence of Article 2 of Protocol 1 (which requires education to be provided in conformity with parents' religious and philosophical convictions). The United Kingdom has accepted this provision only so far as it is compatible with the provision of efficient instruction and training and the avoidance of unreasonable public expenditure. The reservation is set out in Part II of sch. 3 to the Act.

8.20.4 Human Rights Act Decisions

The Court of Appeal considered the scope of the right to education in *Holub and another v Secretary of State for the Home Department* [2001] 1 WLR 1359. It affirmed the content of the right as identified in the *Belgian Linguistics Case* (see 8.20.2 above). Regarding the particular right to an effective education, the Court emphasized that this is not a right to the most effective possible education and it does not invite comparison between educational systems (at 1367). The Article does not confer a right to remain in the UK after the state, exercising its immigration control, has refused leave to remain.

The meaning of 'religious and philosophical convictions' was considered by the Administrative Court in *R (Williamson) v Secretary of State for Education and Employment* [2001] EWHC Admin 960. There, the court held that a belief in the desirability of corporal punishment could not properly be defined as a religious conviction, even though it derived from Christian convictions. A belief which was in accordance with a particular religion did not thereby become a religious conviction in its own right. By contrast, the court considered that a belief in the undesirability of corporal punishment could properly be classified as a 'philosophical or religious' conviction. The Court of Appeal ([2002] EWCA Civ 1926) upheld the High Court's decision, albeit with different reasoning. See further, Mountfield, 'Spare the Rod and Spoil the Child: A Philosophical Conviction?' [2002] *Education Law Journal* 9.

In *R (Jacob Youngson) v Birmingham City Council* [2001] LGR 218, the court followed the approach of the ECtHR in holding that 'education' does not extend to vocational training.

The issue of whether the rights under Article 2 of Protocol 1 are 'civil rights' for the purposes of Article 6 was considered at first instance in *R (P, C and T) v Alperton School and others* [2001] EWHC Admin 229. It was held that they were public law rights, not private law rights, and so did not engage Article 6, although the Court of Appeal subsequently approached the matter on the basis that this distinction did not matter.

8.21 PROTOCOL 1, ARTICLE 3: RIGHT TO FREE ELECTIONS

The High Contracting Parties undertake to hold free elections at reasonable intervals by secret ballot, under conditions which will ensure the free expression of the opinion of the people in the choice of the legislature.

By Article 3 of Protocol 1, states that have ratified the Protocol undertake to hold free elections. Although the provision appears to impose an obligation upon the state rather than conferring a right upon an individual, it was held in *Mathieu-Mohin v Belgium* (1987) 10 EHRR 1 that Protocol 1, Article 3 does give rise to an individual right and can be the object of a complaint.

Mathieu-Mohin v Belgium is the central case to have been decided by the ECtHR regarding this provision, and concerned the rather complex electoral laws existing in Belgium. Several general principles relating to Protocol 1, Article 3 were established.

An important finding by the ECtHR in *Mathieu-Mohin v Belgium* was that Protocol 1, Article 3 extends to the subjective rights of participation—the right to vote and the right to stand for election to the legislature. However, it went on to state that the rights are not absolute. Accordingly, Protocol 1, Article 3 was held not to preclude a state from imposing conditions on the right to vote and to stand for election, provided that the conditions pursue a legitimate aim, are not disproportionate, and do not thwart the free expression of the opinion of the people in the choice of the legislature. The ECtHR has tended to afford states a wide margin of appreciation in limiting the rights, including in relation to the disenfranchisement of convicted prisoners (*H v Netherlands* (1983) 33 DR 242) or citizens resident abroad (*X v United Kingdom* (1979) 15 DR 137), and language requirements (*Frysky Nasjonale Partij v Netherlands* (1985) 45 DR 240).

Protocol 1, Article 3 concerns only the choice of the 'legislature'. The term 'legislature' is not confined to the national Parliament and its meaning will vary according to the constitutional structure of the state in question (*Mathieu-Mohin*). For example, in the *Mathieu-Mohin* case, concerning Belgium, regional councils were held to be constituent parts of the legislature, yet in the context of a complaint against France, a regional council was held not to come within the Article (*Malarde v France* (App. No. 46813/99), 5 September 2000, ECtHR). The flexibility of the term 'legislature' is demonstrated by the finding in *Matthews v United Kingdom* (1999) 28 EHRR 361 that the European Parliament had the requisite features of a 'legislature' for the residents of Gibraltar. However, the ECmHR has decided that other elected bodies, such as the former metropolitan county councils in England, are not 'legislatures' for the purpose of Protocol 1, Article 3 (*Booth-Clibborn v United Kingdom* (1985) 43 DR 236).

While the meaning of 'legislature' may have a degree of flexibility, a tighter approach is taken to the meaning of 'elections'. The ECmHR has ruled that referenda are not subject to Protocol 1, Article 3 (*X v Germany* (1975) 3 DR 98; *X v United Kingdom* (1975) 3 DR 165).

There is no obligation to introduce a specific system of voting, such as proportional representation. The state again has a wide margin of appreciation. It does not have to introduce a system of voting which ensures that all votes have equal weight as regards the outcome of the election, or that all candidates have equal chances of victory. In *Liberal Party v United Kingdom* (1980) 21 DR 211, a challenge was made to the system of 'first past the post' elections in the United Kingdom, which inevitably disadvantaged smaller political parties. The ECmHR found the complaint inadmissible, stating that the United Kingdom system was a fair one overall and that it did not become unfair because of the results that flowed from it.

The ECtHR in *Mathieu-Mohin v Belgium* observed that for the purpose of Protocol 1, Article 3, any electoral system must be assessed in the light of the political evolution of the country concerned. Features that would be unacceptable in the context of one system may be justified in another, as long as the chosen system provides for conditions which will ensure the 'free expression of the opinion of the people in the choice of the legislature'. The same position was taken by the ECtHR, departing from the view of the ECmHR, in *Gitonas v Greece* (1998) 26 EHRR 691.

In the case of *Bowman v United Kingdom* (1998) 26 EHRR 1, the ECtHR examined the relationship of Article 3 of Protocol 1 to Article 10 of the Convention (freedom of expression) in the context of electoral laws. The impugned legislation limited the amount of money spent by unauthorized persons on publications during an election period. This limit was found to be a disproportionate infringement on the right of free speech, which was not outweighed by the need to hold free elections.

8.21.1 Human Rights Act Decisions

The disenfranchisement of prison inmates was the subject of an unsuccessful challenge in *R (Pearson and Martinez) v Secretary of State for the Home Department; Hirst v Attorney-General* [2001] EWHC Admin 239. The Administrative Court held that s. 3 of the Representation of the People Act 1983, which denies prison inmates the ability to vote, is a legitimate and proportionate element of punishment. This case was communicated to Strasbourg on 31 January 2002 (*Hirst v United Kingdom* (App. No. 74025/01)).

A successful challenge was made to the practice of selling copies of the electoral register to commercial concerns in *R (Robertson) v Wakefield Metropolitan District Council* [2001] EWHC Admin 915. It was held that in the absence of an individual right of objection, such a practice violated Protocol 1, Article 3. Although the economic objective of selling the register was legitimate, the absence of a right of objection rendered the practice a disproportionate interference with the protected right.

8.22 PROTOCOL 4

Protocol 4 was opened for signature in September 1963, and although it has been signed by the United Kingdom it has not yet been ratified. At the time of writing the Government was in the process of reconsidering its position on its ratification of Protocol 4 as a part of its review of the major treaties on human rights. It has been suggested that the principal reason for its failure to ratify this Protocol was that the British Nationality Act 1981, which denies the right of entry to some classes of United Kingdom nationals (British Dependent Territories citizens, British Overseas citizens, British Subjects, and British Nationals (Overseas)), conflicts with Article 3 of the Protocol. Recent changes to nationality and the right to reside in the United Kingdom have made this reason for opposing ratification less significant.

8.22.1 Protocol 4, Article 1

No one shall be deprived of his liberty merely on the ground of inability to fulfil a contractual obligation.

This provision is almost identical to Article 11 of the United Nations' International Covenant on Civil and Political Rights, to which the United Kingdom is subject, and it is impossible to find an example of a United Kingdom law that would breach it. It applies only to contractual obligations, and does not affect imprisonment for breach of a court order, such as inability to pay a fine. It is limited to an 'inability to fulfil a contractual obligation', thus excluding from its application a refusal to fulfil such an obligation by someone with the means to fulfil it. The word 'merely' excludes cases in which the defaulter acts fraudulently or maliciously. Thus in *X v Germany* (1971) 14 YB 692, this Article did not protect a person who was detained for refusing to execute an affidavit in respect of his property at the request of his creditor.

8.22.2 Protocol 4, Article 2

1. Everyone lawfully within the territory of a state shall, within that territory, have the right to liberty of movement and freedom to choose his residence.

2. Everyone shall be free to leave any country, including his own.

3. No restrictions shall be placed on the exercise of these rights other than such as are in accordance with law and are necessary in a democratic society in the interests of national security or public safety, for the maintenance of *ordre public*, for the prevention of crime, for the protection of health or morals, or for the protection of the rights and freedoms of others.

4. The rights set forth in paragraph 1 may also be subject, in particular areas, to restrictions imposed in accordance with law and justified by the public interest in a democratic society.

Freedom of movement within a territory applies to 'everyone', including aliens 'lawfully' in a territory. The power of a state to control the entry of non-nationals is preserved by the inclusion of the word 'lawfully'.

This right of free movement is limited by the restrictions found in Protocol 4, Article 2(3) and (4). The first are the usual ones, concerned with national security or public safety, the maintenance of public order, the prevention of crime, for the protection of health or morals, or for the protection of the rights and freedoms of others. Any restriction is subject to the requirement that it be necessary in a democratic society. These restrictions are similar in content to those found in Articles 8–11 of the Convention. Protocol 4, Article 2(4) creates a further restriction not found elsewhere, that of the 'public interest'. This formulation was preferred by the Committee of Experts, a majority of whom rejected a reference to 'economic welfare' being included. However, commentators have suggested that the term 'public interest' is broad enough to include consideration of the economic welfare of society (Harris, O'Boyle, and Warbrick, *Law of the European Convention on Human Rights* (London: Butterworths, 1995), 560–61; 2nd edn forthcoming (London: Butterworths, 2003); van Dijk and van Hoof (eds), *Theory and Practice of the European Convention on Human Rights*, 3rd edn (The Hague: Kluwer, 1998), 670). All restrictions on freedom of movement are subject to the principle of proportionality, the doctrine of the margin of appreciation, and must be in accordance with law. For examples of cases concerning Protocol 4, Article 2, see *X v Belgium* (1981) 24 DR 198; *Schmid v Austria* (1985) 44 DR 195; *Raimondo v Italy* (1994) 18 EHRR 237.

The freedom to leave a state applies to nationals and aliens alike, and is subject to the same restrictions that apply to freedom of movement within a state (see *X v Germany* (1997) 9 DR 190; *M v Germany* (1984) 37 DR 113; *Piermont v France* (1995) 20 EHRR 301).

Protocol 4, Article 5, which applies to the Protocol as a whole, provides that if a state that ratifies the Protocol declares that it also applies to an external territory, that external territory is to be treated as separate from the state's metropolitan territory for the purposes of Protocol 4, Articles 2 and 3.

8.22.3 Protocol 4, Article 3

1. No one shall be expelled, by means either of an individual or of a collective measure, from the territory of the state of which he is a national.

2. No one shall be deprived of the right to enter the territory of the state of which he is a national.

Protocol 4, Article 3(1) prohibits the expulsion of nationals from the territory of their own state, and Protocol 4, Article 3(2) guarantees the right of a national to enter the territory of his or her state.

An expulsion occurs when 'a person is obliged permanently to leave the territory of the state . . . without being left the possibility of returning later' (*X v Austria* (1974) 46 CD 214). Extradition is not within this definition and is outside the scope of this Article (*Bruckmann v Germany* (1974) 17 YB 458).

Protocol 4, Article 5 applies, so that a state's external territories declared subject to the Article are considered separate from the metropolitan territory. This would have allowed the United Kingdom to distinguish between nationals denied entry under the British Nationality Act 1981.

8.22.4 Protocol 4, Article 4

Collective expulsion of aliens is prohibited

This Article refers to expulsion by a collective measure, as opposed to an expulsion following an individual decision about a particular person. In *A v Netherlands* (1988) 59 DR 274, it was held that it was not a collective expulsion where a number of asylum seekers from the same country had been expelled for similar reasons as each had received an individual, reasoned decision. 'Expulsion' in this context has the same meaning as in Protocol 4, Article 3 (see 8.22.3 above). In such a case the issue of discriminatory treatment may, of course, arise.

8.23 PROTOCOL 6

Article 1
Abolition of the death penalty

The death penalty shall be abolished. No person shall be condemned to such penalty or executed.

Article 2
Death penalty in time of war

A State may make provision in its law for the death penalty in respect of acts committed in time of war or of imminent threat of war; such penalty shall be applied only in the instances laid down in the law and in accordance with its provisions. The state shall communicate to the Secretary General of the Council of Europe the relevant provisions of that law.

Article 3
Prohibition of derogations

No derogation from the provisions of this Protocol shall be made under Article 15 of the Convention.

Article 4
Prohibition of reservations

No reservation may be made under Article 57 of the Convention in respect of the provisions of this Protocol.

This Protocol extends the protection of life provided by Article 2 of the Convention by expressly abolishing the death penalty in peacetime, and by creating an enforceable personal right not to be condemned to death or executed. Protocol 6, Articles 3 and 4 disallow any derogations or reservations. This protection provided by this Protocol has now been extended by Protocol 13.

The Protocol was opened to signature in April 1983 and came into force in March 1985. It was ratified by the United Kingdom in 1999. The death penalty was suspended for the offence of murder in 1959 and abolished in 1965 by domestic United Kingdom law, but remained in relation to treason, piracy, and a number of offences under military law. The Crime and Disorder Act 1998 abolishes the death penalty for these offences.

The ECtHR considered the relationship between Protocol 6 and Articles 2 and 3 of the Convention in *Soering v United Kingdom* (1989) 11 EHRR 439, at paras 101–4, in response to an argument advanced by Amnesty International that capital punishment should now be considered inhuman and degrading within the meaning of Article 3 of the Convention in light of evolving standards with regard to the existence and use of such punishment in Western Europe. The ECtHR rejected this submission, pointing to the facts that Protocol 6 had been introduced to create a new obligation to abolish the death penalty, optional for each state, and that Article 2 of the Convention, concerning the right to life, expressly preserved the option of the death penalty.

8.24 PROTOCOL 7

Following the adoption by the General Assembly of the United Nations of the International Covenant on Civil and Political Rights in 1966, the Council of Europe commissioned its Committee of Experts to investigate any problems that may have arisen from the coexistence of the Covenant and the European Convention. That report was the basis of further work in 1976 aimed at extending the human and political rights and freedoms set forth in the Convention. Protocol 7, which was opened for signature in 1984, seeks to bring the Convention into line with the International Covenant. The United Kingdom is not as yet a signatory. It is likely, however, that this Protocol will be ratified in the near future, after the amendment of anachronistic laws which created inequality between spouses.

There have been no ECtHR decisions concerning any of the Articles in Protocol 7, and few ECmHR decisions. The Council of Europe has published an explanatory memorandum, *Text of Protocol No. 7 and Explanatory Memorandum*, CE Doc H (84) 5 (Strasbourg: Council of Europe, 1984), which, although not binding upon either the ECtHR or the ECmHR, will serve as an aid to interpretation in the future.

8.24.1 Protocol 7, Article 1

1.   An alien lawfully resident in the territory of a state shall not be expelled therefrom except in pursuance of a decision reached in accordance with law and shall be allowed:
    (a)   to submit reasons against his expulsion;
    (b)   to have his case reviewed, and
    (c)   to be represented for these purposes before the competent authority or a person or persons designated by that authority.

2. An alien may be expelled before the exercise of his rights under paragraph 1. a, b and c of this article, when such expulsion is necessary in the interests of public order or is grounded on reasons of national security.

This provision affords a minimum guarantee that the procedural rights specified are complied with by a state seeking to expel a lawfully resident alien.

It is a precondition that the person is 'lawfully resident'. The Article does not therefore apply to an alien who has arrived but not yet passed through immigration control, a person in transit or admitted for a limited period for a non-residential purpose, or to those awaiting a decision on a residence application (*Explanatory Memorandum*, para. 9).

The term 'lawfully' refers to domestic law, and it is for that law to determine the conditions under which the person's presence is lawful. The provision applies to aliens who enter unlawfully but who have regularized their position, but not to those whose permits have expired, who are in breach of conditions, or who entered unlawfully and remain so (*ibid.*).

Expulsion means any measure compelling the departure of an alien from the territory, except extradition, and is a concept independent of any national law definition. A decision to expel must be made in 'accordance with law' (see 2.2). The subparagraphs then set out three guarantees, namely, that the person concerned may submit reasons against his or her expulsion, have the case reviewed, and be represented before the relevant authority. In exceptional cases, which involve the interests of public order or reasons of national security, an alien may be expelled before the exercise of his or her rights. The principles of proportionality should be taken into account in this regard, and the rights to review are to be available after expulsion (see *Chahal v United Kingdom* (1997) 23 EHRR 413).

The *Explanatory Memorandum* explains the right to have the case reviewed further. It does not require a two-stage process before different authorities, only that the 'competent authorities' should review the case in the light of the reasons against expulsion. The competent authority does not have to afford the alien an oral hearing—a written procedure will suffice. It does not need to be the authority upon whom the final decision to expel rests, but may have only power of recommendation to the body that does make the final decision. This Article does not relate to the appeal against review procedures that some states have. It is further noted in the *Memorandum* that a decision to deport does not involve a determination of the person's civil rights or of a criminal charge within the meaning of Article 6 of the Convention, and accordingly Protocol 7, Article 1 does not affect the interpretation of Article 6. The competent authority docs not have to comply with the Article 6 characteristics of a judicial body. As Harris, O'Boyle, and Warbrick observe (*Law of the European Convention on Human Rights* (London: Butterworths, 1995), 566; 2nd edn forthcoming (London: Butterworths, 2003)), this interpretation of Protocol 7, Article 1 merely requires that the executive takes into account the arguments of an alien against his or her expulsion, and 'offers only a modest guarantee of procedural due process'.

8.24.2 Protocol 7, Article 2

1.   Everyone convicted of a criminal offence by a tribunal shall have the right to have his conviction or sentence reviewed by a higher tribunal. The exercise of this right, including the grounds on which it may be exercised, shall be governed by law.

2.   This right may be subject to exceptions in regard to offences of a minor character, as prescribed by law, or in cases in which the person concerned was tried in the first instance by the highest tribunal or was convicted following an appeal against acquittal.

Protocol 7, Article 2 extends the general right to a fair trial provided by Article 6 of the Convention. While the latter Article has been interpreted to control any right to an appeal that the state, in its discretion, provides, it does not require that there be such a right. Protocol 7, Article 2 establishes such a right.

The right is restricted to offences which are tried by bodies that are 'tribunals' for the purpose of Article 6 of the Convention. This would exclude cases of a disciplinary nature. Other limits are found in Article 2(2): offences of a 'minor character' are excluded, as are cases where the person was convicted by the highest tribunal or following an appeal against acquittal. Where a person has pleaded guilty, the right to appeal may be limited to one against sentence only, and may be satisfied by leave to appeal proceedings where leave is not granted. The appeal may be limited to law, or may include questions of fact also—'the modalities for the exercise of the right and the grounds on which it may be exercised' are matters to be determined by domestic law (*Explanatory Memorandum*, para. 18).

8.24.3 Protocol 7, Article 3

When a person has by a final decision been convicted of a criminal offence and when subsequently his conviction has been reversed, or he has been pardoned, on the ground that a new or newly discovered fact shows conclusively that there has been a miscarriage of justice, the person who has suffered punishment as a result of such conviction shall be compensated according to the law or the practice of the state concerned, unless it is proved that the non-disclosure of the unknown fact in time is wholly or partly attributable to him.

A right to compensation for miscarriages of justice is thus established, subject to conditions. The person must have been convicted of a criminal offence by a final decision, and suffered punishment as a result. The *Explanatory Memorandum* quotes another Council of Europe memorandum relating to the validity of criminal judgments, which defines a final decision as one which has acquired the force of *res judicata*. A decision is final where it is irrevocable in that no further ordinary remedies are available, the parties have exhausted such remedies, or have allowed the time limit to expire without availing themselves of the remedy. Thus Protocol 7, Article 3 does not apply in cases where a conviction is overturned on an ordinary appeal, or when charges are dismissed in the trial court.

The right to compensation arises, the *Explanatory Memorandum* states, only 'where the person's conviction has been reversed or he has been pardoned, in either case on the grounds that a new or newly discovered fact shows conclusively that there has been a miscarriage of justice—that is, some serious failure in the judicial process involving grave prejudice to the convicted person' (para. 32).

There will be no right to compensation if it is shown that the non-disclosure of the unknown fact in time was wholly or partly attributable to the convicted person.

The nature of the procedures to establish a miscarriage of justice is a matter of domestic law or practice for the state. In the United Kingdom the relevant provision is s. 133 of the Criminal Justice Act 1988. Once established, the intention of the Article is that compensation should be paid by the state. If it is not, presumably a violation of this Article will have occurred.

8.24.4 Protocol 7, Article 4

1. No one shall be liable to be tried or punished again in criminal proceedings under the jurisdiction of the same state for an offence of which he has already been finally acquitted or convicted in accordance with the law and penal procedure of that state.

2. The provisions of the preceding paragraph shall not prevent the reopening of the case in accordance with the law and penal procedure of the state concerned, if there is evidence of new or newly discovered facts, or if there has been a fundamental defect in the previous proceedings, which could affect the outcome of the case.

3. No derogation from this Article shall be made under Article 15 of the Convention.

Article 4 of Protocol 7 incorporates the protection against double jeopardy into the Convention. It is limited to the same national jurisdiction, so that it remains possible to be convicted of the same offence in different jurisdictions. It applies only to criminal proceedings. A 'final' conviction must have been recorded, the meaning of which, the *Explanatory Memorandum* suggests (para. 29), will be the same as that suggested for Protocol 7, Article 3.

Paragraph 2 allows the reopening of a case in exceptional circumstances, where there is evidence of new or newly discovered facts, or where there has been a fundamental defect in the previous proceedings. The *Macpherson Report on the Stephen Lawrence Inquiry* recommended a review of the current protection against double jeopardy and the Law Commission published a report on the subject in March 2001. The Criminal Justice Bill (introduced in the 2002–2003 parliamentary session) contains a proposal to abolish the double jeopardy rule in certain circumstances. Concerns have been raised as to the Convention compliance of these measures by the Government.

8.24.5 Protocol 7, Article 5

Spouses shall enjoy equality of rights and responsibilities of a private law character between them, and in their relations with their children, as to marriage, during marriage and in the event of its dissolution. This Article shall not prevent states from taking such measures as are necessary in the interests of the children.

This Article places an obligation on the state to provide a system of laws by which spouses have equal rights and responsibilities concerning matters of private law, such as property rights and their relations with their children. It does not apply to areas of law external to the relationship of marriage, such as administrative, fiscal, criminal, social, ecclesiastical, or labour laws.

It is concerned only with spouses, and specifically precludes the period before marriage. The Article is not meant in any way to prevent the state from taking such measures as are necessary in the interests of children. Neither is it to prevent the state taking due account of all relevant factors when reaching decisions about the distribution of property upon the dissolution of marriage. There is no obligation imposed on states to provide for dissolution of marriage (*Explanatory Memorandum*, para. 35).

8.25 PROTOCOL 12

1.   The enjoyment of any right set forth by law shall be secured without discrimination on any ground such as sex, race, colour, language, religion, political or other opinion, national or social origin, association with a national minority, property, birth or other status.

2.   No one shall be discriminated against by any public authority on any ground such as those mentioned in paragraph 1.

Protocol 12 is not yet part of the European Convention on Human Rights. However, it is now open for signature and will enter into force following ratification by 10 member states. At present only four states have ratified the Protocol, although a further 28 states are signatories. The United Kingdom has not yet signed the Protocol and has given no indication that it is likely to do so in the near future.

Protocol 12 provides a substantive right to equality of treatment in like situations. Unlike Article 14, this is a free-standing equality right, which does not need to be tied to an existing Convention right. If it were to be adopted as part of the Convention and scheduled to the Human Rights Act, it would bring the Convention into line with Article 26 of the United Nations' International Covenant on Civil and Political Rights. It would be of great importance to English discrimination law, significantly broadening the bases for discrimination in relation to fields in which it could operate.

8.26 PROTOCOL 13

1.   The death penalty shall be abolished. No one shall be condemned to such penalty or executed.

Protocol 13 abolishes the death penalty in all circumstances. In so doing, it closes the gap left by Protocol 6, which does not exclude the death penalty in respect of acts committed in time of war or of imminent threat of war. The Protocol is non-derogable and no reservations may be made in respect of it.

Protocol 13 was opened for signature on 3 May 2002 and, as it has received the necessary 10 ratifications, it will enter into force on 1 July 2003.

9

WHEN RIGHTS HAVE NOT BEEN BROUGHT HOME: TAKING A CASE TO STRASBOURG

9.1 INTRODUCTION

The Human Rights Act 1998 will not, of course, mean the end of cases from the UK in Strasbourg. First, the Human Rights Act 1998 maintains parliamentary sovereignty, so it is likely that there will be cases in which breaches of Convention rights will still arise in primary legislation, and which cannot be rectified in domestic courts. Secondly, there will be cases of a failure to legislate in order to give effect to Convention rights, which cannot be rectified by the common law or statutory interpretation. Lastly, the domestic courts have not always been as robust in their protection of human rights as the Court in Strasbourg. In such circumstances the Strasbourg Court will be available for litigants who consider that the domestic courts have failed to remedy a Convention violation.

The ECtHR is a last resort: it has never been permissible to take a case to Strasbourg without exhausting domestic remedies first, and this requirement is even more crucial now that the Convention is part of domestic law. However, it is unlikely that a declaration of incompatibility (see 6.3 above) will be regarded as an effective remedy for the purposes of Article 13 (which has been confirmed by the admissibility decision in *Hobbs v UK* (App. No. 63684/00), 18 June 2002), so the ECtHR is unlikely to require the applicant to seek such a declaration in order to exhaust domestic remedies.

Greater interest in and understanding of the Convention since the Human Rights Act was passed has led to more rather than fewer cases being taken to the ECtHR. There was, for instance, an increase of 49 per cent in registered applications in the Court against the United Kingdom between the years 1999 and 2000. So practitioners still need to understand Strasbourg procedure.

This chapter outlines the procedure for making applications to the European Court in Strasbourg. It is included to ensure that those who have exhausted their domestic remedies in the United Kingdom have information on how to proceed further. The system for dealing with applications changed on 1 November 1998 and this chapter refers to the new procedure. Prior to this date, the process involved two organs: the Commission and the Court of Human Rights. Protocol 11 to the Convention abolished these two institutions and created in their place a new Court to 'ensure the observance' by the states of their duties under the Convention, in conjunction with the Committee of Ministers. For detailed information on the procedure see Leach, *Taking a Case Under the Convention* (London: Blackstone Press, 2001).

9.2 THE STRUCTURE AND JURISDICTION OF THE COURT

The Court consists of one judge nominated by each of the countries belonging to the Council of Europe (Article 20). These persons act in their individual capacity and cannot be government officials (though they can be ex-government lawyers). For the vast majority of cases the Court will sit in Chambers of seven judges (Article 27(1)). Reserve judges may also sit, so that the case does not need to be reheard if one judge falls ill, or cannot for some other reason deliberate. Where the Chamber considers that a case raises a serious question affecting the interpretation of the Convention, or where the resolution of a question before it might result in an inconsistency in the Court's case law, it may relinquish jurisdiction to a Grand Chamber of 17 judges, under Article 30 of the Convention. Alternatively, within three months of a decision of a Chamber, any of the parties may request that the case be referred to the Grand Chamber under Article 43. This is an exceptional procedure, and the request should be accepted only if the case raises a serious question affecting the interpretation or application of the Convention, or a serious issue of general importance. The first case referred to the Grand Chamber from the United Kingdom under Article 43, *Hatton v UK* (App. No. 36022/97), was decided on 8 July 2003.

The Court can hear complaints of alleged violations of the Convention brought by other member states—as occurred, for example, when the Republic of Ireland complained against the United Kingdom about interrogation practices used in Northern Ireland ((1978) 2 EHRR 25). But this is rare.

The majority of applications are brought by individuals against states.

9.3 MAKING A COMPLAINT

A complaint does not have to be made initially on any special application form, although it will be necessary to complete one eventually. Complaints should be directed to:

Secretary of the European Court of Human Rights
Council of Europe
F-67075 Strasbourg-Cedex
France
Tel: 00 33 03 88 41 2018
Fax: 00 33 03 41 27 30

The following information will be required and should, therefore, be provided in the letter to the Court (Rules of Procedure of the European Court of Human Rights, r. 47):

(a) The applicant's name, age, address, and occupation.

(b) The name, address, and occupation of anyone acting as the representative.

(c) The respondent country.

(d) A clear and concise statement of the facts, including, of course, the exact dates.

(e) The relevant domestic law.

(f) The provisions of the Convention on which the application relies, with any relevant case law.

(g) The object of the application (for example, the repeal or amendment of certain legislation, or the reversal of a decision and compensation).

(h) The details of all remedies (including any appeal) which have been pursued within the country concerned and, where appropriate, an explanation of why any available remedies have not been pursued.

(i) The judgments, decisions, and any other documents relating to the complaint.

The applicant should write a short initial letter to the Court setting out the basic details of the complaint, which should be no longer than three or four pages, if possible. It should include the name, address, date, and place of birth of the applicant. The essence of the complaint and the Convention Articles that are alleged to have been violated should be set out as succinctly as possible, in clear and simple language.

(In the text that follows, references to rules are to the Rules of Procedure of the European Court of Human Rights.)

9.3.1 Urgent Cases

The Court's procedures take some time, but it will give priority to urgent cases (for example, where a person's life or well-being are immediately threatened as in the case of a Motor Neurone Disease sufferer in *Pretty v United Kingdom* (2002) 35 EHRR 1. In urgent cases, the Court should be contacted directly by telephone or fax, to ask it to request the government to refrain from acting until the application has been considered.

9.3.2 Court's Response to a Letter of Introduction

The Court will reply by sending the standard application form. It may also indicate whether it considers any aspect of the complaint to be inadmissible, and may perhaps include a case which it considers relevant. The Court will also indicate that if it receives the application form within a specified period (usually six weeks), it will register the complaint as having been received on the date the initial letter was received.

9.3.3 Representation

Legal representation must be by a lawyer authorized to practise in any Convention country and resident in one of them, unless the President of the Chamber decides otherwise (see r. 36). The Court has the power to direct that an applicant be so represented (r. 36(2)), and at any hearing representation is required unless the President of the Court decides otherwise.

9.3.4 Application Form

All complaints must be made on the application form provided by the Registry (r. 47). A copy of the application form is included in this book as Appendix 6.

9.4 ADMISSIBILITY

The Court's jurisdiction is limited and complaints can be considered only if they meet the admissibility criteria set out in Article 35, which are rigorously applied and which are dealt with in turn below. More than nine out of 10 cases are dismissed as being 'inadmissible', and it is therefore critically important to ensure that an application complies with the admissibility requirements set out below, and contains all of the facts and arguments of law. To have a real chance of success, it is necessary for an application to set out the facts, the relevant domestic law, and detailed submissions on the law of the Convention. One of the best ways of setting out the application is to model it on a decision of the Court.

Article 34 provides that a complaint under the Convention can brought by 'any person, non-governmental organisation or group of individuals claiming to be the victim of a violation'. Neither individuals nor legal persons have to be citizens of the state concerned, nor of any member state. They do not have to be resident or physically present in the territory. Complaints may not be brought by governmental organizations or other 'emanations of the state'.

Although complaints may be brought by groups of individuals and non-governmental organizations (NGOs), a complaint cannot be brought to challenge an action of a state as a matter of principle; the organization or group must itself be a victim of a violation. Trade unions and NGOs can complain about an action directed towards them, and can, of course, provide their members with representation, but cannot complain on behalf of their members.

9.4.1 Who is a 'Victim'?

An applicant must be one of three types of victim: actual, potential, and indirect. An *actual victim* is someone who is personally affected by the alleged violation. It is not necessary to show that any detriment has been suffered, although this will be relevant to the remedy. A *potential victim* is one who is at risk of being directly affected by a law or administrative act. See, for example, *Dudgeon v UK* (1981) 4 EHRR 149. An *indirect victim* is one who is immediately affected by a violation which directly affects another, such as a family member of someone imprisoned or killed.

9.4.2 Against Whom Can a Complaint be Brought?

Only states are parties to the Convention, and therefore only those states can commit violations. Where there are several state organs involved, it will not be necessary for this purpose to identify which level of the state organization is responsible. Complaints cannot be brought against private persons or institutions. However, the complaints may include failure to fulfil positive obligations to ensure that human rights are respected by private persons within the state's jurisdiction (see 2.3.2 above).

9.4.3 Extent of Jurisdiction

Under Article 1, signatory states are required to 'secure to everyone *within their jurisdiction*' (emphasis added) the rights and freedoms protected by the Convention. This means that states are liable for all events that take place in territory for which they are responsible, not just those affecting their own nationals, and even if the effects of the events might be felt outside the Council of Europe area, for example, in cases restraining deportation to places where torture might occur, such as in *Chahal v UK* (1997) 23 EHRR 413. But the jurisdiction of a state may also extend to the acts of state servants that take place beyond the physical territory of the state: for example, see *Loizdou v Turkey* (1997) 23 EHRR 513, concerning the effects of Turkish-sponsored troops in Cyprus. The crucial test for jurisdiction is whether or not the state was exercising *de facto* control over the events in question. For a general discussion of the principles, see *Bankovich v UK & Others* (App. No. 52207/99), 12 December 2001, ECtHR.

9.4.4 Complaint Must Concern a Convention Issue

The Court's jurisdiction extends only to complaints relating to the rights and freedoms contained in the Convention and the protocols that the member state in question has ratified.

9.4.5 Exhaustion of Domestic Remedies

This is discussed above. The ECtHR has consistently held that it 'may only deal with the matter after all domestic remedies have been exhausted'.

This rule is applied strictly in practice. It applies only to the remedies that are available, sufficient, and which relate to the breaches alleged. If in doubt, the remedy should be pursued, though a 'protective' application to the ECtHR may be lodged simultaneously.

9.4.6 Six-month Time Limit

Complaints to the ECtHR must be made within six months of the violation of the Convention or the final decision in the pursuit of alternative remedies. There is very little flexibility for cases brought outside this time limit, though lack of knowledge of the violation may make a later application possible. For example, in *Hilton v UK* (1998) 57 DR 108, a journalist was refused a job within the BBC, but discovered that this was as a result of a secret vetting process only nine years later. This time limit may not be relevant in the case of continuing violations.

9.4.7 Other Inadmissibility Grounds

Under Article 35(2) and (3), the Court may also declare a complaint inadmissible on further grounds, which are dealt with in turn below.

Anonymity
Anonymous complaints are inadmissible, although the complainant may request on the application form that he wishes his identity to be kept confidential (apart from disclosure to the member state itself).

Petition is 'Substantially the Same as' Previous Applications
This restriction prevents successive applications by the same applicant in respect of the same facts, and is not interpreted by the Court to restrict applications in respect of the different instances even if the issues are substantially the same. Similarly, the provision does not act to bar a second application where new facts have arisen since the first complaint.

Examination by Another International Body
If the matter has already been submitted to and dealt with by another procedure of international investigation or settlement and contains no new information, it will be inadmissible.

Incompatible with the Provisions of the Convention
This ground covers complaints which do not concern the rights and freedoms protected by the Convention, as well as situations in which the applicant is not within the jurisdiction of a member state or where the complaint is not directed against the state at all, for example.

Manifestly Ill-founded
This is the most difficult criterion to assess. Ostensibly, this term is applied to complaints that, on a preliminary examination, do not disclose any possible ground on which a violation could be established. Although the test is a *prima facie* one used to screen out clearly unmeritorious complaints, it is applied very strictly: approximately 90 per cent of complaints to the ECtHR are dismissed under this heading. In effect, the Court's assessment of whether a complaint is 'ill-founded' is a strict merits test. The Court's assertion that a case is 'manifestly ill-founded' is not the same as saying that it is unarguable. Many cases that are plainly arguable are excluded on this ground.

Abuse of the Right of Petition
The fact that an applicant does not come to the Court with 'clean hands' or for a proper motive will not itself be a reason to reject the complaint. An inadmissibility ruling on this ground may arise, rather, if the complaint contains obviously untrue evidence, or where the applicant is demonstrably vexatious.

9.4.8 Decision on Admissibility

This may take several months, or even longer. The ECtHR will give its decision on admissibility in writing. It may decide this question without communicating the case to the government concerned, or it may seek the government's observations, and even seek a hearing before deciding the issue of admissibility.

9.4.9 Communication to the Government

The Chamber to which the case has been assigned will decide on what further action needs to be taken in respect of the complaint. It may be that the complaint is immediately declared inadmissible. Alternatively, the Chamber may decide that further information is required from the applicant and/or state concerned. The complaint is therefore formally 'communicated' to the state, which is then invited to make any observations it thinks fit relating to the complaint. In such cases, the state is sent the

Rapporteur's report (with the exception of the section on the preliminary view on admissibility), together with questions to answer. The applicant will be notified of this step and sent a copy of the papers. It may take well over 12 months for the complaint to reach this stage.

Once the government has responded, the applicant is given a chance to reply.

9.4.10 Oral Hearing

If a hearing is to take place (whether for an admissibility decision or otherwise), the applicant will be notified and contacted by the Registry to fix a date. The parties will also be invited to send their final arguments to the Court so that they can be translated and available for the judges at the hearing. The languages of the Court are English and French.

Hearings are held in the Human Rights Building. In practice, hearings take about half a day, with the parties each being allowed 45 minutes in all to clarify their case. The Court's reasoned decision will usually be sent out about six weeks after the hearing, after the record of both parties' submissions has been checked and returned to the Registry.

9.5 THE MERITS STAGE

9.5.1 Assessing the Merits

Once the Court has made a positive admissibility decision it will generally undertake an investigation into the merits of the complaint. At this stage, it will usually invite the parties to submit further evidence and/or to provide their responses to specific questions. The Court also requires the applicant to provide (within two months of the admissibility decision) a detailed final account of any claim for compensation or costs.

9.5.2 Court's Investigative Powers

The Court is empowered to obtain any evidence that it considers capable of providing clarification of the facts of the case, either of its own motion or at the request of any party to the complaint (or a third party, see 9.5.3 below) (r. 42). This can even include deputing one of its judges to conduct an enquiry or take evidence in some other way. In practice, however, this process occurs only very rarely.

9.5.3 Third Party Interventions

Under Article 36 and r. 61, the President of the Court may permit any state, or any natural or legal person, to submit written observations about the complaint. Such applications can arise because a possible lacuna exists in areas of the argument, which neither the state nor the applicant is willing to fill; alternatively, NGOs often intervene to strengthen an applicant's case against the overwhelming resources of the state, or because the case raises an issue of particular interest to them. Liberty has frequently intervened in cases, as, for example, in *Sheffield v UK* (1999) 27 EHRR 163. Businesses also intervene on occasion: for example, in the case of *Hatton v UK* (App. No. 36022/97), 8 July 2003 (concerning night flights from Heathrow airport and the effect on the private lives of those living on the flight path), both British Airways and an environmental pressure group, Friends of the Earth, submitted written interventions.

9.5.4 Oral Hearing

If there has been no oral hearing on admissibility then the Court will usually give the parties an opportunity to make oral submissions (r. 54(4)). The hearing procedure will be very similar to that of an admissibility hearing (see 9.4.10 above).

9.5.5 Judgment

After the private deliberations of the Court, the Registry will consult the parties on the accuracy of the record of their arguments. The judgment will be read in open court, after which printed copies are made available. The judgment of a Chamber does not become final either until the parties declare that they will not be referring the case to the Grand Chamber, or three months after the date of the judgment, or when the Grand Chamber rejects the request for a rehearing.

9.5.6 Appeals to the Grand Chamber

Under Article 43, either party can seek leave to appeal to the Grand Chamber. In order to gain leave, it must satisfy the vetting panel of five judges that there exists either a serious question affecting the interpretation of the Convention or the protocols thereto, or a serious issue of general importance. This request must be made within three months of the Chamber judgment. It is very rare for a case to be referred to the Grand Chamber on review after a hearing by a Chamber. The first application from the United Kingdom, *Hatton v UK* (App. No. 36022/97), was decided on 8 July 2003.

9.5.7 Friendly Settlements

Article 38(1)(b) provides that once the Court has declared an application admissible, it shall place itself at the disposal of the parties concerned with a view to securing a friendly settlement. This phase runs in parallel with the Court's investigation of the merits. Thus, after a positive admissibility decision, the Court writes to the parties, asking whether or not they wish to explore the possibility of a settlement and, if so, inviting proposals on the subject. The Court acts as a go-between if the parties do enter into negotiations.

9.5.8 Remedies

Where the Court finds that a violation of the Convention has occurred, it is required under Article 41 to consider whether the applicant is entitled to any compensation and/or costs, under the term 'just satisfaction'. Any award is at the complete discretion of the Court and a specific claim must have been made by the applicant. A claim can include pecuniary loss and non-pecuniary loss. The Court has also left open the issue of aggravated damages in a suitable case, but has generally declined to award any form of exemplary or punitive damages. Further, the Court cannot order a state to take or refrain from taking any action.

9.6 FUNDING FOR CASES IN STRASBOURG

It is not easy to obtain funding for cases to Strasbourg. However, it is important for potential applicants to be aware that there are no circumstances in which they can be held liable to pay the government's costs, and that if their application is successful, at least most of their costs will be met by the government.

9.6.1 Domestic Legal Services Commission Funding

The United Kingdom's scheme for Legal Services Commission funding is unlikely to cover applications to the ECtHR. The Access to Justice Act 1999 provides in s. 19 that the Legal Services Commission 'may not fund as part of the Community Legal Service or Criminal Defence services relating to any law other than that of England and Wales, unless any such law is relevant for determining any issue relating to the law of England and Wales'. That section currently gives the Lord Chancellor a discretion (by order) to extend the coverage of legal help.

The structure of the Human Rights Act 1998 does not make the Convention part of the law of England and Wales directly. It might be possible to argue that Convention law could be 'relevant for determining any issue relating to the law of England and Wales', but an applicant will generally have had to exhaust domestic remedies first, and the ECtHR, unlike the European Court of Justice, does not allow interim references to resolve the interpretation of a Convention issue.

9.6.2 Other Sources of Funding

Trade unions or pressure groups may fund litigation, or lawyers may act *pro bono* or on a conditional fee basis in important cases.

9.6.3 Strasbourg Legal Aid

The Court itself may provide legal aid, but only towards the end of the examination of a complaint's admissibility and not before it is lodged. Furthermore, legal costs are recoverable where a complaint is successful (r. 91). There are no fees payable to the Court and there is no liability to meet the costs of the government in any event.

Once communication has occurred, legal aid will be available for those who would qualify on income and capital grounds for civil legal aid in the United Kingdom. Legal aid is available from Strasbourg, although the assessment of the legal aid is carried out by the civil legal aid authorities in the United Kingdom. Legal aid once granted will pay a standard amount for the preparation of the original application (approximately 300 euros) and for the drafting of the reply to the government's response to the application. If the case is never communicated, no legal aid is available.

A further payment can be made to cover representation by one lawyer at any hearing, and the travel and accommodation costs of the lawyer and the applicant. In certain circumstances Strasbourg legal aid will stretch to two lawyers. Even if an application is unsuccessful, applicants are never required to pay the government's costs.

10

RESEARCHING HUMAN RIGHTS JURISPRUDENCE

10.1 INTRODUCTION

Lawyers need to understand how to research human rights case law as s. 2 of the Human Rights Act 1998 imposes a statutory duty on courts to 'take into account' Strasbourg jurisprudence in cases concerning Convention concepts. This has opened up a new field of jurisprudence which practitioners need to be aware of, know how to access, and how to interpret. The Strasbourg institutions have taken on an increasing caseload over the last five decades, with over 33,000 cases being disposed of and 889 judgments delivered by the Court in 2001 alone (*2002 Statistical Information Note on Caselaw from the European Court of Human Rights*). It is therefore important for lawyers to understand how to find their way through this vast jurisprudence to locate the most relevant and important cases. This chapter gives details of the practicalities of locating Convention case law, useful books explaining the detailed functioning of the Convention, and highlights domestic law reports and books which focus specifically on the Human Rights Act 1998.

A brief overview of researching comparative case law and the jurisprudence relating to other international human rights instruments is also given. The Convention, and the Universal Declaration of Human Rights from which it grew, have been used as a model for the written constitutional guarantees of human rights in many Commonwealth constitutions. Not only do UN instruments provide important resources for practitioners to be aware of, but judgments from fora such as the

Privy Council, the Constitutional Court of South Africa, and the Supreme Courts of Canada and New Zealand often contain useful and considered guidance on questions involving fundamental rights.

10.2 CONVENTION JURISPRUDENCE

The European Convention for the Protection of Human Rights and Fundamental Freedoms ('the Convention') is an international treaty of the Council of Europe and is set out in full at Appendix 5. The Convention was adopted in 1950, ratified by the UK in 1951, and entered into force in 1953. To understand the case law, it is necessary to understand how cases are, and were (before 1998), brought in the Strasbourg institutions. Any individual, non-governmental organization, or group of individuals can petition the European Court of Human Rights (ECtHR) in Strasbourg alleging a violation of Convention rights following the UK's adoption of the right of individual petition in 1966. States can also petition the ECtHR alleging a violation of Convention rights by another Council of Europe member state. Chapter 9 outlines in more detail the procedural requirements to be fulfilled.

10.2.1 Pre-Protocol 11

Since it was originally adopted, a number of Protocols have been added to the Convention. Protocol 11 was adopted in 1998 and replaced the old system of adjudication with a new, more streamlined one. Prior to 1 November 1998, a two-tier system was employed to examine applications lodged in Strasbourg. Initially, the European Commission on Human Rights (an entirely separately staffed body) (ECmHR) would examine the facts of the application and deliver an admissibility decision on the case, together with a decision on the merits if the Commission did decide to declare the petition admissible. This decision, although critical for determining whether or not a case would go forward to a full hearing, was not binding on the ECtHR itself. Often the ECtHR would adopt a final judgment which was substantially different to the decision reached by the Commission.

Although the ECmHR no longer exists, its decisions detailing the admissibility or otherwise of applications and opinions on the merits of individual cases are still of relevance to the proper interpretation of the Convention. As with judgments from the ECtHR itself, this jurisprudence 'must be taken into account' under the Human Rights Act by any domestic court or tribunal determining a question involving Convention rights.

10.2.2 Protocol 11

Since 1 November 1998, this two-tier system has been replaced with a single, permanent Court. The Rules of Court of the European Court of Human Rights (see 10.3.3

below) adopted on 4 November 1998 set out in full the competence of and procedure before the new institution. Now, three judges of the ECtHR sit in Committee to determine whether an application is 'admissible'. If it is, seven judges sitting as a Chamber determine the merits of the petition. However, cases involving important questions affecting the interpretation of the Convention may be dealt with by a Grand Chamber of 17 judges, either because the original Chamber cedes jurisdiction, or (rarely) where the Grand Chamber re-hears an important case on a review (Article 43). Judgments of the new Court emerge from each of the different Sections (from I through to IV), which are headed by designated Presidents of Sections and are composed of a varying number of judges. This new system has created the possibility of different Chambers taking different views until an issue is resolved by the Grand Chamber (see, for example, the case of *Hatton v UK* (App. No. 36022/97), 8 July 2003).

In both pre- and post-Protocol 11 systems the Committee of Ministers (www.coe.int/t/e/committee_of_ministers) has a supervisory role to play under Article 46(2). This encompasses not only supervising the execution of judgments, but also ensuring that future violations do not take place with equivalent facts to the ones already dealt with. Reports and Resolutions are issued to monitor compliance with judgments and the steps that have been taken to implement the European Court's decisions.

10.2.3 Weight of Authorities

As the Convention is a 'living instrument' and is to be interpreted in the light of present-day conditions, there is no formal doctrine of precedent binding the European Court. However, there are a number of factors to be taken into account when considering how much weight should be given to a particular decision from Strasbourg:

(a) Court judgments are of more importance than decisions of the Commission or the Committee of Ministers. Decisions of the Committee of Ministers are made by politicians, not judges, and without the benefit of legal argument, and are less commonly cited than Court or Commission judgments.

(b) Judgments of the plenary Court (now the Grand Chamber) and decisions or opinions of the plenary Commission are the most authoritative. Decisions which are unanimous or which have large majorities are more likely to be followed or to be influential than those decided by a narrow majority.

(c) Recent decisions are more valuable than decisions made some time ago because the Convention is interpreted as a 'living instrument'. As such its meaning will develop over time, and new case law will develop in an organic way without old case law being specifically overruled.

(d) Caution is needed where Strasbourg organs have relied on the 'margin of appreciation' in concluding that there was no violation of the Convention, as this doctrine has no direct application in domestic law (see 2.5 above).

(e) Admissibility decisions rarely set out the Commission's own view and are less helpful than merits decisions which give the Commission's opinion on the law. While the Commission has often decided that cases are inadmissible because they are 'manifestly ill-founded', this is not the same as a finding that the point of law involved is unarguable. It may depend on the facts in issue, or application of the margin of appreciation. Nevertheless, a decision that a particular case is inadmissible, on the basis it is manifestly unfounded, may be the only indication of the view of the Strasbourg institutions on the point of law in issue, as such cases never go further. Since there is no strict doctrine of precedent, these decisions need not prevent a well-founded case on the same point being raised in an English court.

(f) From November 1998, the Committee of Ministers no longer made decisions on the merits and the Commission ceased to exist. New learning will emerge only from admissibility decisions and judgments by the Chambers and the Grand Chamber. A decision of the Grand Chamber on review is a 'second hearing' of an important case, and so may command greater authority than the previous plenary Court.

10.2.4 Referencing System

Once lodged, all applications to Strasbourg are given a number commencing with five digits, and then two digits representing the year of the application. Occasionally, the case before the Court involves sensitive issues and demands confidentiality, and so the applicant is referred to by a letter, for example, *W v United Kingdom* (App. No. 25678/90). These numbers can be found 'attached' to the names of the parties in all ECtHR or ECmHR documentation and are an important aid when searching for case law.

10.3 FINDING CONVENTION CASE LAW

The Practice Direction issued under the Human Rights Act 1998 relating to the use of human rights material (see Appendix 2) outlines the procedures to be adopted when citing authority in court. The sources highlighted below (both paper and electronic) are acceptable for this purpose.

10.3.1 European Court Judgments: Official Reports

Judgments of the ECtHR before 1996 are published by the Council of Europe in 'Series A' and 'Series B'. Series A contains the full text of the ECtHR's judgments, and from 1985 it also contains extracts of the ECmHR's decisions on the merits of applications. Series B contains selective extracts from the pleadings, arguments, and relevant documentation lodged at the ECtHR for individual cases. These reports are cited as 'Series A, No. 152' or 'A/152' (or 'Series B, No. 123', 'B/123'). Judgments from 1996 onwards are published in the *Reports of Judgments and Decisions* (RJD) (Carl Heymanns Verlag publishers). Every judgment has numbered paragraphs to help locate specific passages. These reports are very specialist and can be difficult to find. However, if a case is reported in either Series A or the RJD, this fact is recorded in the ECtHR's own online database, HUDOC (see 10.3.3 below).

A widely available domestic alternative is the *European Human Rights Reports* (EHRR) (published by Sweet & Maxwell), although it should be noted that not all judgments of the European Court are reported in this series. The first volume was published in 1979 and references to these reports take the form of year of publication, followed by volume number, and lastly a numbered reference. Prior to 2001, this final number referred to the page at which the judgment was reported, but since 2001 (and volume 34) this number refers to the case itself. For example, *Tolstoy Miloslavsky v United Kingdom* (1995) 20 EHRR 442 refers to the 20th volume of the EHRR at page 442; whereas *Hatton v United Kingdom* (2002) 34 EHRR 1 refers to the first case printed in the 34th volume of the EHRR.

Other useful sources of judgments include *Butterworths' Human Rights Cases* (BHRC) and digests in the *European Human Rights Law Review* (EHRLR).

These reports are the most widely used source of ECtHR judgments in UK courts.

10.3.2 European Commission

The majority of the decisions from the ECmHR are published by the Council of Europe in the *Decisions and Reports* series (DR). These numerical volumes contain cases from 1974 to 1995. There are several indexes (published at 15–20 volume intervals) which contain lists of names, application numbers, and, usefully, summaries of judgments by keyword and article numbers. References to these reports appear as year, volume number, and page number. For example, *Rayner v United Kingdom* (1986) 47 DR 5 refers to the 47th volume of the DRs at page 5. DRs are difficult to locate and are available only in good law libraries or, for some volumes, via The Stationery Office (www.tso.co.uk).

The EHRR series (see 10.3.1 above) contains extracts and summaries of some ECmHR decisions. In volumes 1 to 14 these are part of the ordinary text, but from volume 15 onwards (approximately 1993) they appear in a separate section at the end of the bound copies of the series. References to these Commission Decisions are abbreviated as 'EHRR CD'.

Other useful sources of judgments include the *Digest of Strasbourg Case Law* and, for early, pre-1974 decisions, the *Yearbook of the European Convention on Human Rights* (cited as 'YB'), both of which are published by the Council of Europe.

10.3.3 Website

The ECtHR maintains a free, searchable database of all recent Court judgments (and a number of older ones from pre-1988) and most Commission judgments. The HUDOC database can be accessed via www.echr.coe.int and has an online users' guide to help navigate through the search engine. However, general tips to remember include selecting the appropriate databases to search at the top of the screen (language, type of judgment, and so on) and, if known, using the application number and rough date of judgment to focus searches. The database is comprehensive, constantly updated, and is the best way to locate very recent judgments. It also contains press releases summarizing important judgments. The Council of Europe also publishes the free 'Case Law and Information Notes', which give overviews of judgments issued on a monthly basis. The Rules of Court of the ECtHR can be read online at www.echr.coe.int.

In addition, the 'Human Rights Web' (www.coe.int/T/E/Human_rights/) contains useful information about initiatives and programmes under the auspices of Europe's Directorate of Human Rights. Specifically, the 'Human Rights Information Bulletin' (www.humanrights.coe.int/Bulletin/eng/presenting.htm) contains valuable information on current activities. The European Social Charter, another Council of Europe treaty, and its opinions database can be accessed via www.coe.int/T/E/Human_Rights/Esc.

The Council of Europe is investing heavily in upgrading the online resource it currently offers, and it is envisaged that from mid-2003 all old and new decisions (from both the ECtHR and the ECmHR) will be accessible from its website.

10.3.4 Bibliographic Resources on Convention Case Law

Berger, *Case Law of the European Court of Human Rights* (Dublin: Round Hall Press, 1989–95), 3 volumes.

European Human Rights Law Review (EHRLR) (London: Sweet & Maxwell, 1996 to date).

Farran, *The United Kingdom before the European Court of Human Rights* (London: Blackstone Press, 1996).

Gordon, Ward, and Eicke, *The Strasbourg Case Law: Leading Cases from the European Human Rights Reports* (London: Sweet & Maxwell, 2001).

Harris and O'Boyle, *Cases and Materials on the European Convention on Human Rights* (London: Butterworths, 2001).

Harris, O'Boyle, and Warbrick, *Law of European Convention on Human Rights*, 2nd edn (London: Butterworths, 2003).

Jacobs, White, and Ovey, *The European Convention on Human Rights*, 3rd edn (Oxford: Clarendon Press, 2002).

Janis, Kay, and Bradley, *European Human Rights Law: Text and Materials*, 2nd edn (Oxford: Clarendon Press, 2000).

Kempees, *A Systematic Guide to the Case Law of the European Court of Human Rights 1960–1994* (The Hague: Martinus Nijhoff, 1996), 2 volumes.

Livingstone, *The European Convention on Human Rights* (Oxford: Oxford University Press, 2002).

Reid, *A Practitioners Guide to the European Convention on Human Rights* (London: Sweet & Maxwell, 1998).

Robertson and Merrills, *Human Rights in Europe: A Study of the European Convention on Human Rights*, 4th edn (Manchester: Manchester University Press, 2001).

Simor, *Human Rights Practice* (London: Sweet & Maxwell, 2001).

Starmer, *Blackstone's Human Rights Digest* (London: Blackstone Press, 2001).

van Dijk and van Hoof, *Theory and Practice of the European Convention on Human Rights*, 3rd edn (The Hague: Kluwer, 1998).

10.3.5 *Travaux Préparatoires*

In interpreting the Convention, the ECtHR has very occasionally considered the *travaux préparatoires*, or preparatory documents, relating to the drafting of the Convention. They are published by the Council of Europe in *The Collected Edition of the Travaux Préparatoires of the European Convention on Human Rights* and are available through specialist law libraries. The *travaux préparatoires* are used rarely by the ECtHR, and as a means of confirming its interpretation of a Convention provision only when such an interpretation leaves the meaning ambiguous or obscure, or leads to a result that is manifestly absurd.

However, such a means of interpretation can conflict with the principle of the Convention as a 'living instrument' (see Chapter 2), and as a result the ECtHR has been prepared to adopt a construction which appears to conflict with the *travaux préparatoires* if it considers such an interpretation necessary to ensure that Convention rights are 'practical and effective' in a modern context. For example, in the case of *Sigurjonsson v Iceland* (1993) 16 EHRR 462, the ECtHR was determining whether Article 11 guarantees a right not to be compelled to join a trade union. Ignoring the *travaux préparatoires* showing that such a right was deliberately omitted, the ECtHR held that the Convention had to be interpreted as a 'living instrument' and, as there was recognition at the international and domestic level of the right not to join an association, this was also inherent in Article 11 of the Convention.

10.4 FINDING HUMAN RIGHTS ACT MATERIALS

Researching domestic human rights jurisprudence should be carried out in exactly the same way as other domestic legal research. Since the Act specifically provides that 'human rights' cases are not decided by a specialist court or tribunal but can arise in any existing forum, the well-known sets of law reports (Law Reports, Weekly Law Reports, Administrative Court Digest, etc.) will contain details of cases raising human rights points and are an important point of reference. However, since the implementation of the Human Rights Act 1998, several series of specialist reports, journals, and books have been published to help lawyers understand the human rights context and locate relevant materials more easily.

10.4.1 Law Reports, Journals, and Books

From 2000, two new series of reports—the *Human Rights Law Reports—UK Cases* (Sweet & Maxwell, 2000 to date) and the *United Kingdom Human Rights Reports* (Jordans, 2000 to date)—report the most important decisions on human rights points determined by UK courts.

The *European Human Rights Law Review* (see 10.3.1 above) also contains articles and commentary on domestic cases raising human rights issues. Particularly useful are the tables of cases and commentaries produced by the Human Rights Act Research Unit, which comprehensively index relevant decisions. Other useful publications include *Human Rights and UK Practice* (Jordans) and the *Human Rights Alerter* (Sweet & Maxwell), which cover some Strasbourg decisions as well as domestic cases. *Public Law* (Sweet & Maxwell), *Criminal Law Review* (Sweet & Maxwell), *Modern Law Review* (Sweet & Maxwell), and *Judicial Review* (Hart Publishing) are journals which all regularly contain articles and case digests of interest to those researching human rights points.

Books which provide a good, detailed commentary on the framework and issues involved with the incorporation of the Human Rights Act include:

Coppel, *The Human Rights Act 1998: Enforcing the European Convention on Human Rights in the Domestic Courts* (Chichester: John Wiley and Son, 1999)

Grosz, Beatson, and Duffy, *Human Rights: The 1998 Act and European Convention* (London: Sweet & Maxwell, 2000)

Huscroft and Rishworth (eds), *Litigating Rights* (London: Hart, 2002)

Jowell and Cooper (eds), *Understanding Human Rights Principles* (London: Hart/JUSTICE, 2001)

Jowell and Cooper (eds), *Delivering Rights? How the Human Rights Act is Working and for Whom* (London: Hart, 2003)

Lester and Pannick, *Human Rights Law and Practice* (London: Butterworths, 1999) (and supplements)

Simpson, *Human Rights and the End of Empire: Britain and the Genesis of the European Convention* (Oxford: Oxford University Press, 2001)

Singh and Hunt, *Assessing the Impact of the Human Rights Act 1998* (London: Hart, 2003)

Starmer, *European Human Rights Law* (London: Legal Action Group, 1999)

Tomlinson and Clayton, *Human Rights Law* (Oxford: Oxford University Press, 2000) (and annual supplements).

10.4.2 Electronic and Online Resources

The main legal publishers provide subscription-based online services incorporating a mixture of different law reports and texts according to their publishing lists. For example:

- Butterworths' Human Rights Direct (www.butterworths.co.uk) offers the BHRC and some ECtHR decisions alongside Lester and Pannick's key text and a current awareness service.

- Westlaw UK's Human Rights subscription package (www.sweetandmaxwell. co.uk) offers access to the EHRR, EHRLR, and Simor's *Human Rights Practice.*

- JUSTIS' Human Rights service (www.justis.com) indexes a large number of ECtHR decisions for ease of searching.

- Lawtel (www.lawtel.co.uk) offers a Human Rights Service encompassing recent transcripts of judgments from domestic courts and commentary provided by experts.

However, there is a growing number of free websites that offer valuable information on human rights jurisprudence. For locating case law, the database BAILII (www.bailii.org) offers a good starting point. Institutionally, as the former Lord Chancellor's Department (now the Department for Constitutional Affairs) (www.lcd.gov.uk/hract) has responsibility for human rights in government, its website indexes a wealth of resources, including a 'Study Guide on the Human Rights Act'; speeches by ministers on human rights; statistics on the impact of the Act; and other useful materials. Additionally, the webpage of the Parliamentary Joint Committee on Human Rights (JCHR) (www.parliament.uk/commons/selcom/ hrhome.htm) indexes a number of detailed reports and evidence taken in support of the JCHR's remit of scrutinizing all new legislation presented to Parliament.

Several organizations also provide free information on human rights issues, including:

- Liberty www.liberty-human-rights.org.uk and www.yourrights.org.uk

- Justice www.justice.org.uk

- Matrix www.matrixlaw.co.uk

- The Human Rights Update hosted by One Crown Office Row http://www.humanrights.1cor.com/5/text.nc

- The Human Rights Act Research Unit's webpage hosted by Doughty Street Chambers www.doughtystreet.co.uk/hrarp/index.cfm

- Human Rights Directory www.echr.net, designed and maintained by the University of West England.

10.4.3 Use of Hansard

Since the landmark decision of the House of Lords in *Pepper v Hart* [1993] AC 593, parliamentary statements by ministers may, in certain circumstances, be admissible in order to interpret an Act of Parliament. The principles are set out in the speech of Lord Browne-Wilkinson and state that references to Hansard may be admissible where:

(a) legislation is obscure, or ambiguous, or leads to an absurdity;

(b) the material relied upon consists of one or more statements by a minister or other promoter of the Bill, and such other material as is necessary to understand such statements and their effect; and

(c) the statements relied upon are clear.

There has rarely, if ever, been a series of parliamentary debates in which Members of Parliament have referred quite so repeatedly and self-consciously to the *Pepper v Hart* principle as during the passage of the Human Rights Bill. Since there are aspects of the Act which could be ambiguous we have included relevant Hansard statements (at Appendix 4), which may be admissible in court when arguing what the Act is intended to mean, and parliamentary debates grouped by subject.

For a detailed examination of the parliamentary debates leading up to the passing of the Human Rights Act, see Cooper and Marshall-Williams, *Legislating for Human Rights: Parliamentary Debates on the Human Rights Bill* (London: Hart/JUSTICE, 2000). Additionally, The former Lord Chancellor's Department (now the Department for Constitutional Affairs) has produced a user-friendly database indexing the parliamentary debates on the Bill (www.lcd.gov.uk/hract/lawlist2.htm).

It should be borne in mind, however, that some of the Hansard statements are controversial, and it is by no means clear that they should be regarded as any more than 'persuasive' by the courts that consider them.

Indeed, this was illustrated by the case of *Wilson v First County Trust Ltd* [2003] UKHL 40, decided by the House of Lords on 10 July 2003. The Court of Appeal had had recourse to the parliamentary debates in order to decide what aim the Consumer Credit Act 1974 had been intended to address, and whether the legislation was proportionate. The Court of Appeal's decision was successfully appealed to the House of Lords, and during the course of the appeal, the authorities of the Houses of Parliament intervened to question whether it was proper to 'question' proceedings in Parliament in this way.

The House of Lords in the *Wilson* case held that recourse to parliamentary materials was allowed in order to adjudicate on the justification for, and the proportionality of, a measure impugned under the Human Rights Act. Their Lordships distinguished between 'questioning' proceedings in Parliament (which they said would be improper) and considering matters which arose during parliamentary debates as background information tending to show the likely practical impact of a statutory measure, or to identify the policy objective of statutory provision, in order to assess the social policy aim of the legislation or its proportionality (which was permissible). However, Lord Nicholls, in the leading speech, warned against the conceptual and constitutional difficulties of treating the intentions of the Government revealed in debates as reflecting the will of Parliament, and emphasized that Hansard debates used in this way should be treated as no more than a source of relevant background information. And Lord Hobhouse pointed out (at para. 144) that questions of justification and proportionality had to be answered by reference to the time the events took place to which a statutory provision was being applied, and not at the date when the legislation was passed. He observed that, 'to look for justification only in the parliamentary debates at the time the statute was originally passed invites error'.

10.5 FINDING RELEVANT MATERIALS FROM OTHER JURISDICTIONS

The Convention has been incorporated into the law of other European states for many years and there are numerous decisions of their national courts that interpret the Convention.

The Convention (and the Universal Declaration of Human Rights from which it grew) have also been used as a model for the written constitutional guarantees of human rights in many common law jurisdictions. UK courts (particularly the Privy Council) have often looked to the jurisprudence of other Commonwealth constitutions for guidance as to the construction and application of human rights and fundamental freedoms (see *A-G of Hong Kong v Lee Kwong-kut* [1993] AC 951). These decisions are not binding authority, but could be persuasive—especially in cases where there is no settled Convention jurisprudence on the point at issue. As a result, judgments from the Privy Council, the Constitutional Court of South Africa, and the Supreme Courts of Canada, New Zealand, and the US often contain useful guidance for practitioners. For a further examination of this approach see: Lord Lester, 'The Relevance of Comparative Constitutional Case Law' [2001] JR 13, and Tomlinson and Shukla, *Interpreting Convention Rights—Essential Human Rights Cases of the Commonwealth* (London: Butterworths, 2001). Detailed consideration of jurisprudence from a diverse number of countries is given in Tomlinson and Clayton, *Law of Human Rights* (Oxford: Oxford University Press, 2000).

Some comparative material can be freely obtained from a variety of national law reports and databases online. The LLRX website (www.llrx.com/comparative_and_ foreign_law.html) regularly commissions and updates comprehensive guides to researching comparative law in other jurisdictions. These offer not only details of web links to legislative and case law databases around the world, but also a clear overview of the legal framework in the countries concerned. WORLDLII (www.worldlii.org/catalog/303.html) provides a key resource with the ability to search across case law of many jurisdictions and links to a multitude of national links. Similarly, the Interights Human Rights Case Law Databases dealing with International Case Law (www.interights.org/icl) and Commonwealth Case Law (www.interights.org/ccl) are good sources of summaries of important decisions. Broadly relevant materials can also be found in the BHRC (see 10.3.1 above), the *Law Reports of the Commonwealth* (Butterworths), and the journal *International and Comparative Law Quarterly* (Oxford University Press), which subscribers can access electronically via the OUP website (www.oup.com).

10.5.1 Canada

The Canadian Charter of Rights and Freedoms was enacted in 1982, and since that date Canadian courts have drawn upon international human rights jurisprudence when considering cases before them (see Schabas, *International Human Rights Law and the Canadian Charter* (Toronto: Carswell, 1991)). Decisions of the Supreme Court of Canada can be searched by keyword via www.lexum.umontreal.ca/csc-scc/en/, and the Canadian Legal Information Institute (http://www.canlii.org/) contains judgments from most Canadian courts and relevant legislation. The Canadian Human Rights Commission (www.chrc-ccdp.ca/menu.asp?l=e) produces an annual 'Legal Report' that gives useful overviews of the most important legal developments. For a broad overview of the operation of Charter system see Hogg, *Constitutional Law of Canada*, 4th edn (Toronto: Carswell, 1996), or the *Canadian Rights Reporter*.

10.5.2 New Zealand

The New Zealand Bill of Rights Act was enacted in 1990. The looseleaf publication, *Human Rights Reports of New Zealand* (which can be purchased through Sweet & Maxwell), reports the most important cases. Court of Appeal judgments from 1998 can be searched for and downloaded free of charge from www.austlii.edu.au/nz/cases/NZCA. Institutionally, the New Zealand Human Rights Commission (www.hrc.co.nz) has links and resources on relevant legal issues.

10.5.3 South Africa

The South African Constitutional Court determines questions on the interpretation of the 1996 Bill of Rights (and subsequent amendments to the legislation), and the text of both the statutes and the Court's judgments can be accessed via www.concourt.gov.za. *Butterworths' Constitutional Law Reports* publish the most important decisions, and the *South African Journal on Human Rights* (published by Juta and available in the UK through Butterworths) regularly contains articles of interest. The South African Human Rights Commission (www.sahrc.org.za/main_frameset.htm) indexes a series of useful domestic links to help locate other South African resources.

10.5.4 Australia

AUSTLII (www.austlii.edu.au) is a comprehensive, free database of case law, legislation, and other materials that serves as the main resource for finding Australian materials. The Australian Human Rights Resource Centre (www.austlii.edu.au/au/other/ahric) offers a variety of links and useful shortcuts—including to the specialist *Australian Journal of Human Rights* which provides insightful articles on key issues.

10.5.5 Hong Kong

The Bill of Rights Ordinance in Hong Kong incorporates the International Covenant on Civil and Political Rights into domestic law and adds to the constitutional guarantees in the Basic Law. The *Basic Law and Human Rights Bulletin* covers many of the debates involving human rights in Hong Kong. In addition, the Hong Kong Human Rights Commission's website (www.hkhrc.org.hk/homepage/index_e.htm), a coalition of non-governmental organizations, provides useful updates on current issues. The Hong Kong Human Rights Monitor (www.hkhrm.org.hk/) also publishes a regular updating newsletter.

10.5.6 United States

The US Constitution's Bill of Rights and Thirteenth to Fifteenth Amendments have a complex and detailed jurisprudence associated with them. The leading guides to understanding these constitutional protections are *Tribe* or *Nowak and Rotunda* (both available in good law libraries or via www.amazon.com). Additionally, the *Harvard Human Rights Journal* (www.law.harvard.edu/studorgs/hrj/) publishes many relevant articles of interest to the UK lawyer. Online, the vast majority of federal and state case law can be found at www.findlaw.com, which has a separate, fully searchable section for Supreme Court judgments.

10.6 FINDING OTHER INTERNATIONAL AND REGIONAL HUMAN RIGHTS MATERIALS

As highlighted in Chapters 1, 2, and 7, there are a number of international instruments and treaties relating to the protection of human rights in international law which, although they are not incorporated into domestic law, may be of use to courts when determining human rights issues. In the same way that the ECtHR has used international law to help determine the scope of rights, domestic courts may find useful guidance contained in these materials. This could either be because the UK is a signatory to the treaties (as is the case with many UN treaties) and is under an international obligation to comply with the provisions of the instrument, or they may help to give guidance on the scope of the fundamental freedom in question (for example, jurisprudence from the UN Human Rights Committee). The resources listed below are useful starting points for researchers interested in tracking the wider legal context in which the Convention, and human rights law generally, operate.

10.6.1 EC/EU Law

Chapter 7 highlights the developing doctrine of fundamental rights in EC and EU law, and particularly the role of the Charter of Fundamental Rights which is included in Appendix 7. In addition, the homepage of the Charter can be accessed via www.europa.eu.int/comm/justice_home/unit/charte/index_en.html, where visitors can find not only the text of the Charter, but also overviews of its provisions and useful 'Frequently Asked Questions' that outline the important issues. The European Court of Justice's website (www.curia.eu.int) has a searchable database indexing all judgments and decisions since 1996. Key texts that are easily available in good bookshops and law libraries include Craig and de Búrca, *EU Law: Text, Cases and Materials* (Oxford: Oxford University Press, 2002) and Alston, *The EU and Human Rights* (Oxford: Oxford University Press, 1999).

10.6.2 International Human Rights Law

The American Society for International Law, *Guide to Electronic Resources for International Law* (www.asil.org/resource/humrts1.htm) is not only a comprehensive resource with many links to international human rights resources, but is also an excellent step-by-step guide to researching international human rights law. In addition, both the International Law (www.un.org/law) and the Human Rights' (www.un.org/rights) sections of the UN website and the homepage of the International Court of Justice (www.icj-cij.org) provide important general resources on international law which set the international human rights regime in context.

10.6.3 UN Charter and Treaty Body System

The UN has produced a concise guide to researching human rights issues (www.un.org/Depts/dhl/resguide/spechr.htm) to help users navigate their way through the site to the information they need. The majority of international human rights instruments are indexed by subject and accessible via www.unhchr.ch/html/intlinst.htm.

The UN High Commissioner for Human Rights (www.unhchr.ch) oversees the two complementary systems that implement protection of human rights. When researching human rights issues, a distinction has to be made between Charter-based and treaty-based human rights bodies. Reflecting this division, the human rights documentation posted on the website of the High Commissioner is organized into two databases:

(a) *Charter-based organs* derive their establishment from provisions contained in the Charter of the United Nations, hold broad human rights mandates, address an unlimited audience, and take action based on majority voting. They include the Commission on Human Rights and the Sub-Commission on the Promotion and Protection of Human Rights, the Commission on the Status of Women, and the various thematic and country mechanisms established by the Commission (for example, the Special Rapporteur on the Right to Freedom of Expression). These bodies issue reports, resolutions, and decisions, and a searchable database can be found at www.unhchr.ch/huridocda/huridoca.nsf/Documents?OpenFrameset.

(b) The *Treaty-based organs* derive their existence from provisions contained in a specific legal instrument (that is, the Convenant on Civil and Political Rights), hold more narrow mandates (that is, the set of issues codified in the legal instrument involved), address a limited audience (that is, only those countries that have ratified the legal instrument in question), and base their decision-making on consensus. They include the Human Rights Committee formed under the International Covenant on Civil and Political Rights (ICCPR), and the other bodies which grew up under the International Covenant on Social and Economic Rights (IESCR), the Convention on the Rights of the Child (CRC), Convention on the Elimination of Discrimination Against Women (CEDAW), and the Convention on the Elimination of Racial Discrimination (CERD). These bodies monitor compliance with the provisions in the Treaties (in the form of periodic state reports and through the individual petition procedure that Optional Protocols to some of the Treaties provide). In addition to legal opinions on the cases that come before them, these bodies may also issue important 'General Comments' on treaty articles which flesh out the scope of the rights in question. A searchable database can be found on www.unhchr.ch/tbs/doc.nsf.

This is a complex area and specialist texts such as Alston (ed.), *The United Nations and Human Rights: A Critical Appraisal* (Oxford: Clarendon Press, 1992); Steiner and Alston, *International Human Rights in Context* (Oxford: Oxford University Press, 2000); Joseph, Schultz, and Castan, *Covenant on Civil and Political Rights: Case Materials and Commentary* (Oxford: Oxford University Press, 2000); Craven, *The International Covenant on Economic, Social and Cultural Rights* (Oxford: Oxford University Press, 1995) offer more detailed explanation and commentary on how these systems operate.

10.6.4 Inter-American System

The Inter-American System for the protection of human rights does not have as developed a jurisprudence as the European Convention on Human Rights, but has given some key judgments on issues such as the right to life. Both the Inter-American Commission on Human Rights (www.cidh.oas.org) and the Inter-American Court of Human Rights' websites (www.corteidh.or.cr) provide information on judgments and opinions. The leading text by Harris and Livingstone, *The Inter-American System of Human Rights* (Oxford: Oxford University Press, 1998), explains the jurisdiction and workings of the Inter-American System.

10.6.5 African Charter on Human and People's Rights

Case law and primary documentation from the African Commission on Human and People's Rights can be difficult to obtain. Some material, including case law, can be found online through the University of Minnesota's *African Human Rights Resources Centre* (www1.umn.edu/humanrts/africa/comision.html) and at the Derechos *Human Rights in Subsaharan Africa* web-pages (www.derechos.org/human-rights/afr). The African Commission's sessions are also the subject of regular reports in the *Netherlands Quarterly of Human Right* (published by Kluwer).

Appendix 1
Human Rights Act 1998

CHAPTER 42
ARRANGEMENT OF SECTIONS

Introduction

Parliamentary procedure

19.   Statements of compatibility.

Supplemental

20.   Orders etc. under this Act.
21.   Interpretation, etc.
22.   Short title, commencement, application and extent.

SCHEDULES:

Human Rights Act 1998

1998 CHAPTER 42

An Act to give further effect to rights and freedoms guaranteed under the European Convention on Human Rights; to make provision with respect to holders of certain judicial offices who become judges of the European Rights; and for connected purposes.

[9th November 1998]

BE IT ENACTED by the Queen's most Excellent Majesty, by and with the advice and consent of the Lords Spiritual and Temporal, and Commons, in this present Parliament assembled, and by the authority of the same, as follows:—

Introduction

1. The Convention Rights

(1)   In this Act 'the Convention rights' means the rights and fundamental freedoms set out in—

    (a)   Articles 2 to 12 and 14 of the Convention,
    (b)   Articles 1 to 3 of the First Protocol, and
    (c)   Articles 1 and 2 of the Sixth Protocol,
as read with Articles 16 to 18 of the Convention.

(2)   Those Articles are to have effect for the purposes of this Act subject to any designated derogation or reservation (as to which see sections 14 and 15).

(3)   The Articles are set out in Schedule 1.

(4)   The Lord Chancellor may by order make such amendments to this Act as he considers appropriate to reflect the effect, in relation to the United Kingdom, of a protocol.

(5)   In subsection (4) 'protocol' means a protocol to the Convention—

    (a)   which the United Kingdom has ratified; or

    (b)   which the United Kingdom has signed with a view to ratification.

(6)   No amendment may be made by an order under subsection (4) so as to come into
force before the protocol concerned is in force in relation to the United Kingdom.

[This section was amended by the Transfer of Functions (Miscellaneous) Order 2001, SI
2001/3500, Art. 8, sch. 2, Pt I, para. 7(a).]

2. Interpretation of Convention rights

(1)   A court or tribunal determining a question which has arisen in connection with a
Convention right must take into account any—

    (a)   judgment, decision, declaration or advisory opinion of the European Court of
Human Rights,

    (b)   opinion of the Commission given in a report adopted under Article 31 of the
Convention,

    (c)   decision of the Commission in connection with Article 26 or 27(2) of the
Convention, or

    (d)   decision of the Committee of Ministers taken under Article 46 of the Convention,
whenever made or given, so far as, in the opinion of the court or tribunal, it is relevant to the
proceedings in which that question has arisen.

(2)   Evidence of any judgment, decision, declaration or opinion of which account may
have to be taken under this section is to be given in proceedings before any court or tribunal in
such manner as may be provided by rules.

(3)   In this section 'rules' means rules of court or, in the case of proceedings before a
tribunal, rules made for the purposes of this section—

    (a)   by the Lord Chancellor or the Secretary of State, in relation to any proceedings
outside Scotland;

    (b)   by the Secretary of State, in relation to proceedings in Scotland; or

    (c)   by a Northern Ireland department, in relation to proceedings before a tribunal in
Northern Ireland—

        (i)   which deals with transferred matters; and

        (ii)   for which no rules made under paragraph (a) are in force.

Legislation

3. Interpretation of legislation

(1)   So far as it is possible to do so, primary legislation and subordinate legislation must
be read and given effect in a way which is compatible with the Convention rights.

(2)   This section—

    (a)   applies to primary legislation and subordinate legislation whenever enacted;

    (b)   does not affect the validity, continuing operation or enforcement of any incom-
patible primary legislation; and

(c)   does not affect the validity, continuing operation or enforcement of any incompatible subordinate legislation if (disregarding any possibility of revocation) primary legislation prevents removal of the incompatibility.

4. Declaration of incompatibility

(1)   Subsection (2) applies in any proceedings in which a court determines whether a provision of primary legislation is compatible with a Convention right.

(2)   If the court is satisfied that the provision is incompatible with a Convention right, it may make a declaration of that incompatibility.

(3)   Subsection (4) applies in any proceedings in which a court determines whether a provision of subordinate legislation, made in the exercise of a power conferred by primary legislation, is compatible with a Convention right.

(4)   If the court is satisfied—

(a)   that the provision is incompatible with a Convention right, and

(b)   that (disregarding any possibility of revocation) the primary legislation concerned prevents removal of the incompatibility, it may make a declaration of that incompatibility.

(5)   In this section 'court' means—

(a)   the House of Lords;

(b)   the Judicial Committee of the Privy Council;

(c)   the Courts-Martial Appeal Court;

(d)   in Scotland, the High Court of Justiciary sitting otherwise than as a trial court or the Court of Session;

(e)   in England and Wales or Northern Ireland, the High Court or the Court of Appeal.

(6)   A declaration under this section ('a declaration of incompatibility')—

(a)   does not affect the validity, continuing operation or enforcement of the provision in respect of which it is given; and

(b)   is not binding on the parties to the proceedings in which it is made.

5. Right of Crown to intervene

(1)   Where a court is considering whether to make a declaration of incompatibility, the Crown is entitled to notice in accordance with rules of court.

(2)   In any case to which subsection (1) applies—

(a)   a Minister of the Crown (or a person nominated by him),

(b)   a member of the Scottish Executive,

(c)   a Northern Ireland Minister,

(d)   a Northern Ireland department,

is entitled, on giving notice in accordance with rules of court, to be joined as a party to the proceedings.

(3)   Notice under subsection (2) may be given at any time during the proceedings.

(4)   A person who has been made a party to criminal proceedings (other than in Scotland) as the result of a notice under subsection (2) may, with leave, appeal to the House of Lords against any declaration of incompatibility made in the proceedings.

(5)   In subsection (4)—

'criminal proceedings' includes all proceedings before the Courts-Martial Appeal Court; and

'leave' means leave granted by the court making the declaration of incompatibility or by the House of Lords.

Public authorities

6. Acts of public authorities

(1)   It is unlawful for a public authority to act in a way which is incompatible with a Convention right.

(2)   Subsection (1) does not apply to an act if—

(a)   as the result of one or more provisions of primary legislation, the authority could not have acted differently; or

(b)   in the case of one or more provisions of, or made under, primary legislation which cannot be read or given effect in a way which is compatible with the Convention rights, the authority was acting so as to give effect to or enforce those provisions.

(3)   In this section 'public authority' includes—

(a)   a court or tribunal, and

(b)   any person certain of whose functions are functions of a public nature,

but does not include either House of Parliament or a person exercising functions in connection with proceedings in Parliament.

(4)   In subsection (3) 'Parliament' does not include the House of Lords in its judicial capacity.

(5)   In relation to a particular act, a person is not a public authority by virtue only of subsection (3)(b) if the nature of the act is private.

(6)   'An act' includes a failure to act but does not include a failure to—

(a)   introduce in, or lay before, Parliament a proposal for legislation; or

(b)   make any primary legislation or remedial order.

7. Proceedings

(1)   A person who claims that a public authority has acted (or proposes to act) in a way which is made unlawful by section 6(1) may—

(a)   bring proceedings against the authority under this Act in the appropriate court or tribunal, or

(b)   rely on the Convention right or rights concerned in any legal proceedings,

but only if he is (or would be) a victim of the unlawful act.

(2)   In subsection (1)(a) 'appropriate court or tribunal' means such court or tribunal as may be determined in accordance with rules; and proceedings against an authority include a counterclaim or similar proceeding.

(3)   If the proceedings are brought on an application for judicial review, the applicant is to be taken to have a sufficient interest in relation to the unlawful act only if he is, or would be, a victim of that act.

(4)   If the proceedings are made by way of a petition for judicial review in Scotland, the applicant shall be taken to have title and interest to sue in relation to the unlawful act only if he is, or would be, a victim of that act.

(5)   Proceedings under subsection (1)(a) must be brought before the end of

(a)   the period of one year beginning with the date on which the act complained of took place; or

(b)   such longer period as the court or tribunal considers equitable having regard to all the circumstances,

but that is subject to any rule imposing a stricter time limit in relation to the procedure in question.

(6)   In subsection (1)(b) 'legal proceedings' includes—

(a)   proceedings brought by or at the instigation of a public authority; and

(b)   an appeal against the decision of a court or tribunal.

(7)   For the purposes of this section, a person is a victim of an unlawful act only if he would be a victim for the purposes of Article 34 of the Convention if proceedings were brought in the European Court of Human Rights in respect of that act.

(8)   Nothing in this Act creates a criminal offence.

(9)   In this section 'rules' means—

(a)   in relation to proceedings before a court or tribunal outside Scotland, rules made by the Lord Chancellor or the Secretary of State for the purposes of this section or rules of court,

(b)   in relation to proceedings before a court or tribunal in Scotland, rules made by the Secretary of State for those purposes,

(c)   in relation to proceedings before a tribunal in Northern Ireland—

(i)   which deals with transferred matters; and

(ii)   for which no rules made under paragraph (a) are in force,

rules made by a Northern Ireland department for those purposes,

and includes provision made by order under section 1 of the Courts and Legal Services Act 1990.

(10)   In making rules, regard must be had to section 9.

(11)   The Minister who has power to make rules in relation to a particular tribunal may, to the extent he considers it necessary to ensure that the tribunal can provide an appropriate remedy in relation to an act (or proposed act) of a public authority which is (or would be) unlawful as a result of section 6(1), by order add to—

(a)   the relief or remedies which the tribunal may grant; or

(b)   the grounds on which it may grant any of them.

(12)   An order made under subsection (11) may contain such incidental, supplemental, consequential or transitional provision as the Minister making it considers appropriate.

(13)   'The Minister' includes the Northern Ireland department concerned.

8. Judicial remedies

(1)   In relation to any act (or proposed act) of a public authority which the court finds is (or would be) unlawful, it may grant such relief or remedy, or make such order, within its powers as it considers just and appropriate.

(2)   But damages may be awarded only by a court which has power to award damages, or to order the payment of compensation, in civil proceedings.

(3)   No award of damages is to be made unless, taking account of all the circumstances of the case, including—

(a)   any other relief or remedy granted, or order made, in relation to the act in question (by that or any other court), and

(b)   the consequences of any decision (of that or any other court) in respect of that act,

the court is satisfied that the award is necessary to afford just satisfaction to the person in whose favour it is made.

(4)   In determining—

(a)   whether to award damages, or

(b)   the amount of an award,

the court must take into account the principles applied by the European Court of Human Rights in relation to the award of compensation under Article 41 of the Convention.

(5)   A public authority against which damages are awarded is to be treated—

(a)   in Scotland, for the purposes of section 3 of the Law Reform (Miscellaneous Provisions) (Scotland) Act 1940 as if the award were made in an action of damages in which the authority has been found liable in respect of loss or damage to the person to whom the award is made;

(b)   for the purposes of the Civil Liability (Contribution) Act 1978 as liable in respect of damage suffered by the person to whom the award is made.

(6)   In this section—

'court' includes a tribunal;

'damages' means damages for an unlawful act of a public authority; and

'unlawful' means unlawful under section 6(1).

9. Judicial acts

(1)   Proceedings under section 7(1)(a) in respect of a judicial act may be brought only—

(a)   by exercising a right of appeal;

(b)   on an application (in Scotland a petition) for judicial review; or

(c)   in such other forum as may be prescribed by rules.

(2)   That does not affect any rule of law which prevents a court from being the subject of judicial review.

(3)   In proceedings under this Act in respect of a judicial act done in good faith, damages may not be awarded otherwise than to compensate a person to the extent required by Article 5(5) of the Convention.

(4)   An award of damages permitted by subsection (3) is to be made against the Crown but no award may be made unless the appropriate person, if not a party to the proceedings, is joined.

(5)   In this section—

'appropriate person' means the Minister responsible for the court concerned, or a person or government department nominated by him;

'court' includes a tribunal;

'judge' includes a member of a tribunal, a justice of the peace and a clerk or other officer entitled to exercise the jurisdiction of a court;

'judicial act' means a judicial act of a court and includes an act done on the instructions, or on behalf, of a judge; and

'rules' has the same meaning as in section 7(9).

[This section is amended by the Justice (Northern Ireland) Act 2002, s. 10(6), sch. 4, para. 39, not in force as at 1 October 2002.]

Remedial action

10. Power to take remedial action

(1)   This section applies if—

(a)   a provision of legislation has been declared under section 4 to be incompatible with a Convention right and, if an appeal lies

(i)   all persons who may appeal have stated in writing that they do not intend to do so;

(ii)   the time for bringing an appeal has expired and no appeal has been brought within that time; or

(iii)   an appeal brought within that time has been determined or abandoned; or

(b)   it appears to a Minister of the Crown or Her Majesty in Council that, having regard to a finding of the European Court of Human Rights made after the coming into force of this section in proceedings against the United Kingdom, a provision of legislation is incompatible with an obligation of the United Kingdom arising from the Convention.

(2)   If a Minister of the Crown considers that there are compelling reasons for proceeding under this section, he may by order make such amendments to the legislation as he considers necessary to remove the incompatibility.

(3)   If, in the case of subordinate legislation, a Minister of the Crown considers—

(a)   that it is necessary to amend the primary legislation under which the subordinate legislation in question was made, in order to enable the incompatibility to be removed, and

(b)   that there are compelling reasons for proceeding under this section,

he may by order make such amendments to the primary legislation as he considers necessary.

(4)   This section also applies where the provision in question is in subordinate legislation and has been quashed, or declared invalid, by reason of incompatibility with a Convention right and the Minister proposes to proceed under paragraph 2(b) of Schedule 2.

(5)   If the legislation is an Order in Council, the power conferred by subsection (2) or (3) is exercisable by Her Majesty in Council.

(6)   In this section 'legislation' does not include a Measure of the Church Assembly or of the General Synod of the Church of England.

(7)   Schedule 2 makes further provision about remedial orders.

Other rights and proceedings

11. Safeguard for existing human rights

A person's reliance on a Convention right does not restrict—

(a)   any other right or freedom conferred on him by or under any law having effect in any part of the United Kingdom; or

(b)   his right to make any claim or bring any proceedings which he could make or bring apart from sections 7 to 9.

12. Freedom of expression

(1)   This section applies if a court is considering whether to grant any relief which, if granted, might affect the exercise of the Convention right to freedom of expression.

(2)   If the person against whom the application for relief is made ('the respondent') is neither present nor represented, no such relief is to be granted unless the court is satisfied—

(a)   that the applicant has taken all practicable steps to notify the respondent; or

(b)   that there are compelling reasons why the respondent should not be notified.

(3)   No such relief is to be granted so as to restrain publication before trial unless the court is satisfied that the applicant is likely to establish that publication should not be allowed.

(4)   The court must have particular regard to the importance of the Convention right to freedom of expression and, where the proceedings relate to material which the respondent claims, or which appears to the court, to be journalistic, literary or artistic material (or to conduct connected with such material), to—

(a) the extent to which—
(i) the material has, or is about to, become available to the public; or
(ii) it is, or would be, in the public interest for the material to be published
(b) any relevant privacy code.
(5) In this section—
'court' includes a tribunal; and .
'relief' includes any remedy or order (other than in criminal proceedings).

13. Freedom of thought, conscience and religion

(1) If a court's determination of any question arising under this Act might affect the exercise by a religious organisation (itself or its members collectively) of the Convention right to freedom of thought, conscience and religion, it must have particular regard to the importance of that right.
(2) In this section 'court' includes a tribunal.

Derogations and reservations

14. Derogations

(1) In this Act 'designated derogation' means any derogation by the United Kingdom from an Article of the Convention, or of any protocol to the Convention, which is designated for the purposes of this Act in an order made by the Lord Chancellor.
(2) ...
(3) If a designated derogation is amended or replaced it ceases to be a designated derogation.
(4) But subsection (3) does not prevent the Lord Chancellor from exercising his power under subsection (1) to make a fresh designation order in respect of the Article concerned.
(5) The Lord Chancellor must by order make such amendments to Schedule 3 as he considers appropriate to reflect—
(a) any designation order; or
(b) the effect of subsection (3).
(6) A designation order may be made in anticipation of the making by the United Kingdom of a proposed derogation.

[This section was amended by the Human Rights Act (Amendment) Order 2001, SI 2001/1216, Art. 2. It was further amended by the Transfer of Functions (Miscellaneous) Order 2001, SI 2001/3500, Art. 8, sch. 2, Pt I, para. 7(b).]

15. Reservations

(1) In this Act 'designated reservation' means—
(a) the United Kingdom's reservation to Article 2 of the First Protocol to the Convention; and
(b) any other reservation by the United Kingdom to an Article of the Convention, or of any protocol to the Convention, which is designated for the purposes of this Act in an order made by the Lord Chancellor.
(2) The text of the reservation referred to in subsection (1)(a) is set out in Part II of Schedule 3.
(3) If a designated reservation is withdrawn wholly or in part it ceases to be a designated reservation.

(4)   But subsection (3) does not prevent the Lord Chancellor from exercising his power under subsection (1)(b) to make a fresh designation order in respect of the Article concerned.

(5)   The Lord Chancellor must by order make such amendments to this Act as he considers appropriate to reflect—

(a)   any designation order; or

(b)   the effect of subsection (3).

[This section was amended by the Transfer of Functions (Miscellaneous) Order 2001, SI 2001/3500, Art. 8, sch. 2, Pt I, para. 7(c).]

16. Period for which designated derogations have effect

(1)   If it has not already been withdrawn by the United Kingdom, a designated derogation ceases to have effect for the purposes of this Act at the end of the period of five years beginning with the date on which the order designating it was made.

(2)   At any time before the period—

(a)   fixed by subsection (1), or

(b)   extended by an order under this subsection,

comes to an end, the Lord Chancellor may by order extend it by a further period of five years.

(3)   An order under section 14(1) ceases to have effect at the end of the period for consideration, unless a resolution has been passed by each House approving the order.

(4)   Subsection (3) does not affect—

(a)   anything done in reliance on the order; or

(b)   the power to make a fresh order under section 14(1).

(5)   In subsection (3) 'period for consideration' means the period of forty days beginning with the day on which the order was made.

(6)   In calculating the period for consideration, no account is to be taken of any time during which—

(a)   Parliament is dissolved or prorogued; or

(b)   both Houses are adjourned for more than four days.

(7)   If a designated derogation is withdrawn by the United Kingdom, the Lord Chancellor must by order make such amendments to this Act as he considers are required to reflect that withdrawal.

17. Periodic review of designated reservations

(1)   The appropriate Minister must review the designated reservation referred to in section 15(1)(a)—

(a)   before the end of the period of five years beginning with the date on which section 1(2) came into force; and

(b)   if that designation is still in force, before the end of the period of five years beginning with the date on which the last report relating to it was laid under subsection (3).

(2)   The appropriate Minister must review each of the other designated reservations (if any)—

(a)   before the end of the period of five years beginning with the date on which the order designating the reservation first came into force; and

(b)   if the designation is still in force, before the end of the period of five years beginning with the date on which the last report relating to it was laid under subsection (3).

(3)   The Minister conducting a review under this section must prepare a report on the result of the review and lay a copy of it before each House of Parliament.

Judges of the European Court of Human Rights

18. Appointment to European Court of Human Rights

(1)   In this section 'judicial office' means the office of—

(a)   Lord Justice of Appeal, Justice of the High Court or Circuit judge, in England and Wales;

(b)   judge of the Court of Session or sheriff, in Scotland;

(c)   Lord Justice of Appeal, judge of the High Court or county court judge, in Northern Ireland.

(2)   The holder of a judicial office may become a judge of the European Court of Human Rights ('the Court') without being required to relinquish his office.

(3)   But he is not required to perform the duties of his judicial office while he is a judge of the Court.

(4)   In respect of any period during which he is a judge of the Court—

(a)   a Lord Justice of Appeal or Justice of the High Court is not to count as a judge of the relevant court for the purposes of section 2(1) or 4(1) of the Supreme Court Act 1981 (maximum number of judges) nor as a judge of the Supreme Court for the purposes of section 12(1) to (6) of that Act (salaries etc.);

(b)   a judge of the Court of Session is not to count as a judge of that court for the purposes of section 1(1) of the Court of Session Act 1988 (maximum number of judges) or of section 9(1)(c) of the Administration of Justice Act 1973 ('the 1973 Act') (salaries etc.);

(c)   a Lord Justice of Appeal or judge of the High Court in Northern Ireland is not to count as a judge of the relevant court for the purposes of section 2(1) or 3(1) of the Judicature (Northern Ireland) Act 1978 (maximum number of judges) nor as a judge of the Supreme Court of Northern Ireland for the purposes of section 9(1)(d) of the 1973 Act (salaries etc.);

(d)   a Circuit judge is not to count as such for the purposes of section 18 of the Courts Act 1971 (salaries etc.);

(e)   a sheriff is not to count as such for the purposes of section 14 of the Sheriff Courts (Scotland) Act 1907 (salaries etc.);

(f)   county court judge of Northern Ireland is not to count as such for the purposes of section 106 of the County Courts Act (Northern Ireland) 1959 (salaries etc.).

(5)   If a sheriff principal is appointed a judge of the Court, section 11(1) of the Sheriff Courts (Scotland) Act 1971 (temporary appointment of sheriff principal) applies, while he holds that appointment, as if his office is vacant.

(6)   Schedule 4 makes provision about judicial pensions in relation to the holder of a judicial office who serves as a judge of the Court.

(7)   The Lord Chancellor or the Secretary of State may by order make such transitional provision (including, in particular, provision for a temporary increase in the maximum number of judges) as he considers appropriate in relation to any holder of a judicial office who has completed his service as a judge of the Court.

Parliamentary procedure

19. Statements of compatibility

(1)   A Minister of the Crown in charge of a Bill in either House of Parliament must, before Second Reading of the Bill—

(a)   make a statement to the effect that in his view the provisions of the Bill are compatible with the Convention rights ('a statement of compatibility'); or

(b)   make a statement to the effect that although he is unable to make a statement of compatibility the government nevertheless wishes the House to proceed with the Bill.

(2)   The statement must be in writing and be published in such manner as the Minister making it considers appropriate.

Supplemental

20. Orders etc. under this Act

(1)   Any power of a Minister of the Crown to make an order under this Act is exercisable by statutory instrument.

(2)   The power of the Lord Chancellor or the Secretary of State to make rules (other than rules of court) under section 2(3) or 7(9) is exercisable by statutory instrument.

(3)   Any statutory instrument made under section 14, 15 or 16(7) must be laid before Parliament.

(4)   No order may be made by the Lord Chancellor or the Secretary of State under section 1(4), 7(11) or 16(2) unless a draft of the order has been laid before, and approved by, each House of Parliament.

(5)   Any statutory instrument made under section 18(7) or Schedule 4, or to which subsection (2) applies, shall be subject to annulment in pursuance of a resolution of either House of Parliament.

(6)   The power of a Northern Ireland department to make—

(a)   rules under section 2(3)(c) or 7(9)(c), or

(b)   an order under section 7(11),

is exercisable by statutory rule for the purposes of the Statutory Rules (Northern Ireland) Order 1979.

(7)   Any rules made under section 2(3)(c) or 7(9)(c) shall be subject to negative resolution and section 41(6) of the Interpretation Act (Northern Ireland) 1954 (meaning of 'subject to negative resolution') shall apply as if the power to make the rules were conferred by an Act of the Northern Ireland Assembly.

(8)   No order may be made by a Northern Ireland department under section 7(11) unless a draft of the order has been laid before, and approved by, the Northern Ireland Assembly.

21. Interpretation etc.

(1)   In this Act—

'amend' includes repeal and apply (with or without modifications);

'the appropriate Minister' means the Minister of the Crown having charge of the appropriate authorised government department (within the meaning of the Crown Proceedings Act 1947);

'the Commission' means the European Commission of Human Rights;

'the Convention' means the Convention for the Protection of Human Rights and Fundamental Freedoms, agreed by the Council of Europe at Rome on 4th November 1950 as it has effect for the time being in relation to the United Kingdom;

'declaration of incompatibility' means a declaration under section 4;

'Minister of the Crown' has the same meaning as in the Ministers of the Crown Act 1975;

'Northern Ireland Minister' includes the First Minister and the deputy First Minister in Northern Ireland;

'primary legislation' means any—

(a)   public general Act;

(b)   local and personal Act;

(c)   private Act;

(d)   Measure of the Church Assembly;

(e)   Measure of the General Synod of the Church of England;

(f)   Order in Council—

    (i)   made in exercise of Her Majesty's Royal Prerogative;

    (ii)   made under section 38(1)(a) of the Northern Ireland Constitution Act 1973 or the corresponding provision of the Northern Ireland Act 1998; or

    (iii)   amending an Act of a kind mentioned in paragraph (a), (b) or (c);

and includes an order or other instrument made under primary legislation (otherwise than by the National Assembly for Wales, a member of the Scottish Executive, a Northern Ireland Minister or a Northern Ireland department) to the extent to which it operates to bring one or more provisions of that legislation into force or amends any primary legislation;

'the First Protocol' means the protocol to the Convention agreed at Paris on 20th March 1952;

'the Sixth Protocol' means the protocol to the Convention agreed at Strasbourg on 28th April 1983;

'the Eleventh Protocol' means the protocol to the Convention (restructuring the control machinery established by the Convention) agreed at Strasbourg on 11th May 1994;

'remedial order' means an order under section 10;

'subordinate legislation' means any—

(a)   Order in Council other than one—

    (i)   made in exercise of Her Majesty's Royal Prerogative;

    (ii)   made under section 38(1)(a) of the Northern Ireland Constitution Act 1973 or the corresponding provision of the Northern Ireland Act 1998; or

    (iii)   amending an Act of a kind mentioned in the definition of primary legislation

(b)   Act of the Scottish Parliament;

(c)   Act of the Parliament of Northern Ireland;

(d)   Measure of the Assembly established under section 1 of the Northern Ireland Assembly Act 1973;

(e)   Act of the Northern Ireland Assembly;

(f)   order, rules, regulations, scheme, warrant, byelaw or other instrument made under primary legislation (except to the extent to which it operates to bring one or more provisions of that legislation into force or amends any primary legislation);

(g)   order, rules, regulations, scheme, warrant, byelaw or other instrument made under legislation mentioned in paragraph (b), (c), (d) or (e) or made under an Order in Council applying only to Northern Ireland;

(h)   order, rules, regulations, scheme, warrant, byelaw or other instrument made by a member of the Scottish Executive, a Northern Ireland Minister or a Northern Ireland department in exercise of prerogative or other executive functions of Her Majesty which are exercisable by such a person on behalf of Her Majesty;

'transferred matters' has the same meaning as in the Northern Ireland Act 1998; and

'tribunal' means any tribunal in which legal proceedings may be brought.

(2)   The references in paragraphs (b) and (c) of section 2(1) to Articles are to Articles of the Convention as they had effect immediately before the coming into force of the Eleventh Protocol.

(3)   The reference in paragraph (d) of section 2(1) to Article 46 includes a reference to Articles 32 and 54 of the Convention as they had effect immediately before the coming into force of the Eleventh Protocol.

(4)   The references in section 2(1) to a report or decision of the Commission or a decision of the Committee of Ministers include references to a report or decision made as provided by paragraphs 3, 4 and 6 of Article 5 of the Eleventh Protocol (transitional provisions).

(5)   Any liability under the Army Act 1955, the Air Force Act 1955 or the Naval Discipline Act 1957 to suffer death for an offence is replaced by a liability to imprisonment for life or any less punishment authorised by those Acts and those Acts shall accordingly have effect with the necessary modifications.

22. Short title, commencement, application and extent

(1)   This Act may be cited as the Human Rights Act 1998.

(2)   Sections 18, 20 and 21(5) and this section come into force on the passing of this Act.

(3)   The other provisions of this Act come into force on such day as the Secretary of State may by order appoint and different days may be appointed for different purposes.

(4)   Paragraph (b) of subsection (1) of section 7 applies to proceedings brought by or at the instigation of a public authority whenever the act in question took place but otherwise that subsection does not apply to an act taking place before the coming into force of that section.

(5)   This Act binds the Crown.

(6)   This Act extends to Northern Ireland.

(7)   Section 21(5), so far as it relates to any provision contained in the Army Act 1955, the Air Force Act 1955 or the Naval Discipline Act 1957, extends to any place to which that provision extends.

SCHEDULES

Section 1(3)

SCHEDULE 1
THE ARTICLES

PART I
THE CONVENTION

RIGHTS AND FREEDOMS

Article 2
Right to life

1.   Everyone's right to life shall be protected by law. No one shall be deprived of his life intentionally save in the execution of a sentence of a court following his conviction of a crime for which this penalty is provided by law.

2.   Deprivation of life shall not be regarded as inflicted in contravention of this Article when it results from the use of force which is no more than absolutely necessary:

(a)   in defence of any person from unlawful violence;

(b)   in order to effect a lawful arrest or to prevent the escape of a person lawfully detained;

(c)   in action lawfully taken for the purpose of quelling a riot or insurrection.

Article 3
Prohibition of torture

No one shall be subjected to torture or to inhuman or degrading treatment or punishment.

Article 4
Prohibition of slavery and forced labour

1.   No one shall be held in slavery or servitude.

2.   No one shall be required to perform forced or compulsory labour.

3.   For the purpose of this Article the term 'forced or compulsory labour' shall not include:

(a)   any work required to be done in the ordinary course of detention imposed according to the provisions of Article 5 of this Convention or during conditional release from such detention;

(b)   any service of a military character or, in case of conscientious objectors in countries where they are recognised, service exacted instead of compulsory military service;

(c)   any service exacted in case of an emergency or calamity threatening the life or well-being of the community;

(d)   any work or service which forms part of normal civic obligations.

Article 5
Right to liberty and security

1. Everyone has the right to liberty and security of person. No one shall be deprived of his liberty save in the following cases and in accordance with a procedure prescribed by law:

   (a) the lawful detention of a person after conviction by a competent court;

   (b) the lawful arrest or detention of a person for non-compliance with the lawful order of a court or in order to secure the fulfilment of any obligation prescribed by law;

   (c) the lawful arrest or detention of a person effected for the purpose of bringing him before the competent legal authority on reasonable suspicion of having committed an offence or when it is reasonably considered necessary to prevent his committing an offence or fleeing after having done so;

   (d) the detention of a minor by lawful order for the purpose of educational supervision or his lawful detention for the purpose of bringing him before the competent legal authority;

   (e) the lawful detention of persons for the prevention of the spreading of infectious diseases, of persons of unsound mind, alcoholics or drug addicts or vagrants;

   (f) the lawful arrest or detention of a person to prevent his effecting an unauthorised entry into the country or of a person against whom action is being taken with a view to deportation or extradition.

2. Everyone who is arrested shall be informed promptly, in a language which he understands, of the reasons for his arrest and of any charge against him.

3. Everyone arrested or detained in accordance with the provisions of paragraph 1(c) of this Article shall be brought promptly before a judge or other officer authorised by law to exercise judicial power and shall be entitled to trial within a reasonable time or to release pending trial. Release may be conditioned by guarantees to appear for trial.

4. Everyone who is deprived of his liberty by arrest or detention shall be entitled to take proceedings by which the lawfulness of his detention shall be decided speedily by a court and his release ordered if the detention is not lawful.

5. Everyone who has been the victim of arrest or detention in contravention of the provisions of this Article shall have an enforceable right to compensation.

Article 6
Right to a fair trial

1. In the determination of his civil rights and obligations or of any criminal charge against him, everyone is entitled to a fair and public hearing within a reasonable time by an independent and impartial tribunal established by law. Judgment shall be pronounced publicly but the press and public may be excluded from all or part of the trial in the interest of morals, public order or national security in a democratic society, where the interests of juveniles or the protection of the private life of the parties so require, or to the extent strictly necessary in the opinion of the court in special circumstances where publicity would prejudice the interests of justice.

2. Everyone charged with a criminal offence shall be presumed innocent until proved guilty according to law.

3.   Everyone charged with a criminal offence has the following minimum rights:

(a)   to be informed promptly, in a language which he understands and in detail, of the nature and cause of the accusation against him;

(b)   to have adequate time and facilities for the preparation of his defence;

(c)   to defend himself in person or through legal assistance of his own choosing or, if he has not sufficient means to pay for legal assistance, to be given it free when the interests of justice so require;

(d)   to examine or have examined witnesses against him and to obtain the attendance and examination of witnesses on his behalf under the same conditions as witnesses against him;

(e)   to have the free assistance of an interpreter if he cannot understand or speak the language used in court.

Article 7
No punishment without law

1.   No one shall be held guilty of any criminal offence on account of any act or omission which did not constitute a criminal offence under national or international law at the time when it was committed. Nor shall a heavier penalty be imposed than the one that was applicable at the time the criminal offence was committed.

2.   This Article shall not prejudice the trial and punishment of any person for any act or omission which, at the time when it was committed, was criminal according to the general principles of law recognised by civilised nations.

Article 8
Right to respect for private and family life

1.   Everyone has the right to respect for his private and family life, his home and his correspondence.

2.   There shall be no interference by a public authority with the exercise of this right except such as is in accordance with the law and is necessary in a democratic society in the interests of national security, public safety or the economic well being of the country, for the prevention of disorder or crime, for the protection of health or morals, or for the protection of the rights and freedoms of others.

Article 9
Freedom of thought, conscience and religion

1.   Everyone has the right to freedom of thought, conscience and religion; this right includes freedom to change his religion or belief and freedom, either alone or in community with others and in public or private, to manifest his religion or belief, in worship, teaching, practice and observance.

2.   Freedom to manifest one's religion or beliefs shall be subject only to such limitations as are prescribed by law and are necessary in a democratic society in the interests of public safety, for the protection of public order, health or morals, or for the protection of the rights and freedoms of others.

Article 10
Freedom of expression

1. Everyone has the right to freedom of expression. This right shall include freedom to hold opinions and to receive and impart information and ideas without interference by public authority and regardless of frontiers. This Article shall not prevent States from requiring the licensing of broadcasting, television or cinema enterprises.

2. The exercise of these freedoms, since it carries with it duties and responsibilities, may be subject to such formalities, conditions, restrictions or penalties as are prescribed by law and are necessary in a democratic society, in the interests of national security, territorial integrity or public safety, for the prevention of disorder or crime, for the protection of health or morals, for the protection of the reputation or rights of others, for preventing the disclosure of information received in confidence, or for maintaining the authority and impartiality of the judiciary.

Article 11
Freedom of assembly and association

1. Everyone has the right to freedom of peaceful assembly and to freedom of association with others, including the right to form and to join trade unions for the protection of his interests.

2. No restrictions shall be placed on the exercise of these rights other than such as are prescribed by law and are necessary in a democratic society in the interests of national security or public safety, for the prevention of disorder or crime, for the protection of health or morals or for the protection of the rights and freedoms of others. This Article shall not prevent the imposition of lawful restrictions on the exercise of these rights by members of the armed forces, of the police or of the administration of the State.

Article 12
Right to marry

Men and women of marriageable age have the right to marry and to found a family, according to the national laws governing the exercise of this right.

Article 14
Prohibition of discrimination

The enjoyment of the rights and freedoms set forth in this Convention shall be secured without discrimination on any ground such as sex, race, colour, language, religion, political or other opinion, national or social origin, association with a national minority, property, birth or other status.

Article 16
Restrictions on political activity of aliens

Nothing in Articles 10, 11 and 14 shall be regarded as preventing the High Contracting Parties from imposing restrictions on the political activity of aliens.

Article 17
Prohibition of abuse of rights

Nothing in this Convention may be interpreted as implying for any State, group or person any right to engage in any activity or perform any act aimed at the destruction of any of the rights and freedoms set forth herein or at their limitation to a greater extent than is provided for in the Convention.

Article 18
Limitation on use of restrictions on rights

The restrictions permitted under this Convention to the said rights and freedoms shall not be applied for any purpose other than those for which they have been prescribed.

PART II

THE FIRST PROTOCOL

Article 1
Protection of property

Every natural or legal person is entitled to the peaceful enjoyment of his possessions. No one shall be deprived of his possessions except in the public interest and subject to the conditions provided for by law and by the general principles of international law.

The preceding provisions shall not, however, in any way impair the right of a State to enforce such laws as it deems necessary to control the use of property in accordance with the general interest or to secure the payment of taxes or other contributions or penalties.

Article 2
Right to education

No person shall be denied the right to education. In the exercise of any functions which it assumes in relation to education and to teaching, the State shall respect the right of parents to ensure such education and teaching in conformity with their own religious and philosophical convictions.

Article 3
Right to free elections

The High Contracting Parties undertake to hold free elections at reasonable intervals by secret ballot, under conditions which will ensure the free expression of the opinion of the people in the choice of the legislature.

PART III

THE SIXTH PROTOCOL

Article 1

Abolition of the death penalty

The death penalty shall be abolished. No one shall be condemned to such penalty or executed.

Article 2

Death penalty in time of war

A State may make provision in its law for the death penalty in respect of acts committed in time of war or of imminent threat of war; such penalty shall be applied only in the instances laid down in the law and in accordance with its provisions. The State shall communicate to the Secretary General of the Council of Europe the relevant provisions of that law.

SCHEDULE 2

REMEDIAL ORDERS

Orders

1.—(1)   A remedial order may—

    (a)   contain such incidental, supplemental, consequential or transitional provision as the person making it considers appropriate;

    (b)   be made so as to have effect from a date earlier than that on which it is made;

    (c)   make provision for the delegation of specific functions;

    (d)   make different provision for different cases.

  (2)   The power conferred by sub-paragraph (1)(a) includes—

    (a)   power to amend primary legislation (including primary legislation other than that which contains the incompatible provision); and

    (b)   power to amend or revoke subordinate legislation (including subordinate legislation other than that which contains the incompatible provision).

  (3)   A remedial order may be made so as to have the same extent as the legislation which it affects.

  (4)   No person is to be guilty of an offence solely as a result of the retrospective effect of a remedial order.

Procedure

2.   No remedial order may be made unless—

    (a)   a draft of the order has been approved by a resolution of each House of Parliament made after the end of the period of 60 days beginning with the day on which the draft was laid; or

    (b)   it is declared in the order that it appears to the person making it that, because of the urgency of the matter, it is necessary to make the order without a draft being so approved.

Orders laid in draft

3.—(1)   No draft may be laid under paragraph 2(a) unless—

(a)   the person proposing to make the order has laid before Parliament a document which contains a draft of the proposed order and the required information; and

(b)   the period of 60 days, beginning with the day on which the document required by this sub-paragraph was laid, has ended.

(2)   If representations have been made during that period, the draft laid under paragraph 2(a) must be accompanied by a statement containing—

(a)   a summary of the representations; and

(b)   if, as a result of the representations, the proposed order has been changed, details of the changes.

Urgent cases

4.—(1)   If a remedial order ('the original order') is made without being approved in draft, the person making it must lay it before Parliament, accompanied by the required information, after it is made.

(2)   If representations have been made during the period of 60 days beginning with the day on which the original order was made, the person making it must (after the end of that period) lay before Parliament a statement containing—

(a)   a summary of the representations; and

(b)   if, as a result of the representations, he considers it appropriate to make changes to the original order, details of the changes.

(3)   If sub-paragraph (2)(b) applies, the person making the statement must—

(a)   make a further remedial order replacing the original order; and

(b)   lay the replacement order before Parliament.

(4)   If, at the end of the period of 120 days beginning with the day on which the original order was made, a resolution has not been passed by each House approving the original or replacement order, the order ceases to have effect (but without that affecting anything previously done under either order or the power to make a fresh remedial order).

Definitions

5.   In this Schedule—

'representations' means representations about a remedial order (or proposed remedial order) made to the person making (or proposing to make) it and includes any relevant Parliamentary report or resolution; and

'required information' means—

(a)   an explanation of the incompatibility which the order (or proposed order) seeks to remove, including particulars of the relevant declaration, finding or order; and

(b)   a statement of the reasons for proceeding under section 10 and for making an order in those terms.

Calculating periods

6.   In calculating any period for the purposes of this Schedule, no account is to be taken of any time during which—

(a)   Parliament is dissolved or prorogued; or

(b)   both Houses are adjourned for more than four days.

7.—(1)   This paragraph applies in relation to—

(a)   any remedial order made, and any draft of such an order proposed to be made,—

(i)   by the Scottish Ministers; or

(ii)   within devolved competence (within the meaning of the Scotland Act 1998) by Her Majesty in Council; and

(b)   any document or statement to be laid in connection with such an order (or proposed order).

(2)   This Schedule has effect in relation to any such order (or proposed order), document or statement subject to the following modifications.

(3)   Any reference to Parliament, each House of Parliament or both Houses of Parliament shall be construed as a reference to the Scottish Parliament.

(4)   Paragraph 6 does not apply and instead, in calculating any period for the purposes of this Schedule, no account is to be taken of any time during which the Scottish Parliament is dissolved or is in recess for more than four days.

[This Schedule was amended by the Scotland Act 1998 (Consequential Modifications) Order 2000, SI 2000/2040, Art. 2(1), Schedule, Pt I, para. 21.]

SCHEDULE 3
DEROGATION AND RESERVATION

PART I
DEROGATION

United Kingdom's derogation from Article 5(1)

The United Kingdom Permanent Representative to the Council of Europe presents his compliments to the Secretary General of the Council, and has the honour to convey the following information in order to ensure compliance with the obligations of Her Majesty's Government in the United Kingdom under Article 15(3) of the Convention for the Protection of Human Rights and Fundamental Freedoms signed at Rome on 4 November 1950.

Public emergency in the United Kingdom

The terrorist attacks in New York, Washington, DC and Pennsylvania on 11th September 2001 resulted in several thousand deaths, including many British victims and others from 70 different countries. In its resolutions 1368 (2001) and 1373 (2001), the United Nations Security Council recognised the attacks as a threat to international peace and security.

The threat from international terrorism is a continuing one. In its resolution 1373 (2001), the Security Council, acting under Chapter VII of the United Nations Charter, required all States to take measures to prevent the commission of terrorist attacks, including by denying safe haven to those who finance, plan, support or commit terrorist attacks.

There exists a terrorist threat to the United Kingdom from persons suspected of involvement in international terrorism. In particular, there are foreign nationals present in the United

Kingdom who are suspected of being concerned in the commission, preparation or instigation of acts of international terrorism, of being members of organisations or groups which are so concerned or of having links with members of such organisations or groups, and who are a threat to the national security of the United Kingdom.

As a result, a public emergency, within the meaning of Article 15(1) of the Convention, exists in the United Kingdom.

The Anti-terrorism, Crime and Security Act 2001

As a result of the public emergency, provision is made in the Anti-terrorism, Crime and Security Act 2001, inter alia, for an extended power to arrest and detain a foreign national which will apply where it is intended to remove or deport the person from the United Kingdom but where removal or deportation is not for the time being possible, with the consequence that the detention would be unlawful under existing domestic law powers. The extended power to arrest and detain will apply where the Secretary of State issues a certificate indicating his belief that the person's presence in the United Kingdom is a risk to national security and that he suspects the person of being an international terrorist. That certificate will be subject to an appeal to the Special Immigration Appeals Commission ('SIAC'), established under the Special Immigration Appeals Commission Act 1997, which will have power to cancel it if it considers that the certificate should not have been issued. There will be an appeal on a point of law from a ruling by SIAC. In addition, the certificate will be reviewed by SIAC at regular intervals. SIAC will also be able to grant bail, where appropriate, subject to conditions. It will be open to a detainee to end his detention at any time by agreeing to leave the United Kingdom.

The extended power of arrest and detention in the Anti-terrorism, Crime and Security Act 2001 is a measure which is strictly required by the exigencies of the situation. It is a temporary provision which comes into force for an initial period of 15 months and then expires unless renewed by Parliament. Thereafter, it is subject to annual renewal by Parliament. If, at any time, in the Government's assessment, the public emergency no longer exists or the extended power is no longer strictly required by the exigencies of the situation, then the Secretary of State will, by Order, repeal the provision.

Domestic law powers of detention (other than under the Anti-terrorism, Crime and Security Act 2001)

The Government has powers under the Immigration Act 1971 ('the 1971 Act') to remove or deport persons on the ground that their presence in the United Kingdom is not conducive to the public good on national security grounds. Persons can also be arrested and detained under Schedules 2 and 3 to the 1971 Act pending their removal or deportation. The courts in the United Kingdom have ruled that this power of detention can only be exercised during the period necessary, in all the circumstances of the particular case, to effect removal and that, if it becomes clear that removal is not going to be possible within a reasonable time, detention will be unlawful (*R* v *Governor of Durham Prison, ex parte Singh* [1984] 1 All ER 983).

Article 5(1)(f) of the Convention

It is well established that Article 5(1)(f) permits the detention of a person with a view to deportation only in circumstance where 'action is being taken with a view to deportation'

(*Chahal* v *United Kingdom* (1996) 23 EHRR 413 at paragraph 112). In that case the European Court of Human Rights indicated that detention will cease to be permissible under Article 5(1)(f) if deportation proceedings are not prosecuted with due diligence and that it was necessary in such cases to determine whether the duration of the deportation proceedings was excessive (paragraph 113).

In some cases, where the intention remains to remove or deport a person on national security grounds, continued detention may not be consistent with Article 5(1)(f) as interpreted by the Court in the *Chahal* case. This may be the case, for example, if the person has established that removal to their own country might result in treatment contrary to Article 3 of the Convention. In such circumstances, irrespective of the gravity of the threat to national security posed by the person concerned, it is well established that Article 3 prevents removal or deportation to a place where there is a real risk that the person will suffer treatment contrary to that article. If no alternative destination is immediately available then removal or deportation may not, for the time being, be possible even though the ultimate intention remains to remove or deport the person once satisfactory arrangements can be made. In addition, it may not be possible to prosecute the person for a criminal offence given the strict rules on the admissibility of evidence in the criminal justice system of the United Kingdom and the high standard of proof required.

Derogation under Article 15 of the Convention

The Government has considered whether the exercise of the extended power to detain contained in the Anti-terrorism, Crime and Security Act 2001 may be inconsistent with the obligations under Article 5(1) of the Convention. As indicated above, there may be cases where, notwithstanding a continuing intention to remove or deport a person who is being detained, it is not possible to say that 'action is being taken with a view to deportation' within the meaning of Article 5(1)(f) as interpreted by the Court in the *Chahal* case. To the extent, therefore, that the exercise of the extended power may be inconsistent with the United Kingdom's obligations under Article 5(1), the Government has decided to avail itself of the right of derogation conferred by Article 15(1) of the Convention and will continue to do so until further notice.

Strasbourg, 18 December 2001

PART II
RESERVATION

At the time of signing the present (First) Protocol, I declare that, in view of certain provisions of the Education Acts in the United Kingdom, the principle affirmed in the second sentence of Article 2 is accepted by the United Kingdom only so far as it is compatible with the provision of efficient instruction and training, and the avoidance of unreasonable public expenditure.

Dated 20 March 1952. Made by the United Kingdom Permanent Representative to the Council of Europe.

[This Schedule was amended by the Human Rights Act (Amendment) Order 2001, SI 2001/1216, Art. 4. It was further amended by the Human Rights Act 1998 (Amendment No. 2) Order 2001, SI 2001/4032, Art. 2, Schedule.]

SCHEDULE 4
JUDICIAL PENSIONS

Duty to make orders about pensions

1.—(1)   The appropriate Minister must by order make provision with respect to pensions payable to or in respect of any holder of a judicial office who serves as an ECHR judge.

(2)   A pensions order must include such provision as the Minister making it considers is necessary to secure that—

(a)   an ECHR judge who was, immediately before his appointment as an ECHR judge, a member of a judicial pension scheme is entitled to remain as a member of that scheme;

(b)   the terms on which he remains a member of the scheme are those which would have been applicable had he not been appointed as an ECHR judge; and

(c)   entitlement to benefits payable in accordance with the scheme continues to be determined as if, while serving as an ECHR judge, his salary was that which would (but for section 18(4)) have been payable to him in respect of his continuing service as the holder of his judicial office.

Contributions

2. A pensions order may, in particular, make provision—

(a)   for any contributions which are payable by a person who remains a member of a scheme as a result of the order, and which would otherwise be payable by deduction from his salary, to be made otherwise than by deduction from his salary as an ECHR judge; and

(b)   for such contributions to be collected in such manner as may be determined by the administrators of the scheme.

Amendments of other enactments

3. A pensions order may amend any provision of, or made under, a pensions Act in such manner and to such extent as the Minister making the order considers necessary or expedient to ensure the proper administration of any scheme to which it relates.

Definitions

4.   In this Schedule
'appropriate Minister' means—

(a)   in relation to any judicial office whose jurisdiction is exercisable exclusively in relation to Scotland, the Secretary of State; and

(b)   otherwise, the Lord Chancellor;

'ECHR judge' means the holder of a judicial office who is serving as a judge of the Court;

'judicial pension scheme' means a scheme established by and in accordance with a pensions Act;

'pensions Act' means—

    (a)   the County Courts Act (Northern Ireland) 1959;

    (b)   the Sheriffs' Pensions (Scotland) Act 1961;

    (c)   the Judicial Pensions Act 1981; or

    (d)   the Judicial Pensions and Retirement Act 1993; and

'pensions order' means an order made under paragraph 1.

Appendix 2
A. Civil Procedure Rules and Practice Directions

CIVIL PROCEDURE (AMENDMENT NO. 4) RULES 2000
(SI 2000, No. 2092) (L. 16)

The Civil Procedure Rule Committee, having power under section 2 of the Civil Procedure Act 1997 to make rules of court under section 1 of that Act, after consulting in accordance with section 2(6)(a) of that Act, make the following Rules—

1. Citation, commencement and interpretation
These Rules may be cited as the Civil Procedure (Amendment No. 4) Rules 2000 and shall come into force on 2 October 2000.

2. In these Rules—
   (a) a reference to a Part or rule by number alone means the Part or rule so numbered in the Civil Procedure Rules 1998;
   (b) a reference to an Order by number and prefixed by 'RSC' means the RSC Order so numbered in Schedule 1 to those Rules; and
   (c) a reference to an Order by number and prefixed by 'CCR' means the CCR Order so numbered in Schedule 2 to those Rules.

3. Amendments to Civil Procedure Rules 1998

. . .

6.   After rule 7.10, insert—
   '7.11   Human Rights
   (1)   A claim under section 7(1)(a) of the Human Rights Act 1998 in respect of a judicial act may be brought only in the High Court.
   (2)   Any other claim under section 7(1)(a) of that Act may be brought in any court.'

. . .

8.   After rule 19.4, insert—
   '19.4A Human Rights

   Section 4 of the Human Rights Act 1998

   (1)   The court may not make a declaration of incompatibility in accordance with section 4 of the Human Rights Act 1998 unless 21 days' notice, or such other period of notice as the court directs, has been given to the Crown.

   (2)   Where notice has been given to the Crown a Minister, or other person permitted by that Act, shall be joined as a party on giving notice to the court.

   (Only courts specified in section 4 of the Human Rights Act 1998 can make a declaration of incompatibility.)

Section 9 of the Human Rights Act 1998

(3)   Where a claim is made under that Act for damages in respect of a judicial act—
    (a)   that claim must be set out in the statement of case or the appeal notice; and
    (b)   notice must be given to the Crown.

(4)   Where paragraph (3) applies and the appropriate person has not applied to be joined as a party within 21 days, or such other period as the court directs, after the notice is served, the court may join the appropriate person as a party.

(A practice direction makes provision for these notices.)'

. . .

13.   In rule 30.3(2)—
    (a)   for the full stop at the end of sub-paragraph (f) substitute a semicolon; and
    (b)   after sub-paragraph (f), insert—
        '(g)   whether the making of a declaration of incompatibility under section 4 of the Human Rights Act 1998 has arisen or may arise.'

. . .

15.   After rule 33.8, insert—
'33.9   Human Rights
(1)   This rule applies where a claim is—
    (a)   for a remedy under section 7 of the Human Rights Act 1998 in respect of a judicial act which is alleged to have infringed the claimant's Article 5 Convention rights; and
    (b)   based on a finding by a court or tribunal that the claimant's Convention rights have been infringed.

(2)   The court hearing the claim—
    (a)   may proceed on the basis of the finding of that other court or tribunal that there has been an infringement but it is not required to do so, and
    (b)   may reach its own conclusion in the light of that finding and of the evidence heard by that other court or tribunal.'

. . .

PART 54
JUDICIAL REVIEW

Contents of this Part

54.1 Scope and interpretation

(1)   This Part contains rules about judicial review.

(2)   In this Part—

    (a)   a 'claim for judicial review' means a claim to review the lawfulness of—

        (i)   an enactment; or

        (ii)   a decision, action or failure to act in relation to the exercise of a public function.

    (b)   an order of mandamus is called a 'mandatory order';

    (c)   an order of prohibition is called a 'prohibiting order';

    (d)   an order of certiorari is called a 'quashing order';

    (e)   'the judicial review procedure' means the Part 8 procedure as modified by this Part;

    (f)   'interested party' means any person (other than the claimant and defendant) who is directly affected by the claim; and

    (g)   'court' means the High Court, unless otherwise stated.

(Rule 8.1 (6)(b) provides that a rule or practice direction may, in relation to a specified type of proceedings, disapply or modify any of the rules set out in Part 8 as they apply to those proceedings.)

54.2 When this Part must be used

The judicial review procedure must be used in a claim for judicial review where the claimant is seeking—

    (a)   a mandatory order;

    (b)   a prohibiting order;

    (c)   a quashing order; or

    (d)   an injunction under section 30 of the Supreme Court Act 1981 (restraining a person from acting in any office in which he is not entitled to act).

54.3   When this Part may be used

(1)   The judicial review procedure may be used in a claim for judicial review where the claimant is seeking—

    (a)   a declaration; or

    (b)   an injunction 0007(gl).

(Section 31(2) of the Supreme Court Act 1981 sets out the circumstances in which the court may grant a declaration or injunction in a claim for judicial review.)

(Where the claimant is seeking a declaration or injunction in addition to one of the remedies listed in rule 54.2, the judicial review procedure must be used.)

(2) A claim for judicial review may include a claim for damages but may not seek damages alone.

(Section 31(4) of the Supreme Court Act 1981 sets out the circumstances in which the court may award damages on a claim for judicial review.)

54.4 Permission required

The court's permission to proceed is required in a claim for judicial review whether started under this Part or transferred to the Administrative Court.

54.5 Time limit for filing claim form

(1) The claim form must be filed—

(a) promptly; and

(b) in any event not later than 3 months after the grounds to make the claim first arose.

(2) The time limit in this rule may not be extended by agreement between the parties.

(3) This rule does not apply when any other enactment specifies a shorter time limit for making the claim for judicial review.

54.6 Claim form

(1) In addition to the matters set out in rule 8.2 (contents of the claim form) the claimant must also state—

(a) the name and address of any person he considers to be an interested party;

(b) that he is requesting permission to proceed with a claim for judicial review; and

(c) any remedy (including any interim remedy) he is claiming.

(Part 25 sets out how to apply for an interim remedy.)

(2) The claim form must be accompanied by the documents required by the relevant practice direction.

54.7 Service of claim form

The claim form must be served on—

(a) the defendant; and

(b) unless the court otherwise directs, any person the claimant considers to be an interested party, within 7 days after the date of issue.

54.8 Acknowledgment of service

(1) Any person served with the claim form who wishes to take part in the judicial review must file an acknowledgment of service in the relevant practice form in accordance with the following provisions of this rule.

(2) Any acknowledgment of service must be—

(a) filed not more than 21 days after service of the claim form; and

(b) served on

(i) the claimant; and

(ii) subject to any direction under rule 54.7(b), any other person named in the claim form, as soon as practicable and, in any event, not later than 7 days after it is filed.

(3) The time limits under this rule may not be extended by agreement between the parties.

(4) The acknowledgement of service—

(a) must—

(i)   where the person filing it intends to contest the claim, set out a summary of his grounds for doing so; and

(ii)   state the name and address of any person the person filing it considers to be an interested party; and

(b)   may include or be accompanied by an application for directions.

(5)   Rule 10.3(2) does not apply.

54.9 Failure to file acknowledgement of service

(1)   Where a person served with the claim form has failed to file an acknowledgement of service in accordance with rule 54.8, he—

(a)   may not take part in a hearing to decide whether permission should be given unless the court allows him to do so; but

(b)   provided he complies with rule 54.14 or any other direction of the court regarding the filing and service of—

(i)   detailed grounds for contesting the claim or supporting it on additional grounds; and

(ii)   any written evidence, may take part in the hearing of the judicial review.

(2)   Where that person takes part in the hearing of the judicial review, the court may take his failure to file an acknowledgment of service into account when deciding what order to make about costs.

(3)   Rule 8.4 does not apply.

54.10 Permission given

(1)   Where permission to proceed is given the court may also give directions.

(2)   Directions under paragraph (1) may include a stay 0007(gl) of proceedings to which the claim relates.

(Rule 3.7 provides a sanction for the non-payment of the fee payable when permission to proceed has been given.)

54.11 Service of order giving or refusing permission

The court will serve—

(a)   the order giving or refusing permission; and

(b)   any directions,

on—

(i)   the claimant;

(ii)   the defendant; and

(iii) any other person who filed an acknowledgement of service.

54.12 Permission decision without a hearing

(1)   This rule applies where the court, without a hearing—

(a)   refuses permission to proceed; or

(b)   gives permission to proceed—

(i)   subject to conditions; or

(ii)   on certain grounds only.

(2)   The court will serve its reasons for making the decision when it serves the order giving or refusing permission in accordance with rule 54.11.

(3)   The claimant may not appeal but may request the decision to be reconsidered at a hearing.

(4)   A request under paragraph (3) must be filed within 7 days after service of the reasons under paragraph (2).

(5)   The claimant, defendant and any other person who has filed an acknowledgement of service will be given at least 2 days' notice of the hearing date.

54.13 Defendant, etc. may not apply to set aside[(gl)]

Neither the defendant nor any other person served with the claim form may apply to set aside[(gl)] an order giving permission to proceed.

54.14 Response

(1)   A defendant and any other person saved with the claim form who wishes to contest the claim or support it on additional grounds must file and serve—

(a)   detailed grounds for contesting the claim or supporting it on additional grounds; and

(b)   any written evidence, within 35 days after service of the order giving permission.

(2)   The following rules do not apply—

(a)   rule 8.5(3) and 8.5(4) (defendant to file and serve written evidence at the same time as acknowledgement of service); and

(b)   rule 8.5(5) and 8.5(6) (claimant to file and serve any reply within 14 days).

54.15 Where claimant seeks to rely on additional grounds

The court's permission is required if a claimant seeks to rely on grounds other than those for which he has been given permission to proceed.

54.16 Evidence

(1)   Rule 8.6 does not apply.

(2)   No written evidence may be relied on unless—

(a)   it has been served in accordance with any—

(i)   rule under this Part; or

(ii)   direction of the court; or

(b)   the court gives permission.

54.17 Court's powers to hear any person

(1)   Any person may apply for permission—

(a)   to file evidence; or

(b)   make representations at the hearing of the judicial review.

(2)   An application under paragraph (1) should be made promptly.

54.18 Judicial review may be decided without a hearing

The court may decide the claim for judicial review without a hearing where all the parties agree.

54.19 Court's powers in respect of quashing orders

(1)   This rule applies where the court makes a quashing order in respect of the decision to which the claim relates.

(2)   The court may—

(a)   remit the matter to the decision-maker; and

(b)   direct it to reconsider the matter and reach a decision in accordance with the judgment of the court.

(3)   Where the court considers that there is no purpose to be served in remitting the matter

to the decision-maker it may, subject to any statutory provision, take the decision itself. (Where a statutory power is given to a tribunal, person or other body it may be the case that the court cannot take the decision itself).

54.20 Transfer
The court may—

      (a)   order a claim to continue as if it had not been started under this Part; and

      (b)   where it does so, give directions about the future management of the claim.

(Part 30 (transfer) applies to transfers to and from the Administrative Court.)

CPR PRACTICE DIRECTIONS RELATING TO HUMAN RIGHTS

CPR Practice Direction Supplementing Part 7
Where to Start Proceedings

2.10

(1)   The normal rules apply in deciding in which court and specialist list a claim that includes issues under the Human Rights Act 1998 should be started. They also apply in deciding which procedure to use to start the claim; this Part or CPR Part 8 or CPR Part 54 (judicial review).

(2)   The exception is a claim for damages in respect of a judicial act, which should be commenced in the High Court. If the claim is made in a notice of appeal then it will be dealt with according to the normal rules governing where that appeal is heard.

(A county court cannot make a declaration of incompatibility in accordance with section 4 of the Human Rights Act 1998. Legislation may direct that such a claim is to be brought before a specified tribunal.)

CPR Practice Direction Supplementing Part 16
Statements of Case

HUMAN RIGHTS

15.1

A party who seeks to rely on any provision of or right arising under the Human Rights Act 1998 or seeks a remedy available under that Act—

    (1)   must state that fact in his statement of case; and

    (2)   must in his statement of case—

      (a)   give precise details of the Convention right which it is alleged has been infringed and details of the alleged infringement;

      (b)   specify the relief sought;

      (c)   state if the relief sought includes—

          (i)   a declaration of incompatibility in accordance with section 4 of that Act, or

          (ii)   damages in respect of a judicial act to which section 9(3) of that Act applies;

      (d)   where the relief sought includes a declaration of incompatibility in accordance with section 4 of that Act, give precise details of the legislative provision alleged to be incompatible and details of the alleged incompatibility; where the relief sought includes a declaration of incompatibility in accordance with section 4 of that Act, give precise details of the legislative provision alleged to be incompatible and details of the alleged incompatibility;

(e)   where the claim is founded on a finding of unlawfulness by another court or tribunal, give details of the finding; and

(f)   where the claim is founded on a judicial act which is alleged to have infringed a Convention right of the party as provided by section 9 of the Human Rights Act 1998, the judicial act complained of and the court or tribunal which is alleged to have made it.

(The practice direction to Part 19 provides for notice to be given and parties joined in the circumstances referred to in (c), (d) and (f).)

15.2

A party who seeks to amend his statement of case to include the matters referred to in paragraph 15.1 must, unless the court orders otherwise, do so as soon as possible.

(Part 17 provides for the amendment of a statement of case.)

CPR Practice Direction Supplementing Part 19
Addition and Substitution of Parties

HUMAN RIGHTS, JOINING THE CROWN

Section 4 of the Human Rights Act 1998

Where a party has included in his statement of case—

6.1

(1)   a claim for a declaration of incompatibility in accordance with section 4 of the Human Rights Act 1998, or

(2)   an issue for the court to decide which may lead to the court considering making a declaration, then the court may at any time consider whether notice should be given to the Crown as required by that Act and give directions for the content and service of the notice. The rule allows a period of 21 days before the court will make the declaration but the court may vary this period of time.

6.2

The court will normally consider the issues and give the directions referred to in paragraph 6.1 at the case management conference.

6.3

Where a party amends his statement of case to include any matter referred to in paragraph 6.1, then the court will consider whether notice should be given to the Crown and give directions for the content and service of the notice.

(The practice direction to CPR Part 16 requires a party to include issues under the Human Rights Act 1998 in his statement of case.)

6.4

(1)   The notice given under rule 19.4A must be served on the person named in the list published under section 17 of the Crown Proceedings Act 1947.

(The list, made by the Minister for the Civil Service, is annexed to this practice direction.)

(2)   The notice will be in the form directed by the court but will normally include the directions given by the court and all the statements of case in the claim. The notice will also be served on all the parties.

(3)   The court may require the parties to assist in the preparation of the notice.

(4)   In the circumstances described in the National Assembly for Wales (Transfer of Functions) (No. 2) Order 2000 the notice must also be served on the National Assembly for Wales.

(Section 5(3) of the Human Rights Act 1998 provides that the Crown may give notice that it intends to become a party at any stage in the proceedings once notice has been given.)

6.5

Unless the court orders otherwise, the Minister or other person permitted by the Human Rights Act 1998 to be joined as a party must, if he wishes to be joined, give notice of his intention to be joined as a party to the court and every other party. Where the Minister has nominated a person to be joined as a party the notice must be accompanied by the written nomination.

(Section 5(2)(a) of the Human Rights Act 1998 permits a person nominated by a Minister of the Crown to be joined as a party. The nomination may be signed on behalf of the Minister.)

Section 9 of the Human Rights Act 1998

6.6

(1)   The procedure in paragraphs 6.1 to 6.5 also applies where a claim is made under sections 7(1)(a) and 9(3) of the Human Rights Act 1998 for damages in respect of a judicial act.

(2)   Notice must be given to the Lord Chancellor and should be served on the Treasury Solicitor on his behalf, except where the judicial act is of a Court-Martial when the appropriate person is the Secretary of State for Defence and the notice must be served on the Treasury Solicitor on his behalf.

(3)   The notice will also give details of the judicial act, which is the subject of the claim for damages, and of the court or tribunal that made it.

(Section 9(4) of the Human Rights Act 1998 provides that no award of damages may be made against the Crown as provided for in section 9(3) unless the appropriate person is joined in the proceedings. The appropriate person is the Minister responsible for the court concerned or a person or department nominated by him (section 9(5) of the Act).)

CPR Practice Direction Supplementing Rule 30
Transfer

TRANSFER ON THE CRITERION IN RULE 30.3(2)(G)

7.

A transfer should only be made on the basis of the criterion in rule 30.3(2)(g) where there is a real prospect that a declaration of incompatibility will be made.

CPR Practice Direction Supplementing Rule 39
Miscellaneous Provisions Relating to Hearings

CITATION OF AUTHORITIES HUMAN RIGHTS

8.1

If it is necessary for a party to give evidence at a hearing of an authority referred to in section 2 of the Human Rights Act 1998—

    (1)   the authority to be cited should be an authoritative and complete report; and

    (2)   the party must give to the court and any other party a list of the authorities he intends to cite and copies of the reports not less than three days before the hearing.

(Section 2(1) of the Human Rights Act 1998 requires the court to take into account the authorities listed there.)

    (3)   Copies of the complete original texts issued by the European Court and Commission either paper based or from the Court's judgment database (HUDOC), which is available on the Internet, may be used.

CPR Practice Direction Supplementing Part 52
Appeals

HUMAN RIGHTS

5.1A

Where the appellant is seeking to rely on any issue under the Human Rights Act 1998, or seeks a remedy available under that Act, for the first time in an appeal he must include in his appeal notice the information required by paragraph 15.1 of the practice direction to CPR Part 15. Paragraph 15.2 of that practice direction also applies as if references.

5.1B

CPR rule 19.4A and the practice direction supplementing it shall apply as if references to the case management conference were to the application for permission to appeal.

(The practice direction to Part 19 provides for notice to be given and parties joined in certain circumstances to which this paragraph applies.)

B. Family Proceedings Rules

FAMILY PROCEEDINGS (AMENDMENT) RULES 2000
(SI 2000, No. 2267)

We, the authority having the power under section 40(1) of the Matrimonial and Family Proceedings Act 1984 to make rules of court for the purposes of family proceedings in the High Court and county courts, in the exercise of the powers conferred by section 40 make the following rules:

1. Citation and commencement

    (1)   These rules may be cited as the Family Proceedings (Amendment) Rules 2000.

(2)   Rules 3, 4 and 10 and this rule shall come into force on 2nd October 2000, and the remainder of these Rules shall come into force on 1st December 2000.

2. Transitional provisions

(1)   Subject to paragraphs (2) and (3), the Family Proceedings Rules 1991, as amended by these rules, shall apply to all proceedings for divorce, nullity of marriage or judicial separation, whether commenced before, on or after 1st December 2000.

(2)   This paragraph applies where before 1st December 2000—

(a)   an application for ancillary relief has been made, or notice of intention to proceed with the application has been given, in Form A; and

(b)   that application or notice specified that the relief sought includes provision to be made under section 25B or 25C of the Matrimonial Causes Act 1973, or a request for such provision has been added to the application.

(3)   Where paragraph (2) applies—

(a)   the Family Proceedings Rules 1991 shall have effect as if rules 4(a), 5–9 and 11 of these Rules had not come into force; but

(b)   in rule 2.70(5) and (6), any reference to an affidavit in support of an application shall be construed as referring to paragraph 2.16 of the statement in Form E, and any reference to an affidavit in reply shall be construed as meaning a statement in reply.

3. Interpretation

A reference to a rule by number alone refers to the rule so numbered in the Family Proceedings Rules 1991, and a reference to a Form by letter refers to the Form identified by that letter in Appendix 1A to those Rules.

10.   After rule 10.25 there shall be inserted the following—

'Human Rights Act 1998

10.26—(1)   In this rule—

'originating document' means a petition, application, originating application, originating summons or other originating process;

'answer' means an answer or other document filed or served by a party in reply to an originating document (but not an acknowledgement of service);

'Convention right' has the same meaning as in the Human Rights Act 1998;

'declaration of incompatibility' means a declaration of incompatibility under section 4 of the Human Rights Act 1998.

(2)   A party who seeks to rely on any provision of or right arising under the Human Rights Act 1998 or seeks a remedy available under that Act—

(a)   shall state that fact in his originating document or (as the case may be) answer; and

(b)   shall in his originating document or (as the case may be) answer:—

(i)   give precise details of the Convention right which it is alleged has been infringed and details of the alleged infringement;

(ii)   specify the relief sought;

(iii)   state if the relief sought includes a declaration of incompatibility.

(3)   A party who seeks to amend his originating document or (as the case may be) answer to include the matters referred to in paragraph (2) shall, unless the court orders otherwise, do so as soon as possible and in any event not less than 28 days before the hearing.

(4)   The court shall not make a declaration of incompatibility unless 21 days' notice, or such other period of notice as the court directs, has been given to the Crown.

(5)   Where notice has been given to the Crown a Minister, or other person permitted by the Human Rights Act 1998, shall be joined as a party on giving notice to the court.

(6)   Where a party has included in his originating document or (as the case may be) answer:

(a)   a claim for a declaration of incompatibility; or

(b)   an issue for the court to decide which may lead to the court considering making a declaration of incompatibility,

then the court may at any time consider whether notice should be given to the Crown as required by the Human Rights Act 1998 and give directions for the content and service of the notice.

(7)   In the case of an appeal for which permission to appeal is required, the court shall, unless it decides that it is appropriate to do so at another stage in the proceedings, consider the issues and give the directions referred to in paragraph (6) when deciding whether to give such permission.

(8)   If paragraph (7) does not apply, and a hearing for directions would, but for this rule, be held, the court shall, unless it decides that it is appropriate to do so at another stage in the proceedings, consider the issues and give the directions referred to in paragraph (6) at the hearing for directions.

(9)   If neither paragraph (7) nor paragraph (8) applies, the court shall consider the issues and give the directions referred to in paragraph (6) when it considers it appropriate to do so, and may fix a hearing for this purpose.

(10)   Where a party amends his originating document or (as the case may be) answer to include any matter referred to in paragraph (6)(a), then the court will consider whether notice should be given to the Crown and give directions for the content and service of the notice.

(11)   In paragraphs (12) to (16), 'notice' means the notice given under paragraph (4).

(12)   The notice shall be served on the person named in the list published under section 17 of the Crown Proceedings Act 1947.

(13)   The notice shall be in the form directed by the court.

(14)   Unless the court orders otherwise, the notice shall be accompanied by the directions given by the court and the originating document and any answers in the proceedings.

(15)   Copies of the notice shall be served on all the parties.

(16)   The court may require the parties to assist in the preparation of the notice.

(17)   Unless the court orders otherwise, the Minister or other person permitted by the Human Rights Act 1998 to be joined as a party shall, if he wishes to be joined, give notice of his intention to be joined as a party to the court and every other party, and where the Minister has nominated a person to be joined as a party the notice must be accompanied by the written nomination.

(18)   Where a claim is made under section 9(3) of the Human Rights Act 1998 in respect of a judicial act the procedure in paragraphs (6) to (17) shall also apply, but the notice to be given to the Crown:

(a)   shall be given to the Lord Chancellor and shall be served on the Treasury Solicitor on his behalf; and

(b)   shall also give details of the judicial act which is the subject of the claim and of the court that made it.

(19)   Where in any appeal a claim is made in respect of a judicial act to which sections 9(3) and (4) of that Act applies—

    (a)   that claim must be set out in the notice of appeal; and

    (b)   notice must be given to the Crown in accordance with paragraph (18).

(20)   The appellant must in a notice of appeal to which paragraph (19)(a) applies—

    (a)   state that a claim is being made under section 9(3) of the Human Rights Act 1998; and

    (b)   give details of—

        (i)   the Convention right which it is alleged has been infringed;

        (ii)   the infringement;

        (iii)   the judicial act complained of; and

        (iv)   the court which made it.

(21)   Where paragraph (19) applies and the appropriate person (as defined in section 9(5) of the Human Rights Act 1998) has not applied within 21 days, or such other period as the court directs, after the notice is served to be joined as a party, the court may join the appropriate person as a party.

(22)   On any application or appeal concerning—

    (a)   a committal order;

    (b)   a refusal to grant habeas corpus; or

    (c)   a secure accommodation order made under section 25 of the Act of 1989, if the court ordering the release of the person concludes that his Convention rights have been infringed by the making of the order to which the application or appeal relates, the judgment or order should so state, but if the court does not do so, that failure will not prevent another court from deciding the matter.

C. Criminal Appeal Rules

CRIMINAL APPEAL (AMENDMENT) RULES 2000
(SI 2000, No. 2036)

We, the Crown Court Rule Committee, in exercise of the powers conferred on us by sections 84(1), 84(2) and 86 of the Supreme Court Act 198 and section 5 of the Human Rights Act 1998, hereby makes the following Rules:

1. Citation and commencement
These Rules may be cited as the Criminal Appeal (Amendment) Rules 2000 and shall come into force on 2 October 2000.

2. Amendment of Criminal Appeal Rules 1968
The Criminal Appeal Rules 1968 shall be amended as follows—

    (a)   in rule 2, after paragraph (2)(a) there shall be inserted—

    '(aa)   A notice of the grounds of appeal or application set out in Form 3 shall include notice—

        (i)   of any application to be made to the court for a declaration of incompatibility under section 4 of the Human Rights Act 1998; or

(ii)   of any issue for the court to decide which may lead to the court making such a declaration.

(ab) Where the grounds of appeal or application include notice in accordance with paragraph (aa) above, a copy of the notice shall be served on the prosecutor by the appellant.'

(b)   after rule 14 there shall be inserted—

'14.A   Human Rights Act

(1)   The court shall not consider making a declaration of incompatibility under section 4 of the Human Rights Act 1998 unless it has given written notice to the Crown.

(2)   Where notice has been given to the Crown, a Minister, or other person entitled under the Human Rights Act 1998 to be joined as a party, shall be so joined on giving written notice to the court.

(3)   A notice given under paragraph (1) above shall be given to—

(a)   the person named in the list published under section 17(1) of the Crown Proceedings Act 1947; or

(b)   in the case of doubt as to whether any and if so which of those departments is appropriate, the Treasury Solicitor.

(4)   A notice given under paragraph (1) above, shall provide an outline of the issues in the case and specify—

(a)   the prosecutor and appellant;

(b)   the date, judge and court of the trial in the proceedings from which the appeal lies;

(c)   the provision of primary legislation and the Convention right under question.

(5)   Any consideration of whether a declaration of incompatibility should be made, shall be adjourned for—

(a)   21 days from the date of the notice given under paragraph (1) above; or

(b)   such other period (specified in the notice), as the court shall allow in order that the relevant Minister or other person, may seek to be joined and prepare his case.

(6)   Unless the court otherwise directs, the Minister or other person entitled under the Human Rights Act 1998 to be joined as a party shall, if he is to be joined, give written notice to the court and every other party.

(7)   Where a Minister of the Crown has nominated a person to be joined as a party by virtue of section 5(2)(a) of the Human Rights Act 1998, a notice under paragraph (6) above shall be accompanied by a written nomination signed by or on behalf of the Minister.'

(c)   in rule 15 after paragraph (1)(d) there shall be inserted—

'(e)   in the case of a declaration of incompatibility under section 4 of the Human Rights Act 1998, the declaration shall be served on—

(i)   all of the parties to the proceedings; and

(ii)   where a Minister of the Crown has not been joined as a party, the Crown (in accordance with rule 14A(3) above).'

Appendix 3
The Government's White Paper

RIGHTS BROUGHT HOME: THE HUMAN RIGHTS BILL

Presented to Parliament by the The Secretary of State for the Home Department
by Command of Her Majesty
October 1997
(Cm 3782)

PREFACE BY THE PRIME MINISTER

The Government is pledged to modernise British politics. We are committed to a comprehensive programme of constitutional reform. We believe it is right to increase individual rights, to decentralise power, to open up government and to reform Parliament.

The elements are well known:

— a Scottish Parliament and a Welsh Assembly giving the people of Scotland and Wales more control over their own affairs within the United Kingdom;
— new rights, based on bringing the European Convention on Human Rights into United Kingdom law;
— an elected Mayor and new strategic authority for London with more accountability in the regions of England;
— freedom of information;
— a referendum on the voting system for the House of Commons; and
— reform of the House of Lords.

This White Paper explains the proposals contained in the Human Rights Bill which we are introducing into Parliament. The Bill marks a major step forward in the achievement of our programme of reform. It will give people in the United Kingdom opportunities to enforce their rights under the European Convention in British courts rather than having to incur the cost and delay of taking a case to the European Human Rights Commission and Court in Strasbourg. It will enhance the awareness of human rights in our society. And it stands alongside our decision to put the promotion of human rights at the forefront of our foreign policy.

I warmly commend these proposals to Parliament and to the people of this country.

Tony Blair

INTRODUCTION AND SUMMARY

The Government has a Manifesto commitment to introduce legislation to incorporate the European Convention on Human Rights into United Kingdom law. The Queen's Speech at the opening of the new Parliament announced that the Government would bring forward a Bill for this purpose in the current Session. We are now introducing the Human Rights Bill into Parliament. This White Paper explains what the Bill does, and why.

Before the General Election the Labour Party published a consultation document, *Bringing Rights Home*, setting our in some detail the case for incorporation and its preliminary proposals for the way this should be done. A number of individuals and organisations responded helpfully with a range of comments on the paper, and have continued to make their knowledge and advice available to the Government. The Government's proposals for the Bill take full account of the responses to Bringing Rights Home. Any further comments in response to this White Paper or on the Bill should be sent to:

Human Rights Unit
Home Office
50 Queen Anne's Gate
London SW1H 9AT.

We may make any comments we receive publicly available. Respondents who would prefer their comments to be treated in confidence are invited to indicate this expressly.

Chapter 1 of this White Paper explains the content and status of the European Convention on Human Rights and why the Government considers it desirable to give people in this country easier access to their Convention rights.

The United Kingdom is bound in international law to observe the Convention, which it ratified in 1951, and is answerable for any violation. In some limited circumstances, the United Kingdom courts can already take the Convention into account in domestic proceedings. But public authorities in the United Kingdom are not required as a matter of domestic law to comply with the Convention and, generally speaking, there is no means of having the application of the Convention rights tested in the United Kingdom courts. The Government believes that these arrangements are no longer adequate, given the importance which it attaches to the maintenance of basic human rights in this country, and that the time has come to 'bring rights home'.

Chapter 2 explains the Government's proposals to make the Convention rights enforceable directly in this country. The Bill makes it unlawful for public authorities to act in a way which is incompatible with the Convention rights. This will make it possible for people to invoke their rights in any proceedings—criminal or civil—brought against them by a public authority, or in proceedings which they may bring against a public authority. The Government prefers a system in which Convention rights can be called upon as they arise, in normal court proceedings, rather than confirming their consideration to some kind of constitutional court. Courts and tribunals will be able to award whatever remedy, within their normal powers, is appropriate in the circumstances.

Although the courts will not, under the proposals in the Bill be able to set aside Acts of the United Kingdom Parliament, the Bill requires them to interpret legislation as far as possible in accordance with the Convention. If this is not possible, the higher courts will be able to issue a formal declaration to the effect that the legislative provisions in question are incompatible with the Convention rights. It will then be up to the Government and Parliament to put matters right. The Bill makes a 'fast-track' procedure available for the purpose of amending the law so as to bring it into conformity with the Convention.

Chapter 3 sets out the other measures which the Government intends to take to ensure that the Convention rights are taken more fully into account in the development of new policies and of legislation. It also suggests that Parliament should itself establish a new Human Rights Committee. Amongst the matters on which the Government would welcome advice from a Parliamentary Committee is the possible establishment of a Human Rights Commission, but for the time being the Government has concluded that a new Commission should not be set up by means of this Bill.

Chapter 4 reviews the position on the derogation and reservation which the United Kingdom currently has in place in respect of the Convention and its First Protocol. The Government has concluded that these must remain for the time being, but the Bill requires any derogation to be subject to periodic renewal by Parliament and reservations to be subject to periodic review.

Chapter 4 also reviews the position in respect of those Protocols to the Convention which guarantee other rights (Protocols 4, 6 and 7) and which the United Kingdom has not so far accepted. The Government does not propose that the United Kingdom should ratify at present Protocol 4 or Protocol 6, but it does propose to sign and ratify Protocol 7 once some existing legislation has been amended.

The Annex [which is not reprinted here] sets out the text of the Convention rights themselves.

CHAPTER 1 THE CASE FOR CHANGE

The European Convention on Human Rights

1.1   The European Convention for the Protection of Human Rights and Fundamental Freedoms is a treaty of the Council of Europe. This institution was established at the end of the Second World War, as part of the Allies' programme to reconstruct durable civilisation on the mainland of Europe. The Council was established before the European Union and, although many nations are members of both, the two bodies are quite separate.

1.2   The United Kingdom played a major part in drafting the Convention, and there was a broad agreement between the major political parties about the need for it (one of its draftsmen later became, as Lord Kilmuir, Lord Chancellor in the Conservative Administration from 1954 to 1962). The United Kingdom was among the first group of countries to sign the Convention. It was the very first country to ratify it, in March 1951. In 1966 the United Kingdom accepted that an individual person, and not merely another State, could bring a case against the United Kingdom in Strasbourg (the home of the European Commission of Human Rights and Court of Human Rights, which were established by the Convention). Successive administrations in the United Kingdom have maintained these arrangements.

1.3   The European Convention is not the only international human rights agreement to which the United Kingdom and other like-minded countries are party, but over the years it has become one of the premier agreements defining standards of behaviour across Europe. It was also for many years unique because of the system which it put in place for people from signatory countries to take complaints to Strasbourg and for those complaints to be judicially determined. These arrangements are by now well tried and tested. The rights and freedoms which are guaranteed under the Convention are ones with which the people of this country are plainly comfortable. They therefore afford an excellent basis for the Human Rights Bill which we are now introducing.

1.4   The constitutional arrangements in most continental European countries have meant that their acceptance of the Convention went hand in hand with its incorporation into their domestic law. In this country it was long believed that the rights and freedoms guaranteed by the Convention could be delivered under our common law. In the last two decades, however, there has been a growing awareness that it is not sufficient to rely on the common law and that incorporation is necessary

1.5   The Liberal Democrat Peer, Lord Lester of Herne Hill QC, recently introduced two Bills on incorporation in the House of Lords (in 1994 and 1996). Before that, the then Conservative MP Sir Edward Gardener QC introduced a private member's Bill on incorporation into the House of Commons in 1987. At the time of introducing his Bill he commented on the language of the articles in the Convention saying: 'It is language which echoes right down the corridors of history. It goes deep into our history and as far back as Magna Carta.' (Hansard HC, 6 February 1987. col. 1224.) In preparing this White Paper the Government has paid close attention to earlier debates and proposals for incorporation.

The Convention rights

1.6   The Convention contains articles which guarantee a number of basic human rights. They deal with the right to life (Article 2): torture or inhuman or degrading treatment or punishment (Article 3); slavery and forced labour (Article 4); liberty and security of person (Article 5); fair trial (Article 6); retrospective criminal laws (Article 7): respect for private and family life, home and correspondence (Article 8): freedom of thought, conscience and religion (Article 9); freedom of expression (Article 10); freedom of peaceful assembly and freedom of association, including the right to join a trade union (Article 11); the right to marry and to found a family (Article 12); and discrimination in the enjoyment of these rights and freedoms (Article 14).

1.7   The United Kingdom is also a party to the First Protocol to the Convention, which guarantees the right to the peaceful enjoyment of possessions (Article 1), the right to education (Article 2) and the right to free elections (Article 3).

1.8   The rights in the Convention are set out in general terms, and they are subject in the Convention to a number of qualifications which are also of a general character. Some of these qualifications are set out in the substantive Articles themselves (see, for example, Article 10, concerning freedom of expression); others are set out in Articles 16 to 18 of the Convention. Sometimes too the rights guaranteed under the Convention need to be balanced against each other (for example, those guaranteed by Article 8 and Article 10).

Applications under the Convention

1.9   Anyone within the United Kingdom jurisdiction who is aggrieved by an action of the executive or by the effect of the existing law and who believes it is contrary to the European Convention can submit a petition to the European Commission of Human Rights. The Commission will first consider whether the petition is admissible. One of the conditions of admissibility is that the applicant must have gone through all the steps available to him or her at home for challenging the decision which he or she is complaining about. If the Commission decides that a complaint is admissible and if a friendly settlement cannot be secured, it will send a confidential report to the Committee of Ministers of the Council of Europe, stating its opinion on whether there has been a violation. The matter may end there with a decision by the Committee (which in practice always adopts the opinion of the Commission), or the case may be referred on to the European Court of

Human Rights[1] for consideration. If the Court finds that there has been a violation it may itself 'afford just satisfaction' to the injured party by an award of damages or an award of costs and expenses. The Court may also find that a formal finding of a violation is sufficient. There is no appeal from the Court.

Effect of a Court judgment

1.10   A finding by the European Court of Human Rights of a violation of a Convention right does not have the effect of automatically changing United Kingdom law and practice: that is a matter for the United Kingdom Government and Parliament. But the United Kingdom, like all other States who are parties to the Convention, has agreed to abide by the decisions of the Court or (where the case has not been referred to the Court) the Committee of Ministers. It follows that, in cases where a violation has been found the State concerned must ensure that any deficiency in its internal laws is rectified so as to bring them into line with the Convention. The State is responsible for deciding what changes are needed, but it must satisfy the Committee of Minister that the steps taken are sufficient. Successive United Kingdom administrations have accepted these obligations in full.

Relationship to current law in the United Kingdom

1.11   When the United Kingdom ratified the Convention the view was taken that the rights and freedoms which the Convention guarantees were already, in substance, fully protected in British law. It was not considered necessary to write the Convention itself into British law, or to introduce any new laws in the United Kingdom in order to be sure of being able to comply with the Convention.

1.12   From the point of view of the *international* obligation which the United Kingdom was undertaking when it signed and ratified the Convention, this was understandable. Moreover, the European Court of Human Rights explicitly confirmed that it was not a necessary part of proper observance of the Convention that it should be incorporated into the laws of the States concerned.

1.13   However, since its drafting nearly 50 years ago, almost all the States which are party to the European Convention on Human Rights have gradually incorporated it into their domestic law in one way or another. Ireland and Norway have not done so, but Ireland has a Bill of Rights which guarantees rights similar to those guaranteed by the Convention and Norway is also in the process of incorporating the Convention. Several other countries with which we have close links and which share the common law tradition, such as Canada and New Zealand, have provided similar protection for human rights in their own legal systems.

The case for incorporation

1.14   The effect of non-incorporation on the British people is a very practical one. The rights, originally developed with major help from the United Kingdom Government, are no longer actually seen as British rights. And enforcing them takes too long and costs too much. It takes on average five years to get an action into the European Court of Human Rights once all domestic remedies have been exhausted; and it costs an average of £30,000. Bringing these rights home will mean that the British people will be able to argue for their rights in the British courts—without this inordinate delay and cost. It will also mean that the rights will be brought

---

[1] Protocol 11 to the Convention, which will come into force on 1 November 1998, will replace the existing part-time European Commission and Court of Human Rights with a single full-time Court.

much more fully into the jurisprudence of the courts throughout the United Kingdom and their interpretation will thus be far more subtly and powerfully woven into our law. And there will be another distinct benefit. British judges will be enabled to make a distinctively British contribution to the development of the jurisprudence of human rights in Europe.

1.15   Moreover in the Government's view the approach which the United Kingdom has so far adopted towards the Convention does not sufficiently reflect its importance and has not stood the test of time.

1.16   The most obvious proof of this lies in the number of cases in which the European Commission and Court have found that there have been violations of the Convention rights in the United Kingdom. The causes vary. The Government recognises that interpretations of the rights guaranteed under the Convention have developed over the years reflecting changes in society and attitudes. Sometimes United Kingdom laws have proved to be inherently at odds with the Convention rights. On other occasions, although the law has been satisfactory, something has been done which our courts have held to be lawful by United Kingdom standards but which breaches the Convention. In other cases again, there has simply been no framework within which the compatibility with the Convention rights of an executive act or decision can be tested in the British courts: these courts can of course review the exercise of executive discretion, but they can do so only on the basis of what is lawful or unlawful according to the law in the United Kingdom as it stands. It is plainly unsatisfactory that someone should be the victim of a breach of the Convention standards by the State yet cannot bring any case at all in the British courts, simply because British law does not recognise the right in the same terms as one contained in the Convention.

1.17   For individuals and for those advising them, the road to Strasbourg is long and hard. Even when they get there, the Convention enforcement machinery is subject to long delays This might be convenient for a government which was half-hearted about the Convention and the right of individuals to apply under it, since it postpones the moment at which changes in domestic law or practice must be made. But it is not in keeping with the importance which this Government attaches to the observance of basic human rights.

Bringing rights home

1.18   We therefore believe that the time has come to enable people to enforce their Convention rights against the State in the British courts, rather than having to incur the delays and expense which are involved in taking a case to the European Human Rights Commission and Court in Strasbourg and which may altogether deter some people from pursuing their rights. Enabling courts in the United Kingdom to rule on the application of the Convention will also help to influence the development of case law on the Convention by the European Court of Human Rights on the basis of familiarity with our laws and customs and of sensitivity to practices and procedures in the United Kingdom. Our courts' decisions will provide the European Court with a useful source of information and reasoning for its own decisions. United Kingdom judges have a very high reputation internationally, but the fact that they do not deal in the same concepts as the European Court of Human Rights limits the extent to which their judgments can be drawn upon and followed. Enabling the Convention rights to be judged by British courts will also lead to closer scrutiny of the human rights implications of new legislation and new policies. If legislation is enacted which is incompatible with the Convention a ruling by the domestic courts to that effect will be much more direct and immediate than a ruling from the European Court of Human Rights. The Government of the day and Parliament, will want to minimise the risk of that happening.

1.19   Our aim is a straightforward one. It is to make more directly accessible the rights which the British people already enjoy under the Convention. In other words, to bring those rights home.

CHAPTER 2 THE GOVERNMENT'S PROPOSALS FOR ENFORCING THE CONVENTION RIGHTS

2.1   The essential feature of the Human Rights Bill is that the United Kingdom will not be bound to give effect to the Convention rights merely as a matter of international law, but will also give them further effect directly in our domestic law. But there is more than one way of achieving this. This chapter explains the choices which the Government has made for the Bill.

A new requirement on public authorities

2.2   Although the United Kingdom has an international obligation to comply with the Convention there at present is no requirement in our domestic law on central and local government, or others exercising similar executive powers, to exercise those powers in a way which is compatible with the Convention. This Bill will change that by making it unlawful for public authorities to act in a way which is incompatible with the Convention rights. The definition of what constitutes a public authority is in wide terms. Examples of persons or organisations whose acts or omissions it is intended should be able to be challenged include central government (including executive agencies); local government; the police; immigration officers; prisons; courts and tribunals themselves: and, to the extent that they are exercising public functions, companies responsible for areas of activity which were previously within the public sector, such as the privatised utilities. The actions of Parliament, however, are excluded.

2.3   A person who is aggrieved by an act or omission on the part of a public authority which is incompatible with the Convention rights will be able to challenge the act or omission in the courts. The effects will be wide-ranging. They will extend both to legal actions which a public authority pursues against individuals (for example, where a criminal prosecution is brought or where an administrative decision is being enforced through legal proceedings) and to cases which individuals pursue against a public authority (for example, for judicial review of an executive decision). Convention points will normally be taken in the context of proceedings instituted against individuals or already open to them, but if none is available, it will be possible for people to bring cases on Convention grounds alone. Individuals or organisations seeking judicial review of decisions by public authorities on Convention grounds will need to show that they have been directly affected as they must if they take a case to Strasbourg.

2.4   It is our intention that people or organisations should be able to argue that their Convention rights have been infringed by a public authority in our courts at any level. This will enable the Convention rights to be applied from the outset against the facts and background of a particular case, and the people concerned to obtain their remedy at the earliest possible moment. We think this is preferable to allowing cases to run their ordinary course but then referring them to some kind of separate constitutional court which, like the European Court of Human Rights, would simply review cases which had already passed through the regular legal machinery. In considering Convention points our courts will be required to take account of relevant decisions of the European Commission and Court of Human Rights (although these will not be binding).

2.5 The Convention is often described as a 'living instrument' because it is interpreted by the European Court in the light of present-day conditions and therefore reflects changing social attitudes and the changes in the circumstances of society. In future our judges will be able to contribute to this dynamic and evolving interpretation of the Convention. In particular, our courts will be required to balance the protection of individuals' fundamental rights against the demands of the general interest of the community, particularly in relation to Articles 8–11 where a State may restrict the protected right to the extent that this is 'necessary in a democratic society'.

Remedies for a failure to comply with the Convention

2.6 A public authority which is found to have acted unlawfully by failing to comply with the Convention will not be exposed to criminal penalties. But the court or tribunal will be able to grant the injured person any remedy which is within its normal powers to grant and which it considers appropriate and just in the circumstances. What remedy is appropriate will of course depend both on the facts of the case and on a proper balance between the rights of the individual and the public interest. In some cases, the right course may be for the decision of the public authority in the particular case to be quashed. In other cases, the only appropriate remedy may be an award of damages. The Bill provides that, in considering an award of damages on Convention grounds, the courts are to take into account the principles applied by the European Court of Human Rights in awarding compensation, so that people will be able to receive compensation from a domestic court equivalent to what they would have received in Strasbourg.

Interpretation of legislation

2.7 The Bill provides for legislation—both Acts of Parliament and secondary legislation—to be interpreted so far as possible so as to be compatible with the Convention. This goes far beyond the present rule which enables the courts to take the Convention into account in resolving any ambiguity in a legislative provision. The courts will be required to interpret legislation so as to uphold the Convention rights unless the legislation itself is so clearly incompatible with the Convention that it is impossible to do so.

2.8 This 'rule of construction' is to apply to past as well as to future legislation. To the extent that it affects the meaning of a legislative provision the courts will not be bound by previous interpretations. They will be able to build a new body of case law, taking into account the Convention rights.

A declaration of incompatibility with the Convention rights

2.9 If the courts decide in any case that it is impossible to interpret an Act of Parliament in a way which is compatible with the Convention, the Bill enables a formal declaration to be made that its provisions are incompatible with the Convention. A declaration of incompatibility will be an important statement to make, and the power to make it will be reserved to the higher courts. They will be able to make a declaration in any proceedings before them, whether the case originated with them (as, in the High Court, on judicial review of an executive act) or in considering an appeal from a lower court or tribunal. The Government will have the right to intervene in any proceedings where such a declaration is a possible outcome. A decision by the High Court or Court of Appeal, determining whether or not such a declaration should be made, will itself be appealable.

Effect of court decisions on legislation

2.10   A declaration that legislation is incompatible with the Convention rights will not of itself have the effect of changing the law, which will continue to apply. But it will almost certainly prompt the Government and Parliament to change the law.

2.11   The Government has considered very carefully whether it would be right for the Bill to go further, and give the courts in the United Kingdom the power to set aside an Act of Parliament which they believe is incompatible with the Convention rights. In considering this question we have looked at a number of models. The Canadian Charter of Rights and Freedoms 1982 enables the courts to strike down any legislation which is inconsistent with the Charter, unless the legislation contains an explicit statement that it is to apply 'notwithstanding' the provisions of the Charter. But legislation which has been struck down may be re-enacted with a 'notwithstanding' clause. In New Zealand, on the other hand, although there was an earlier proposal for legislation on lines similar to the Canadian Charter, the human rights legislation which was eventually enacted after wide consultation took a different form. The New Zealand Bill of Rights Act 1990 is an 'interpretative' statute which requires past and future legislation to be interpreted consistently with the rights contained in the Act as far as possible but provides that legislation stands if that is impossible. In Hong Kong, a middle course was adopted. The Hong Kong Bill of Rights Ordinance 1991 distinguishes between legislation enacted before and after the Ordinance took effect: previous legislation is subordinated to the provisions of the Ordinance, but subsequent legislation takes precedence over it.

2.12   The Government has also considered the European Communities Act 1972 which provides for European law, in cases where that law has 'direct effect', to take precedence over domestic law. There is, however, an essential difference between European Community law and the European Convention on Human Rights, because it is a *requirement* of membership of the European Union that Member States give priority to directly effective EC law in their own legal systems. There is no such requirement in the Convention.

2.13   The Government has reached the conclusion that courts should not have the power to set aside primary legislation past or future, on the ground of incompatibility with the Convention, this conclusion arises from the importance which the Government attaches to Parliamentary sovereignty. In this context, Parliamentary sovereignty means that Parliament is competent to make any law on any matter of its choosing and no court may question the validity of any Act that is passed. In enacting legislation, Parliament is making decisions about important matters of public policy. The authority to make those decisions derives from a democratic mandate. Members of Parliament in the House of Commons possess such a mandate because they are elected, accountable and representative. To make provision in the Bill for the courts to set aside Act of Parliament would confer on the judiciary a general power over the decisions of Parliament which under our present constitutional arrangements they do not possess, and would be likely on occasions to draw the judiciary into serious conflict with Parliament. There is no evidence to suggest that they desire this power, nor that the public wish them to have it. Certainly this Government has no mandate for any such change.

2.14   It has been suggested that the courts should be able to uphold the rights in the Human Rights Bill in preference to any provisions of earlier legislation which are incompatible with those rights. This in on the basis that a later Act of Parliament takes precedence over an earlier Act if there is a conflict. But the Human Rights Bill is intended to provide a new basis for judicial interpretation of all legislation, not a basis for striking down any part of it.

2.15   The courts will, however, be able to strike down or set aside secondary legislation which is incompatible with the Convention, unless the terms of the parent statute make this impossible. The courts can already strike down or set aside secondary legislation when they consider it to be outside the powers conferred by the statute under which it is made, and it is right that they should be able to do so when it is incompatible with the Convention rights and could have been framed differently.

Entrenchment

2.16   On one view, human rights legislation is so important that it should be given added protection from subsequent amendment or repeal. The Constitution of the United States of America, for example, guarantees rights which can be amended or repealed only by securing qualified majorities in both the House of Representatives and the Senate and among the States themselves. But an arrangement of this kind could not be reconciled with our own constitutional traditions, which allow any Act of Parliament to be amended or repealed by a subsequent Act of Parliament. We do not believe that it is necessary or would be desirable to attempt to devise such a special arrangement for this Bill.

Amending legislation

2.17   Although the Bill does not allow the courts to set aside Acts of Parliament, it will nevertheless have a profound impact on the way that legislation is interpreted and applied, and it will have the effect of putting the issues squarely to the Government and Parliament for further consideration. It is important to ensure that the Government and Parliament, for their part, can respond quickly. In the normal way, primary legislation can be amended only by further primary legislation, and this can take a long time. Given the volume of Government business, an early opportunity to legislate may not arise; and the process of legislating is itself protracted. Emergency legislation can be enacted very quickly indeed, but it is introduced only in the most exceptional circumstances.

2.18   The Bill provides for a fast-track procedure for changing legislation in response either to a declaration of incompatibility by our own higher courts or to a finding of a violation of the Convention in Strasbourg. The appropriate Government Minister will be able to amend the legislation by Order so as to make it compatible with the Convention. The Order will be subject to approval by both Houses of Parliament before taking effect, except where the need to amend the legislation is particularly urgent, when the Order will take effect immediately but will expire after a short period if not approved by Parliament.

2.19   There are already precedents for using secondary legislation to amend primary legislation in some circumstances, and we think the use of such procedure is acceptable in this context and would be welcome as a means of improving the observance of human rights. Plainly the Minister would have to exercise this power only in relation to the provisions which contravene the Convention, together with any necessary consequential amendments. In other words, Ministers would not have carte blanche to amend unrelated parts of the Act in which the breach is discovered.

Scotland

2.20   In Scotland, the position with regard to Acts of the Westminster Parliament will be the same as in England and Wales. All courts will be required to interpret the legislation in a way which is compatible with the Convention so far as possible. If a provision is found to be incompatible with the Convention, the Court of Session or the High Court will be able to make a declarator to that effect, but this will not affect the validity or continuing operation of the provision.

2.21   The position will be different, however, in relation to Acts of the Scottish Parliament when it is established. The Government has decided that the Scottish Parliament will have no power to legislate in a way which is incompatible with the Convention: and similarly that the Scottish Executive will have no power to make subordinate legislation or to take executive action which is incompatible with the Convention. It will accordingly be possible to challenge such legislation and actions in the Scottish courts on the ground that the Scottish Parliament or Executive has incorrectly applied its powers. If the challenge is successful then the legislation or action would be held to the unlawful. As with other issues concerning the powers of the Scottish Parliament there will be a procedure for inferior courts to refer such issues to the superior Scottish courts; and those courts in turn will be able to refer the matter to the Judicial Committee of the Privy Council. If such issues are decided by the superior Scottish courts, an appeal from their decision will be to the Judicial Committee. These arrangements are in line with the Government's general approach to devolution.

Wales
2.22   Similarly the Welsh Assembly will not have power to make subordinate legislation or take executive action which is incompatible with the Convention. It will be possible to challenge such legislation and action in the courts and for them to be quashed, on the ground that the Assembly has exceeded its powers.

Northern Ireland
2.23   Acts of the Westminster Parliament will be treated in the same way in Northern Ireland as in the rest of the United Kingdom. But Orders in Council and other related legislation will be treated as subordinate legislation. In other words, they will be struck down by the courts if they are incompatible with the Convention. Most such legislation is a temporary means of enacting legislation which would otherwise be done by measures of a devolved Northern Ireland legislature.

CHAPTER 3 IMPROVING COMPLIANCE WITH THE CONVENTION RIGHTS

3.1   The enforcement of Convention rights will be a matter for the courts, whilst the Government and Parliament will have the different but equally important responsibility of revising legislation where necessary. But it is also highly desirable for the Government to ensure as far as possible that legislation which it places before Parliament in the normal way is compatible with the Convention rights, and for Parliament to ensure that the human rights implications of legislation are subject to proper consideration before the legislation is enacted.

Government legislation
3.2   The Human Rights Bill introduces a new procedure to make the human rights implications of proposed Government legislation more transparent. The responsible Minister will be required to provide a statement that in his or her view the proposed Bill is compatible with the Convention. The Government intends to include this statement alongside the Explanatory and Financial Memorandum which accompanies a Bill when it is introduced into each House of Parliament.

3.3   There may be occasions where such a statement cannot be provided, for example because it is essential to legislate on a particular issue but the policy in question requires a risk to be taken in relation to the Convention, or because the arguments in relation to the Convention issues raised are not clear-cut. In such cases, the Minister will indicate that he or she cannot provide a positive statement but that the Government nevertheless wishes Parliament to proceed to consider the Bill. Parliament would expect the Minister to explain his or her reasons during the normal course of the proceedings on the Bill. This will ensure that the human rights implications are debated at the earliest opportunity.

Consideration of draft legislation within Government

3.4   The new requirement to make a statement about the compliance of draft legislation with the Convention will have a significant and beneficial impact on the preparation of draft legislation within Government before its introduction into Parliament. It will ensure that all Ministers their departments and officials are fully seised of the gravity of the Convention's obligations in respect of human rights. But we also intend to strengthen collective Government procedures so as to ensure that a proper assessment is made of the human rights implications when collective approval is sought for a new policy, as well as when any draft Bill is considered by Ministers. Revised guidance to Departments on these procedures will, like the existing guidance by publicly available.

3.5   Some central coordination will also be extremely desirable in considering the approach to be taken to Convention points in criminal or civil proceedings or in proceedings for judicial review to which a Government department is a party. This is likely to require an interdepartmental group of lawyers and administrators meeting on a regular basis to ensure that a consistent approach is taken and to ensure that developments in case law are well understood by all those in Government who are involved in proceeding on Convention points. We do not, however, see any need to make a particular Minister responsible for promoting human rights across Government, or to set up a separate new Unit for this purpose. The responsibility for complying with human rights requirements rests on the Government as a whole.

A Parliamentary Committee on Human Rights

3.6   *Bringing Rights Home* suggested that 'Parliament itself should play a leading role in protecting the rights which are at the heart of a parliamentary democracy'. How this is achieved is a matter for Parliament to decide, but in the Government's view the best course would be to establish a new Parliamentary Committee with functions relating to human rights. This would not require legislation or any change in Parliamentary procedure. There could be a Joint Committee of both Houses of Parliament or each House could have its own Committee; or there could be Committee which met jointly for some purposes and separately for others.

3.7   The new Committee might conduct enquiries on a range of human rights issues relating to the Convention and produce reports so as to assist the Government and Parliament in deciding what action to take. It might also want to range more widely, and examine issues relating to the other international obligations of the United Kingdom such as proposals to accept new rights under other human rights treaties.

Should there be a Human Rights Commission?

3.8   *Bringing Rights Home* canvassed views on the establishment of a Human Rights Commission, and this possibility has received a good deal of attention. No commitment to establish a Commission was, however, made in the Manifesto on which the Government was elected. The Government's priority is implementation of its Manifesto commitment to give further effect to the Convention rights in domestic law so that people can enforce those rights in United Kingdom courts. Establishment of a new Human Rights Commission is not central to that objective and does not need to form part of the current Bill.

3.9   Moreover, the idea of setting up a new human rights body is not universally acclaimed. Some reservations have been expressed particularly from the point of view of the impact on existing bodies concerned with particular aspects of human rights, such as the Commission for Racial Equality and the Equal Opportunities Commission, whose primary concern is to protect the rights for which they were established. A quinquennial review is currently being conducted of the Equal Opportunities Commission, and the Government has also decided to establish a new Disability Rights Commission.

3.10   The Government's conclusion is that, before a Human Rights Commission could be established by legislation, more consideration needs to be given to how it would work in relation to such bodies, and to the new arrangements to be established for Parliamentary and Government scrutiny of human rights issues. This is necessary not only for the purposes of framing the legislation but also to justify the additional public expenditure needed to establish and run a new Commission. A range of organisational issues need more detailed consideration before the legislative and financial case for a new Commission is made, and there needs to be a greater degree of consensus on an appropriate model among existing human rights bodies.

3.11   However, the Government has not closed its mind to the idea of a new Human Rights Commission at some stage in the future in the light of practical experience of the working of the new legislation. If Parliament establishes a Committee on Human Rights, one of its main tasks might be to conduct an inquiry into whether a Human Rights Commission is needed and how it should operate. The Government would want to give full weight to the Committee's report in considering whether to create a statutory Human Rights Commission in future.

3.12   It has been suggested that a new Commission might be funded from non-Government sources. The Government would not wish to deter a move towards a non-statutory, privately financed body if its role was limited to functions such as public education and advice to individuals. However, a non-statutory body could not absorb any of the functions of the existing statutory bodies concerned with aspects of human rights.

CHAPTER 4 DEROGATIONS, RESERVATIONS AND OTHER PROTOCOLS

Derogations

4.1   Article 15 of the Convention permits a State to derogate from certain Articles of the Convention in time of war or other public emergency threatening life of the nation. The United Kingdom has one derogation in place, in respect of art. 5(3) of the Convention.

4.2   The derogation arose from a case in 1988 in which the European Court of Human Rights held that the detention of the applicants in the case before it under the Prevention of Terrorism (Temporary Provisions) Act 1984 for more than four days constituted a breach of art. 5(3) of the Convention, because they had not been brought promptly before a judicial authority. The Government of the day entered a derogation following the judgment in order to preserve the Secretary of State's power under the Act to extend the period of detention of persons suspected of terrorism connected with the affairs of Northern Ireland for a total of up to seven days. The validity of the derogation was subsequently upheld by the European Court of Human Rights in another case in 1993.

4.3   We are considering what change might be made to the arrangements under the prevention of terrorism legislation. Substituting judicial for executive authority for extensions, which would mean that the derogation could be withdrawn, would require primary legislation. In the meantime, however, the derogation remains necessary. The Bill sets out the text of the derogation, and art. 5(3) will have effect in domestic law for the time being subject to its terms.

4.4   Given our commitment to promoting human rights, however, we would not want the derogation to remain in place indefinitely without good reasons. Accordingly its effect in domestic law will be time-limited. If not withdrawn earlier, it will expire five years after the Bill comes into force unless both Houses of Parliament agree that it should be renewed and similarly thereafter. The Bill contains similar provision in respect of any new derogation which may be entered in future.

Reservations

4.5   Article 64 of the Convention allows a state to enter a reservation when a law in force is not in conformity which a Convention provision. The United Kingdom is a party to the First Protocol to the Convention, but has a reservation in place in respect of Article 2 of the Protocol. Article 2 sets out two principles. The first states that no person shall be denied the right to eduction. The second is that in exercising any functions in relation to education and teaching, the State shall respect the right of parents to ensure that such education and teaching is in conformity with their own religious and philosophical convictions. The reservation makes it clear that the United Kingdom accepts this second principle only so far as it is compatible with the provision of efficient instruction and training, and the avoidance of unreasonable public expenditure.

4.6   The reservation reflects the fundamental principle originally enacted in the Education Act 1944, and now contained in section 9 of the Education Act 1996, 'that pupils are to be educated in accordance with the wishes of their parents so far as that is compatible with the provision of efficient instruction and training and the avoidance of unreasonable public expenditure'. There is similar provision in Scottish legislation. The reservation does not affect the right to education in Article 2. Nor does it deny parents the right to have account taken of their religious or philosophical convictions. Its purpose is to recognise that in the provision of State-funded education a balance must be struck in some cases between the convictions of parents and what is educationally sound and affordable.

4.7   Having carefully considered this, the Government has concluded that the reservation should be kept in place. Its text is included in the Bill, and Article 2 of the First Protocol will have effect in domestic law subject to its terms.

4.8   Whilst derogations are permitted under the Convention only in times of war or other public emergency, and so are clearly temporary, there is no such limitation in respect of reservations. We do not therefore propose to make the effect of the reservation in domestic law subject to periodic renewal by Parliament, but the Bill requires the Secretary of State (the Secretary of State for Education and Employment) to review the reservation every five years and to lay a report before Parliament.

Other Protocols

4.9   Protocols 4, 6 and 7 guarantee a number of rights additional to those in the original Convention itself and its First Protocol. These further rights have been added largely to reflect the wider range of rights subsequently included under the International Covenant on Civil and Political Rights. There is no obligation upon States who are party to the original Convention to accept these additional Protocols, but the Government has taken the opportunity to review the position of the United Kingdom on Protocols 4, 6 and 7.

4.10   Protocol 4 contains a prohibition on the deprivation of liberty on grounds of inability to fulfil contractual obligations; a right to liberty of movement; a right to non-expulsion from the home State; a right of entry to the State of which a person is a national; and a prohibition on the collective expulsion of aliens. These provisions largely reflect similar (but not identical) rights provided under the International Covenant on Civil and Political Rights. Protocol 4 was signed by the United Kingdom in 1963 but not subsequently ratified because of concerns about what is the exact extent of the obligation regarding a right of entry.

4.11   These are important rights, and we would like to see them given formal recognition in our law. But we also believe that existing laws in relation to different categories of British nationals must be maintained. It will be possible to ratify Protocol 4 only if the potential conflicts with our domestic laws can be resolved. This remains under consideration but we do not propose to ratify Protocol 4 at present.

4.12   Protocol 6 requires the complete abolition of the death penalty other than in time of war or imminent threat of war. It does not permit any derogation or reservation. The Protocol largely parallels the Second Optional Protocol to the International Covenant on Civil and Political Rights, which the United Kingdom has not accepted.

4.13   The death penalty was abolished as a sentence for murder in 1965 following a free vote in the House of Commons. It remains as a penalty for treason, piracy with violence, and certain armed forces offences. No execution for these offences has taken place since 1946, when the wartime Nazi propagandist William Joyce (known as Lord Haw-Haw) was hanged at Wandsworth prison. The last recorded execution for piracy was in 1830. Thus there might appear to be little difficulty in our ratifying Protocol 6. This would, however, make it impossible for a United Kingdom Parliament to reintroduce the death penalty for murder, short of denouncing the European Convention. The view taken so far is that the issue is not one of basic constitutional principle but is a matter of judgment and conscience to be decided by Members of Parliament as they see fit. For these reasons we do not propose to ratify Protocol 6 at present.

4.14   Protocol 7 contains a prohibition on the expulsion of aliens without a decision in accordance with the law or opportunities for review; a right to a review of conviction or sentence after criminal conviction; a right to compensation following a miscarriage of justice; a prohibition on double jeopardy in criminal cases; and a right to equality between spouses. These rights reflect similar rights protected under the International Covenant on Civil and Political Rights.

4.15   In general the provisions of Protocol 7 reflect principles already inherent in our law. In view of concerns in some of these areas in recent years, the Government believes that it would be particularly helpful to give these important principles the same legal status as other rights in the Convention by ratifying and incorporating Protocol 7. There is, however, a difficulty with this because a few provisions of our domestic law, for example in relation to the property rights of spouses, could not be interpreted in a way which is compatible with Protocol 7. The Government intends to legislate to remove these inconsistencies when a suitable opportunity occurs, and then to sign and ratify the Protocol.

4.16   The Secretary of State will be able to amend the Human Rights Act by Order so as to insert into it the rights contained in any Protocols to the Convention which the United Kingdom ratifies in future. The Order will be subject to approval by both Houses of Parliament. The Bill also enables any reservation to a Protocol to be added, but as with the existing reservation it will have to be reviewed every five years if not withdrawn earlier.

Appendix 4
Extracts from Hansard

This is a selection of some of the statements made during the Parliamentary debates on the Human Rights Act 1998 by introducing ministers. The extracts are given section by section in the following format:

Place, [Stage]
Hansard reference
Speaker: text

For example:

House of Commons, Committee Stage
Hansard HC, 20 May 1998, col. 981
The Secretary of State for the Home Department (Mr Jack Straw): . . . I wish future Judicial Committees of the House of Lords luck in working through these debates. One sometimes wonders about the wisdom of the *Pepper* v *Hart* judgment in terms of the work that it has given the higher judiciary.

Unless the wording of a provision changed after a ministerial explanation was given, we have given final section numbers rather than clause numbers.

For reasons of space, we have only given the ministerial rationale underlying individual sections (and the ministerial understanding of the margin of appreciation) where it illustrates underlying policy motives, or may be admissible under the rule in *Pepper* v *Hart* [1993] AC 593. (See Preface, pp. xii and xiii.)

Other passages which may be of particular interest to practitioners are as follows:

(a) The introduction by Lord Irvine of Lairg LC to the purposes of the Act and its place in the British constitution (Hansard HL, 3 November 1997, col. 1227–38).

(b) The introduction by the Home Secretary (Jack Straw) to the purposes of the Act (Hansard HC, 16 February 1998, col. 769–82).

(c) The introduction by the Parliamentary Under-Secretary of State for the Home Department (Mike O'Brien) to the purposes of the Act (Hansard HC, 16 February 1998, col. 858–61).

(d) General remarks by Jack Straw in committee on 'the British approach' to incorporation (Hansard HC, 3 June 1998, col. 419 ff.)

(e) Arguments in favour of the Act on second reading in the House of Lords by Lord Bingham of Cornhill CJ (Hansard HL, 3 November 1997, col. 1245–6). Lord Scarman (retired Law Lord and long-time advocate of incorporation) (Hansard HL, 3 November 1997, col. 1256) and Lord Cooke of Thordon (retired senior New Zealand judge who has sat on appellate committees of the House of Lords) (Hansard HL, 3 November 1997, col. 1271–3). Of particular interest is Lord Cooke's analysis of section 3 of the Act, and the difference it will make to statutory interpretation (at col. 1272–3):

[Section 3] will require a very different approach to interpretation from that to which United Kingdom courts are accustomed. Traditionally, the search has been for the true meaning; now it will be for a possible meaning that would prevent the making of a declaration of incompatibility. . . . The shift of the criterion to a search for possible compatible meanings will confront the courts with delicate responsibilities. Even for lawyers, a must is a must. For surely the difference between mandatory and directory provisions can have no place in interpreting the Human Rights [Act], which will itself be primary legislation. Consider, say, an Act making a certain kind of disclosure a criminal offence, enacting one specific defence, but not specifically excluding a defence under art. 10 (freedom to impart information). Without expressing any opinion as to the outcomes, one can see that there will be a new kind of problem. In effect, the courts are being asked to solve these problems by applying a rebuttable presumption in favour of the Convention rights.

LONG TITLE

Bill does not make European Convention 'part of our law'—meaning of 'give further effect'

House of Lords, Report Stage
Hansard HL, 29 January 1998, col. 421
The Lord Chancellor (Lord Irvine of Lairg): . . . The word 'further' is included in the Long Title because, in our national arrangements, the Convention can, and is, already applied in a variety of different circumstances and is relied on in a range of ways by our own courts.

The Bill will greatly increase the ability of our courts to enforce Convention rights, but it is not introducing a wholly new concept. As I have said before, the Bill as such does not incorporate Convention rights into domestic law but, in accordance with the language of the Long Title, it gives further effect in the United Kingdom to Convention rights by requiring the courts in [s. 3(1)], 'So far as it is possible to do so' to construe—in the language of the statute, to read and give effect to—primary legislation and subordinate legislation in a way which is compatible with the Convention rights. That is an interpretative principle. . . .

I have to make this point absolutely plain. The European Convention on Human Rights under this [Act] is not made part of our law. The [Act] gives the European Convention on Human Rights a special relationship which will mean that the courts will give effect to the interpretative provisions to which I have already referred, but it does not make the Convention directly justiciable as it would be if it were expressly made part of our law. I want there to be no ambiguity about that. . . . [col. 422] The short point is that if the Convention rights were incorporated into our law, they would be directly justiciable and would be enforced by our courts. That is not the scheme of this [Act]. If the courts find it impossible to construe primary legislation in a way which is compatible with the Convention rights, the primary legislation remains in full force and effect. All that the courts may do is to make a declaration of incompatibility.

SECTION 1. THE CONVENTION AND THE FIRST PROTOCOL

Section 1 sets out which Convention rights are incorporated. Controversial issues were the non-incorporation of art. 13 and the addition, at a late stage, by a free vote in the House of Commons, of the Sixth Protocol. Only those matters are considered here.

Failure to incorporate art. 13

House of Lords, Second Reading
Hansard HL, 3 November 1997, col. 1308
The Parliamentary Under-Secretary of State, Home Office (Lord Williams of Mostyn):
. . . Our view is, quite unambiguously, that art. 13 is met by the passage of the [Art].

House of Lords, Committee Stage
Hansard HL, 18 November 1997, col. 475
The Lord Chancellor: . . . The [Act] gives effect to art. 1 by securing to people in the United Kingdom the rights and freedoms of the Convention. It gives effect to art. 13 by establishing a scheme under which Convention rights can be raised before our domestic courts. To that end, remedies are provided in [s. 8]. If the concern is to ensure that the [Act] provides an exhaustive code of remedies for those whose Convention rights have been violated, we believe that [s. 8] already achieves that and that nothing further is needed.

We have set out in the [Act] a scheme to provide remedies for violation of Convention rights and we do not believe that it is necessary to add to it. We also believe that it is undesirable to provide for arts 1 and 13 in the [Act] in this way. The courts would be bound to ask themselves what was intended beyond the existing scheme of remedies set out in the [Act]. It might lead them to fashion remedies other than the [s. 8] remedies, which we regard as sufficient and clear. We believe that [s. 8] provides effective remedies before our courts. . . .

Lord Lester of Herne Hill: Is it the intention of the Government that the courts should not be entitled to have regard to art. 13 and the case law of the Strasbourg Court on that article in cases where it would otherwise be relevant? . . . Is it the intention of the Government that in cases where the European Court has said that the right provision is art. 13 and not art. 6 our courts should wear blinkers and are not allowed to look at art. 13 or the Court's case law?

The Lord Chancellor: One always has in mind *Pepper* v *Hart* when one is asked questions of that kind. I shall reply as candidly as I may. [Section 2(1)] provides:

> A court or tribunal determining a question which has arisen under this Act in connection with a Convention right must take into account any . . . judgment, decision, declaration or advisory opinion of the European Court of Human Rights.

That means what it says. The court must take into account such material. . . .

My response to the second part of the question posed by the noble Lord, Lord Lester, is that the courts may have regard to art. 13. In particular, they may wish to do so when considering the very ample provisions of [s. 8(1)].

. . . to incorporate expressly art. 13 may lead to the courts fashioning remedies about which we know nothing other than the [s. 8] remedies which we regard as sufficient and clear. Until we are told in some specific respect how [s. 8] is or may reasonably be anticipated to be deficient we maintain our present position.

House of Commons, Committee Stage
Hansard HC, 20 May 1998, col. 979
Secretary of State for the Home Department (Mr Jack Straw): We decided it was inappropriate to include art. 13, for the following reasons.

First and foremost, it is the Bill that gives effect to art. 13, so there was an issue of duplication. The Bill sets out clearly how the Convention rights will be given further effect in our domestic law, and what remedies are to be available when a court or tribunal finds that a person has been the victim of an unlawful act. . . . In our judgment, [the existing provisions of the Act] afford ample protection for individuals' rights under the Convention. In particular, [s. 8(1)] gives the courts considerable scope for doing justice when unlawful acts have been committed. Indeed, no one has been able to suggest any respect in which the [Act] is deficient in providing effective remedies to those who have been victims of an unlawful act. . . . If we were to include art. 13 in the Bill in addition to the remedies provided in [ss 3, 6, 7 and 8], the question would inevitably arise what the courts would make of the amendment, which, on the face of it, contains nothing new. I suggest that the amendment would either cause confusion or prompt the courts to act in ways not intended by the Bill—for example, by creating remedies beyond those available in s. 8. Whatever the outcome, the result would be undesirable. . . . [col. 981] The Convention has been international law for 50 years, and any tribunal will consider the bare text of any original Convention by considering the way in which its application has developed there is, indeed, a requirement to do so so, in practice, the courts must take account of the large body of Convention jurisprudence when considering remedies. Obviously, in doing so, they are bound to take judicial notice of art. 13, without specifically being bound by it.

That is my judgment about the way in which the law will work. I wish future Judicial Committees of the House of Lords luck in working through these debates. One sometimes wonders about the wisdom of the *Pepper* v *Hart* judgment in terms of the work that it has given the higher judiciary. It is a fine point, but since we saw that there was no purpose, and indeed that there were some dangers, in including art. 13, we thought that it was best omitted. . . . [col. 986] As far as I am concerned, we are indeed legislating by black-letter law on the face of the Bill. [col. 987] We could have a separate debate about the wisdom of the decision in *Pepper* v *Hart*: I know why the Judicial Committee made that decision and, to some extent, there is common sense in seeking to tease out the meaning of words where they are ambiguous, but I have always taken the view that what Parliament passes is not what Ministers say, but what is on the face of a Bill. That is of profound importance to the manner in which we make legislation.

Incorporation of arts. 1 and 2 of the Sixth Protocol

House of Lord, Report Stage
Hansard HL, 29 October 1998, col. 2084
Lord Williams of Mostyn: My Lords, I beg to move that the House do agree with the Commons in their Amendment [to add arts 1 and 2 of the Sixth Protocol to the list of Convention rights in sch. 1]. . . . that would make it impossible for Parliament to reintroduce the death penalty in future, except for acts committed in time of war or imminent threat of war, without denouncing the Convention itself. . . . [I]f those articles were added to the [Act], when we had not signed or ratified the sixth protocol, there would be a certain degree of lack of kilter with our international obligations. . . .

Amendment No. 54 inserts a new subsection into [s. 21—interpretation] which provides that any liability to the death penalty under the service discipline Acts is to be treated as a liability to life imprisonment or some lesser penalty. This general statement will be supplemented by detailed amendments to the service discipline Acts when the next legislation to consolidate those Acts is announced.

Amendment No. 55 provides that the new subsection inserted by Amendment No. 54

comes into force, when the Human Rights Bill receives Royal Assent. . . . that is consistent with our intention to proceed without delay to sign and ratify the sixth protocol.

Amendment No. 57 provides that the new subsection inserted by Amendment No. 54 has effect in any place in which the service discipline Acts have effect. This is needed because the Acts, unlike the Human Rights Bill, are not limited in their territorial extent to the United Kingdom. It is consistent with our intention, subject to their agreement, to extend the ratification of the sixth protocol to the Channel Islands and the Isle of Man.

SECTION 2. INTERPRETATION OF CONVENTION RIGHTS

House of Lords, Second Reading
Hansard HL, 3 November 1997, col. 1230
The Lord Chancellor (Lord Irvine of Lairg): . . . [Section 2] requires courts in the United Kingdom to take account of the decisions of the Convention institutions in Strasbourg in their consideration of Convention points which come before them. It is entirely appropriate that our courts should draw on the wealth of existing jurisprudence on the Convention.

House of Commons, Second Reading
Hansard HC, 16 February 1998, col. 780
The Secretary of State for the Home Department (Mr Jack Straw): . . . [Section 2] ensures that, in giving effect to those rights, our domestic courts and tribunals have regard to Strasbourg jurisprudence.

Amendment seeking to make decisions of the European Convention bodies
'binding' undesirable

House of Lords, Report Stage
Hansard HL, 19 January 1998, col. 1270
The Lord Chancellor (Lord Irvine of Lairg): As other noble Lords have said, the word 'binding' is the language of strict precedent but the Convention has no rule of precedent. . . . We take the view that the expression 'take in account' is clear enough. Should a United Kingdom court ever have a case before it which is a precise mirror of one that has been previously considered by the European Court of Human Rights, which I doubt, it may be appropriate for it to apply the European court's findings directly to that case; but in real life cases are rarely as neat and tidy as that. The courts will often be faced with cases that involve factors perhaps specific to the United Kingdom which distinguish them from cases considered by the European court. . . . [col. 1271] it is important that our courts have the scope to apply that discretion so as to aid in the development of human rights law.

There may also be occasions when it would be right for the United Kingdom courts to depart from Strasbourg decisions. We must remember that the interpretation of the Convention rights develops over the years. Circumstances may therefore arise in which a judgment given by the European Court of Human Rights decades ago contains pronouncements which it would not be appropriate to apply to the letter in the circumstances of today in a particular set of circumstances affecting this country. The [Act] would allow our courts to use their common sense in applying the European Court's judgment to such a case. We feel that to accept this amendment removes from the judges the flexibility and discretion that they require in developing human rights law. . . . [Section 2] requires the courts to pay heed to all the judgments of the European Court of Human Rights regardless of whether they have been given in cases involving the United Kingdom.

SECTION 3. LEGISLATION

House of Lords, Second Reading
Hansard HL, 3 November 1997, col. 1230
The Lord Chancellor (Lord Irvine of Lairg): . . . [Section 3] provides that legislation, whenever enacted, must as far as possible be read and given effect in a way which is compatible with the Convention rights. This will ensure that, if it is possible to interpret a statute in two ways—one compatible with the Convention and one not—the courts will always choose the interpretation which is compatible. In practice, this will prove a strong form of incorporation . . . however, the Bill does not allow the courts to set aside or ignore Acts of Parliament. [Section 3] preserves the effect of primary legislation which is [col. 1231] incompatible with the Convention. It does the same for secondary legislation where it is inevitably incompatible because of the terms of the parent statute. . . .

[col. 1294] The [Act] sets out a scheme for giving effect to the Convention rights which maximises the protection to individuals while retaining the fundamental principle of Parliamentary sovereignty. [Section 3] is the central part of this scheme. [Section 3(1)] requires legislation to be read and given effect to so far as it is possible to do so in a way that is compatible with the Convention rights. [Section 3(2)] provides that where it is not possible to give a compatible construction to primary legislation or to subordinate legislation whose incompatibility flows from the terms of the parent Act, that does not affect its validity, continuing operation or enforcement. This ensures that the courts are not empowered to strike down Acts of Parliament which they find to be incompatible with the Convention rights. Instead, [s. 4] together with [s. 10] introduces a new mechanism through which the courts can signal to the Government that a provision of legislation is, in their view, incompatible. It is then for government and Parliament to consider what action should be taken. I believe that this will prove to be an effective procedure and it is also one which accords with our traditions of Parliamentary sovereignty. That is why the [Act] adopts it.

House of Commons, Second Reading
Hansard HC, 16 February 1998, col. 780
The Secretary of State for the Home Department (Mr Jack Straw): . . . [Section 3] provides that legislation, whenever enacted, must as far as possible be read and given effect in such a way as to be compatible with Convention rights. We expect that, in almost all cases, the courts will be able to interpret legislation compatibly with the Convention. However, we need to provide for the rare cases where that cannot be done. Consistent with maintaining Parliamentary sovereignty, [section 3] therefore provides that if a provision of primary legislation cannot be interpreted compatibly with the Convention rights, that legislation will continue to have force and effect.

House of Commons, Committee Stage
Hansard HC, 3 June 1998, col. 421
The Secretary of State for the Home Department (Mr Jack Straw): . . . we want the courts to strive to find an interpretation of legislation that is consistent with Convention rights, so far

as the plain words of the [col. 422] legislation allow, and only in the last resort to conclude that the legislation is simply incompatible with them. . . . there was a time when all the courts could do to divine the intention of Parliament was to apply themselves to the words on the face of any Act. Now, following *Pepper* v *Hart*, they are able to look behind that and, not least, to look at the words used by Ministers. I do not think that courts will need to apply themselves to the words that I am about to use, but, for the avoidance of doubt, I will say that it is not our intention that the courts, in applying [s. 3], should contort the meaning of words to produce implausible or incredible meanings. I am talking about plain words in what is actually a clear [Act] with plain language—with the intention of Parliament set out in Hansard, should the courts wish to refer to it. . . . Ever since the *Wednesbury* decision, the courts have chided others for being unreasonable, so it is difficult to imagine them not being reasonable. If we had used just the word 'reasonable', we would have created a subjective test. 'Possible' is different. It means, [col. 423] 'What is the possible interpretation? Let us look at this set of words and the possible interpretations.'

SECTIONS 4 AND 5. DECLARATIONS OF INCOMPATIBILITY

House of Lords, Second Reading
Hansard HL, 3 November 1997, col. 1231
The Lord Chancellor (Lord Irvine of Lairg): . . . [Section 4] provides for the rare cases where the courts may have to make declarations of incompatibility. Such declarations are serious. That is why [s. 5] gives the Crown the right to have notice of any case where a court is considering making a declaration of incompatibility and the right to be joined as a party to the proceedings, so that it can make representations on the point.

A declaration of incompatibility will not itself change the law. The statute will continue to apply despite its incompatibility. But the declaration is very likely to prompt the Government and Parliament to respond.

House of Commons, Second Reading
Hansard HC, 16 February 1997, col. 780
The Secretary of State for the Home Department (Mr Jack Straw): . . . A declaration of incompatibility will not affect the continuing validity of the legislation in question. That would be contrary to the principle of the [Act]. However, it will be a clear signal to Government and Parliament that, in the court's view, a provision of legislation does not conform to the standards of the Convention. To return to a matter that I discussed earlier, it is likely that the Government and Parliament would wish to respond to such a situation and would do so rapidly. We have discussed how that would operate and no doubt there will be further detailed discussions in committee on the floor of the House.

House of Commons, Third Reading
Hansard HC, 21 October 1998, col. 1306
Jack Straw: . . . The right hon. and learned Gentleman asked me what would happen with the lower courts, and whether they would follow the judgment. No, they would not, because [s. 4(6)] is clear; a declaration does not affect the validity, continuing operation or enforcement of the provisions in respect of which it is given. There is absolute clarity there. In a judicial and political sense, the status quo ante would apply. Then, obviously, the Government would

have to consider, and in most cases they would consider the position pretty rapidly. No time limit is set down, but the reverse could not apply. We could not, for example, say that the declaration of incompatibility would have force unless or until the Government said the reverse. That would create considerable uncertainty.

SECTION 6. ACTS OF PUBLIC AUTHORITIES

House of Lords, Second Reading
Hansard HL, 16 November 1997, col. 1231
The Lord Chancellor (Lord Irvine of Lairg): . . . [Section 6] makes it unlawful for a public authority to act in a way which is incompatible with the Convention.

House of Commons, Second Reading
Hansard HC, 16 February 1998, col. 780
The Secondary of State for the Home Department (Mr Jack Straw): . . . [Section 6] makes it unlawful for public authorities to act in a way that is incompatible with a Convention right, unless they are required to do so to give effect to primary legislation.

House of Lords, Second Reading
Hansard HL, 16 November 1997, col. 1231
The Lord Chancellor (Lord Irvine of Lairg): . . . We decided . . . that a provision of this kind should apply only to public authorities, [col. 1231] however defined, and not to private individuals. . . . We also decided that we should apply the Bill to a wide rather than a narrow range of public authorities, so as to provide as much protection as possible to those who claim that their rights have been infringed.

[Section 6] is designed to apply not to obvious public authorities such as government departments and the police, but also to bodies which are public in certain respects but not others. Organisations of this kind will be liable under [s. 6] of the Bill for any of their acts, unless the act is of a private nature. Finally, [section 6] does not impose a liability on organisations which have no public functions at all.

House of Lords, Committee Stage
Hansard HL, 24 November 1997, col. 784
The Lord Chancellor: I want to tackle the concerns of the press directly. They are essentially twofold. First, will the courts develop a law of privacy, and, secondly, is the PCC itself to be regarded as a public authority which should act consistently with the convention? First, as I have often said, the judges are pen-poised regardless of incorporation of the convention to develop a right to privacy to be protected by the common law. This is not me saying so; they have said so. It must be emphasised that the judges are free to develop the common law in their own independent judicial sphere. What I say positively is that it will be a better law if the judges develop it after incorporation because they will have regard to arts 8 and 10, giving art. 10 its due high value. . . . [col. 785]

I would not agree with any proposition that the courts as pubic authorities will be obliged to fashion a law on privacy because of the terms of the Bill. That is simply not so. If it were so, whenever a law cannot be found either in the statute book or as a rule of common law to protect a convention right, the courts would in effect be obliged to legislation by way of judicial decision and to make one. That is not the true position. If it were—in my view, it is not—the courts would also have in effect to legislate where Parliament had acted, but incompatibly with the convention. Let us suppose that an Act of Parliament provides for detention on suspicion of drug trafficking but that the legislation goes too far and conflicts with art. 5. The court would so hold and would make a declaration of incompatibility. The scheme of the Bill is that Parliament may act to remedy a failure where the judges cannot.

In my opinion, the court is not obliged to remedy the failure by legislating via the common law either where a convention right is infringed by incompatible legislation or where, because of the absence of legislation—say, privacy legislation—a convention right is left unprotected. In my view, the courts may not act as legislators and grant new remedies for infringement of convention rights unless the common law itself enables them to develop new rights or remedies. I believe that the true view is that the courts will be able to adapt and develop the common law by relying on existing domestic principles in the laws of trespass, nuisance, copyright, confidence and the like, to fashion a common law right to privacy. . . . I repeat my view that any privacy law developed by the judges will be a better law after incorporation of the convention because the judges will have to balance and have regard to arts 10 and 8, giving art. 10 its due high value. What I have said is in accord with European jurisprudence.

I tend to believe that the important function of the PCC to adjudicate on complaints from the public about the press may well be held to be a function of a public nature, so that . . . the PCC might well be held to be a public authority under the Human Rights [Act]. [col. 796] . . . There are some bodies which are obviously public authorities such as the police, the courts, government departments and prisons. They are obviously public authorities under [s. 6(1)]. However, under [s. 6(3)(c)] the term 'public authority' includes, 'any person certain of whose functions are functions of a public nature'. . . . [One should] abstain from asking . . . the question: is this a public authority just looking at the body in the round? That is what [s. 6(1)] invites us to do. However, [s. 6(3)(c)] asks whether the body in question has certain functions—not all—which are functions of a public nature. If it has any functions of a public nature, it qualifies as a public authority. However, it is certain acts by public authorities which this Act makes unlawful. In [s. 6(5)] the [Act] provides: 'In relation to a particular act, a person is not a public authority by virtue only of subsection (3)(c) if the nature of the act is private'. Therefore Railtrack, as a public utility, obviously qualifies as a public authority because some of its functions, for example its functions in relation to safety on the railway, qualify it as a public authority. However, acts carried out in its capacity as a private property developer would no doubt be held by the courts to be of a private nature and therefore not caught by the [Act].

. . . we took a policy decision to avoid a list. . . . There are obvious public authorities—I have mentioned some—which are covered in relation to the whole of their functions by [s. 6(1)]. Then there are some bodies some of whose functions are public and some private. If there are some public functions the body qualifies as a public authority but not in respect of acts which are of a private nature. Those statutory principles will have to be applied case by case by the courts when issues arise.

What we have sought to do in [s. 6] is to set out a principle: first, that the effects of [ss. 6 to 8] should apply in the first place to bodies which are quite plainly public authorities such as government departments; and, secondly, to other bodies whose functions include functions of a public nature, and therefore the focus should be on their functions and not on their nature as an authority. In the latter case the provisions of the Bill would not apply to the private acts of the bodies in question. That is the principled approach that we have chosen.

House of Lords, Committee Stage
Hansard HL, 24 November 1997, col. 758
The Parliamentary Under-Secretary of State, Home Office (Lord Williams of Mostyn):
. . . 'public authority' is plainly defined in [s. 6]. . . . one will be dealing with two types of public authority—those which everyone would recognise as being plainly public authorities in the exercise of their functions, and those public authorities which are public authorities because, in part of their functions, they carry out what would be regarded as public functions. Examples vary, but I believe that the courts will have in mind changing social economic and cultural conditions when they come to consider particular decisions on particular aspects of a public authority.

. . . [Section 6(3)(c)] provides that a 'public authority' includes, 'any person certain of whose functions are of a public nature'. [Section 6(5)] provides that: 'In relation to a particular act, a person is not a public authority by virtue only of subsection (3)(c) if the nature of the act is private'. I believe that my noble and learned friend the Lord Chancellor gave an illustration on an earlier occasion. For example, Railtrack has statutory public powers and functions as the safety regulatory authority; but, equally, it may well carry out private transactions, such as the disposal of, the acquisition of, or the development of property.

If one follows the scheme through, we suggest that it is perfectly capable of being understood. The amendment would except from the prohibition in [col. 759] [s. 6(1)] a public authority falling within [s. 6(3)] in respect of its private acts. However, I venture to suggest to the Committee that that is already achieved, we say satisfactorily, by subsection (5). The other public authorities specified in [s. 6(3)] are courts and tribunals which, we think, are in a very similar position to obvious public authorities, such as government departments, in that all their acts are to be treated as being of such a public nature as to engage the convention.

House of Commons, Second Reading
Hansard HC, 16 February 1998, col. 775
The Secretary of State for the Home Department (Mr Jack Straw): . . . the media and the Churches . . . have concerns that centre on the provisions of [s. 6], relating to public authorities, so I must briefly explain the principles underlying that clause.

Under the convention, the Government are answerable in Strasbourg for any acts or omissions of the state about which an individual has a complaint under the convention. The Government have a direct responsibility for core bodies, such as central Government and the police, but they also have a responsibility for other public authorities, in so far as the actions of such authorities impinge on private individuals.

The Bill had to have a definition of a public authority that went at least as wide and took account of the fact that, over the past 20 years, an increasingly large number of private bodies, such as companies or charities, have come to exercise public functions that were previously exercised by public authorities. Under United Kingdom domestic common law, such bodies have increasingly been held to account under the processes of judicial review. . . . it was not practicable to list all the bodies to which the Bill's provisions should apply. Nor would it have been wise to do so. What was needed instead was a statement of principle to which the courts could give effect. [Section 6] therefore adopts a non-exhaustive definition of a public authority. Obvious public authorities, such as central government and the police, are caught in respect of everything they do. Public—but not private—acts of bodies that have a mix of public and private functions are also covered.

House of Commons, Second Reading
Hansard HC, 16 February 1998, col. 860
Sir Britain Mawhinney: Does a body that spends taxpayers' money, or fulfils a statutory function, or has Government appointees on its governing body constitute a public authority for the purposes of the Bill?
The Parliamentary Under-Secretary of State for the Home Department (Mr Mike O'Brien): That will be a matter for the courts, but it would appear to be likely to be so.

Definition of persons for s. 6(3)

House of Lords, Committee Stage
Hansard HL, 24 November 1997, col. 803
Lord Williams of Mostyn: . . . [Section 6(3)(c)] refers to 'any person'. . . . the term is well known as a term of art in our law. It is defined in the Interpretation Act 1978 and is relied upon throughout the statute book as including any person or body of persons corporate or unincorporate. I suggest that that is clearly wide enough to cover the natural or legal person to which the amendment refers.

Status of media bodies

House of Commons, Second Reading
Hansard HC, 16 December 1998, col. 778
Mr David Ruffley (Bury St Edmunds): In the context of arts 8 and 10, would the BBC and independent television companies be public authorities for the purposes of [s. 6]?
The Secretary of State for the Home Department (Mr Jack Straw): That is ultimately a matter for the courts, but our judgment is that the BBC will be regarded as a public authority under [s. 6]; independent television companies will not, but the Independent Television Commission will be.

Parliamentary sovereignty

House of Commons, Second Reading
Hansard HC, 16 February 1998, col. 773
The Secretary of State for the Home Department (Mr Jack Straw): The [Act] makes the position clear, in [s. 6(3)] and elsewhere. [Section 6] excludes the Houses of Parliament from the category of public authorities, for very good reasons. What the [Act] makes clear is that Parliament is supreme, and that if Parliament wishes to maintain the position enshrined in an Act that it has passed, but which is incompatible with the convention in the eyes of a British court, it is that Act which will remain in force.

There is, however, a separate question, which is why, in most instances, Parliament and Government will wish to recognise the force of a declaration of incompatibility by the High Court. Let us suppose that a case goes to Strasbourg, where the European Court decides that an action by the British Government, or the British Parliament, is outwith the convention. According to 50 years of practice on both sides, we always put the action right, and bring it into line with the convention. One of the questions that will always be before Government, in practice, will be, 'Is it sensible to wait for a further challenge to Strasbourg, when the British courts have declared the provision to be outwith the convention?'

House of Commons, Committee Stage
Hansard HC, 20 May 1998, col. 1018
The Secretary of State for the Home Department (Mr Jack Straw): There will be occasions—it is the nature of British society—on which various institutions that are private in terms of their legal personality carry out public functions. That includes the churches in the narrow circumstances that I have described. I would suggest that it also includes the Jockey Club. . . . The Jockey Club is a curious body; it is entirely private, but exercises public functions in some respects, and to those extents, but to no other, it would be regarded as falling within [s. 6].

SECTION 7. PROCEEDINGS

'Victims', standing and third party interventions

House of Lords, Second Reading
Hansard HL, 3 November 1997, col. 1232
The Lord Chancellor (Lord Irvine of Lairg): If people believe that their convention rights have been infringed by a public authority, what can they do about it? Under [s. 7] they will be able to rely on convention points in any legal proceedings involving a public authority; for example as part of a defence to criminal or civil proceedings, or when acting as plaintiff in civil proceedings, or in seeking judicial review, or on appeal. They will also be able to bring proceedings against public authorities purely on convention grounds even if no other cause of action is open to them.

House of Commons, Second Reading
Hansard HC, 16 February 1998, col. 780
The Secretary of State for the Home Department (Mr Jack Straw): . . . [Section 7] enables individuals who believe that they have been a victim of an unlawful act of a public authority to rely on the convention rights in legal proceedings. They may do so in a number of ways: by bringing proceedings under the [Act] in an appropriate court or tribunal; in seeking judicial review; as part of a defence against a criminal or civil action brought against them by a public authority; or in the case of an appeal. [Section 7] ensures that an individual will always have a means by which to raise his or her convention rights. It is intended that existing court procedures will, wherever possible, be used for that purpose.

House of Commons, Second Reading
Hansard HC, 16 February 1998, col. 856
The Parliamentary Under-Secretary of State for the Home Department (Mr Mike O'Brien): . . . My hon. Friend . . . asked us to consider allowing organisations that are not themselves victims to bring class actions and to anticipate issues. We considered doing that, but decided to follow the convention practice and enable victims of breaches to raise issues as they occur.

Effect of Section 7 rules on standing and third-party interventions

House of Lords, Second Reading
Hansard HL, 24 November 1997, col. 830
The Lord Chancellor (Lord Irvine of Lairg): The purposes of the [Act] is to give greater effect in our domestic law to the convention rights. It is in keeping with this approach that

persons should be able to rely [col. 831] on the convention rights before our domestic courts in precisely the same circumstances as they can rely upon them before the Strasbourg institutions. The wording of [s. 7] therefore reflects the terms of the convention, which stipulates that petitions to the European Commission (or to the European Court once the Eleventh Protocol comes into force) will be ruled inadmissible unless the applicant is the victim of the alleged violation.

I acknowledge that a consequence of that approach is that a narrower test will be applied for bringing applications by judicial review on convention grounds than will continue to apply in applications for judicial review on other grounds. But interest groups will still be able to provide assistance to victims who bring cases under the [Act] and to bring cases directly where they themselves are victims of an unlawful act.

I also point out that [s. 7], consistently with the position in Strasbourg, also treats as victims those who are faced with the threat of a public authority proposing to act in a way which would be unlawful under [s. 6(1)]. So potential victims are included. Interest groups will similarly be able to assist potential victims to bring challenges to action which is threatened before it is actually carried out.

Lord Goodhart: Can the noble and learned Lord and Lord Chancellor say what is the position of a public interest group which, having perfectly properly brought proceedings under [s. 11] of the [Act] on grounds [col. 832] which do not involve convention rights, then finds that in those same proceedings it is unable to raise issues of convention rights because of [s. 7]?

The Lord Chancellor: . . . I do not believe, for reasons I shall explain in a moment, that that consequence will follow.

. . . Essentially we believe the victim/potential victim test to be right. If there is unlawful action or if unlawful action is threatened, then there will be victims or potential victims who will complain and who will in practice be supported by interest groups. If there are no victims, the issue is probably academic and the courts should not be troubled.

We are right to mirror the law as Strasbourg applies it.

. . . in relation to third-party intervention. The European Court of Human Rights rules of procedure allow non-parties such as national and international non-governmental organisations to make written submissions in the form of a brief. There is no reason why any change to primary legislation in this [Act] is needed to allow the domestic courts to develop a similar practice in human rights cases, which is the answer to the noble Lord's question on how I would respond to the point that an interest group would have the right to be heard in a judicial review case under the English domestic test but that, if there was not a victim, could the individual interest group be heard on the convention point? So now . . . I address an answer to that question.

This is a development—that is to say, allowing third parties to intervene and be heard—which has already begun in the higher courts of this country in public law cases. Provisions as to standing are quite different. They determine who can become parties to the proceedings. The standing rule which the Bill proposes in relation to convention cases *simpliciter* is identical to that operated at Strasbourg; and why not? Is that not right in principle? It would not, however, prevent the acceptance by the courts in this country of non-governmental organisational briefs here any more than it does in Strasbourg.

Your Lordships' House, in its judicial capacity, has recently given leave for non-governmental organisations to intervene and file amicus briefs. It has done that in [col. 833] *R v Khan* for the benefit of Liberty and it has done that in *R v Secretary of State for the Home Department, ex parte Venables* for the benefit of Justice. So it appears to me . . . that the natural position to take is to adopt the victim test as applied by Strasbourg when complaint is made of a denial of convention rights, recognising that our courts will be ready to permit amicus written briefs from non-governmental organisations; that is to say briefs, but not to treat them as full parties. [col. 834] . . . [Section 7(1)(b)] does not touch a third party who has not *ex hypothesi* been the victim of the infringement of a convention right. It in no way precludes a third party from making submissions about the implication of convention rights in written briefs if a written brief is invited or accepted by the court, as I believe will happen.

As regards oral interventions by a third party, I dare say that the courts will be equally hospitable to oral interventions provided that they are brief.

. . . It is no part of the intention of this [Act] to alter the standing rules in relation to judicial review in either England or Scotland. It is part of the intention of this [Act] to import the Strasbourg victim test in relation to complaints based solely on denial of convention rights.

House of Commons, Committee Stage
Hansard HC, 20 May 1998, col. 1084
The Parliamentary Under-Secretary of State for the Home Department (Mr Mike O'Brien): . . . It is clear that [in s. 7(5)] we are appropriating the text of art. 34 and the jurisprudence that goes with it. The intention is that a victim under the [Art] should be in the same position as a victim in Strasbourg. A local [col. 1085] authority cannot be a victim under s. 7 because it cannot be a victim in Strasbourg under current Strasbourg jurisprudence. . . . On the definition, the convention provides that

> The Commission may receive petitions . . . from any person, non-governmental organisation or group of individuals claiming to be a victim of a violation by one of the High Contracting Parties of the rights set forth in this Convention.

Applying the victim requirement, the basic approach of the Commission and the Court has been to require that the applicant must claim to be directly affected in some way by the matter complained of. In some cases, they have interpreted fairly flexibly the requirement for the applicant to be directly affected, although the jurisprudence on the issue is not always entirely consistent. . . . Applications have been allowed not only by the person immediately affected—sometimes referred to as the direct victim—but by indirect victims. Where there has been an alleged violation of the right to life and the direct victim is dead, for example, close relatives of the deceased can be treated as victims on the basis that they were indirectly affected by the alleged violation. . . . Obviously, [family members] can be victims in appropriate circumstances. For example, a decision to deport someone might allow the family of the person to claim to be a victim of a violation of article 8—the right to respect for family life. . . . I can confirm that we have no intention of restricting guardians *ad litem* or [col. 1086] others who could normally undertake cases from doing so. Likewise, a case can be brought on behalf of a dead victim by his or her family or relatives. The best known case, of which we have all heard, is the 'Death on the Rock' case, brought on behalf of a dead IRA terrorist shot in Gibraltar. That is the sort of area that we are considering. A person may be able to claim that he or she is directly affected as a consequence of a violation of the rights of someone else. Where complaints are brought by persons threatened by deportation, that may arise.

. . . Interest groups, such as professional associations and NGOs, can bring an application in Strasbourg only if they can demonstrate that they themselves are victims of a breach—that is, that they are in some way affected by the measure complained of. It is not enough that the actual victim, whether a member of the organisation or not, consents to them acting on his behalf. In *B* v *United Kingdom*, both Mrs B and the Society for the Protection of the Unborn Child brought an application complaining of the way in which the law affected electoral expenses. The Commission ruled the application by SPUC inadmissible because it was not directly affected by the law—only Mrs B had been prosecuted. On the other hand, in *Council of Civil Service Unions* v *United Kingdom*, the Commission accepted that the CCSU was itself a victim of the GCHQ ban and could therefore bring an application, although it was rejected on different grounds. An NGO may represent its members in certain contexts and, in that case, it needs to identify them and produce the evidence of authority. In such circumstances, the NGO does not, however, thereby become a party itself.

Our courts will develop their own jurisprudence on the issue, taking account of Strasbourg cases and the Strasbourg jurisprudence. As a Government, our aim is to grant access to victims.

House of Commons, Committee Stage
Hansard HC, 24 June 1998, col. 1083

The Parliamentary Under-Secretary of State for the Home Department (Mr Mike O'Brien): ... The purposes of the [Act] is to give effect in our domestic law to the Convention rights. It is in keeping with that approach that people should be able to rely on those rights before our courts in the same circumstances as they can rely on them before the Strasbourg institutions. [Section 7] accordingly seeks to mirror the approach taken by Strasbourg—reliance on the Convention rights is restricted to victims or potential victims of unlawful acts and the definition of a victim for this purpose is tied to art. 34 of the Convention as amended by the 11th protocol. . . .

I acknowledge that, as a consequence, a narrower test will be applied for bringing applications by judicial review on Convention grounds than in applications for judicial review on other grounds. However, interest groups will still be able to provide assistance to victims who bring cases under the Bill, including the filing of amicus briefs. Interest groups will also be able to bring cases directly where they are victims of an unlawful act.

I do not believe that the different tests for Convention and non-Convention cases will cause undue difficulty for the courts, or prevent interest groups from helping individuals who are victims of unlawful acts.

. . . the [Act] does not prevent interest groups from providing assistance to a victim once a case is brought.

, *Limitation periods*

(Section 7(5) of the Act was added by amendment during the House of Commons committee stage.)

House of Commons, Committee Stage
Hansard HC, 20 May 1998, col. 1094

The Parliamentary Under-Secretary of State for the Home Department (Mr Mike O'Brien): ... proceedings brought on Convention grounds alone and not under any pre-existing cause of action . . . should be no different from other civil proceedings in having a limitation period. . . . our amendment relates only to proceedings under [s. 7(1)(a)]. If a plaintiff proceeded under [s. 7(1)(b)]—that is to say, he brought proceedings under an existing cause of action and relied on his Convention rights as an additional argument in support of his case—the limitation period would be the one that applies in the normal way to the existing cause of action.

The Government amendment provides that proceedings under [s. 7(1)(a)] must be brought within one year, beginning with the date on which the act complained of took place, or within such longer period as the court or tribunal considers equitable, having regard to all the circumstances. However, that time limit is subject to any stricter time limit in relation to the procedure in question. The most obvious such case is judicial review. Assuming that the new rules of court that will be needed for the [Act] provide that a procedure analogous to judicial review may [col. 1095] be used for cases under [s. 7(1)(a)], it is reasonable that the time limit for that procedure—which is three months—should continue to apply. It would not be right for applicants who choose to bring their claims by way of judicial review to benefit from the longer 12-month period proposed for claims under the [Act]. . . . There is no off-the-shelf answer to the question of how long the limitation period for claims under [s. 7(1)(a)] should be. What we have tried to do in our amendment is to strike a balance between the legitimate needs of the plaintiff and the legitimate needs of the defendant, which is what all limitation periods should do. . . . We believe that the right balance is provided by a 12-month period, with a power to extend it for the benefit of the complainant. . . . We recognise . . . that there may be circumstances where a rigid one-year cut-off could lead to injustice. [Section 7(5)] does not therefore seek to provide a rigid limit, but enables a court to extend the period where it is appropriate to do so. There will be cases in which an individual has a good reason for delay. In judicial review cases, for example, the courts have extended time where the applicant has been seeking redress by other proper means, such as by pursuing internal grievance procedures, or where he has had to apply for legal aid. I have no doubt that the courts will continue to exercise their discretion so as to prevent prejudice to one party or the other where an application is made to extend time. . . . We do not wish to narrow the range of circumstances which might influence the court. . . . [col. 1097] It is not our intention to create a vast array of novel features that would allow litigants to pursue cases in courts in a way that the courts and Parliament had not intended. However, someone with a genuine human rights grievance will be entitled to pursue it under [s. 7(1)(a)], whether or not he is within the time limit for judicial review. We accept that that should be so. The . . . one-year time limit for [s. 7(1)(a)] [is] so that the courts have time to make a judgment. We have not sought to constrain that time too much because [s. 7(5)(b)] allows the courts to decide when they wish to go beyond the 12-month period, should it be equitable to do so.

We are conscious that it is important that the person is allowed to pursue any action under [s. 7(1)(a)]. We do not want to create an artificial time limit of three months . . . without giving the level of flexibility that is needed [which] would tie the procedure too tightly to the judicial review procedure. The courts will develop their own jurisprudence on this issue, over time.

SECTION 8. REMEDIES

House of Lords, Second Reading
Hansard HL, 3 November 1997, col. 1232
The Lord Chancellor (Lord Irvine of Lairg): . . . If a court or tribunal finds that a public authority has acted in a way which is incompatible with the Convention . . . [u]nder [s. 8] it may provide whatever remedy is available to it and which seems just and appropriate. That might include awarding damages against the public authority.

House of Lords, Committee Stage

Hansard HL, 24 November 1997, col. 844

The Lord Chancellor: [Section 8] provides the courts and tribunals with wide powers to grant such relief or remedy which they consider just and appropriate where they find that a public authority has acted unlawfully by virtue of [s. 6(1)] of the [Act]. [Section 8(2) and (3)] . . . [is] a comprehensive and comprehensible code. However, it is necessary to put down certain limits on what remedies a court or tribunal can provide. Subsection (2) . . . provides one such restriction. . . . [quoted] . . . Quite clearly, this means that a criminal court will not be able to award damages for a Convention breach, even if it currently has the power to make a compensation order unless it also has the power to award damages in civil proceedings. . . .

[col. 855] So as to make the intention plain, it is not the [Act's] aim that, for example, the Crown Court should be able to make an award of damages where it finds, during the course of a trial, that a violation of a person's Convention rights has occurred. We believe that it is appropriate for an individual who considers that his rights have been infringed in such a case to pursue any matter of damages through the civil courts where this type of issue is normally dealt with; in other words, to pursue the matter in the courts that are accustomed to determining whether it is necessary and appropriate to award damages and what the proper amount should be. For that reason, we regard the inclusion of subsection (2) as an entirely proper part of the scheme.

We say that the Crown Court, in cases of crime, should not award damages. The remedy that the defendant wants in a criminal court is not to be convicted. We see very considerable practical difficulties about giving a new power to award damages to a criminal court in Convention cases. It would seem to me to open up the need for representation in the Crown Court to any person who it might appear in the course of criminal proceedings might be at risk of damages. We believe that that would be potentially disruptive of a criminal trial. Similarly, a magistrates' court is a criminal court. . . . We believe that it is appropriate that the civil courts, which traditionally make awards of damages, should, alone, be enabled to make awards of damages in these Convention cases.

House of Lords, Committee Stage

Hansard HL, 18 November 1997, col. 479

The Lord Chancellor (Lord Irvine of Lairg): . . . I cannot conceive of any state of affairs in which an English court, having held an Act to be unlawful because of its infringement of a Convention right, would under [s. 8(1)], be disabled from giving an effective remedy. I believe that the English law is rich in remedies and I cannot conceive of a case in which English law under [s. 8(1)] would be unable to provide an effective remedy.

However, during the earlier course of the debate I did not say that art. 13 was incorporated. The debate is about the fact that it is not incorporated. . . . in my view the English courts . . . would be able to have regard to art. 13.

House of Lords, Report Stage

Hansard HL, 19 January 1998, col. 1266

The Lord Chancellor (Lord Irvine of Lairg): My Lords, I have not the least idea what the remedies the courts might develop outside [s. 8] could be if art. 13 was included. . . . [Section 8(1)] is of the widest amplitude. No one is [col. 1267] contending that it will not do the job. When we have challenged the proponents of the amendment on a number of occasions in Committee to say how [s. 8] might not do the job, they have been unable to offer a single example. Therefore, the argument is all one way. What we have done is sufficient.

House of Commons, Second Reading
Hansard HC, 16 February 1998, col. 780
The Secretary of State for the Home Department (Mr Jack Straw): . . . [Section] 8 deals with remedies. . . . If a court or tribunal finds that a public authority has acted unlawfully, it may grant whatever remedy is available to it that it considers just and appropriate.

House of Common, Committee Stage
Hansard HC, 20 May 1998, col. 979
Mr Garnier: Will the right hon. Gentleman give one or two examples of the remedies he envisages [under art. 13] that would go beyond those set out in [s. 8]?
The Secretary of State for the Home Department (Mr Jack Straw): In considering article 13, the courts could decide to grant damages in more circumstances than we had envisaged. We had to consider that matter carefully, because of the effect on the public purse. . . . We had to think carefully about the scope of the remedies that we should provide.

House of Commons, Committee Stage
Hansard HC, 24 June 1998, col. 1113
The Parliamentary Under-Secretary of State for the Home Department (Mr Mike O'Brien): . . . The Civil Liability (Contribution) Art 1978 provides a right to contribution when more than one person is liable for the same damage. We see no reason why that standard provision should not apply when damages are awarded against a public authority under [s. 8] of the [Act]. . . . the terms of the 1978 Act . . . apply to the award of such damages. . . .
   [col. 1114] the requirement to take into account the principles applied in Strasbourg . . . allows the court to have regard to the conduct of the applicant.

SECTION 10. REMEDIAL ORDERS

(In the original Bill, the provisions which were eventually enacted as s. 10 and sch. 2 were set out as clauses 10, 11 and 12. The circumstances in which a remedial order could be made was also amended during the passage of the Bill, so that this may now be done only in 'compelling' circumstances. Because of these substantial changes, references in relation to this section have been retained as references to clauses of the Bill except where referring to language which was adopted as part of the final section, where references have been given to the final provision.)

House of Lords, Second Reading
Hansard HL, 3 November 1997, col. 1231
The Lord Chancellor (Lord Irvine of Lairg): . . . if legislation has been declared incompatible, a prompt Parliamentary remedy should be available. Clauses 10 to 12 of the Bill provide how that is to be achieved. A Minister of the Crown will be able to make what is to be known as a remedial order. The order will be available in response to a declaration of incompatibility by the higher courts. It will also be available if legislation appears to a Minister to be incompatible because of a finding by the European Court of Human Rights.
   We recognise that a power to amend primary legislation by means of a statutory instrument is not a power to be conferred or exercised lightly. Those clauses therefore place a number of procedural and other restrictions on its use. First, a remedial order must be

approved by both Houses of Parliament. That will normally require it to be laid in draft and subject to the affirmative resolution procedure before it takes effect. In urgent cases, it will be possible to make the order without it being approved in that way, but even then it will cease to have effect after 40 days unless it is approved by Parliament. So we have built in as much Parliamentary scrutiny as possible.

In addition, the power to make a remedial order may be used only to remove an incompatibility or a possible incompatibility between legislation and the Convention. It may therefore be used only to protect human rights, not to infringe them. And the Bill also specifically provides that no person is to be guilty of a criminal offence solely as a result of any retrospective effect of a remedial order.

House of Commons, Second Reading
Hansard HC, 16 February 1998, col. 773
The Secretary of State for the Home Department (Mr Jack Straw): . . . occasions on which the courts will declare an Act of this Parliament to be incompatible are rare; there will be very few such cases. Secondly, the purposes of remedial action is to try to resolve the current paralysis, which is to nobody's advantage. It is not to take away anyone's rights; it is to confer rights.

Rationale behind and intended effect of s. 10(1)(a)

House of Lords, Report Stage
Hansard HL, 29 January 1998, col. 393
Lord Williams of Mostyn: . . . Amendments Nos. 41—[the words after 'right' in s. 10(1)(a)] and 42 [which inserted the words after 'rights' in s. 10(1)(b)] place limits on the power of a Minister to make a remedial order under Clause 10 following a declaration of Convention incompatibility by a court. Both are specific responses to concerns expressed by your Lordships in Committee. . . .

House of Commons, Committee Stage
Hansard HC, 20 June 1998, col. 42
The Secretary of State for the Home Department (Mr Jack Straw): . . . [O]our intention is not that the procedure under clause 10 should be used to by-pass the will of the House, but simply to deal with practical problems that may arise. . . . Even on the most dismal interpretation of clause 10, the will of the House still prevails. It may be a truncated procedure, but it certainly does not give the courts the power to say what the law of the land should be . . .

Meaning of 'compelling' in s. 10(2)

House of Commons, Committee Stage
Hansard HC, 24 June 1998, col. 1140
The Secretary of State for the Home Department (Mr Jack Straw): I am answering ad lib and without the benefit of a legal dictionary, but the situation that I described in the Chahal case, where the liberty of a subject would be adversely affected by a delay in producing primary legislation, was a compelling case. I am not certain that it would be an exceptional case, because one could ask, 'To what is it exceptional?' but it would certainly be a compelling case. Frankly, only in that situation would remedial orders be necessary and appropriate.

House of Commons, Third Reading
Hansard HC, 21 October 1998, col. 1300
The Secretary of State for the Home Department (Mr Jack Straw): The Government thought—there was no great argument about the manner, but it was important that we should deal with all the arguments—that it was important to enshrine Parliament's sovereignty in the Bill. We therefore developed the scheme of declarations of incompatibility. We did not propose that the Judicial Committee of the House of Lords should have the power to override Acts of Parliament by stating that, because they were incompatible with the Convention, they were unenforceable and of no effect.

[col. 1301] We said that the Judicial Committee of the House of Lords would be able to declare whether, in its opinion, an Act of Parliament was incompatible with the Convention, and subsequently to refer the matter back to the Government, which is answerable to Parliament. In the overwhelming majority of cases, regardless of which party was in government. I think that Ministers would examine the matter and say, 'A declaration of incompatibility has been made, and we shall have to accept it. We shall therefore have to remedy the defeat in the law spotted by the Judicial Committee of the House of Lords.' Therefore—as has been discussed in previous debates, and will be discussed again today—we have included in the Bill procedures for remedial orders. It is also always open to Ministers to introduce amending legislation in the normal way.

It is possible that the Judicial Committee of the House of Lords could make a declaration that, subsequently, Ministers propose, and Parliament accepts, should not be accepted. . . . the issue of abortion . . . provides a good example. . . .

Mr Mike O'Brien: [col. 1330] The requirement for compelling reasons in [s. 10(2)] is itself a response to concern expressed here and in another place about the remedial order provisions. It is there to make it absolutely clear that a remedial order is not a routine response in preference to fresh primary legislation. We would not want to go further . . . and limit 'compelling reasons' to [likely jeopardy to national security, public health or the liberty of the individual]. There may be other circumstances that constitute compelling reasons sufficient to justify a remedial order: for example, a decision of the higher courts in relation to basic provisions of criminal procedure affecting the way in which, perhaps, all criminal cases must be handled. An example is a provision that might invalidate a crucial part of the codes of practice under the Police and Criminal Evidence Act 1984, or provisions relating to the detention of suspects. Therefore, there are a number of issues where we would want to proceed with care. We also might need to respond very quickly simply to avoid the criminal justice system in such cases either collapsing or not being able to deliver justice and proper convictions.

'Compelling' is a strong word. We see no need to define it by reference to particular categories. In both the outstanding cases . . . put to me, our view is likely to be that those would not create the compelling reasons that would justify a remedial order In any event, on those issues—electoral law and chastising children—everyone would expect primary legislation rather than a remedial order. . . .

[col. 1331] It would be open to the Government to take no action in response to a declaration of incompatibility . . . but, where a declaration is made, a Government who are committed to promoting human rights, as we are, will want to do something about the law in question. It is possible for primary legislation to be introduced and passed quickly, but the pressures on the timetable can make it very difficult to find a slot.

The power to make a remedial order is there for cases where there is a very good reason to amend the law following a declaration of incompatibility or a finding by the Strasbourg court, but no suitable legislative vehicle is available. Where a remedial order is made or proposed, we accepted that the procedures for Parliamentary scrutiny needed to be strengthened. That is why the requirement to provide a document containing all the relevant information and a statement providing a summary of any representations on an order or draft order was added to [sch. 2] in Committee.

Mr Straw: [col. 1357] Three sets of changes have been made as a result of concerns expressed. . . . The first concerns remedial orders. We continue to believe that it should be possible to amend Acts of Parliament by a remedial order so as to bring them into line with the Convention rights, but we have . . . considerably restricted the circumstances in which they can be made, and we have significantly enhanced the Parliamentary opportunities for scrutiny of those orders.

[col. 1358] We have explained that any response to a declaration of incompatibility by the courts, whether by fresh primary legislation or by a remedial order, is a matter on which the Government will propose, but it is for Parliament to dispose. One of the [Act's] many strengths is that it promotes human rights while maintaining the sovereignty of Parliament and the separation of powers which underpins our constitutional arrangements.

SECTION 11. SAVING FOR EXISTING HUMAN RIGHTS PROTECTION

House of Lords, Report Stage
Hansard HL, 29 January 1998, col. 410
Lord Williams of Mostyn: . . . [Section 11] is simply to provide a saving for other human rights. It is there to ensure that if a person has existing rights, nothing in this [Act] shall detract from them in any way. . . . [col. 411] There are, of course, two kinds of relationship created in the [Act] between Convention and domestic law: the interpretive principle in [ss. 3 to 5], and the right to reply on Convention rights against a public authority in [ss. 6 to 9]. We do not wish to have any misunderstanding.

House of Commons, Second Reading
Hansard HC, 16 February 1998, col. 738
The Secretary of State for the Home Department (Mr Jack Straw): . . . [Section 11] confirms that a person's reliance on a Convention right does not restrict any other right or freedom that he enjoys under United Kingdom law.

SECTION 12. THE PRESS

[The provision enacted as s. 12 was introduced as new clause 13 in committee in the House of Commons on 2 July 1998, by Jack Straw.]

When restrictions on press freedom permissible

House of Commons, Committee Stage
Hansard HC, 2 July 1998, col. 535
The Secretary of State for the Home Department (Mr Jack Straw): . . . Subsection (1) provides for the new clause to apply in any case where a court is considering granting relief—

for example, an injunction restraining a threatened breach of confidence; but it could be any relief apart from that [col. 536] relating to criminal proceedings—which might affect the exercise of the art. 10 right to freedom of expression. It applies to the press, broadcasters or anyone whose right to freedom of expression might be affected. It is not limited to cases to which a public authority is a party. We have taken the opportunity to enhance press freedom in a wider way than would arise simply from the incorporation of the Convention into our domestic law.

Subsection (2) provides that no relief is to be granted if the person against whom it is sought—the respondent—is not present or represented, unless the applicant has taken all practicable steps to notify the respondent or there are compelling reasons why the respondent should not be notified. The courts are well able to deal with the first limb of that exception relating to whether all practical steps have been taken to notify the respondent, and in the case of broadcasting authorities and the press, rarely would an applicant not be able to serve notice of the proceedings on the respondent.

The latter circumstance—compelling reasons—might arise in a case raising issues of national security where the mere knowledge that an injunction was being sought might cause the respondent to publish the material immediately. We do not anticipate that that limb would be used often. In the past, such applications have been rare, but there has been at least one recent case involving the Ministry of Defence.

. . . the provision is intended overall to ensure that *ex parte* injunctions are granted only in exceptional circumstances. Even where both parties are represented, we expect that injunctions will continue to be rare, as they are at present.

. . . we believe that the courts should consider the merits of an application when it is made and should not grant an interim injunction simply to preserve the status quo ante between the parties.

[col. 537] . . . we believe that the new clause would protect a respondent potential publisher from what amounts to legal or legalised intimidation. We have already discussed the difficulty of getting interlocutory relief. It will be very difficult to get it unless the applicant can satisfy the court that the applicant is likely to establish that publication should not be allowed. That is a much higher test than that there should simply be a prima facie case to get the matter into court . . .

[I was asked about a case where] a respondent who succeeded in preventing an injunction at the interlocutory stage and then published but it turned [col. 538] out that there had been some breach of the law. [I was] asked whether that could be weighed in the balance in respect of damages. . . .

Subsection (4) requires the court to have particular regard to the importance of the art. 10 right to freedom of expression. Where the proceedings concern journalistic, literary or artistic material, the court must also have particular regard to the extent to which the material has or is about to become available to the public—in other words, a question of prior publication—and the extent to which publication would be in the public interest. If the court and the parties to the proceedings know that a story will shortly be published anyway, for example, in another country or on the Internet, that must affect the decision whether it is appropriate to restrain publication by the print or broadcast media in this country.

Under subsection (4), the court must also have particular regard to any relevant privacy code. Depending on the circumstances, that could be the newspaper industry code of practice operated by the Press Complaints Commission, the Broadcasting Standards Commission code, the Independent Television Commission code, or a broadcaster's internal code such as that operated by the BBC. The fact that a newspaper has complied with the terms of the code operated by the [col. 539] PCC—or conversely, that it has breached the code—is one of the factors that we believe the courts should take into account in considering whether to grant relief.

Definition of public interest

House of Commons, Second Reading
Hansard HC, 2 July 1998, col. 539
The Secretary of State for the Home Department (Mr Jack Straw): . . . The courts are well versed in making judgments about the balance between a private interest of an applicant before them and the wider public interest. That is inherent in any case in a clash between art. 10 and art. 8. It is also inherent in the way in which the courts until now have dealt with many issues surrounding proceedings for defamation. The European Commission and the European Court of Human Rights have devoted quite a lot of time and effort to developing the concept of the public interest. Without being too tautologous, one of the points of the public interest is, to quote the words of the Strasbourg court in *Handyside* v *United Kingdom* in 1976, that 'freedom of expression constitutes one of the essential foundations of a democratic society, one of the basic conditions for its progress, and for the development of every man'—and these days, I have no doubt, every woman. That is a brief sketch of a subject on which I have every confidence in the courts' ability to make good judgments in particular cases. . . .

[col. 540] There is no direct qualification to the word 'public' in the new clause. Ultimately, it would be a matter for the courts to decide, based on common sense and proportionality. The fact that the information was available across the globe in very narrow circumstances would be weighed in the balance. . . . The courts would be bound to take such facts into account. . . . they would also take into account the extent to which the information was available in another country or on the Internet, but in each case, the courts would have to apply balance and proportionality.

House of Commons, Committee Stage
Hansard HC, 2 July 1998, col. 562
The Parliamentary Under-Secretary of State for the Home Department (Mr Mike O'Brien): . . . I am perhaps tempting further interventions by going into the issue of what the public interest is, but the basic question is whether the public should have particular information. For example, information might have an effect on proper political discourse, or a matter of public policy. It might also affect individual behaviour. For example, information about BSE might have affected decisions on whether to eat beef. Those are areas in which there is a proper public interest in the press revealing information. The judge would have to ask the same question put by the hon. and learned Member for Harborough: is a matter only of interest to the public, or is it a matter of public interest? There should be some good reason why the public should know. [col. 563] It is arguable whether there should be a good reason for the public not to know something. That takes us into realms of philosophy and jurisprudence, and I do not want to go too far into them. However, judges will debate that matter among themselves as they reach their decisions.

Intended effect of subsection (3)

House of Commons, Committee Stage
Hansard HC, 2 July 1998, col. 562
The Parliamentary Under-Secretary of State for the Home Department (Mr Mike O'Brien): . . . We suggest . . . that the law on granting injunctions is flexible in privacy cases, and we are tightening it to ensure that the applicant will in all cases need to establish a stronger case.

Subsection (4): 'conduct connected with such material'

House of Commons, Committee Stage
Hansard HC, 2 July 1998, col. 540
The Secretary of State for the Home Department (Mr Jack Straw): . . . The reference in the new clause to 'conduct connected with such material' is intended for cases where journalistic inquiries suggest the presence of a story, but no actual material yet exists—perhaps because the story has not yet been written.

Subsection (5)

House of Commons, Committee Stage
Hansard HC, 2 July 1998, col. 540
The Secretary of State for the Home Department (Mr Jack Straw): . . . Subsection (5) provides that references to a court include references to a tribunal, and that references to relief include references to any remedy or order, other than in criminal proceedings. We drafted the amendment with civil, rather than criminal, proceedings against the media in mind. Without such an exclusion, judges wanting to impose reporting restrictions in a criminal trial would, for example, have to consider any relevant privacy code, although plainly it would not be appropriate in that context.

Nevertheless, as public authorities, the criminal courts will of course, in the same way as other courts, be required not to act in a way that is incompatible with arts. 8 and 10 and other Convention rights. The special provision that we are making in [s. 12] does not therefore exempt criminal courts from the general obligations imposed by other provisions of the Bill. However, had we included criminal proceedings under [s. 12], we would have made the running of criminal trials very complicated.

SECTION 13. THE CHURCHES

(The provision enacted as s. 13 was introduced as new clause 9 in committee in the House of Commons on 20 May 1998 by Jack Straw.)

House of Commons, Committee Stage
Hansard HC, 20 May 1998, col. 1020
The Secretary of State for the Home Department (Mr Jack Straw): . . . [Section 13] would come into play in any case in which a court's determination of any question arising out

of the [Act] might affect the exercise by a religious organisation of the Convention right of freedom of thought, conscience and religion. In such a case, it provides for the court to have particular regard—not [col. 1021] just to have regard, going back to the earlier debate, but to have particular regard—to the importance of that right. Its purpose is not to exempt Churches and other religious organisations from the scope of the [Act]—they have not sought that—any more than from that of the Convention. It is to reassure them against the [Act] being used to intrude upon genuinely religious beliefs or practices based on their beliefs. I emphasise the word 'practices', as well as 'beliefs'.

There is ample reassurance available on this point from Convention jurisprudence. Apart from stating the importance of the courts having due regard to art. 9, [s. 13] is designed to bring out the point that art. 9 rights attach not only to individuals but to the Churches. The idea that Convention rights typically attach only to individuals and not the Churches caused considerable anxiety. I understood that, and that is why the new clause has been phrased so that the Churches have its protection as well as individuals.

There is Convention jurisprudence to the effect that a Church body or other association with religious objectives is capable of possessing and exercising the rights in art. 9 as a representative of its members. [Section 13] will emphasise that point to our courts. The intention is to focus the courts' attention in any proceedings on the view generally held by the Church in question, and on its interest in protecting the integrity of the common faith of its members against attack, whether by outsiders or by individual dissidents. That is a significant protection.

. . . [Section 13] refers to the exercise of the right to freedom of thought, conscience and religion by a 'religious organisation', but leaves that expression undefined . . . [the reason is] partly that no definition is readily available, at home or in Strasbourg.

We considered the issue with great care, and took the advice of Parliamentary counsel. I have already referred to the difficulty arising from this point in the amendments made in another place in discriminating between some religions and others. We are seeking to reflect precisely the Strasbourg case law. The Convention institutions have not offered a definition, but we are confident that the term 'religious organisation' is recognisable in terms of the Convention. . . .

The key concept that we are talking about is organisations with religious objectives.

[col. 1022] . . . [s. 13] is flexible enough to cover cases involving religious charities where Church issues form a backdrop to the case. . . . it applies to a court's determination of any question arising under the Human Rights [Act] that might affect the exercise by a religious organisation of the rights guaranteed by art. 9. It is therefore not tied to circumstances in which a religious organisation is directly involved, as a body, in the court proceedings.

If a case is brought against a charity, and the charity can show that what it is doing is to maintain and practise the religious beliefs which it shares with its parent Church, we consider that [s. 13] would come into play so as to ensure that due consideration was given to those beliefs. . . .

[col. 1023] Nothing in the [Act] applies to any organisation unless the organisation is a public body—charities are not of themselves public bodies. . . . Provided the employment practices of a charity came within the general law—nothing to do with the Convention—[the Act] would have no effect.

SECTION 19. STATEMENTS OF COMPATIBILITY

Statements of compatibility

House of Lords, Second Reading
Hansard HL, 3 November 1997, col. 1233
The Lord Chancellor (Lord Irvine of Lairg): . . . [Section 19] imposes a new requirement on government Ministers when introducing legislation. In future, they will have to make a statement either that the provisions of the legislation are compatible with the Convention or that they cannot make such a statement but nevertheless wish Parliament to proceed to consider the Bill.

Ministers will obviously want to make a positive statement whenever possible. That requirement should therefore have a significant impact on the scrutiny of draft legislation with government. Where such a statement cannot be made, Parliamentary scrutiny of the Bill would be intense.

House of Lords, Second Reading
Hansard HL, 27 November 1997, col. 1228
Lord Williams of Mostyn: The design of the Bill is to give the courts as much space as possible to protect human rights, short of a power to set aside or ignore Acts of Parliament. In the very rare cases where the higher courts will find it impossible to read and give effect to any statute in a way which is compatible with Convention rights, they [col. 1229] will be able to make a declaration of incompatibility. Then it is for Parliament to decide whether there should be remedial legislation. Parliament may, not must, and generally will, legislate. If a Minister's prior assessment of compatibility (under [s. 19]) is subsequently found by declaration of incompatibility by the courts to have been mistaken, it is hard to see how a Minister could withhold remedial action.

House of Commons, Second Reading
Hansard HC, 16 February 1998, col. 780
The Secretary of State for the Home Department (Mr Jack Straw): . . . [Section 19] is a further demonstration of our determination to improve compliance with Convention rights. It places a requirement on a Minister to publish a statement in relation to any Bill that he or she introduces. The statement will either be that the provisions of the legislation are compatible with Convention rights or that he or she cannot make such a statement, but that the Government nevertheless wish to proceed with the Bill.

I am sure that Ministers will want to make a positive statement whenever possible. The requirement to make a statement will have a significant impact on the scrutiny of draft legislation within Government and by Parliament. In my judgment, it will greatly assist Parliament's consideration of Bills by highlighting the potential implications for human rights.

COMMENT ON THE MARGIN OF APPRECIATION

House of Commons, Committee Stage
Hansard HC, 3 June 1998, col. 424
The Secretary of State for the Home Department (Mr Jack Straw): . . . [Section 8] would require the courts, in considering whether legislation was compatible with Convention rights,

to have full regard to the margin of appreciation accorded to states by Strasbourg institutions. Presumably, that is intended to signal to the courts that they should recognise the primary responsibility of Governments for detailed decisions on how Convention rights are given effect in domestic law. [col. 424] The doctrine of the margin of appreciation—it is an important one—recognises that a state is allowed a certain measure of discretion, subject to European supervision, when it takes legislative, judicial or administrative action in respect of some Convention rights. In other words, it is best placed to decide in the first place whether—and, if so, what—action is required.

My first point about the margin of appreciation is that it is more relevant to some Convention rights than to others. It is especially relevant to arts 8 to 11, which enable restrictions to be placed on rights where that is necessary in a democratic society, for any one of a number of reasons. It is less relevant to some of the other articles, for example, art. 2 on the right to life and art. 3 on the prohibition on torture or inhuman and degrading treatment or punishment. The doctrine of the margin of appreciation means allowing this country a margin of appreciation when it interprets our law and the action of our Governments in an international court, perhaps the European Court of Human Rights. Through incorporation we are giving a profound margin of appreciation to British courts to interpret the Convention in accordance with British jurisprudence as well as European jurisprudence.

One of the frustrations of non-incorporation has been that our own judges . . . have not been able to bring their intellectual skills and our great tradition of common law to bear on the development of European Convention jurisprudence. . . .

The margin of appreciation is laid down in many commission and court judgments. Therefore, it is spelt out in the meaning of [s. 2].

Appendix 5
European Convention for the Protection of Fundamental Rights and Freedoms

The governments signatory hereto, being members of the Council of Europe,

Considering the Universal Declaration of Human Rights proclaimed by the General Assembly of the United Nations on 10th December 1948;

Considering that this Declaration aims at securing the universal and effective recognition and observance of the Rights therein declared;

Considering that the aim of the Council of Europe is the achievement of greater unity between its members and that one of the methods by which that aim is to be pursued is the maintenance and further realisation of human rights and fundamental freedoms;

Reaffirming their profound belief in those fundamental freedoms which are the foundation of justice and peace in the world and are best maintained on the one hand by an effective political democracy and on the other by a common understanding and observance of the human rights upon which they depend;

Being resolved, as the governments of European countries which are like-minded and have a common heritage of political traditions, ideals, freedom and the rule of law, to take the first steps for the collective enforcement of certain of the rights stated in the Universal Declaration,

Have agreed as follows:

Article 1
Obligation to respect human rights

The High Contracting Parties shall secure to everyone within their jurisdiction the rights and freedoms defined in Section I of this Convention.

Section I—Rights and freedoms

Article 2
Right to life

1 Everyone's right to life shall be protected by law. No one shall be deprived of his life intentionally save in the execution of a sentence of a court following his conviction of a crime for which this penalty is provided by law.

2 Deprivation of life shall not be regarded as inflicted in contravention of this article when it results from the use of force which is no more than absolutely necessary:

a   in defence of any person from unlawful violence;

b   in order to effect a lawful arrest or to prevent the escape of a person lawfully detained;

c   in action lawfully taken for the purpose of quelling a riot or insurrection.

Article 3
Prohibition of torture

No one shall be subjected to torture or to inhuman or degrading treatment or punishment.

Article 4
Prohibition of slavery and forced labour

1 No one shall be held in slavery or servitude.

2 No one shall be required to perform forced or compulsory labour.

3 For the purpose of this article the term 'forced or compulsory labour' shall not include:

a any work required to be done in the ordinary course of detention imposed according to the provision of Article 5 of this Convention or during conditional release from such detention;

b any service of a military character or, in case of conscientious objectors in countries where they are recognised, service exacted instead of compulsory military service;

c any service exacted in case of an emergency or calamity threatening the life or well-being of the community;

d any work or service which forms part of normal civil obligations.

Article 5
Right to liberty and security

1 Everyone has the right to liberty and security of person. No one shall be deprived of his liberty save in the following cases and in accordance with a procedure prescribed by law:

a the lawful detention of a person after conviction by a competent court;

b the lawful arrest or detention of a person for non-compliance with the lawful order of a court or in order to secure the fulfilment of any obligation prescribed by law;

c the lawful arrest or detention of a person effected for the purpose of bringing him before the competent legal authority on reasonable suspicion of having committed an offence or when it is reasonably considered necessary to prevent his committing an offence or fleeing after having done so;

d the detention of a minor by lawful order for the purpose of educational supervision or his lawful detention for the purpose of bringing him before the competent legal authority;

e the lawful detention of persons for the prevention of the spreading of infectious diseases, of persons of unsound mind, alcoholics or drug addicts or vagrants;

f the lawful arrest or detention of a person to prevent his effecting an unauthorised entry into the country or of a person against whom action is being taken with a view to deportation or extradition.

2 Everyone who is arrested shall be informed promptly, in a language which he understands, of the reasons for his arrest and of any charge against him.

3 Everyone arrested or detained in accordance with the provision of paragraph 1.c of this article shall be brought promptly before a judge or other officer authorised by law to exercise judicial power and shall be entitled to trial within a reasonable time or to release pending trial. Release may be conditioned by guarantees to appear for trial.

4 Everyone who is deprived of his liberty by arrest or detention shall be entitled to take proceedings by which the lawfulness of his detention shall be decided speedily by a court and his release ordered if the detention is not lawful.

5   Everyone who has been the victim of arrest or detention in contravention of the provisions of this article shall have an enforceable right to compensation.

Article 6
Right to a fair trial

1   In the determination of his civil rights and obligations or of any criminal charge against him, everyone is entitled to a fair and public hearing within a reasonable time by an independent and impartial tribunal established by law. Judgment shall be pronounced publicly but the press and public may be excluded from all or part of the trial in the interests of morals, public order or national security in a democratic society, where the interests of juveniles or the protection of the private life of the parties so require, or to the extent strictly necessary in the opinion of the court in special circumstances where publicity would prejudice the interests of justice.

2   Everyone charged with a criminal offence shall be presumed innocent until proved guilty according to law.

3   Everyone charged with a criminal offence has the following minimum rights:

a   to be informed promptly, in a language which he understands and in detail, of the nature and cause of the accusation against him;

b   to have adequate time and facilities for the preparation of his defence;

c   to defend himself in person or through legal assistance of his own choosing or, if he has not sufficient means to pay for legal assistance, to be given it free when the interests of justice so require;

d   to examine or have examined witnesses against him and to obtain the attendance and examination of witnesses on his behalf under the same conditions as witnesses against him;

e   to have the free assistance of an interpreter if he cannot understand or speak the language used in court.

Article 7
No punishment without law

1   No one shall be held guilty of any criminal offence on account of any act or omission which did not constitute a criminal offence under national or international law at the time when it was committed. Nor shall a heavier penalty be imposed than the one that was applicable at the time the criminal offence was committed.

2   This article shall not prejudice the trial and punishment of any person for any act or omission which, at the time when it was committed, was criminal according to the general principles of law recognised by civilised nations.

Article 8
Right to respect for private and family life

1   Everyone has the right to respect for his private and family life, his home and his correspondence.

2   There shall be no interference by a public authority with the exercise of this right except such as is in accordance with the law and is necessary in a democratic society in the interests of national security, public safety or the economic well-being of the country, for the prevention of disorder or crime, for the protection of health or morals, or for the protection of the rights and freedoms of others.

Article 9
Freedom of thought, conscience and religion

1   Everyone has the right to freedom of thought, conscience and religion; this right includes freedom to change his religion or belief and freedom, either alone or in community with others and in public or private, to manifest his religion or belief, in worship, teaching, practice and observance.

2   Freedom to manifest one's religion or beliefs shall be subject only to such limitations as are prescribed by law and are necessary in a democratic society in the interests of public safety, for the protection of public order, health or morals, or for the protection of the rights and freedoms of others.

Article 10
Freedom of expression

1   Everyone has the right to freedom of expression. This right shall include freedom to hold opinions and to receive and impart information and ideas without interference by public authority and regardless of frontiers. This article shall not prevent States from requiring the licensing of broadcasting, television or cinema enterprises.

2   The exercise of these freedoms, since it carries with it duties and responsibilities, may be subject to such formalities, conditions, restrictions or penalties as are prescribed by law and are necessary in a democratic society, in the interests of national security, territorial integrity or public safety, for the prevention of disorder or crime, for the protection of health or morals, for the protection of the reputation or rights of others, for preventing the disclosure of information received in confidence, or for maintaining the authority and impartiality of the judiciary.

Article 11
Freedom of assembly and association

1   Everyone has the right to freedom of peaceful assembly and to freedom of association with others, including the right to form and to join trade unions for the protection of this interests.

2   No restrictions shall be placed on the exercise of these rights other than such as are prescribed by law and are necessary in a democratic society in the interests of national security or public safety, for the prevention of disorder or crime, for the protection of health or morals or for the protection of the rights and freedoms of others. This article shall not prevent the imposition of lawful restrictions on the exercise of these rights by members of the armed forces, of the police or of the administration of the State.

Article 12
Right to marry

Men and women of marriageable age have the right to marry and to found a family, according to the national laws governing the exercise of this right.

Article 13
Right to an effective remedy

Everyone whose rights and freedoms as set forth in this Convention are violated shall have an effective remedy before a national authority notwithstanding that the violation has been committed by persons acting in an official capacity.

Article 14
Prohibition of discrimination

The enjoyment of the rights and freedoms set forth in this Convention shall be secured without discrimination on any ground such as sex, race, colour, language, religion, political or other opinion, national or social origin, association with a national minority, property, birth or other status.

Article 15
Derogation in time of emergency

1   In time of war or other public emergency threatening the life of the nation any High Contracting Party may take measures derogating from its obligations under this Convention to the extent strictly required by the exigencies of the situation, provided that such measures are not inconsistent with its other obligations under international law.

2   No derogation from Article 2, except in respect of deaths resulting from lawful acts of war, or from Articles 3, 4 (paragraph 1) and 7 shall be made under this provision.

3   Any High Contracting Party availing itself of this right of derogation shall keep the Secretary General of the Council of Europe fully informed of the measures which it has taken and the reasons therefor. It shall also inform the Secretary General of the Council of Europe when such measures have ceased to operate and the provisions of the Convention are again being fully executed.

Article 16
Restrictions on political activity of aliens

Nothing in Articles 10, 11 and 14 shall be regarded as preventing the High Contracting Parties from imposing restrictions on the political activity of aliens.

Article 17
Prohibition of abuse of rights

Nothing in this Convention may be interpreted as implying for any State, group or person any right to engage in any activity or perform any act aimed at the destruction of any of the rights and freedoms set forth herein or at their limitation to a greater extent than is provided for in the Convention.

Article 18
Limitation on use of restrictions on rights

The restrictions permitted under this Convention to the said rights and freedoms shall not be applied for any purpose other than those for which they have been prescribed.

Section II—European Court of Human Rights

Article 19
Establishment of the Court

To ensure the observance of the engagements undertaken by the High Contracting Parties in the Convention and the Protocols thereto, there shall be set up a European Court of Human Rights, hereinafter referred to as 'the Court'. It shall function on a permanent basis.

Article 20
Number of judges

The Court shall consist of a number of judges equal to that of the High Contracting Parties.

Article 21
Criteria for office

1   The judges shall be of high moral character and must either possess the qualifications required for appointment to high judicial office or be jurisconsults of recognised competence.

2   The judges shall sit on the Court in their individual capacity.

3   During their term of office the judges shall not engage in any activity which is incompatible with their independence, impartiality or with the demands of a full-time office; all questions arising from the application of this paragraph shall be decided by the Court.

Article 22
Election of judges

1   The judges shall be elected by the Parliamentary Assembly with respect to each High Contracting Party by a majority of votes cast from a list of three candidates nominated by the High Contracting Party.

2   The same procedure shall be followed to complete the Court in the event of the accession of new High Contracting Parties and in filling casual vacancies.

Article 23
Terms of office

1   The judges shall be elected for a period of six years. They may be re-elected. However, the terms of office of one-half of the judges elected at the first election shall expire at the end of three years.

2   The judges whose terms of office are to expire at the end of the initial period of three years shall be chosen by lot by the Secretary General of the Council of Europe immediately after their election.

3   In order to ensure that, as far as possible, the terms of office of one-half of the judges are renewed every three years, the Parliamentary Assembly may decide, before proceeding to any subsequent election, that the term or terms of office of one or more judges to be elected shall be for a period other than six years but not more than nine and not less than three years.

4   In cases where more than one term of office is involved and where the Parliamentary Assembly applies the preceding paragraph, the allocation of the terms of office shall be effected by a drawing of lots by the Secretary General of the Council of Europe immediately after the election.

5   A judge elected to replace a judge whose term of office has not expired shall hold office for the remainder of his predecessor's term.

6   The terms of office of judges shall expire when they reach the age of 70.

7   The judges shall hold office until replaced. They shall, however, continue to deal with such cases as they already have under consideration.

Article 24
Dismissal

No judge may be dismissed from his office unless the other judges decide by a majority of two-thirds that he has ceased to fulfil the required conditions.

Article 25
Registry and legal secretaries

The Court shall have a registry, the functions and organisation of which shall be laid down in the rules of the Court. The Court shall be assisted by legal secretaries.

Article 26
Plenary Court

The plenary Court shall
    a   elect its President and one or two Vice-Presidents for a period of three years; they may be re-elected;
    b   set up Chambers, constituted for a fixed period of time;
    c   elect the Presidents of the Chambers of the Court; they may be re-elected;
    d   adopt the rules of the Court, and
    e   elect the Registrar and one or more Deputy Registrars.

Article 27
Committees, Chambers and Grand Chamber

1   To consider cases brought before it, the Court shall sit in committees of three judges, in Chambers of seven judges and in a Grand Chamber of seventeen judges. The Court's Chamber shall set up committees for a fixed period of time.

2   There shall sit as an *ex officio* member of the Chamber and the Grand Chamber the judge elected in respect of the State Party concerned or, if there is none or if he is unable to sit, a person of its choice who shall sit in the capacity of judge.

3   The Grand Chamber shall also include the President of the Court, the Vice-Presidents, the Presidents of the Chambers and other judges chosen in accordance with the rules of the Court. When a case is referred to the Grand Chamber under Article 43, no judge from the Chamber which rendered the judgment shall sit in the Grand Chamber, with the exception of the President of the Chamber and the judge who sat in respect of the State Party concerned.

Article 28
Declarations of inadmissibility by committees

A committee may, by a unanimous vote, declare inadmissible or strike out of its list of cases an application submitted under Article 34 where such a decision can be taken without further examination. The decision shall be final.

Article 29
Decisions by Chambers on admissibility and merits

1   If no decision is taken under Article 28, a Chamber shall decide on the admissibility and merits of individual applications submitted under Article 34.

2   A Chamber shall decide on the admissibility and merits of inter-State applications submitted under Article 33.

3   The decision on admissibility shall be taken separately unless the Court, in exceptional cases, decides otherwise.

Article 30
Relinquishment of jurisdiction to the Grand Chamber

Where a case pending before a Chamber raises a serious question affecting the interpretation of the Convention or the protocols thereto, or where the resolution of a question before the Chamber might have a result inconsistent with a judgment previously delivered by the Court, the Chamber may, at any time before it has rendered its judgment, relinquish jurisdiction in favour of the Grand Chamber, unless one of the parties to the case objects.

Article 31
Powers of the Grand Chamber

The Grand Chamber shall

a   determine applications submitted either under Article 33 or Article 34 when a Chamber has relinquished jurisdiction under Article 30 or when the case has been referred to it under Article 43; and

b   consider requests for advisory opinions submitted under Article 47.

Article 32
Jurisdiction of the Court

1   The jurisdiction of the Court shall extend to all matters concerning the interpretation and application of the Convention and the protocols thereto which are referred to it as provided in Articles 33, 34 and 47.

2   In the event of dispute as to whether the Court has jurisdiction, the court shall decide.

Article 33
Inter-State cases

Any High Contracting Party may refer to the Court any alleged breach of the provisions of the Convention and the protocols thereto by another High Contracting Party.

Article 34
Individual applications

The Court may receive applications from any person, non-governmental organisation or group of individuals claiming to be the victim of a violation by one of the High Contracting Parties of the rights set forth in the Convention or the protocols thereto. The High Contracting Parties undertake not to hinder in any way the effective exercise of this right.

Article 35
Admissibility criteria

1   The Court may only deal with the matter after all domestic remedies have been exhausted, according to the generally recognised rules of international law, and within a period of six months from the date on which the final decision was taken.

2   The Court shall not deal with any application submitted under Article 34 that

a   is anonymous; or

b   is substantially the same as a matter that has already been examined by the Court or has already been submitted to another procedure of international investigation or settlement and contains no relevant new information.

3   The Court shall declare inadmissible any individual application submitted under Article 34 which it considers incompatible with the provisions of the Convention or the protocols thereto, manifestly ill-founded, or an abuse of the right of application.

4   The Court shall reject any application which it considers inadmissible under this Article. It may do so at any stage of the proceedings.

Article 36
Third party intervention

1   In all cases before a Chamber of the Grand Chamber, a High Contracting Party one of whose nationals is an applicant shall have the right to submit written comments and to take part in hearings.

2   The President of the Court may, in the interest of the proper administration of justice, invite any High Contracting Party which is not a party to the proceedings or any person concerned who is not the applicant to submit written comments or take part in hearings.

Article 37
Striking out applications

1   The Court may at any stage of the proceedings decide to strike an application out of its list of cases where the circumstances lead to the conclusion that

a   the applicant does not intend to pursue his application; or

b   the matter has been resolved; or

c   for any other reason established by the Court, it is no longer justified to continue the examination of the application.

However, the Court shall continue the examination of the application if respect for human rights as defined in the Convention and the protocols thereto so requires.

2   The Court may decide to restore an application to its list of cases if it considers that the circumstances justify such a course.

Article 38
Examination of the case and friendly settlement proceedings

1   If the Court declares the application admissible, it shall

a   pursue the examination of the case, together with the representatives of the parties, and if need be, undertake an investigation, for the effective conduct of which the States concerned shall furnish all necessary facilities;

b   place itself at the disposal of the parties concerned with a view to securing a friendly settlement of the matter on the basis of respect for human rights as defined in the Convention and the protocols thereto.

2   Proceedings conducted under paragraph 1.b shall be confidential.

Article 39
Finding of a friendly settlement

If a friendly settlement is effected, the court shall strike the case out of its list by means of a decision which shall be confined to a brief statement of the facts and of the solution reached.

Article 40
Public hearings and access to documents

1   Hearings shall be in public unless the Court in exceptional circumstances decides otherwise.

2   Documents deposited with the Registrar shall be accessible to the public unless the President of the Court decides otherwise.

Article 41
Just satisfaction

If the Court finds that there has been a violation of the Convention or the protocols thereto, and if the internal law of the High Contracting Party concerned allows only partial reparation to be made, the Court shall, if necessary afford just satisfaction to the injured party.

Article 42
Judgments of Chambers

Judgments of Chambers shall become final in accordance with the provisions of Article 44, paragraph 2.

Article 43
Referral to the Grand Chamber

1   Within a period of three months from the date of the judgment of the Chamber, any party to the case may, in exceptional cases, request that the case be referred to the Grand Chamber.

2   A panel of five judges of the Grand Chamber shall accept the request if the case raises a serious question affecting the interpretation or application of the Convention or the protocols thereto, or a serious issue of general importance.

3   If the panel accepts the request, the Grand Chamber shall decide the case by means of a judgment.

Article 44
Final judgments

1   The judgment of the Grand Chamber shall be final.

2   The judgment of a Chamber shall become final

   a   when the parties declare that they will not request that the case be referred to the Grand Chamber; or

   b   three months after the date of the judgment, if reference of the case to the Grand Chamber has not been requested; or

   c   when the panel of the Grand Chamber rejects the request to refer under Article 43.

3   The final judgment shall be published.

Article 45
Reasons for judgments and decisions

1   Reasons shall be given for judgments as well as for decisions declaring applications admissible or inadmissible.

2   If a judgment does not represent, in whole or in part, the unanimous opinion of the judges, any judge shall be entitled to deliver a separate opinion.

Article 46
Binding force and execution of judgments

1   The High Contracting Parties undertake to abide by the final judgment of the Court in any case to which they are parties.

2   The final judgment of the court shall be transmitted to the Committee of Ministers, which shall supervise its execution.

Article 47
Advisory opinions

1   The Court may, at the request of the Committee of Ministers, give advisory opinions on legal questions concerning the interpretation of the Convention and the protocols thereto.

2   Such opinions shall not deal with any question relating to the content or scope of the rights or freedoms defined in Section I of the Convention and the protocols thereto, or with any other question which the Court or the Committee of Ministers might have to consider in consequence of any such proceedings as could be instituted in accordance with the Convention.

3   Decisions of the Committee of Ministers to request an advisory opinion of the Court shall require a majority vote of the representatives entitled to sit on the Committee.

Article 48
Advisory jurisdiction of the Court

The Court shall decide whether a request for an advisory opinion submitted by the Committee of Ministers is within its competence as defined in Article 47.

Article 49
Reasons for advisory opinions

1   Reasons shall be given for advisory opinions of the court.

2   If the advisory opinion does not represent, in whole or in part, the unanimous opinion of the judges, any judge shall be entitled to deliver a separate opinion.

3   Advisory opinions of the Court shall be communicated to the Committee of Ministers.

Article 50
Expenditure on the Court

The expenditure on the Court shall be borne by the Council of Europe.

Article 51
Privileges and immunities of judges

The judges shall be entitled, during the exercise of their functions, to the privileges and immunities provided for in Article 40 of the Statute of the Council of Europe and in the agreements made thereunder.

Section III—Miscellaneous provisions

Article 52
Inquiries by the Secretary General

On receipt of a request from the Secretary General of the Council of Europe any High Contracting Party shall furnish an explanation of the manner in which its internal law ensures the effective implementation of any of the provision of the Convention.

Article 53
Safeguard for existing human rights

Nothing in this Convention shall be construed as limiting or derogating from any of the human rights and fundamental freedoms which may be ensured under the laws of any High Contracting Party or under any other agreement to which it is a Party.

Article 54
Powers of the Committee of Ministers

Nothing in this Convention shall prejudice the powers conferred on the Committee of Ministers by the Statute of the Council of Europe.

Article 55
Exclusions of other means of dispute settlement

The High Contracting Parties agree that, except by special agreement, they will not avail themselves of treaties, conventions or declarations in force between them for the purpose of submitting, by way of petition, a dispute arising out of the interpretation or application of this Convention to a means of settlement other than those provided for in this Convention.

Article 56
Territorial application

1   Any State may at the time of its ratification or at any time thereafter declare by notification addressed to the Secretary General of the Council of Europe that the present Convention shall, subject to paragraph 4 of this Article, extend to all or any of the territories for whose international relations it is responsible.

2   The Convention shall extend to the territory or territories named in the notification as from the thirtieth day after the receipt of this notification by the Secretary General of the Council of Europe.

3   The provisions of this Convention shall be applied in such territories with due regard, however, to local requirements.

4   Any State which has made a declaration in accordance with paragraph 1 of this article may at any time thereafter declare on behalf of one or more of the territories to which the declaration related that it accepts the competence of the Court to receive applications from individuals, non-governmental organisations or groups of individuals as provided by Article 34 of the Convention.

Article 57
Reservations

1   Any State may, when signing this Convention or when depositing its instrument of ratification, make a reservation in respect of any particular provision of the Convention to the extent that any law then in force in its territory is not in conformity with the provision. Reservations of a general character shall not be permitted under this article.

2   Any reservation made under this article shall contain a brief statement of the law concerned.

Article 58
Denunciation

1   A High Contracting Party may denounce the present Convention only after the expiry of five years from the date on which it became a party to it and after six months' notice contained in a notification addressed to the Secretary General of the Council of Europe, who shall inform the other High Contracting Parties.

2   Such a denunciation shall not have the effect of releasing the High Contracting Party concerned from its obligations under this Convention in respect of any act which, being capable of constituting a violation of such obligations, may have been performed by it before the date at which the denunciation became effective.

3   Any High Contracting Party which shall cease to be a member of the Council of Europe shall cease to be a Party to this Convention under the same conditions.

4   The Convention may be denounced in accordance with the provisions of the preceding paragraphs in respect of any territory to which it has been declared to extend under the terms of Article 56.

Article 59
Signature and ratification

1   This Convention shall be open to the signature of the members of the Council of Europe. It shall be ratified. Ratifications shall be deposited with the Secretary General of the Council of Europe.

2   The present Convention shall come into force after the deposit of ten instruments of ratification.

3   As regards any signatory ratifying subsequently, the Convention shall come into force at the date of the deposit of its instrument of ratification.

4   The Secretary General of the Council of Europe shall notify all the members of the Council of Europe of the entry into force of the Convention, the names of the High Contracting Parties who have ratified it, and the deposit of all instruments of ratification which may be effected subsequently.

Done at Rome this 4th day of November 1950, in English and French, both texts being equally authentic, in a single copy which shall remain deposited in the archives of the Council of Europe.

The Secretary General shall transmit certified copes to each of the signatories.

PROTOCOL [NO. 1] TO THE CONVENTION FOR THE PROTECTION OF HUMAN RIGHTS AND FUNDAMENTAL FREEDOMS, AS AMENDED BY PROTOCOL NO. 11

The governments signatory hereto, being members of the Council of Europe,

Being resolved to take steps to ensure the collective enforcement of certain rights and freedoms other than those already included in Section I of the Convention for the Protection of Human Rights and Fundamental Freedoms signed at Rome on 4 November 1950 (hereinafter referred to as 'the Convention'),

Have agreed as follows:

Article 1
Protection of property

Every natural or legal person is entitled to the peaceful enjoyment of his possessions. No one shall be deprived of his possessions except in the public interest and subject to the conditions provided for by law and by the general principles of international law.

The preceding provisions shall not, however, in any way impair the right of a State to enforce such laws as it deems necessary to control the use of property in accordance with the general interest or to secure the payment of taxes or other contributions or penalties.

Article 2
Right to education

No person shall be denied the right to education. In the exercise of any functions which it assumes in relation to education and to teaching, the State shall respect the right of parents to ensure such education and teaching in conformity with their own religious and philosophical convictions.

Article 3
Right to free elections

The High Contracting Parties undertake to hold free elections at reasonable intervals by secret ballot, under conditions which will ensure the free expression of the opinion of the people in the choice of the legislature.

Article 4
Territorial application

Any High Contracting Party may at the time of signature or ratification or at any time thereafter communicate to the Secretary General of the Council of Europe a declaration stating the extent to which it undertakes that the provisions of the present Protocol shall apply to such of the territories for the international relations of which it is responsible as are named therein.

Any High Contracting Party which has communicated a declaration in virtue of the preceding paragraph may from time to ttme communicate a further declaration modifying the terms of any former declaration or terminating the application of the provisions of this Protocol in respect of any territory.

A declaration made in accordance with this article shall be deemed to have been made in accordance with paragraph 1 of Article 56 of the Convention.

Article 5
Relationship to the Convention

As between the High Contracting Parties the provisions of Articles 1, 2, 3 and 4 of this Protocol shall be regarded as additional articles to the Convention and all the provisions of the Convention shall apply accordingly.

Article 6
Signature and ratification

This Protocol shall be open for signature by the members of the Council of Europe, who are the signatories of the Convention; it shall be ratified at the same time as or after the ratification of the Convention. It shall enter into force after the deposit of ten instruments of ratification. As regards any signatory ratifying subsequently, the Protocol shall enter into force at the date of the deposit of its instrument of ratification.

The instruments of ratification shall be deposited with the Secretary General of the Council of Europe, who will notify all members of the names of those who have ratified.

Done at Paris on the 20th day of March 1952, in English and French, both texts being equally authentic, in a single copy which shall remain deposited in the archives of the Council of Europe. The Secretary General shall transmit certified copies to each of the signatory governments.

PROTOCOL NO. 4 TO THE CONVENTION FOR THE PROTECTION OF HUMAN RIGHTS AND FUNDAMENTAL FREEDOMS, SECURING CERTAIN RIGHTS AND FREEDOMS OTHER THAN THOSE ALREADY INCLUDED IN THE CONVENTION AND IN THE FIRST PROTOCOL THERETO, AS AMENDED BY PROTOCOL NO. 11

The governments signatory hereto, being members of the Council of Europe,

Being resolved to take steps to ensure the collective enforcement of certain rights and freedoms other than those already included in Section 1 of the Convention for the Protection of Human Rights and Fundamental Freedoms signed at Rome on 4th November 1950 (hereinafter referred to as the 'Convention') and in Articles 1 to 3 of the First Protocol to the Convention, signed at Paris on 20th March 1952,

Have agreed as follows:

Article 1
Prohibition of imprisonment for debt

No one shall be deprived of his liberty merely on the ground of inability to fulfil a contractual obligation.

Article 2
Freedom of movement

1   Everyone lawfully within the territory of a State shall, within that territory, have the right to liberty of movement and freedom to choose his residence.

2   Everyone shall be free to leave any country, including his own.

3   No restrictions shall be placed on the exercise of these rights other than such as are in accordance with law and are necessary in a democratic society in the interests of national security or public safety, for the maintenance of *ordre public*, for the prevention of crime, for the protection of health or morals, or for the protection of the rights and freedoms of others.

4   The rights set forth in paragraph 1 may also be subject, in particular areas, to restrictions imposed in accordance with law and justified by the public interest in a democratic society.

Article 3
Prohibition of expulsion of nationals

1   No one shall be expelled, by means either of an individual or of a collective measure, from the territory of the State of which he is a national.

2   No one shall be deprived of the right to enter the territory of the state of which he is a national.

Article 4
Prohibition of collective expulsion of aliens

Collective expulsion of aliens is prohibited.

Article 5
Territorial application

1   Any High Contracting Party may, at the time of signature or ratification of this Protocol, or at any time thereafter, communicate to the Secretary General of the Council of Europe a declaration stating the extent to which it undertakes that the provision of this Protocol shall apply to such of the territories for the international relations of which it is responsible as are named therein.

2   Any High Contracting Party which has communicated a declaration in virtue of the preceding paragraph may, from time to time, communicate a further declaration modifying the terms of any former declaration or terminating the application of the provisions of this Protocol in respect of any territory.

3   A declaration made in accordance with this article shall be deemed to have been made in accordance with paragraph 1 of Article 56 of the Convention.

4   The territory of any State to which this Protocol applies by virtue of ratification or acceptance by that State, and each territory to which this Protocol is applied by virtue of a

declaration by that State under this article, shall be treated as separate territories for the purpose of the references in Articles 2 and 3 to the territory of a State.

5   Any State which has made a declaration in accordance with paragraph 1 or 2 of this Article may at any time thereafter declare on behalf of one or more of the territories to which the declaration relates that it accepts the competence of the Court to receive applications from individuals, non-governmental organisations or groups of individuals as provided in Article 34 of the Convention in respect of all or any of Articles 1 to 4 of this Protocol.

Article 6
Relationship to the Convention

As between the High Contracting Parties the provisions of Articles 1 to 5 of this Protocol shall be regarded as additional Articles to the Convention, and all the provisions of the Convention shall apply accordingly.

Article 7
Signature and ratification

1   This Protocol shall be open for signature by the members of the Council of Europe who are the signatories of the Convention; it shall be ratified at the same time as or after the ratification of the Convention. It shall enter into force after the deposit of five instruments of ratification. As regards any signatory ratifying subsequently, the Protocol shall enter into force at the date of the deposit of its instrument of ratification.

2   The instruments of ratification shall be deposited with the Secretary General of the Council of Europe, who will notify all members of the names of those who have ratified.

In witness whereof the undersigned, being duly authorised thereto, have signed this Protocol.

Done at Strasbourg, this 16th day of September 1963, in English and in French, both texts being equally authoritative, in a single copy which shall remain deposited in the archives of the Council of Europe. The Secretary General shall transmit certified copies to each of the signatory states.

PROTOCOL NO. 6 TO THE CONVENTION FOR THE PROTECTION OF HUMAN RIGHTS AND FUNDAMENTAL FREEDOMS CONCERNING THE ABOLITION OF THE DEATH PENALTY, AS AMENDED BY PROTOCOL NO. 11

The member States of the Council of Europe, signatory to this Protocol to the Convention for the Protection of Human Rights and Fundamental Freedoms, signed at Rome on 4 November 1950 (hereinafter referred to as 'the Convention'),

Considering that the evolution that has occurred in several member States of the Council of Europe expresses a general tendency in favour of abolition of the death penalty.

Have agreed as follows:

Article 1
Abolition of the death penalty

The death penalty shall be abolished. No-one shall be condemned to such penalty or executed.

Article 2
Death penalty in time of war

A State may make provision in its law for the death penalty in respect of acts committed in time of war or of imminent threat of war; such penalty shall be applied only in the instances laid down in the law and in accordance with its provision. The State shall communicate to the Secretary General of the Council of Europe the relevant provisions of that law.

Article 3
Prohibition of derogations

No derogation from the provisions of this Protocol shall be made under Article 15 of the Convention.

Article 4
Prohibition of reservations

No reservation may be made under Article 57 of the Convention in respect of the provisions of this Protocol.

Article 5
Territorial application

1   Any State may at the time of signature or when depositing its instrument of ratification, acceptance or approval, specify the territory or territories to which this Protocol shall apply.

2   Any State may at any later date, by a declaration addressed to the Secretary General of the Council of Europe, extend the application of this Protocol to any other territory specified in the declaration. In respect of such territory the Protocol shall enter into force on the first day of the month following the date of receipt of such declaration by the Secretary General.

3   Any declaration made under the two preceding paragraphs may, in respect of any territory specified in such declaration, be withdrawn by a notification addressed to the Secretary General. The withdrawal shall become effective on the first day of the month following the date of receipt of such notification by the Secretary General.

Article 6
Relationship to the Convention

As between the States Parties the provisions of Articles 1 to 5 of this Protocol shall be regarded as additional articles to the Convention and all the provisions of the Convention shall apply accordingly.

Article 7
Signature and ratification

The Protocol shall be open for signature by the member States of the Council of Europe, signatories to the Convention. It shall be subject to ratification, acceptance or approval. A member State of the Council of Europe may not ratify, accept or approve this Protocol unless it has, simultaneously or previously, ratified the Convention. Instruments of ratification, acceptance or approval shall be deposited with the Secretary General of the Council of Europe.

Article 8
Entry into force

1   This Protocol shall enter into force on the first day of the month following the date on which five member States of the Council of Europe have expressed their consent to be bound by the Protocol in accordance with the provisions of Article 7.

2   In respect of any member State which subsequently expresses its consent to be bound by it, the Protocol shall enter into force on the first day of the month following the date of the deposit of the instrument of ratification, acceptance or approval.

Article 9
Depositary functions

The Secretary General of the Council of Europe shall notify the member States of the Council of:

a   any signature;
b   the deposit of any instrument of ratification, acceptance or approval;
c   any date of entry into force of this Protocol in accordance with Articles 5 and 8;
d   any other act, notification or communication relating to this Protocol.

In witness whereof the undersigned, being duly authorised thereto, have signed this Protocol.

Done at Strasbourg, this 28th day of April 1983, in English and in French, both texts being equally authentic, in a single copy which shall be deposited in the archives of the Council of Europe. The Secretary General of the Council of Europe shall transmit certified copies to each member State of the Council of Europe.

PROTOCOL NO. 7 TO THE CONVENTION FOR THE PROTECTION OF HUMAN RIGHTS AND FUNDAMENTAL FREEDOMS, AS AMENDED BY PROTOCOL NO. 11

The member States of the Council of Europe signatory hereto,

Being resolved to take further steps to ensure the collective enforcement of certain rights and freedoms by means of the convention for the protection of Human Rights and Fundamental Freedoms signed at Rome on 4 November 1950 (hereinafter referred to as 'the Convention'),

Have agreed as follows

Article 1
Procedural safeguards relating to expulsion of aliens

1   An alien lawfully resident in the territory of s State shall not be expelled therefrom except in pursuance of a decision reached in accordance with law and shall be allowed:

    a   to submit reasons against his expulsion,

    b   to have his case reviewed, and

    c   to be represented for these purposes before the competent authority or a person or persons designated by that authority.

2   An alien may be expelled before the exercise of his rights under paragraph 1.a, b and c of this Article, when such expulsion is necessary in the interests of public order or is grounded on reasons of national security.

Article 2
Right of appeal in criminal matters

1   Everyone convicted of a criminal offence by a tribunal shall have the right to have his conviction or sentence reviewed by a higher tribunal. The exercise of this right, including the grounds on which it may be exercised, shall be governed by law.

2   This right may be subject to exceptions in regard to offences of a minor character, as prescribed by law, or in cases in which the person concerned was tried in the first instance by the highest tribunal or was convicted following an appeal against acquittal.

Article 3
Compensation for wrongful conviction

When a person has by a final decision been convicted of a criminal offence and when subsequently his conviction has been reversed, or he has been pardoned, on the ground that a new or newly discovered fact shows conclusively that there has been a miscarriage of justice, the person who has suffered punishment as a result of such conviction shall be compensated according to the law or the practice of the State concerned, unless it is proved that the non-disclosure of the unknown fact in time is wholly or partly attributable to him.

Article 4
Right not to be tried or punished twice

1   No one shall be liable to be tried or punished again in criminal proceedings under the jurisdiction of the same State for an offence for which he has already been finally acquitted or convicted in accordance with the law and penal procedure of that State.

2   The provisions of the preceding paragraph shall not prevent the reopening of the cases in accordance with the law and penal procedure of the State concerned, if there is evidence of new or newly discovered facts, or if there has been a fundamental defect in the previous proceedings, which could affect the outcome of the case.

3   No derogation from this Article shall be made under Article 15 of the Convention.

Article 5
Equality between spouses

Spouses shall enjoy equality of rights and responsibilities of a private law character between them, and in their relations with their children, as to marriage, during marriage and in the event of its dissolution. This Article shall not prevent States from taking such measures as are necessary in the interests of the children.

Article 6
Territorial application

1   Any State may at the time of signature or when depositing its instrument of ratification, acceptance or approval, specify the territory or territories to which the Protocol shall apply and state the extent to which it undertakes that the provisions of this Protocol shall apply to such territory or territories.

2   Any State may at any later date, by a declaration addressed to the Secretary General of the Council of Europe, extend the application of this Protocol to any other territory specified in the declaration. In respect of such territory the Protocol shall enter into force on the first day of the month following the expiration of a period of two months after the date of receipt by the Secretary General of such declaration.

3   Any declaration made under the two preceding paragraphs may, in respect of any territory specified in such declaration, be withdrawn or modified by a notification addressed to the Secretary General. The withdrawal or modification shall become effective on the first day of the month following the expiration of a period of two months after the date of receipt of such notification by the Secretary General.

4   A declaration made in accordance with this Article shall be deemed to have been made in accordance with paragraph 1 of Article 56 of the Convention.

5   The territory of any State to which this Protocol applies by virtue of ratification, acceptance or approval by that State, and each territory to which this Protocol is applied by virtue of a declaration by that State under this Article, may be treated as separate territories for the purpose of the reference in Article 1 to the territory of a State.

6   Any State which has made a declaration in accordance with paragraph 1 or 2 of this Article may at any time thereafter declare on behalf of one or more of the territories to which the declaration related that it accepts the competence of the Court to receive applications from individuals, non-governmental organisations or groups of individuals as provided in Article 34 of the Convention in respect of Articles 1 to 5 of this Protocol.

Article 7
Relationship to the Convention

As between the States Parties, the provisions of Article 1 to 6 of this Protocol shall be regarded as additional Articles to the Convention, and all the provisions of the Convention shall apply accordingly.

Article 8
Signature and ratification

This Protocol shall be open for signature by member States of the Council of Europe which have signed the Convention. It is subject to ratification, acceptance or approval. A member State of the Council of Europe may not ratify, accept or approve this Protocol without previously or simultaneously ratifying the Convention. Instruments of ratification, acceptance or approval shall be deposited with the Secretary General of the Council of Europe.

Article 9
Entry into force

1   This Protocol shall enter into force on the first day of the month following the expiration of a period of two months after the date on which seven member States of the Council of Europe have expressed their consent to be bound by the Protocol in accordance with the provisions of Article 8.

2   In respect of any member State which subsequently expresses its consent to be bound by it, the Protocol shall enter into force on the first day of the month following the expiration of a period of two months after the date of the deposit of the instrument of ratification, acceptance or approval.

Article 10
Depositary functions

The Secretary General of the Council of Europe shall notify all the member States of the Council of Europe of:

a   any signature;
b   the deposit of any instrument of ratification, acceptance or approval;
c   any date of entry into force of this Protocol in accordance with Articles 6 and 9;
d   any other act, notification or declaration relating to this Protocol.

In witness whereof the undersigned, being duly authorised thereto, have signed this Protocol.

Done at Strasbourg, this 22nd day of November 1984, in English and French, both texts being equally authentic, in a single copy which shall be deposited in the archives of the Council of Europe. The Secretary General of the Council of Europe shall transmit certified copies to each member State of the Council of Europe.

PROTOCOL NO. 12 TO THE CONVENTION FOR THE PROTECTION OF HUMAN RIGHTS AND FUNDAMENTAL FREEDOMS

The member States of the Council of Europe signatory hereto,

Having regard to the fundamental principle according to which all persons are equal before the law and are entitled to the equal protection of the law;

Being resolved to take further steps to promote the equality of all persons through the collective enforcement of a general prohibition of the discrimination by means of the Convention for the Protection of Human Rights and Fundamental Freedoms signed at Rome on 4 November 1950 (hereinafter referred to as 'the Convention');

Reaffirming that the principle of non-discrimination does not prevent States Parties from taking measures in order to promote full and effective equality, provided that there is an objective and reasonable justification for those measures,

Have agreed as follows:

Article 1
General prohibition of discrimination

1   The enjoyment of any right set forth by law shall be secured without discrimination on any ground such as sex, race, colour, language, religion, political or other opinion, national or social origin, association with a national minority, property, birth or other status.

2   No one shall be discriminated against by any public authority on any ground such as those mentioned in paragraph 1.

Article 2
Territorial application

1   Any State may, at the time of signature or when depositing its instrument of ratification, acceptance or approval, specify the territory or territories to which this Protocol shall apply.

2   Any State may at any later date, by a declaration addressed to the Secretary General of the Council of Europe, extend the application of this Protocol to any other territory specified in the declaration. In respect of such territory the Protocol shall enter into force on the first day of the month following the expiration of a period of three months after the date of receipt by the Secretary General of such declaration.

3   Any declaration made under the two preceding paragraphs may, in respect of any territory specified in such declaration, be withdrawn or modified by a notification addressed to the Secretary General of the Council of Europe. The withdrawal or modification shall become effective on the first day of the month following the expiration of a period of three months after the date of receipt or such notification by the Secretary General.

4   A declaration made in accordance with this article shall be deemed to have been made in accordance with paragraph 1 of Article 56 of the Convention.

5   Any State which has made a declaration in accordance with paragraph 1 or 2 of this article may at any time thereafter declare on behalf of one or more of the territories to which the declaration relates that it accepts the competence of the Court to receive applications from individuals, non-governmental organisations or groups of individuals as provided by Article 34 of the Convention in respect of Article 1 of this Protocol.

Article 3
Relationship to the Convention

As between the States Parties, the provisions of Articles 1 and 2 of this Protocol shall be regarded as additional articles to the Convention, and all the provisions of the Convention shall apply accordingly.

Article 4
Signature and ratification

This Protocol shall be open for signature by member States of the Council of Europe which have signed the Convention. It is subject to ratification, acceptance or approval. A member State of the Council of Europe may not ratify, accept or approve this Protocol without previously or simultaneously ratifying the Convention. Instruments of ratification, acceptance or approval shall be deposited with the Secretary General of the Council of Europe.

Article 5
Entry into force

1   This Protocol shall enter into force on the first day of the month following the expiration of a period of three months after the date on which ten member States of the Council of Europe have expressed their consent to be bound by the Protocol in accordance with the provisions of Article 4.

2   In respect of any member State which subsequently expresses its consent to be bound by it, the Protocol shall enter into force on the first day of the month following the expiration of a period of three months after the date of the deposit of the instrument of ratification, acceptance or approval.

Article 6
Depositary functions

The Secretary General of the Council of Europe shall notify all the member States of the Council of Europe of:

a   any signature;
b   the deposit of any instrument of ratification, acceptance or approval;
c   any date of entry into force of this Protocol in accordance with Articles 2 and 5;
d   any other act, notification or communication relating to this Protocol.

In witness whereof the undersigned, being duly authorised thereto, have signed this Protocol.

Done at Rome, this 4th day of November 2000, in English and in French, both texts being equally authentic, in a single copy which shall be deposited in the archives of the Council of Europe. The Secretary General of the Council of Europe shall transmit certified copies to each member State of the Council of Europe.

Appendix 6

Voir Note explicative
See Explanatory Note

COUR EUROPÉENNE DES DROITS DE L'HOMME
EUROPEAN COURT OF HUMAN RIGHTS

Conseil de l'Europe—*Council of Europe*
Strasbourg, France

REQUÊTE
APPLICATION

présentée en application de l'article 34 de la Convention européenne des Droits de l'Homme, ainsi que des articles 45 et 47 du règlement de la Cour

under Article 34 of the European Convention on Human Rights and Rules 45 and 47 of the Rules of Court

IMPORTANT: La présente requête est un document juridique et peut affecter vos droits et obligations.
This application is a formal legal document and may affect your rights and obligations.

I.   LES PARTIES
THE PARTIES

A.   LE REQUÉRANT/LA REQUÉRANTE
THE APPLICANT

(Renseignements à fournir concernant le/la requérant(e) et son/sa représentant(e) éventuel(le))
(*Fill in the following details of the applicant and the representative, if any*)

1. Nom de famille . . . .   2. Prénom(s) . . . .
    Surname   *First name(s)*

              Sexe : masculin /féminin   *Sex: male /female*

3. Nationalité . . . .   4. Profession . . . .
    Nationality   *Occupation*

5. Date et lieu de naissance . . . .
    Date and place of birth

6. Domicile . . . .
    Permanent address

7. Tel. N° . . . .

8. Adresse actuelle (si différente de 6.) . . . .
    Present address (if different from 6.)

9. Nom et prénom du/de la représentant(e)* . . . .
    *Name of representative**

10. Profession du/de la représentant(e) . . . .
    Occupation of representative

11. Adresse du/de la représentant(e) . . . .
    Address of representative

12. Tel. N° . . . .   Fax N° . . . .

B.   LA HAUTE PARTIE CONTRACTANTE
THE HIGH CONTRACTING PARTY

(Indiquer ci-après le nom de l'Etat/des Etats contre le(s)quel(s) la requête est dirigée)
(*Fill in the name of the State(s) against which the application is directed*)

13.   . . . .

---

* Si le/la requérant(e) est représenté(e), joindre une procuration signée par le/la requérant(e) et son/sa
représentant(e).
*If the applicant appoints a representative, attach a form of authority signed by the applicant and his or
her representative.*

II.   EXPOSÉ DES FAITS
STATEMENT OF THE FACTS

(Voir chapitre II de la note explicative)
(*See Part II of the Explanatory Note*)

14.

III. EXPOSÉ DE LA OU DES VIOLATION(S) DE LA CONVENTION ET/OU DES PROTOCOLES ALLÉGUÉE(S), AINSI QUE DES ARGUMENTS À L'APPUI
STATEMENT OF ALLEGED VIOLATION(S) OF THE CONVENTION AND/OR PROTOCOLS AND OF RELEVANT ARGUMENTS

(Voir chapitre III de la note explicative)
(*See Part III of the Explanatory Note*)

15.

IV. EXPOSÉ RELATIF AUX PRESCRIPTIONS DE L'ARTICLE 35 § 1 DE LA CONVENTION
STATEMENT RELATIVE TO ARTICLE 35 § 1 OF THE CONVENTION

(Voir chapitre IV de la note explicative. Donner pour chaque grief, et au besoin sur une feuille séparée, les renseignements demandés sous les points 16 à 18 ci-après)
(See Part IV of the Explanatory Note. If necessary, give the details mentioned below under points 16 to 18 on a separate sheet for each separate complaint)

16. Décision interne définitive (date et nature de la décision, organe—judiciaire ou autre—l'ayant rendue)
Final decision (date, court or authority and nature of decision)

17. Autres décisions (énumérées dans l'ordre chronologique en indiquant, pour chaque décision, sa date, sa nature et l'organe—judiciaire ou autre—l'ayant rendue)
Other decisions (list in chronological order, giving date, court or authority and nature of decision for each of them)

18. Dispos(i)ez-vous d'un recours que vous n'avez pas exercé? Si oui, lequel et pour quel motif n'a-t-il pas été exercé?
Is there or was there any other appeal or other remedy available to you which you have not used? If so, explain why you have not used it.

Si nécessaire, continuer sur une feuille séparée
Continue on a separate sheet if necessary

V. EXPOSÉ DE L'OBJET DE LA REQUÊTE
STATEMENT OF THE OBJECT OF THE APPLICATION

(Voir chapitre V de la note explicative)
(*See Part V of the Explanatory Note*)

19.

VI. AUTRES INSTANCES INTERNATIONALES TRAITANT OU AYANT TRAITÉ L'AFFAIRE
STATEMENT CONCERNING OTHER INTERNATIONAL PROCEEDINGS

(Voir chapitre VI de la note explicative)
(*See Part VI of the Explanatory Note*)

20. Avez-vous soumis à une autre instance internationale d'enquête ou de règlement les griefs énoncés dans la présente requête? Si oui, fournir des indications détaillées à ce sujet.

Have you submitted the above complaints to any other procedure of international investigation or settlement? If so, give full details.

VII. PIÈCES ANNEXÉES
LIST OF DOCUMENTS

**(PAS D'ORIGINAUX,
UNIQUEMENT DES COPIES)**
*(NO ORIGINAL DOCUMENTS,
ONLY PHOTOCOPIES)*

(Voir chapitre VII de la note explicative. Joindre copie de toutes les décisions mentionnées sous ch. IV et VI ci-dessus. Se procurer, au besoin, les copies nécessaires, et, en cas d'impossibilité, expliquer pourquoi celles-ci ne peuvent pas être obtenues. Ces documents ne vous seront pas retournés.)
(See Part VII of the Explanatory Note. Include copies of all decisions referred to in Parts IV and VI above. If you do not have copies, you should obtain them. If you cannot obtain them, explain why not. No documents will be returned to you.)

21. a) ....

    b) ....

    c) ....

VIII.   DÉCLARATION ET SIGNATURE
        DECLARATION AND SIGNATURE

(Voir chapitre VIII de la note explicative)
(*See Part VIII of the Explanatory Note*)

Je déclare en toute conscience et loyauté que les renseignements qui figurent sur la présente formule de requête sont exacts.
I hereby declare that, to the best of my knowledge and belief, the information I have given in the present application form is correct.

Lieu/*Place* . . . .

Date/*Date* . . . .

(Signature du/de la requérant(e) ou du/de la représentant(e))
(*Signature of the applicant or of the representative*)

(Eng)   (29/04/2002)

> **NOTES**
> for the guidance of persons wishing to apply to the
> **EUROPEAN COURT OF HUMAN RIGHTS**

I.   WHAT CASES CAN THE COURT DEAL WITH?

1.   The European Court of Human Rights is an international institution which **in certain circumstances** can examine complaints from persons claiming that their rights under the European Convention on Human Rights have been infringed. This Convention is an international treaty by which a large number of European States have agreed to secure **certain fundamental rights**. The rights guaranteed are set out in the Convention itself, and also in Protocols Nos. 1, 4, 6 and 7 which only some of the States have accepted. You should read these texts and the accompanying reservations, which are all enclosed.

2.   If you consider that you have **personally and directly been the victim** of a breach of one or more of these fundamental rights by one of the States, you may complain to the Court.

3.   The Court can only deal with complaints relating to infringements of one or more of **the rights set forth in the Convention and Protocols**. It is not a court of appeal *vis-à-vis* national courts and cannot annul or alter their decisions. Nor can it intervene directly on your behalf with the authority you are complaining about.

4.   The Court can only examine complaints that are directed against States which have ratified the Convention or the Protocol in question and concern **events after a given date**. The date varies according to the State and according to whether the complaint relates to a right set out in the Convention itself or in one of the Protocols.

5.   You can only complain to the Court about **matters which are the responsibility of a public authority** (legislature, administrative authority, court of law, etc.) of one of these States. **The Court cannot deal with complaints against private individuals or private organisations**.

6.   By the terms of Article 35 § 1 of the Convention, the Court can only deal with an application after **all domestic remedies have been exhausted** and within a period of **six months from the date on which the final decision was taken**. The Court will not be able to consider any application that does not satisfy these admissibility requirements.

7.   It is therefore absolutely essential that before applying to the Court, you should have tried **all judicial remedies** in the State concerned by means of which it might have been possible to redress your grievance; failing that, you will have to show that such remedies would have been ineffective. You must accordingly have first applied to the domestic courts, up to and including the highest court with jurisdiction in the matter, where you must have raised, at least in substance, the complaints that you wish to submit subsequently to the Court.

8.   When availing yourself of the appropriate remedies, you must normally **comply with national rules of procedure**, including time-limits. If, for instance, your appeal is dismissed because you have brought it too late or in the wrong court or have not used the proper procedure, the Court will not be able to examine your case.

9.   However, if you are complaining of a court decision such as a conviction or sentence, it is not necessary to have tried to have your case reopened after going through the normal appeal

procedures in the courts. Nor do you have to have made use of non-contentious remedies or seek a pardon or an amnesty. Petitions (to Parliament, the Head of State or Government, a minister or an ombudsman) are not regarded as effective remedies that you must have used.

10.   After a decision of the highest competent national court or authority has been given, you have **six months** within which you may apply to the Court. The six-month period begins when the final court decision in the ordinary appeal process is served on you or your lawyer, not on the date of any later refusal of an application to reopen your case or of a petition for pardon or amnesty or of any other non-contentious application to an authority.

11.   Time only stops running when the Court first receives from you either your **first letter** clearly setting out—even if only in summary form—the subject-matter of the application you may wish to lodge or a completed application form. A mere request for information is not sufficient to stop time running for the purposes of complying with the six-month time-limit.

II.   How to apply to the Court

12.   The Court's **official languages** are English and French but if it is easier for you, you may alternatively write to the Registry in an official language of one of the States that have ratified the Convention.

13.   Applications to the Court cannot be made by phone or by e-mail unless **confirmed by ordinary post**, nor is any purpose served by your coming to Strasbourg in person to state your case orally.

14.   All correspondence relating to your complaint should be sent to the following **address**:

> The Registrar
> European Court of Human Rights
> Council of Europe
> F–67075 STRASBOURG CEDEX.

15.   On receipt of your first letter or the application form, the Registry of the Court will reply, telling you that **a file (whose number must be mentioned in all subsequent correspondence) has been opened in your name**. Subsequently, you may be asked for further information, documents or particulars of your complaints. On the other hand, the Registry cannot inform you about the law of the State against which you are making your complaint or give legal advice concerning the application and interpretation of national law.

16.   It is in your interests to **be diligent in conducting your correspondence** with the Registry. Any delay in replying or failure to reply is likely to be regarded as a sign that you are not interested in continuing to have your case dealt with. Thus, if you do not answer any letter sent to you by the Registry subsequently within one year of its dispatch to you, your file will be destroyed.

17.   If you consider that your complaint does concern one of the rights guaranteed by the Convention or its Protocols and that the conditions set out above are satisfied, **you should fill in the application form carefully and legibly and return it within six weeks at most**.

18.   By the terms of Rule 47 of the Rules of Court, **it is essential that in your application you**:

(a)   give a brief **summary of the facts** of which you wish to complain and the nature of your complaints;

(b)   indicate which of your **Convention rights** you think have been infringed;

(c)   state **what remedies you have used**;

(d)   list the **official decisions** in your case, giving the date of each decision, the court or authority which took it, and brief details of the decision itself. Attach to your letter a full copy of these decisions. (No documents will be returned to you. It is thus in your interest to **submit only copies, not the originals**.)

19.   Rule 45 of the Rules of Court requires the application form to be **signed** by you as applicant or by your representative.

20.   If you do not wish your identity to be disclosed to the public, you must say so and set out the reasons for such a departure from the normal rule of public access to information in the proceedings. The Court may authorise **anonymity** in exceptional and duly justified cases.

21.   If you wish to apply to the Court through **a lawyer or other representative**, you must send with the form **your authority for him or her to act** on your behalf. A representative of a legal entity (company, association, etc.) or group of individuals must provide proof of his or her legal right to represent it. For the purpose of lodging the initial complaint, your representative (if any) does not have to be a lawyer. It should be noted, however, that at a later stage in the proceedings an applicant's representative must, in the absence of any special exemption, be an advocate authorised to practise in one of the States that have ratified the Convention. The advocate must have at least a passive knowledge of one of the Court's official languages (English and French).

22. The Court does not grant **legal aid** to help you pay for a lawyer to draft your initial complaint. At a later stage of the proceedings—after a decision by the Court to communicate the application to the government concerned for written observations—you may be eligible for free legal aid if you have insufficient means to pay a lawyer's fees and if a grant of such aid is considered necessary for the proper conduct of the case.

23. Your case will be dealt with **free of charge**. As the proceedings are initially in writing, there is no point in coming to the Court's premises in person. You will automatically be informed of any decision taken by the Court.

(Eng)   (02/10/2002)

EXPLANATORY NOTE

for persons completing the Application Form
under Article 34 of the Convention

INTRODUCTION

These notes are intended to assist you in drawing up your application to the Court. **Please read them carefully before completing the form**, and then refer to them as you complete each section of the form.

The completed form will be your application to the Court under Article 34 of the Convention. It will be the basis for the Court's examination of your case. It is therefore important that you **complete it fully and accurately even if this means repeating information you have already given the Registry in previous correspondence.**

You will see that there are eight sections to the form. You should complete all of these so that your application contains all the information required under the Rules of Court. Below you will find an explanatory note relating to each section of the form. You will also find at the end of these notes the text of Rules 45 and 47 of the Rules of Court.

NOTES RELATING TO THE APPLICATION FORM

I.   THE PARTIES—Rule 47 § 1 (a), (b) and (c)
(1–13)

If there is more than one applicant, you should give the required information for each one, on a separate sheet if necessary.

An applicant may appoint a person to represent him. Such representative shall be an advocate authorised to practise in any of the Contracting Parties and resident in the territory of one of them, or any other person approved by the Court. When an applicant is represented, relevant details should be given in this part of the application form, and the Registry will correspond only with the representative.

II.   STATEMENT OF THE FACTS—Rule 47 § 1 (d)
(14)

You should give clear and concise details of the facts you are complaining about. Try to describe the events in the order in which they occurred. Give exact dates. If your complaints relate to a number of different matters (for instance different sets of court proceedings) you should deal with each matter separately.

III.   STATEMENT OF ALLEGED VIOLATION(S) OF THE CONVENTION
(15)   **AND/OR PROTOCOLS AND OF RELEVANT ARGUMENTS**—Rule 47 § 1 (e)

In this section of the form you should explain as precisely as you can what your complaint **under the Convention** is. Say which provisions of the Convention you rely on and explain why you consider that the facts you have set out in Part II of the form involve a violation of these provisions.

You will see that some of the articles of the Convention permit interferences with the rights they guarantee in certain circumstances (see for instance sub-paragraphs (a) to (f) of

Article 5 §§ 1 and 2 of Articles 8 to 11). If you are relying on such an article, try to explain why you consider the interference about which you are complaining is not justified.

IV. STATEMENT RELATIVE TO ARTICLE 35 § 1 OF THE CONVENTION—Rule 47 § 2 (a)
(16–18)

In this section you should set out details of the remedies you have pursued before the national authorities. You should fill in each of the three parts of this section and give the same information separately for each separate complaint. In part 18 you should say whether or not any other appeal or remedy is available which could redress your complaints and which you have not used. If such a remedy is available, you should say what it is (e.g. name the court or authority to which an appeal would lie) and explain why you have not used it.

V. STATEMENT OF THE OBJECT OF THE APPLICATION—Rule 47 § 1 (g)
(19)

Here you should state briefly what you want to achieve through your application to the Court.

VI. STATEMENT CONCERNING OTHER INTERNATIONAL PROCEEDINGS— Rule 47 § 2 (b)
(20)

Here you should say whether or not you have ever submitted the complaints in your application to any other procedure of international investigation or settlement. If you have, you should give full details, including the name of the body to which you submitted your complaints, dates and details of any proceedings which took place and details of decisions taken. You should also submit copies of relevant decisions and other documents.

VII. LIST OF DOCUMENTS—Rule 47 § 1 (h)
(21)   **(NO ORIGINAL DOCUMENTS, ONLY PHOTOCOPIES)**

Do not forget to enclose with your application and to mention on the list all judgments and decisions referred to in Sections IV and VI, as well as any other documents you wish the Court to take into consideration as evidence (transcripts, statements of witnesses, etc.). Include any documents giving the reasons for a court or other decision as well as the decision itself. Only submit documents which are relevant to the complaints you are making to the Court.

VIII. DECLARATION AND SIGNATURE—Rule 45 § 3
(22)

If the application is signed by the representative of the applicant, it should be accompanied by a form of authority signed by the applicant and the representative (unless this has already been submitted).

RULES OF THE EUROPEAN COURT OF HUMAN RIGHTS

Chapter II
Institution of Proceedings

Rule 45
(Signatures)

1.   Any application made under Articles 33 or 34 of the Convention shall be submitted in writing and shall be signed by the applicant or by the applicant's representative.

2.   Where an application is made by a non-governmental organisation or by a group of individuals, it shall be signed by those persons competent to represent that organisation or group. The Chamber or Committee concerned shall determine any question as to whether the persons who have signed an application are competent to do so.

3.   Where applicants are represented in accordance with Rule 36, a power of attorney or written authority to act shall be supplied by their representative or representatives.

Rule 47
(Contents of an individual application)

1.   Any application under Article 34 of the Convention shall be made on the application form provided by the Registry, unless the President of the Section concerned decides otherwise. It shall set out

(a) the name, date of birth, nationality, sex, occupation and address of the applicant;

(b) the name, occupation and address of the representative, if any;

(c) the name of the Contracting Party or Parties against which the application is made;

(d) a succinct statement of the facts;

(e) a succinct statement of the alleged violation(s) of the Convention and the relevant arguments;

(f) a succinct statement on the applicant's compliance with the admissibility criteria (exhaustion of domestic remedies and the six-month rule) laid down in Article 35 § 1 of the Convention; and

(g) the object of the application;

and be accompanied by

(h) copies of any relevant documents and in particular the decisions, whether judicial or not, relating to the object of the application.

2.   Applicants shall furthermore

(a) provide information, notably the documents and decisions referred to in paragraph 1 (h) of this Rule, enabling it to be shown that the admissibility criteria (exhaustion of domestic remedies and the six-month rule) laid down in Article 35 § 1 of the Convention have been satisfied; and

(b) indicate whether they have submitted their complaints to any other procedure of international investigation or settlement.

3.   Applicants who do not wish their identity to be disclosed to the public shall so indicate and shall submit a statement of the reasons justifying such a departure from the normal rule of public access to information in proceedings before the Court. The President of the Chamber may authorise anonymity in exceptional and duly justified cases.

4.   Failure to comply with the requirements set out in paragraphs 1 and 2 of this Rule may result in the application not being examined by the Court.

5.   The date of introduction of the application shall as a general rule be considered to be the date of the first communication from the applicant setting out, even summarily, the object of the application. The Court may for good cause nevertheless decide that a different date shall be considered to be the date of introduction.

6.   Applicants shall keep the Court informed of any change of address and of all circumstances relevant to the application.

Appendix 7
Charter of Fundamental Rights of the European Union

CHARTER OF FUNDAMENTAL RIGHTS OF THE
EUROPEAN UNION
(2000/C 364/01)

PREAMBLE

The peoples of Europe, in creating an ever closer union among them, are resolved to share a peaceful future based on common values.

Conscious of its spiritual and moral heritage, the Union is founded on the indivisible, universal values of human dignity, freedom, equality and solidarity; it is based on the principles of democracy and the rule of law. It places the individual at the heart of its activities, by establishing the citizenship of the Union and by creating an area of freedom, security and justice.

The Union contributes to the preservation and to the development of these common values while respecting the diversity of the cultures and traditions of the peoples of Europe as well as the national identities of the Member States and the organisation of their public authorities at national, regional and local levels; it seeks to promote balanced and sustainable development and ensures free movement of persons, goods, services and capital, and the freedom of establishment.

To this end, it is necessary to strengthen the protection of fundamental rights in the light of changes in society, social progress and scientific and technological developments by making those rights more visible in a Charter.

This Charter reaffirms, with due regard for the powers and tasks of the Community and the Union and the principle of subsidiarity, the rights as they result, in particular, from the constitutional traditions and international obligations common to the Member States, the Treaty on European Union, the Community Treaties, the European Convention for the Protection of Human Rights and Fundamental Freedoms, the Social Charters adopted by the Community and by the Council of Europe and the case law of the Court of Justice of the European Communities and of the European Court of Human Rights.

Enjoyment of these rights entails responsibilities and duties with regard to other persons, to the human community and to future generations.

The Union therefore recognises the rights, freedoms and principles set out hereafter.

CHAPTER I
DIGNITY

Article 1
Human dignity

Human dignity is inviolable. It must be respected and protected.

Article 2
Right to life

1. Everyone has the right to life.
2. No one shall be condemned to the death penalty, or executed.

Article 3
Right to the integrity of the person

1. Everyone has the right to respect for his or her physical and mental integrity.
2. In the fields of medicine and biology, the following must be respected in particular:
   —the free and informed consent of the person concerned, according to the procedures laid down by law,
   —the prohibition of eugenic practices, in particular those aiming at the selection of persons,
   —the prohibition on making the human body and its parts as such a source of financial gain,
   —the prohibition of the reproductive cloning of human beings.

Article 4
Prohibition of torture and inhuman or degrading treatment or punishment

No one shall be subjected to torture or to inhuman or degrading treatment or punishment.

Article 5
Prohibition of slavery and forced labour

1. No one shall be held in slavery or servitude.
2. No one shall be required to perform forced or compulsory labour.
3. Trafficking in human beings is prohibited.

CHAPTER II
FREEDOMS

Article 6
Right to liberty and security

Everyone has the right to liberty and security of person.

Article 7
Respect for private and family life

Everyone has the right to respect for his or her private and family life, home and communications.

Article 8
Protection of personal data

1. Everyone has the right to the protection of personal data concerning him or her.

2. Such data must be processed fairly for specified purposes and on the basis of the consent of the person concerned or some other legitimate basis laid down by law. Everyone has the right of access to data which has been collected concerning him or her, and the right to have it rectified.

3. Compliance with these rules shall be subject to control by an independent authority.

Article 9
Right to marry and right to found a family

The right to marry and the right to found a family shall be guaranteed in accordance with the national laws governing the exercise of these rights.

Article 10
Freedom of thought, conscience and religion

1. Everyone has the right to freedom of thought, conscience and religion. This right includes freedom to change religion or belief and freedom, either alone or in community with others and in public or in private, to manifest religion or belief, in worship, teaching, practice and observance.

2. The right to conscientious objection is recognised, in accordance with the national laws governing the exercise of this right.

Article 11
Freedom of expression and information

1. Everyone has the right to freedom of expression. This right shall include freedom to hold opinions and to receive and impart information and ideas without interference by public authority and regardless of frontiers.

2. The freedom and pluralism of the media shall be respected.

Article 12
Freedom of assembly and of association

1. Everyone has the right to freedom of peaceful assembly and to freedom of association at all levels, in particular in political, trade union and civic matters, which implies the right of everyone to form and to join trade unions for the protection of his or her interests.

2. Political parties at Union level contribute to expressing the political will of the citizens of the Union.

Article 13
Freedom of the arts and sciences

The arts and scientific research shall be free of constraint. Academic freedom shall be respected.

Article 14
Right to education

1. Everyone has the right to education and to have access to vocational and continuing training.

2. This right includes the possibility to receive free compulsory education.

3. The freedom to found educational establishments with due respect for democratic principles and the right of parents to ensure the education and teaching of their children in conformity with their religious, philosophical and pedagogical convictions shall be respected, in accordance with the national laws governing the exercise of such freedom and right.

Article 15
Freedom to choose an occupation and
right to engage in work

1. Everyone has the right to engage in work and to pursue a freely chosen or accepted occupation.

2. Every citizen of the Union has the freedom to seek employment, to work, to exercise the right of establishment and to provide services in any Member State.

3. Nationals of third countries who are authorised to work in the territories of the Member States are entitled to working conditions equivalent to those of citizens of the Union.

Article 16
Freedom to conduct a business

The freedom to conduct a business in accordance with Community law and national laws and practices is recognised.

Article 17
Right to property

1. Everyone has the right to own, use, dispose of and bequeath his or her lawfully acquired possessions. No one may be deprived of his or her possessions, except in the public interest and in the cases and under the conditions provided for by law, subject to fair compensation being paid in good time for their loss. The use of property may be regulated by law insofar as is necessary for the general interest.

2. Intellectual property shall be protected.

Article 18
Right to asylum

The right to asylum shall be guaranteed with due respect for the rules of the Geneva

Convention of 28 July 1951 and the Protocol of 31 January 1967 relating to the status of refugees and in accordance with the Treaty establishing the European Community.

Article 19
Protection in the event of removal, expulsion or extradition

1. Collective expulsions are prohibited.

2. No one may be removed, expelled or extradited to a State where there is a serious risk that he or she would be subjected to the death penalty, torture or other inhuman or degrading treatment or punishment.

CHAPTER III
EQUALITY

Article 20
Equality before the law

Everyone is equal before the law.

Article 21
Non-discrimination

1. Any discrimination based on any ground such as sex, race, colour, ethnic or social origin, genetic features, language, religion or belief, political or any other opinion, membership of a national minority, property, birth, disability, age or sexual orientation shall be prohibited.

2. Within the scope of application of the Treaty establishing the European Community and of the Treaty on European Union, and without prejudice to the special provisions of those Treaties, any discrimination on grounds of nationality shall be prohibited.

Article 22
Cultural, religious and linguistic diversity

The Union shall respect cultural, religious and linguistic diversity.

Article 23
Equality between men and women

Equality between men and women must be ensured in all areas, including employment, work and pay.

The principle of equality shall not prevent the maintenance or adoption of measures providing for specific advantages in favour of the under-represented sex.

Article 24
The rights of the child

1. Children shall have the right to such protection and care as is necessary for their well-being. They may express their views freely. Such views shall be taken into consideration on matters which concern them in accordance with their age and maturity.

2. In all actions relating to children, whether taken by public authorities or private institutions, the child's best interests must be a primary consideration.

3. Every child shall have the right to maintain on a regular basis a personal relationship and direct contact with both his or her parents, unless that is contrary to his or her interests.

Article 25
The rights of the elderly

The Union recognises and respects the rights of the elderly to lead a life of dignity and independence and to participate in social and cultural life.

Article 26
Integration of persons with disabilities

The Union recognises and respects the right of persons with disabilities to benefit from measures designed to ensure their independence, social and occupational integration and participation in the life of the community.

CHAPTER IV
SOLIDARITY

Article 27
Workers' right to information and consultation
within the undertaking

Workers or their representatives must, at the appropriate levels, be guaranteed information and consultation in good time in the cases and under the conditions provided for by Community law and national laws and practices.

Article 28
Right of collective bargaining and action

Workers and employers, or their respective organisations, have, in accordance with Community law and national laws and practices, the right to negotiate and conclude collective agreements at the appropriate levels and, in cases of conflicts of interest, to take collective action to defend their interests, including strike action.

Article 29
Right of access to placement services

Everyone has the right of access to a free placement service.

Article 30
Protection in the event of unjustified dismissal

Every worker has the right to protection against unjustified dismissal, in accordance with Community law and national laws and practices.

Article 31
Fair and just working conditions

1. Every worker has the right to working conditions which respect his or her health, safety and dignity.

2. Every worker has the right to limitation of maximum working hours, to daily and weekly rest periods and to an annual period of paid leave.

Article 32
Prohibition of child labour and protection of young people at work

The employment of children is prohibited. The minimum age of admission to employment may not be lower than the minimum school-leaving age, without prejudice to such rules as may be more favourable to young people and except for limited derogations.

Young people admitted to work must have working conditions appropriate to their age and be protected against economic exploitation and any work likely to harm their safety, health or physical, mental, moral or social development or to interfere with their education.

Article 33
Family and professional life

1. The family shall enjoy legal, economic and social protection.

2. To reconcile family and professional life, everyone shall have the right to protection from dismissal for a reason connected with maternity and the right to paid maternity leave and to parental leave following the birth or adoption of a child.

Article 34
Social security and social assistance

1. The Union recognises and respects the entitlement to social security benefits and social services providing protection in cases such as maternity, illness, industrial accidents, dependency or old age, and in the case of loss of employment, in accordance with the procedures laid down by Community law and national laws and practices.

2. Everyone residing and moving legally within the European Union is entitled to social security benefits and social advantages in accordance with Community law and national laws and practices.

3. In order to combat social exclusion and poverty, the Union recognises and respects the right to social and housing assistance so as to ensure a decent existence for all those who lack sufficient resources, in accordance with the procedures laid down by Community law and national laws and practices.

Article 35
Health care

Everyone has the right of access to preventive health care and the right to benefit from medical treatment under the conditions established by national laws and practices. A high level of human health protection shall be ensured in the definition and implementation of all Union policies and activities.

Article 36
Access to services of general economic interest

The Union recognises and respects access to services of general economic interest as provided for in national laws and practices, in accordance with the Treaty establishing the European Community, in order to promote the social and territorial cohesion of the Union.

Article 37
Environmental protection

A high level of environmental protection and the improvement of the quality of the environment must be integrated into the polices of the Union and ensured in accordance with the principle of sustainable development.

Article 38
Consumer Protection

Union policies shall ensure a high level of consumer protection.

CHAPTER V
CITIZENS' RIGHTS

Article 39
Right to vote and to stand as a candidate at elections
to the European Parliament

1. Every citizen of the Union has the right to vote and to stand as a candidate at elections to the European Parliament in the Member State in which he or she resides, under the same conditions as nationals of that State.

2. Members of the European Parliament shall be elected by direct universal suffrage in a free and secret ballot.

Article 40
Right to vote and to stand as a candidate
at municipal elections

Every citizen of the Union has the right to vote and to stand as a candidate at municipal elections in the Member State in which he or she resides under the same conditions as nationals of that State.

Article 41
Right to good administration

1. Every person has the right to have his or her affairs handled impartially, fairly and within a reasonable time by the institutions and bodies of the Union.

2. This right includes:
— the right of every person to be heard, before any individual measure which would affect him or her adversely is taken;
— the right of every person to have access to his or her file, while respecting the legitimate interests of confidentiality and of professional and business secrecy;
— the obligation of the administration to give reasons for its decisions.

3. Every person has the right to have the Community make good any damage caused by its institutions or by its servants in the performance of their duties, in accordance with the general principles common to the laws of the Member States.

4. Every person may write to the institutions of the Union in one of the languages of the Treaties and must have an answer in the same language.

Article 42
Right of access to documents

Any citizen of the Union, and any natural or legal person residing or having its registered office in a Member State, has a right of access to European Parliament, Council and Commission documents.

Article 43
Ombudsman

Any citizen of the Union and any natural or legal person residing or having its registered office in a Member State has the right to refer to the Ombudsman of the Union cases of maladministration in the activities of the Community institutions or bodies, with the exception of the Court of Justice and the Court of First Instance acting in their judicial role.

Article 44
Right to petition

Any citizen of the Union and any natural or legal person residing or having its registered office in a Member State has the right to petition the European Parliament.

Article 45
Freedom of movement and of residence

1. Every citizen of the Union has the right to move and reside freely within the territory of the Member States.

2. Freedom of movement and residence may be granted, in accordance with the Treaty establishing the European Community, to nationals of third countries legally resident in the territory of a Member State.

Article 46
Diplomatic and consular protection

Every citizen of the Union shall, in the territory of a third country in which the Member State of which he or she is a national is not represented, be entitled to protection by the diplomatic or consular authorities of any Member State, on the same conditions as the nationals of that Member State.

CHAPTER VI
JUSTICE

Article 47
Right to an effective remedy and to a fair trial

Everyone whose rights and freedoms guaranteed by the law of the Union are violated has the right to an effective remedy before a tribunal in compliance with the conditions laid down in this Article.

Everyone is entitled to a fair and public hearing within a reasonable time by an independent and impartial tribunal previously established by law. Everyone shall have the possibility of being advised, defended and represented.

Legal aid shall be made available to those who lack sufficient resources insofar as such aid is necessary to ensure effective access to justice.

Article 48
Presumption of innocence and right of defence

1. Everyone who has been charged shall be presumed innocent until proved guilty according to law.

2. Respect for the rights of the defence of anyone who has been charged shall be guaranteed.

Article 49
Principles of legality and proportionality of criminal
offences and penalties

1. No one shall be held guilty of any criminal offence on account of any act or omission which did not constitute a criminal offence under national law or international law at the time when it was committed. Nor shall a heavier penalty be imposed than that which was applicable at the time the criminal offence was committed. If, subsequent to the commission of a criminal offence, the law provides for a lighter penalty, that penalty shall be applicable.

2. This Article shall not prejudice the trial and punishment of any person for any act or omission which, at the time when it was committed, was criminal according to the general principles recognised by the community of nations.

3. The severity of penalties must not be disproportionate to the criminal offence.

Article 50
Right not to be tried or punished twice in criminal proceedings
for the same criminal offence

No one shall be liable to be tried or punished again in criminal proceedings for an offence for which he or she has already been finally acquitted or convicted within the Union in accordance with the law.

CHAPTER VII
GENERAL PROVISIONS

Article 51
Scope

1. The provisions of this Charter are addressed to the institutions and bodies of the Union with due regard for the principle of subsidiarity and to the Member States only when they are implementing Union law. They shall therefore respect the rights, observe the principles and promote the application thereof in accordance with their respective powers.

2. This Charter does not establish any new power or task for the Community or the Union, or modify powers and tasks defined by the Treaties.

Article 52
Scope of guaranteed rights

1. Any limitation on the exercise of the rights and freedoms recognised by this Charter must be provided for by law and respect the essence of those rights and freedoms. Subject to the principle of proportionality, limitations may be made only if they are necessary and genuinely meet objectives of general interest recognised by the Union or the need to protect the rights and freedoms of others.

2. Rights recognised by this Charter which are based on the Community Treaties or the Treaty on European Union shall be exercised under the conditions and within the limits defined by those Treaties.

3. Insofar as this Charter contains rights which correspond to rights guaranteed by the Convention for the Protection of Human Rights and Fundamental Freedoms, the meaning and scope of those rights shall be the same as those laid down by the said Convention. This provision shall not prevent Union law providing more extensive protection.

Article 53
Level of protection

Nothing in this Charter shall be interpreted as restricting or adversely affecting human rights and fundamental freedoms as recognised, in their respective fields of application, by Union law and international law and by international agreements to which the Union, the Community or all the Member States are party, including the European Convention for the Protection of Human Rights and Fundamental Freedoms, and by the Member States' constitutions.

Article 54
Prohibition of abuse of rights

Nothing in this Charter shall be interpreted as implying any right to engage in any activity or to perform any act aimed at the destruction of any of the rights and freedoms recognised in this Charter or at their limitation to a greater extent than is provided for herein.

Index